THE DEVELOPMENT OF
SPATIAL COGNITION

THE DEVELOPMENT OF
SPATIAL COGNITION

Edited by

Robert Cohen
Memphis State University

LEA LAWRENCE ERLBAUM ASSOCIATES, PUBLISHERS
1985   Hillsdale, New Jersey   London

Hmm
BF
723
S63
D48
1985

Copyright © 1985 by Lawrence Erlbaum Associates, Inc.
    All rights reserved. No part of this book may be reproduced in
any form, by photostat, microform, retrieval system, or any other
means, without the prior written permission of the publisher.

Lawrence Erlbaum Associates, Inc., Publishers
365 Broadway
Hillsdale, New Jersey 07642

Library of Congress Cataloging in Publication Data
The Development of spatial cognition.

  Bibliography: p.
  Includes index.
  1. Space perception in children—Addresses, essays,
lectures.   2. Child development—Addresses, essays,
lectures.   I. Cohen, Robert, 1941–   .
RF723.S63D48   1985   155.4′13   85-1454
ISBN 0-89859-543-6

Printed in the United States of America

Table of Contents

PART IV: SPECIAL VARIABLES

PART V: METHODOLOGICAL AND META-METHODOLOGICAL ISSUES

Foreword

The 1973 publication of *Image and Environment* edited by Roger Downs and David Stea shortly followed in 1975 by Alexander Siegel and Shepard White's seminal paper on the spatial representation of large scale-environments signaled the advent of a decade of intense and sustained interest in spatial cognition. The present book represents a statement of the state of the art in a very important aspect of spatial cognition, its development. Of course there were antecedents to this sudden increase of attention. One important one was Kevin Lynch's book, *Image of the City* (1960). Another was Piaget's classic work on children's spatial cognition reflected in the *Child's Conception of Space* (1956) and his measurement of their spatial egocentrism with the well known three-mountain problem. However, the considerable research activity which started at the time was probably attributable to a happy conjunction of several trends. From the practical side were the pressures of those years for making basic research relevant. Spatial cognition is an excellent arena in which to do this. Spatial orientation is a pervasive facet of our everyday life and in spite of over a hundred years of systematic work on space perception researchers could say little about how we knew where in the world we were. At the same time the problem of spatial orientation is constrained enough and sufficiently subject to experimental control that there is promise of fundamental understanding. From the theoretical side, cognitive psychology was well into the information processing era with the potential of the very detailed and analytic studies characteristic of that approach. At the same time from the theoretical side there were initial signs of dissatisfaction with the artificial and relatively rigid constraints of much of the work done from that point of view. In this context the study of spatial cognition became an attractive focus.

How one maintains spatial orientation was particularly appealing for developmental study. In the first place, here was a practical problem that confronted children in very real form as soon as they began to locomote. The most casual observer can see the extent to which parents monitor their children's whereabouts in crowded, unfamiliar environments, and only slightly more sophistication is required to note the complementary strategies of many children to keep tabs on their caregivers in unfamiliar environments. At the same time who has not heard over the public address system of a shopping mall, amusement park, or sports arena disturbing announcements such as, "Will the parents of a little blond girl wearing a white blouse and red skirt please report to the security office and claim her?" In the second place, in spite of such errors even young children seem to display rather remarkable spatial behavior particularly in familiar environments—finding their way around, searching for objects, making detours, and so on. Such behavior suggested inferential capacity surprisingly in advance of other domains of cognitive performance. Structuring relatively natural situations for investigating these phenomena was quite feasible for young children and even for prelocomoting infants. Perhaps because of the practicality of such realistic and yet rigorous experimental settings, research on the development of spatial cognition proceeded at a faster pace than the study of mature cognition in adults.

Where do we stand now after ten years of such activity? The empirical basis of our knowledge has been greatly increased and much of that information is elegantly and thoroughly reviewed in the present volume. Unfortunately, in my opinion, theoretical progress has not kept up. We have no general and abstract understanding of what this task of maintaining orientation involves and the mechanisms by which it is accomplished. There are, however, some intriguing hints and approaches also spelled out in this volume. One important concern is the nature of our representation of spatial layout. The debate continues over just how the form of our (or children's) spatial knowledge should be characterized. Inferences about this are based primarily on the kinds of operations and manipulations that are possible by subjects with their spatial knowledge. The developmental question, of course, is whether and how these operations and the knowledge on which they are based change with age. A second central issue is the relation of spatial cognition to other aspects of cognition. For example, it is possible to find spatial components in what are seemingly non-spatial tasks. In addition, the spatial metaphor seems in our cognition to be a very powerful one. That is, many non-spatial problems can be conceived of spatially or translated into a spatial form. Think, for example, of spatial diagrams of kinship relations, sociometric descriptions, or diagrams of the logic of analysis of variance, etc. For many such domains as adults it is very natural and easy for us to think in such terms. The developmental question concerns how we come to do this. To what extent is this the way our mind inherently organizes information or do we learn to do it? If experience plays a role what is the underlying mechanism? Is the relevant experience something very specific to particular spatial layouts or is it something very general like the physical nature of the environment or the presence or absence of vision, etc?

The question of the nature of relevant experience raises the possibility that the crucial factors are not even spatial at all. Rather, other aspects of the environment, social as well as physical may be determinant factors that affect a child's reaction to the environment, its willingness to explore, etc. That issue in turn, leads to another central theoretical concern which is the relation between spatial and other forms of environmental cognition. It is not hard to believe that if a space is difficult to traverse it will seem bigger. But what about if the space is interesting or frightening? If we are having a good time are we less likely to maintain orientation? If we are afraid, are we more likely to keep aware of where we are?

The papers in this book represent detailed information and studies that touch on many of these theoretical concerns. There are few final answers. But there are parts of answers. And more important the questions are raised here by Robert Cohen and his authors and there are examples of how relevant information can be obtained. As well as providing a statement of where we are now, this book provides an orientation for the next decade of work.

Herbert L. Pick, Jr.

Acknowledgments

My thoughts and feelings about the processes of planning, organizing, supervising, and editing a text such as this can be described in many ways. I feel a sense of accomplishment, a sense of intellectual satisfaction, and pride in the product. I also feel a tremendous amount of relief. One truly pleasurable component of the whole process is the opportunity to compose an acknowledgments page. I am thankful for the chance to formally recognize those who have supported me and this project.

First, I wish to acknowledge those professionals who contributed to the book. An edited volume is as good as its contributors. The authors of this book are exceptional scholars and have written what I believe to be clear, comprehensive, and innovative chapters spanning diverse domains in the field of spatial cognition. I wish to thank Herb Pick for his efforts as a reviewer of the manuscripts. The book certainly benefitted from his comments.

Second, on the production side of things, I sincerely thank Jack Burton of Lawrence Erlbaum Associates. His seemingly unlimited patience and timely suggestions made my tasks considerably more tolerable than they would have been otherwise. Susan Kasmin Shrader, who served as Production Editor, did an excellent job and I thank her as well.

I wish to acknowledge those individuals who have helped me not in my work on this book per se, but have helped me in a variety of ways. I appreciate the discussions and support from my colleagues at Memphis State University. On a more personal note, I wish to thank my friends and family, many of whom don't really understand what or why I do what I do, but love me just the same. Special thanks to Bradley, Christine, Esther, Milton, Newmamma, and Scott (in alphabetical order). How can I properly acknowledge my appreciation for the contribution of my wife, colleague, and friend, Sheila Cohen, who has the incredible knack of showing me that I'm neither as good nor as bad as my moods dictate?

Finally, I wish to not only acknowledge but dedicate this book to my father, Louis Cohen. My dad has taught me a number of lessons over the years, not the least of which is a healthy respect for learning. I remain forever grateful to him.

THE DEVELOPMENT OF
SPATIAL COGNITION

I INTRODUCTION

1 What's So Special About Spatial Cognition?

Robert Cohen
Memphis State University

Allow me to begin with a personal anecdote that has occurred with some frequency. I'll be at a social gathering and be introduced to a real person (i.e., nonprofessional, nonscientist). Inevitably I will be asked, "And what is your occupation?" To which I reply, "Oh, I'm a psychologist."

"I'm sure that's very interesting," he or she says while backing away and scanning the room for someone else to engage in conversation.

"But really I'm a child psychologist," I hasten to add.

"Oh," the person perks up, "my kid has been sticking peas in his ears quite regularly, and I was wondering if. . . ."

"Actually, I'm a research psychologist."

"How interesting!" says my new friend, now completely at ease. "And what do you research?"

Now of course, I'm interested. "I study spatial cognition in children!"

As puzzlement begins to cloud my listener's face, I then get the question that indirectly formed the concept of this chapter. "What's special cognition?"

This question may be due to an unknown speech impediment on my part, or it may be due to my residing in the South and there being a confusion in dialect. Most likely, however, the layman is unfamiliar with the domain addressed in this book, as in fact I would guess are many social scientists.

The philosophical roots of spatial cognition, of course, are quite old, dating back at least to the rationalism-empiricism debate of Plato and Aristotle. Research interests in the field can be traced to the early part of this century with the research on human factors, to more recently the interest of psychologists, educators, architects, city planners, and others in the impact of physical setting on behavior. It is not my purpose here to provide a detailed history of the field. The

1

reader is directed to Liben, Patterson, and Newcombe (1981), Hart and Moore (1973), and Siegel and White (1975) for excellent accounts. I would like to direct your attention in the present chapter to what I feel is an important issue for researchers and consumers of this field: What constitute the dimensions of inquiry for spatial cognition? Following this discussion, I briefly outline the chapters of the book.

A THEORETICAL NICHE FOR SPATIAL COGNITION

While many researchers continue to focus on experimental independent variables that either deny or ignore the importance of environmental factors, there are several contemporary theories that emphasize the role of context as an influence on behavior. Following is a brief review of some of these theories with an eye toward ferreting out and elaborating the role of spatial cognition.

SOME GENERAL THEORIES OF WHICH SPATIAL COGNITION IS A PART

Ittelson, Proshansky, Rivlin, and Winkel (1974) and others have been leaders in what has been termed "Environmental Psychology." Although I find a formal definition of this field to be somewhat elusive, Ittelson et al. offer some general parameters. Environmental psychology is a multidisciplinary approach to understanding person-environment transactions. Environmental psychologists are interested primarily in field research, viewing people in context, to understand the dynamic interchange between people and settings. Many of them have become interested in social problems that stem from environmental concerns such as crises of urban living and pollution.

Many of the statements in the preceding paragraph may remind the reader of the research on human factors or human engineering, but the perspective of the contemporary environmental psychologist is considerably wider. The environment is broadly conceived of as a total constellation rather than as a set of easily separable elements. A person, as part of that constellation, influences and is influenced by the setting. Thus, it is at best inappropriate to separate out for analysis the physical from the social aspects of any environmental setting. While focusing on social and cultural factors, the environmental psychologist also considers more circumspect person factors. How an individual experiences the world (perception) and how an individual understands the world (cognition) are considered as integral to the dynamic interplay of person and environment.

The work by Roger Barker (e.g., 1968), which has resurfaced in recent years with a new fervor, perhaps best exemplifies a concern for the role of physical setting. The environment is not simply a stage or setting for behavior; rather behavior and physical context exist in a synomorphic relationship. Each contributes to the structure and organization of the other. Yet the laws that govern the impact of the physical setting are different from the laws that govern the behavior in those settings. This implies that the behaviors that can exist in a setting together with the nonbehavioral components of the setting exist independently of any particular person or set of people. As support for this notion, Barker observed that interindividual variations in behavior within a setting are often less than intraindividual variations in behavior across settings.

This is not to deny the existence of individual differences in behavior. Psychological, physiological, and learning factors play a role in how an individual will behave in any setting at any point in time. But the variations themselves will follow a form dictated by the structure of the setting. To use an example we've used elsewhere (Cohen, Poag, & Goodnight, 1982), some children may perceive the classroom as a success arena, whereas others may view it as a scene of frustration and failure. Though the first set of children will arrive on time, be attentive, and participate, the latter may be tardy, inattentive, and disruptive. The point to be made is that all these are "classroom behaviors," albeit some are valued by observers and others are not. Thus the behavior of an individual will be influenced by the structure of a setting, the structure of behavior, and the physical and interpersonal dynamics of people in settings.

While Barker places primary emphasis on physical context, some theorists focus on the social contexts of behavior. Bandura's (1977) contemporary rendition of social learning theory includes the concept of reciprocal determinism in this regard. According to Bandura, behavior, environment, and personal characteristics are interdependent factors. Personal characteristics are primarily defined in cognitive terms such as expectancies, self-efficacy, attentional processes, and so forth. There is some mention of the impact of physical setting, but the role of environment is mainly as an arena where others put behaviors on display for the observational learning of the individual. Thus, like Barker, Bandura believes that behavior is best understood in its relationship to the context in which it is produced. Barker emphasizes the setting, whereas Bandura emphasizes the social learning abilities of the person and the opportunities for observational learning from others in the environment.

Bronfenbrenner (1979) offers a significantly more comprehensive view of the impact of social settings. An individual is embedded within a series of social systems that differ in the degree of directness of impact they have. The most direct level is termed the microsystem. This includes those systems that the person directly experiences, such as the social interactions a child has with parents at home or with peers at school. The next level, mesosystem, refers to the sets of interactions that occur among microsystems. An example here would be a parent-teacher conference. The child has direct access, and is influenced directly by both parents and teacher, and is somewhat less directly influenced by the conference between the two. The child has an even more indirect relationship with the exosystem, or third level, proposed by Bronfenbrenner. Exosystem interactions involve those interactions that the child has no access to but nevertheless affect him or her. Parents' occupations are examples of this influence. Finally, at the broadest (and thus most indirect level), macrosystem influences are cultural (or subcultural) ideologies which play a role in an individual's life.

The implications of Bronfenbrenner's approach are quite far-reaching. Appropriate research becomes defined not as simply doing naturalistic observations (which is sometimes attributed to him) but rather as analyzing and controlling a variety of spheres of influence to assess certain kinds of developmental change. From my perspective, the strength of Bronfenbrenner's position is his explicit and detailed, yet comprehensive groundwork for the analysis of behavior and for development. I also see two weaknesses, both of which can be easily remedied without disruption of the theory. First, I am not as willing as Bronfenbrenner to downplay the role of internal factors such as cognition in favor of interpersonal interactions. Henggeler's (1982) family-ecological systems approach to clinical psychology also noted this shortcoming and incorporated a "mini-microsystem" level of analysis. A second shortcoming, in my opinion, is that Bronfenbrenner gives very little importance to the role of physical setting. Certainly the physical context of behavior at each level of the various systems will play an important role in behavior and in development, from urban versus rural housing for the microsystem, to agrarian versus industrial settings for the macrosystem.

Ittelson et al., Barker, Bandura, and Bronfenbrenner all share an appreciation for the complexity of factors influencing human behavior. They differ in the scope of what they choose to focus on and emphasize. Although integrating their theories into a comprehensive conceptualization would be difficult, they nevertheless offer us some important general dimensions of context (both physical and social) with which to analyze behavior in general and spatial cognition in particular. To make this analysis more comprehensible, I first discuss some current theories that deal more explicitly with spatial cognition.

SOME THEORIES OF SPATIAL COGNITION

Piaget and Inhelder (1967) proposed that the child's understanding of spatial relations develops in concert with the general stages of cognitive development. A preoperational child understands space in terms of topological relations, or qualitative factors such as "next to" or "in front of." The concrete operational child, being able to coordinate and seriate objects, understands projective properties of space. That is, this child recognizes that different views of the arrangement of space will accompany different viewing positions of the space. Finally, as a late concrete operational, early formal operational accomplishment, the individual comes to understand Euclidean or metric properties of space. Not only do objects in space order themselves along the dimensions of space, there is a precise measurement or fixed coordinate system that can exactly define the position of an object.

As an important extension and clarification of Piaget's work, Pick and Lockman (1981) view the development of spatial behaviors in relation to the concept of frames of reference. For these authors, a frame of reference refers to the cue(s) used to define the position of objects in space. For example, objects may be defined egocentrically (i.e., using one's body as the major reference point), or objects may be defined allocentrically (i.e., using reference points external to the person, such as landmarks, container cues, or geographical coordinates). Although the use of frames of reference follows the progression of body-body, body-object, to object-object relations (i.e., primarily egocentric to primarily allocentric), Pick and Lockman note that mastery and complexity of all three types continue to increase throughout development. In addition, it is overly simplistic to consider any but a very few spatial tasks as involving a single frame of reference. More often it is the case that multiple frames of reference must be coordinated.

As an example of a frames of reference analysis, Pick and Lockman (1981) considered body-object and object-object relations for the spatial behaviors of object manipulation and locomotion in infants and young children. They suggested that body-object relations are mastered first for both activities (i.e., the baby can place his or her hand in a box prior to placing objects in other objects; young children can successfully reverse a traveled route prior to making inferences about the location of objects not directly linked by the route). These data are explained as a reliance by the infant and young child on an egocentric frame of reference. It is easier for the child to orient and manipulate objects and locations in space in reference to self than in reference to the other objects/locations. Efficiency is gained by using external loci; with development, the individual is able to perform more sophisticated orientation with the move to allocentric (object-object) reference systems.

Perhaps more than any other publication, Siegel and White (1975) encouraged investigators to examine spatial cognition in large-scale environments. The issue of scale of the environment is related to, but distinct from, the issue of the size of the space. Large-scale spaces surround the individual and require a coordination of multiple views in order to comprehend the structure in its entirety. Siegel and White suggested that the ability to operate within these complex spaces implies the existence of spatial representations. Individuals must have some mental code of the physical world in order to understand, move about, and interact within the world. They further proposed that the development of these spatial representations follows a particular course. This sequence is followed ontogenetically by children mastering spatial relations, and microgenetically by adults learning a new environment.

First, the individual encodes landmarks-in-context. Landmarks are primarily visual configurations of meaningful, route-orienting objects. Thus, a corner grocery, an intersection, or an old maple tree can serve as landmarks. Next, the individual learns sensorimotor routines connecting landmarks, called routes. Landmarks and routes are the organizing features of spatial representations. As the route knowledge of the person becomes more detailed and enriched, eventually a survey representation of part or all of the space is believed to exist. A survey representation offers comprehensive knowledge of the relationship of landmarks and routes. Presented with the problem of a detour, the individual with survey knowledge can deduce an alternative, never experienced, novel route.

Siegel and White's theory of the development of large-scale spatial cognition set the stage for much of the current research on spatial cognition. Issues of relevance from this work that have provoked investigators are the externalization of these covert representations, the impact of different environmental structures, and the role of a variety of acquisition experiences, to name a few.

The proliferation of research on spatial representations has not been without its growing pains. A common issue of debate has been different interpretations concerning the development of spatial competence as a function of using different spatial tasks for externalizing the representation. This also raises the issue of the link between one's covert representation and behavior presumably based upon that representation. Liben (1981) suggested that much of the controversy may be due to a definitional discrepancy. Specifically, researchers of spatial representations may mean different things in their use of the term. As a means of resolving (or at least clarifying) this point, she makes the case quite nicely that there are three types of spatial representations being talked about: spatial products, spatial thought, and spatial storage. Spatial products refer to the concrete outcome of a spatial task such as a map or a verbal description. We know that children's performance will vary as a function of the medium used to externalize the representation. These production factors take on increased importance to the extent that one proposes that the ability to use particular media is inherent to the individual's representational ability.

Liben suggested that much of the confusion in the research literature can be understood by the distinction between spatial thought and spatial storage. Spatial thought refers to any cognitive event that involves spatial information being processed by the individual. Remembering a route or being able to mentally rotate an object for comparison with another are examples of spatial thought. Spatial storage is that body of information about space and spatial relations which an individual has but is not conscious of. By way of analogy Liben points to the work by many linguists who propose elaborate rules that native speakers must follow in order to be competent speakers. These rules are a way of characterizing what the speaker can do and in fact can be used to understand how people speak and understand language. Yet the rules exist explicitly in the head of the linguist, not in the head of the native speaker. If an individual becomes aware of the information in spatial storage, Liben suggests this knowledge then falls within the realm of spatial thought.

This conceptualization clarifies some perplexing issues involved with spatial representations. Although inferences about spatial storage can be made from particular behaviors, inferences about spatial thought require the use of several tasks and convergent findings. Thus, to quote Liben, "Positions that appear to be different with respect to methodologies or with respect to the hypothesized link between representation and action appear to be more readily understood and reconciled by recognizing that there are differences with respect to the construct (type of representation) of interest, that is, with respect to the questions being asked" (Liben, 1981, p. 15).

The research under the heading of spatial cognition has become, as noted by Siegel (1982), "an industry." Some of the best products of this industry are reported in the chapters of this book. Before outlining the remaining chapters for the reader, I would like to make some general statements about the field in light of the two sets of theoretical accounts presented above.

THE LOGIC AND LIMITS OF SPATIAL COGNITION

The first set of theories above asserts the importance of spatial cognition as a component of, and embedded within, a complex network of social and phys-ical/environmental factors. The second set of theories focuses on spatial cog-nitive processes often to the exclusion of the interpersonal factors. It seems to me to be fruitful to explore a possible middle-of-the-road meeting ground for these sets of theories. Although the global theories of environmental influence offer a heuristically appealing framework for understanding a wide range of context influences, I feel much would be gained by fleshing out this framework at the level of the individual's cognitive functioning. The cognitive theorists provide important data on how individuals construct and manipulate knowledge of their physical settings, but much would be gained by expanding the research to in-clude processing of information of the surrounding social systems.

There seem to be two conceptual barriers for expanding the spatial cognition research toward a more comprehensive analysis of context. One is the predomi-nance of the analysis of spatial representations. This term has become nearly synonymous with the more generic term "spatial cognition." An implication one might draw from much of the literature is that when thought involves spatial content, that thought is somehow different from (although related to) other aspects of thinking. It is experienced differently than other forms of knowledge, is transformed and manipulated by different processes, and indeed is represented uniquely in the head.

I am certainly aware that not everyone would share the implication I have drawn above. Also, I am aware that not everyone who agrees with my analysis would be troubled by the implication. Although the growth of the spatial cognition enterprise probably needed a sense of separateness from other cognitive concerns, the time is right to reevaluate this position. Several of the chapters in this book explore this relationship.

Regardless of one's position concerning the equating of spatial cognition with spatial representations and the separateness this implies, the second conceptual barrier that narrows the focus of inquiry of this research is probably the more important limitation. Following the tradition established in the last couple of decades in other areas of psychology, there exists a conceptual and empirical isolation of investigations into cognitive concerns versus social concerns. Cognitive theorists give lip service to social factors and social theorists give lip service to cognitive functioning. Neither is disparaging of the other; they are simply separate concerns. The history of the investigation of the development of social cognition will serve both as an example of what I'm alluding to, and also as a potential resolution for researchers of spatial cognition.

As noted by Shantz (1975) social cognition concerns the investigation of how an individual infers the covert, psychological processes of others. In her extensive review article she classified the research into such things as inferring what another is seeing, feeling, intending, and so forth. The vast majority of this research used a paradigm where the individual was presented with a display or a hypothetical situation from which inferences of various sorts were to be drawn. In general, this work uncovered a progression from an inability to take different perspectives in the preschool-aged child, to an understanding of quite indirect social implications for consideration by the adolescent. As noted by Bearison (1982), two types of findings have been problematic to social cognitive researchers: the age-related changes are not the same across different contents of thought, and the link between social cognition and social behavior has often not been clearly demonstrated. (It is interesting, of course, that these same concerns are often aired by spatial cognition researchers; see for example, Newcombe, 1981.)

Current work in the area of social cognition emphasizes the context of the thought. The typical paradigm mentioned above tells us how children can reflect on the covert processes of others in isolation, but not on how, why, where, or when these reflections occur and influence social interactions. In addition, those in the field of social cognition have been engrossed in a couple of arguments similar to the two I presented above. Some discuss whether social cognition should be considered separate from cognition of nonsocial phenomena (e.g., see Damon, 1979), and others suggest that definitions of separateness aside, social and cognitive concerns must be considered jointly. Bearison (1982), from a Piagetian perspective, suggests that knowledge of social context and of physical context are derived from the same structural base. Reasoning about either is derived from the same laws of knowing. Thus, all cognitive experiences have social origins. To use Bearison's words, "Thus, social cognition not only reflects the development of social knowledge but also the social development of knowledge" (p. 202).

If we can accept that all knowledge has social origins, we also can argue that all knowledge has spatial and temporal properties as well. Can we substitute in the remark above and have the statement, "Thus, spatial cognition not only reflects the development of spatial knowledge but also the spatial development of knowledge"? At the simplest level this statement implies that all knowledge is temporally and spatially tagged by the knower. At a less trivial level, this statement suggests that the properties of environments, as known by an individual, may influence the acquisition and use of information acquired in the environments. A union of spatial knowledge, social knowledge, and an understanding of the physical and social natures of environments—all in relation to the cognitive functioning of the participants—would seem to be a fruitful integration of interests among environmentalists, spatial cognitivists, and those interested in social behavior. Put more simply, studying the processes of thought for different spatial and social contexts is being advocated here.

OUTLINE OF THE REMAINING CHAPTERS

The next three chapters of the book are general reviews that provide a general context for the field of spatial cognition. In the first, Robin West, Carolyn Morris, and Gerry Nichol offer an analysis of spatial thinking on tasks that researchers do not traditionally consider to be spatial tasks. Specifically, they review the work on imagery, selective memory tasks, syllogistic reasoning, semantic integration, and the academic tasks of mathematics, science, and reading. The use of a spatial metaphor for understanding performance on these tasks has proven quite useful. The authors make the interesting point that it would prove to be even more profitable to understand the relationship between tasks that *assess* spatial knowledge and those tasks that *access* spatial knowledge.

In Chapter 3, David Weatherford provides a detailed discussion of the types of environments used by spatial cognition researchers. Although theoretical and operational definitions concerning the size and scale of these spaces abound, David offers what I feel to be an important taxonomy: model/small-scale environments, navigable/small-scale environments, and large-scale environments. Within these three categories he reviews the research on perspective taking, mental rotation, cognitive mapping, and orientation, with an eye toward uncovering important findings attributable to differences in these structural aspects of the environments.

David Weatherford's chapter considers environments experimenters construct for children. In the final introductory chapter, Chloee Poag, Judy Goodnight, and I review the research on the environments in which children typically find themselves as participants. We present research on the home, neighborhood, and school and consider a variety of influences of these settings.

The next three chapters explore the phenomena of spatial cognition for three different age groups. In Chapter 5, Linda Acredolo organizes the burgeoning research on infant's spatial cognition, specifically in terms of spatial orientation abilities. She discusses the research under two headings corresponding to having an understanding of a change in location for an object when one's vantage point is changed versus an understanding when the object has been moved. Linda offers an interesting account of the development of spatial orientation during infancy, noting that infancy is a period of rapid change and should not be considered as a homogeneous period.

Next, Gärling, Böök, and Lindberg present their analysis of the use of certain spatial concepts and skills by adults for adjusting to everyday environments. They take an information-processing approach to this endeavor and present research concerned with delineating the processes of a variety of internal structures for the representation of spatial information, research on the acquisition of this information, and a discussion of movement and orientation in large-scale spaces. Finally, they discuss their ongoing research of other related everyday cognitive skills.

K. C. Kirasic, in Chapter 7, gives us the other end of the age spectrum by reviewing spatial research on the elderly adult. While the research literature is particularly sparse with this age group, K. C. notes the practical importance of understanding how the elderly comprehend and cope with changing environments and with today's urban settings. She reviews the psychometric studies of spatial abilities with the elderly and then reviews the work that more directly assesses the individual's spatial behavior. The issue of the ecological validity of the testing situation seems to be a particularly pertinent one for this age group.

The next three chapters offer an analysis of some special variables of interest to the study of spatial cognition. In Chapter 8, Sheila Cohen and I piece together the work on the role of activity for the construction of spatial representations. First, we infer the influence of activity from studies not specifically designed to do so; then we discuss the research that more directly assesses this influence. We present our most current research, which leads us to suggest that it would be beneficial to conceptualize the role of activity more broadly, particularly in terms of the goals and functions of the person and the activity.

Next, Susan Golbeck contributes a detailed analysis relating a taxonomy of general environmental characteristics, including structural and organizational features, to environmental cognition. Susan uses the school classroom as an example of the use of this framework. This chapter offers an interesting extension of the review provided by Poag, Goodnight, and Cohen in Chapter 4.

In Chapter 10, Judy Goodnight and I review topics of social concerns that have traditionally been of interest to spatial cognition researchers: privacy, crowding, personal space. In the conclusion of the chapter, we consider research on social cognition and two general issues of social development, socialization and individuation, and relate these bodies of work toward developing an integrative analysis of spatial and social cognitive development. We feel that this is an important first step toward a theory, not only of behavior-in-context, but also of development-in-context.

The final four chapters address several methodological and meta-methodological issues of spatial cognition. Nora Newcombe offers a detailed analysis of spatial tasks in Chapter 11. Rather than being troubled by different performances from different tasks, she reminds us that different tasks have different demands and call for different types of spatial processing. It becomes much more important to understand these different demands than to argue over whose techniques are better. Nora presents an analysis of some of these task demands under three headings: the correspondence between performance and some assessment of accuracy; subjects' preferences about which technique best captures their subjective appraisal; and those studies using more than one dependent variable. She points out various strengths and weaknesses of some common research techniques and provides some interesting guidelines for better understanding our methods of spatial cognition research.

Whereas West, Morris, and Nichol in Chapter 2 used spatial metaphors to understand general cognitive development, Gary Allen, in Chapter 12, interprets spatial research within the realm of experimental human cognition. First, he discusses the conceptual problems associated with the use of such terms as "cognitive map." Then, he explores the constructs of metamemory, linear order representations, frames of reference, and production systems first as general interpretive guides and then in relation to Liben's (1981) categories of spatial storage, spatial thought, and spatial products.

As a geographer, Roger Downs, in Chapter 13, notes that cartography plays a central role in our theories of spatial cognition, yet most researchers have a limited grasp of this field. His chapter addresses this weakness by discussing the field of cartography and the use of maps in general, and its application for understanding spatial cognition in particular. Going beyond simply questioning what constitutes an accurate representation, Roger disentangles the knower from what is to be known for both cartography and spatial cognition. This perspective leads him to a broader view of both fields and a series of interesting questions to be explored.

In Chapter 14, Alex Siegel and Jennifer Cousins consider the research on spatial cognition within a broad epistemological and social context. They consider a host of issues relevant to the field: from the issue of accuracy, to the issue of competence versus performance, to the ecological validity of our work, to the agenda of not only the subjects but also the researchers. I find this chapter's appeal to be due not only to its firm historical and empirical documentation but to its commonsensical approach.

In conclusion, this book offers an in-depth analysis of the development of spatial cognition: from an examination of important developmental and environmental variables, to an evaluation of a variety of methodological and theoretical issues, to a consideration of a number of metatheoretical concerns. To assert that the study of spatial cognition is a growing enterprise among social scientists is beyond dispute. The authors of these chapters present both the state of the art and future directions for this enterprise. I'm sure the reader of this book will have ample evidence for answering the opening question of this chapter; the contributors to this book have made admirable progress in making the study of spatial cognition truly special.

REFERENCES

Bandura, A. *Social learning theory.* Englewood Cliffs, NJ: Prentice-Hall, 1977.

Barker, R. G. *Ecological psychology.* Stanford, CA; Stanford University Press, 1968.

Bearison, D. J. New directions in studies of social interaction and cognitive growth. In F. C. Serafica (Ed.), *Social-cognitive development in context.* New York: Guilford Press, 1982.

Bronfenbrenner, U. *The ecology of human development.* Cambridge, MA: Harvard University Press, 1979.

Cohen, R., Poag, C. K., Goodnight, J. A. The impact of physical setting on the adolescent. In S. W. Henggeler (Ed.), *Delinquency and adolescent psychopathology.* Littleton, MA: Wright/PSG, 1982.

Damon, W. Why study social-cognitive development? *Human Development,* 1979, *22,* 206–211.

Hart, R. A., & Moore, G. T. The development of spatial cognition: A review. In R. M. Downs & D. Stea (Eds.), *Image and environment: Cognitive mapping and spatial behavior.* Chicago: Aldine, 1973.

Henggeler, S. W. (Ed.). *Delinquency and adolescent psychopathology.* Littleton, MA: Wright/PSG, 1982.

Ittelson, W. H., Proshansky, H. M., Rivlin, L. G., & Winkel, G. H. *An introduction to environmental psychology.* New York: Holt, Rinehart & Winston, 1974.

Liben, L. S. Spatial representation and behavior: Multiple perspectives. In L. S. Liben, A. H. Patterson, & N. Newcombe (Eds.), *Spatial representation and behavior across the life span.* New York: Academic Press, 1981.

Liben, L. S., Patterson, A. H., & Newcombe, N. *Spatial representation and behavior across the life span.* New York: Academic Press, 1981.

Newcombe, N. Spatial representation and behavior: Retrospect and prospect. In L. S. Liben, A. H. Patterson, & N. Newcombe (Eds.), *Spatial representation and behavior across the life span.* New York: Academic Press, 1981.

Piaget, J., & Inhelder, B. *The child's conception of space.* New York: Norton, 1967.

Pick, H. L., & Lockman, J. J. From frames of reference to spatial representations. In L. S. Liben, A. H. Patterson, & N. Newcombe (Eds.), *Spatial representation and behavior across the life span.* New York: Academic Press, 1981.

Shantz, C. U. The development of social cognition. In E. M. Hetherington (Ed.), *Review of child development research* (Vol. 5). Chicago: University of Chicago Press, 1975.

Siegel, A. W. Towards a social ecology of cognitive mapping. In R. Cohen (Ed.), *Children's conceptions of spatial relationships.* San Francisco: Jossey-Bass, 1982.

Siegel, A. W., & White, S. H. The development of spatial representations of large-scale environments. In H. W. Reese (Ed.), *Advances in child development and behavior* (Vol. 10). New York: Academic Press, 1975.

II SETTING THE STAGE

2
Spatial Cognition on Nonspatial Tasks: Finding Spatial Knowledge When You're Not Looking For It

Robin L. West
Aging and Development Program
Washington University

Carolyn W. Morris
Gerry T. Nichol
Memphis State University

Research on the development of spatial cognition has expanded our knowledge of cognitive development by investigating changes in cognitive structures and processes within a new domain. The accumulated evidence from this research also has revealed a great deal about how children perceive, understand, and remember spatial configurations. Obviously, spatial thinking occurs in the typical spatial cognition paradigms described in this book. Not so obvious, perhaps, is the role that spatial thinking plays in nonspatial tasks. A child's spatial ability, understanding of spatial relationships, and coordination and integration of spatial information affect performance on a wide variety of tasks. The intent of this chapter is to bridge the conceptual gap between research on spatial cognition in particular, and the effects of spatial cognition in a more general sense.

Liben (1981) has defined spatial thought as a type of representation that concerns or makes use of space in some way. It is "knowledge that individuals have access to, can reflect upon, or can manipulate" (Liben, 1981, p. 12). Spatial thought is necessary for integrating and comprehending spatial relationships in different forms, in different contexts. Spatial relationships can be represented in the locations of objects in an array, the arrangements of mental images, the formations of words from letters, or in prose descriptions of an environment. Whether explicit or implicit, information that conveys spatial relationships may be understood or remembered to the extent that a person has developed spatial-cognitive skills.

The influence of spatial thought on nonspatial tasks has largely been overlooked, because at first glance it might seem that spatial cognition has little to offer. From a narrow perspective this would seem true—scholars interested in memory and imagery are not well versed in the spatial cognition research and vice versa. But the theme of this chapter is that this research is interrelated. It is clear that the cognitive processes of memory and imagery affect learning of routes, landmarks, and configurations. However, these relationships are not presented here. Instead, we focus on the proposition that spatial thinking can be looked upon as a metaphor for thinking on nonspatial tasks. People think as if they are using spatial knowledge when performing tasks involving memory, imagery, and inferencing. Careful analysis suggests the usefulness of the spatial metaphor in understanding and explaining performance on these nonspatial tasks.

Rather than focus on theories that have considered the development of spatial thinking (see Hart & Moore, 1973, and Siegel & White, 1975, for reviews), we focus on the influence of spatial thinking on cognitive performance in different areas, beginning with a discussion of spatial cognition in imagery. The second section of the chapter is concerned with spatial aspects of memory tasks and the relationship between memory performance and children's use of locational cues. In addition, we examine the effect of spatial knowledge on the organization and integration of information for recall. The third major section considers how children use spatial inferences both to solve syllogistic reasoning problems and to comprehend and remember written information about spatial relationships. Finally, we explicate the role that spatial thinking plays in children's performance on academic tasks, such as mathematics and reading. The conclusions describe the link between spatial thinking and cognitive performance, focusing on the need for understanding the relationship between tasks that directly *assess* spatial knowledge and tasks that indirectly *access* spatial knowledge.

IMAGERY

The nature of imagery is a topic of interest to psychologists as a result of the revival of concern with cognitive processes. Imagery involves the internal perception or representation of an object. This internal representation may occur when the object is present—to play a role in perceptual processing and identification—or it may occur when the object is absent—to play a role in remembering the object. Although both introspection and experimental evidence indicate that visual imagery often accompanies thought, the exact role that imagery plays is the subject of debate. Pylyshyn (1973, 1981) and Anderson and Bower (1973) deny a functional role to imagery. Rather, they assert that knowledge is stored as either abstract propositions (Anderson & Bower, 1973) or symbolic descriptions (Pylyshyn, 1973). Pylyshyn (1981) sees the term "image" and the picture metaphor as misleading, as they suggest that the image is an entity to be perceived. He stresses that individuals report not the properties of their images but the properties of the objects that they are imaging. In this view, therefore, imagery is seen as a by-product of thought or "mental embroidery." Others, however, attribute a more functional role to imagery. For example, Paivio (1969) postulates two interconnected memory systems, verbal and imaginal, which operate in parallel. Similarly, Kosslyn (1973, 1981), in his analogical position, sees imagery as an important component of cognition.

Regardless of the role attributed to visual imagery, if internal images are generated as part of cognitive processing, they are very likely to have spatial properties. Kosslyn (1973, 1981) has been among the first to investigate the spatial thinking involved in imagery. He defines images as temporal, spatial displays in active memory—displays that are generated from more abstract representations in long-term memory.

Kosslyn's research (1973, 1978b) supports his position that mental images do in fact represent information "pictorially." In a series of experiments, Kosslyn set out to demonstrate that images containing spatial content preserve relative metric distances between objects and portions of objects. In each of these studies, subjects were asked to construct visual images of stimuli to which they had been exposed, for example, pictures of faces, landscapes, maps. Subjects were then asked to scan their image, looking for an object or location specified by the experimenter. Three findings merit attention. First, as greater distances were covered in scanning a mental image to "see" some target, the scan times were longer. In fact, scan times increased linearly with distance scanned (Kosslyn, 1973; Kosslyn, Ball, & Reiser, 1978). Second, subjects required more time to examine subjectively smaller images than larger images when "looking" for a named part. Subjects reported having to "zoom in" to "see" a named part if the imaged object was extremely small (Kosslyn, 1975). Moreover, smaller parts required more time even when the smaller parts were more highly associated with the object in question than were the larger ones. In fact, the smaller parts were verified as appropriate more quickly when imagery was not used (Kosslyn, 1976). Third, there is evidence indicating that imagined representations occur in a medium that is spatially bounded. The size of the image appears to be limited by outer boundaries, and subjects report that larger objects seem to "overflow" at further subjective distances than do smaller objects (Kosslyn, 1978a).

In addition to providing evidence about the spatial aspects of imagery, Kosslyn (1978b) has discussed the development of imagery in children. According to his representational-development hypothesis, young children rely predominantly on imagery for representing information in memory, whereas older children and adults tend to use more abstract linguistic representations. He posits that children use imagery largely by necessity, but adults, having more alternatives, use it by preference. As the individual acquires more information, it becomes more likely that the information will be encoded in an abstract "propositional" code as well as an imagery format. For example, when asked to consider the question "What color is a bee's head?" most adults report picturing the insect's head and examining their image to get the answer. If asked again, however, they report that it is no longer necessary to use imagery. In addition to the influence of experience on how information is represented in memory, Kosslyn points to the influence of maturational factors upon the use of imagery at different ages, e.g., speed of processing may increase as the child matures. This may affect not only how many representations can be held in mind simultaneously, but also how easily the child can make deductions. Children may consult an image rather than deduce answers because of constraints imposed by limits in processing capacity or decay rates. In summary, Kosslyn suggests that imagery will be used if one is asked a question about a concrete object and the information is not stored explicitly. If the required information is not available in an abstract propositional code or if deduction is difficult, imagery is increasingly likely to be used.

Striking evidence for Kosslyn's view comes from the reaction time work of Shepard and his colleagues (Cooper & Shepard, 1973; Shepard, 1978; Shepard & Metzler, 1971). In this research, subjects were shown a target stimulus followed by a rotated comparison and were asked to decide if the two stimuli were the same (e.g., R,R) or mirror images, (e.g., R,Я). Reaction time for such decisions approximated a linear function of the extent of rotation from the original, suggesting that subjects formed an image of the comparison and mentally rotated it to the axis of the original.

Individuals differ in their tendency to invoke and use mental imagery. Developmental differences in ability to compare imaginal representations have been investigated using a reaction time paradigm. Childs and Polich (1979) required third graders, fifth graders, and college students to determine whether a letter of the alphabet was presented in its backward or normal position. Letters were presented at 0°, 60°, 180°, 240°, or 300° orientations from upright. Either subjects were given no advance information about a test letter or they were given identity and orientation information. There were basic similarities in the strategies employed by children and adults when provided with no advance information. The reaction times of all age groups receiving no advance information were slower than those groups receiving information, and these slower reaction times indicated that the children mentally rotated the image. On the other hand, there were basic differences in the strategies employed when a clue letter was provided. The uniformly fast reaction times of the college students in the advance information condition suggested that they compared the test stimulus with the imaginal representation of the clue letter. However, an examination of individual reaction time profiles for the younger age groups revealed that some children could make effective use of the clue letter but others could not. Therefore, individual differences play a significant role in the use of mental imagery by young children.

Imagery and Learning

A considerable amount of evidence leads to the conclusion that imagery increases children's learning of both verbal and pictorial materials. Research on the effect of imagery on learning has most frequently used the paired-associate paradigm. In the paired-associate task, the learner is presented with a list of pairs, typically words or pictures. One part of the pair is the stimulus and the other is the response. The child's task is to learn the appropriate response for each stimulus. In a review of studies on imagery, Pressley (1977) noted three types of imagery commonly studied using this task. These included (1) imposed elaborated images—the experimenter provided images in the form of pictures depicting an interactive scene; (2) imposed unelaborated images—the experimenter provided images in the form of separate pictures presented in a linear arrangement; and (3) induced elaborated images—the subject generated images from separate pictures.

In general, imposed elaborated images facilitate retention of paired associates (Dempster & Rohwer, 1974; Holyoak, Hogeterp, & Yuille, 1972; Pressley, 1977). Pictures presented as interacting pairs were easier to learn than the same items presented in separate pictures, an effect that held for both nursery school children (Reese, 1970, 1972) and older elementary children (Danner & Taylor, 1973; Davidson & Adams, 1970; Holyoak et al., 1972). Young children apparently use the spatial integration of imposed elaborated pictures to spontaneously encode them into thematic relationships. Spatially separated pictures lead to more attention to individual items and result in less retention of the associated pairs (e.g., Mandler & Stein, 1974).

Instructions to generate spatially interacting images from separate pictures also facilitate retention of paired associates in kindergarten children (Danner & Taylor, 1973; Reese, 1972; Yuille & Catchpole, 1973) and in college students (Forbes & Reese, 1974). Yuille and Catchpole (1973), for example, found that kindergarten children given imagery training and children shown pairs of objects interacting recognized about twice as many correctly matched paired associates as children shown the objects presented side by side. Researchers have demonstrated that the ability to benefit from interactive imagery instruction seems to undergo rapid development between the ages of 6 and 12 (Pressley & Levin, 1977); younger children often fail to benefit from induced imagery instruction unless supplementary training methods are used (Varley, Levin, Severson, Wolff, 1974; Wolff & Levin, 1972). Brody, Mattson, and Zuckerwise (1978) suggested that the inability of young children to form imaginal mediators may represent a lack of understanding of what to do rather than an absence of imaginal capabilities.

Other research also has suggested that individual differences in imaginal capacity affect the ability to profit from induced imagery instructions. Hollenberg (1970) identified children as high and low imagers on the basis of tests for imaginal ability and demonstrated that high imagery children learned verbal labels for objects more quickly than did low imagery children. A later study showed that fourth-grade children who were good at learning paired associates from pictures benefited from imagery instructions, whereas those who learned poorly from pictures showed a decrease in performance following imagery instructions (Levin, Divine-Hawkins, Kerst, & Guttmann, 1974). These findings suggest that imagery instructions may be more potent for some children than others.

In addition to increasing children's learning of paired associates, imagery also facilitates comprehension and retention of prose. Experimenter-provided pictures that illustrate the content of stories increase both children's and adults' ability to correctly answer questions about passages (Bransford & Johnson, 1973; Guttman, Levin, & Pressley, 1977; Shimron, 1975). However, it is not until middle childhood that memory for stories is improved by instructions to construct internal images corresponding to story content. Shimron (1975), for example, found that both first- and fourth-grade children shown picture illustrations while listening to stories answered more story-related questions than did control subjects who only listened to the stories. In contrast, instructions to construct mental pictures of the content of the stories improved memory of prose only for fourth graders; first graders given imagery instructions answered no more questions correctly than the control subjects.

Although even very young children benefit from imagery provided by pictures, it is only later that they can generate their own images to help them remember paired associates or prose. Constructing imaginal mediators is difficult for young children unless they are given training in using internal imagery. With training, young children can produce internal visualizations of spatially interacting objects or schematize objects in an appropriate context, thus facilitating their retention of material.

Summary

Although the role of spatial cognition in imagery has only been highlighted here, this does illustrate the complex interrelationship between the two areas. Furthermore, it demonstrates the importance of considering the effects of spatial thinking on performance in imagery tasks. In this section, we discussed how imagery involves spatially organized, internally represented objects that have size, shape, and interlocation cues in a mental environment. Use of these spatial cues affects performance on a variety of tasks requiring imagined representations of objects, much like the presence of landmarks affects the learning of large-scale spaces. The research showed that mentally represented objects with larger interpoint distances or greater size require longer reaction times to scan than imagined objects with smaller sizes. In addition, presenting objects in interacting scenes facilitates recall of these objects in comparison to presenting them in separated scenes. In this section we also emphasized the importance of attending to developmental differences in the use of imagery and the resultant effect on task performance. Young children are less likely than older children to use imagery spontaneously as a mnemonic device to learn paired associates or to learn details from stories.

MEMORY

Memory plays an integral role in spatial cognition. In fact, much of the research investigating spatial cognition uses recall accuracy as a dependent measure, yet this research has not been fully integrated with the traditional memory literature. At the same time, performance on memory tasks may be affected by spatial cognition, and this relationship has largely been ignored. For example, if imagery involves spatial representation, as we suggested earlier, memory tasks with instructions encouraging the use of imagery may be strongly affected by the spatial relationships among the items. However, even if imagery is not involved, there are a variety of memory tasks that may access spatial knowledge. Items presented visually in any kind of array, matrix, or picture will have spatial properties, and these properties may affect the memorability of the items. This section focuses on to-be-remembered information that contains spatial cues or spatial relations.

Encoding of Spatial Information

The influence of spatial knowledge on memory performance has been recognized for centuries. For example, the method of loci has been used since the time of the Greeks (Bower, 1970). This mnemonic method involves imagining to-be-remembered items in locations in a familiar environment, and then remembering the items by taking a "mental walk" through the environment. The spatial layout of a familiar environment does not need to be learned and it can provide cues for remembering. Beyond this simple mnemonic, the memorial function of spatial knowledge has been recognized with respect to the encoding of locational information. As noted, any array of items contains spatial or locational information that could be encoded. Depending on the child's memorizing skills and spatial knowledge, and the task requirements, spatial cues may be derived from the encoded locational information. Or spatial cues may be provided explicitly in the task instructions. In effect, learning an array may be viewed as learning a tiny environment, and the spatial layout of that tiny environment can influence one's ability to recall it.

With children, the type of array used most often in memory research is a horizontal row of 6 to 8 pictures. Using this kind of array, the probe-type locational recall task was initially designed as a means for assessing young children's short-term memory ability (Atkinson, Hansen, & Bernbach, 1964). In this paradigm, a series of pictures are presented one at a time and then turned face down until all items have been presented. Typically, the temporal and spatial order of item presentation are completely redundant. For recall, a cue card is shown and the child is asked to point to the location of the unseen target picture that matches it.

Some investigators have suggested that the encoding of spatial information does not have a strong effect on performance on this task (Atkinson et al., 1964; Rosner, 1972). However, a shadow of doubt was cast on this interpretation when very young children showed primacy effects. Primacy effects are usually interpreted as an indication of some kind of serial rehearsal, yet there is considerable evidence indicating that young children are nonrehearsers (for a review see Hagen, Jongeward, & Kail, 1975). Recent research with this task demonstrated that the primacy effects observed in children as young as 4 may be due to spatial cues rather than rehearsal. When the temporal order of item presentation was not congruent with the left-to-right arrangement, a spatial primacy effect was still observed—that is, the children had higher recall scores for items in the first positions than for items in other positions in the array (Berch, 1978; Siegel, Allik, & Herman, 1976), although this did not occur when the children were asked to label the items (Brown, Brown, & Caci, 1981). Berch (1979) noted that the primacy effects occurring with children under 6 reflect higher recall of the initial array item only. This supports the contextual uniqueness hypothesis (Siegel et al., 1976) that the initial item on the left of the array stands out in contrast to other items within the array.

Even though older children are probably engaging in verbal rehearsal of picture labels, the presence of spatial information appears to facilitate their performance on the probe-type location recall task (Berch, 1978; Brown et al., 1981). A recent reanalysis of a location recall study, with children from 5 to 12 years of age, supports the idea that older children are affected by the availability of spatial cues (West, 1980). After simultaneous presentation, all of the children demonstrated fewer errors and higher clustering scores for pictures presented in the first position in the array than for pictures in other positions. The primacy effect was significantly greater on a reconstruction task requiring subjects to remember locations than on a recognition task not requiring memory for locations. In addition, the spatial primacy effect was strongest for the oldest children given a brief presentation of the array (West, 1980). These findings suggest that older children who demonstrate rehearsal and organizational strategies are still affected by the spatial arrangement of items when they apply those strategies.

Knowing that spatial information affects the recall of children across a wide age range raises another issue: to what extent do children automatically encode locational or spatial cues to memorize visually presented items? There is some evidence that locational information may be encoded by children as young as 4, even when attention is not specifically drawn to it (Ceci, Lea, & Howe, 1980; Mandler, Seegmiller, & Day, 1977; von Wright, Gebhard, & Karttunen, 1975). There is also evidence suggesting that there are minimal developmental differences in the extent to which performance is enhanced by the presence of spatial cues (Geis & Lange, 1976; Henek & Miller, 1976; Samuels, Hiscock, & Kinsbourne, 1978; von Wright et al., 1975). To explain these data, it has been suggested that location is encoded automatically (if other item characteristics are encoded) because the location of the items serves as contextual or environmental information (Altom & Weil, 1977; Schulman, 1973; von Wright et al., 1975). Then, when the item is remembered, its locational context is also remembered. Certainly, if items are remembered through the use of visual imagery, the physical features of the items and the spatial relationships among items in the array probably would be represented in the image. Thus, the item is represented internally in its context.

To suggest that young children encode spatial information is not to say that such information is part of strategic processing. For example, the child may encode locational information without clustering on the basis of location. Locational clustering is far more likely as children get older (West, 1980). Also, children across a wide age range can remember some item locations on the probe-type location recall task, but only the older children use serial rehearsal strategies to remember locations (e.g., Conroy & Weener, 1976). It may be that serial rehearsal involves an internalized image that is spatially organized, with the first and last items serving as anchors (see Brown, 1976). In any case, young children appear to encode some locational information without using it in strategic memory processing. Interestingly, when young elementary school children are required to recall items and their locations, their recall of items often suffers in comparison to conditions where only item recall is required (von Wright et al., 1975; West, 1980). It is as if the young child's attempt to apply an intentional strategy to remember location interferes with the processing of item information. Typically, intentional strategies for remembering location, such as rehearsal and clustering, are not applied until the fifth or sixth grade (Hagen & Kail, 1973; Hagen & Stanovich, 1977).

The benefits of encoding spatial information are not clearly delineated. For example, considerable research has investigated whether spatial or temporal information is more useful for recalling visually presented arrays. It is clear from this research that spatial information plays an important role in memorization, that serial recall of an array is facilitated by the confounding of spatial and temporal order, and that spatial information is more salient than temporal information for some populations, for example, deaf or retarded individuals (see Berch, 1979, for a review).

If there is a memory advantage provided by the addition of spatial information, it is important to determine the reason for this advantage. Underwood (1969) suggested that spatial attributes are encoded by children at a fairly early age and that spatial information may be more useful for item differentiation than for item retrieval. This suggests that spatial cues are useful when other retrieval cues are present or when item retrieval is not required. Item retrieval usually is not required in the probe-type location recall task where the child is asked to identify the location of presented items, nor is it required in reconstruction tasks where the child is asked to recreate an array. Thus, the addition of spatial cues may enhance performance particularly on these tasks. Underwood's ideas are clearly consistent with the notion that spatial information is remembered together with item content, and that it serves as a context for remembering items. The contextual information may serve as a cue for discriminating among items that are retrieved primarily through the use of other kinds of content cues.

The presence of spatial information is often a function of presentation conditions; for example, no spatial cues are provided when items are presented successively in the same location. The improved performance typically obtained under some presentation conditions may be due to the availability of spatial cues to aid memory. For instance, it may be that the advantage of item sorting during a study period (usually seen as a way to improve item organization) include the addition of spatial cues for the items grouped in front of the child. Also, the advantage of simultaneous over successive presentation may be due, in part, to the addition of spatial cues under simultaneous presentation conditions. Unfortunately, there are few studies examining the extent to which locational cues are used for memorizing items seen under different presentation conditions. It is apparent that age differences are reduced under simultaneous presentation conditions (e.g., Henek & Miller, 1976) and that simultaneous presentation facilitates the performance of young children more than older children (e.g., Brown, 1976; Furth & Milgram, 1973). The added spatial cues may help the younger child. There is an alternative view. Brown (1976) suggested that simultaneous presentation facilitates the performance of young children because it allows them to see the items as a unit. The unitized items are more likely to be recalled together than the items that are presented successively. (The effects of unitization will be discussed further in the next section). More data comparing different presentation methods and intentional and incidental learning of locations are needed before any conclusions can be drawn about the benefits of encoding spatial information.

Spatial Representation

Thus far, we have examined the use of spatial information in memory by discussing research related to the encoding of spatial cues or locations in an array. There is a broader sense in which spatial knowledge may affect memory: It may affect the organization or integration of information. Spatial representation is often used to clarify, explain, or enhance conceptual understanding of relationships. For instance, when we want someone to understand the relationships among concepts or members of a group, we often make a diagram, where related concepts or members are explicitly connected with lines. These graphic representations rely on spatial metaphor to convey information about hierarchies and interconnecting ideas. They are useful because they make relationships explicit, and because they provide the necessary guidance for using imagery to remember abstract conceptual relationships that are not easily imaged.

This kind of spatial metaphor is used within the memory literature as well. Memory searches through complex semantic networks have been discussed in terms of semantic distance (see Collins & Loftus, 1975). Knowledge about object relationships or events has been explained through the use of tree diagrams. Although this function of spatial representation is rarely investigated directly, many studies have examined the use of spatial representation as a key to integrating information presented in visual arrays. This integration often requires accessing schemata, or internal representations of the common relationships among familiar objects in the environment. Such schemata help to organize and give meaning to real-world settings. As we shall see, schemata for familiar settings appear to be well learned at a fairly young age, and they affect recall of pictured scenes.

The most interesting studies of spatial representation in memory have been conducted by Mandler and her colleagues. Mandler studied memory for pictured scenes containing 5 to 10 objects. The objects were either depicted randomly on a page or depicted in an arrangement analogous to the common placements of the objects. The latter items were called "organized" because they reflected the normal arrangement or organization of objects in the environment. Organized scenes were much easier to recall than unorganized scenes (Mandler & Robinson, 1978; Mandler & Stein, 1974). Spatial relation information (i.e., distances between objects and left-right positioning) was remembered more accurately in the organized scenes than the unorganized scenes, even for children as young as 7 (Mandler & Johnson, 1976; Mandler & Robinson, 1978; Mandler & Stein, 1974). Developmental differences in performance were larger with the unorganized scenes (Mandler & Robinson, 1978). For the unorganized pictures, spatial composition information (i.e., density of object placement, empty and filled spaces) affected the recognition memory of adults and older children but not younger children (Mandler & Johnson, 1976; Mandler & Robinson, 1978). These authors concluded that older children and adults were able to impose some kind of spatial schemata on unorganized pictures while young children were not, even though the young children appeared to use scene schemata to remember organized pictures. For both adults and children, spatial schemata appear to affect memory for object locations or distances between objects, but such schemata do not affect memory for the details in pictures (Hock, Romanski, Galie, & Williams, 1978; Mandler & Parker, 1976; Mandler & Ritchey, 1977). Thus, age differences in memory for details are probably not due to schema development.

The ability of adults and older children to impose organization on unorganized items is evident in other studies looking at the unitization of pictures. In these studies, children were shown several pictures presented separately or presented as a conceptual unit: "doll sat on the chair with a ball on lap" or "a circus scene with a clown, an elephant, a tiger, and a performing sea lion." Nursery school and young elementary children recalled pictures in the unitized scenes much better than separated items (Horowitz, Lampel, & Takanishi, 1969; Lampel, 1973; von Wright et al., 1975). Furthermore, there is some evidence that unitization facilitates memory in younger children more than older children (von Wright et al., 1975), again suggesting that older children are able to integrate information without the additional cues. This supports the Piagetian view that older children are capable of developing schematic representations in memory that are not within the cognitive capacity of young children (Piaget & Inhelder, 1973).

It is possible, however, that the effects of unitization are not due to the spatial integration of unitized items, but rather to the conceptual or thematic link between items that are unitized. That is, the conceptual theme orients the younger children to the semantic information in the items. Semantic orienting improves the recall of the younger children, whereas the older children have higher levels of recall without this semantic orienting. Baumeister and Smith (1979) addressed this issue in a study utilizing items that were spatially blocked, conceptually related, or both. Preschool and fifth-grade children recalled more and clustered more with pictures that were spatially blocked. However, preschool children were more affected by spatial proximity than conceptual themes, and fifth graders performed better when spatially blocked pictures were given some conceptual theme. Related research suggests that spatial proximity improves the incidental recall of items throughout elementary school (Druker & Hagen, 1969; Wheeler & Dusek, 1973) and that the use of an outside "frame" for items improves children's recall (von Wright, Loikkanen, & Reijonen, 1978). Taken together, these data suggest that unitization, or spatial proximity, facilitates performance by increasing the extent to which items are integrated in memory, regardless of conceptual content.

Summary

Two conclusions can be derived from this research concerning memory for spatial information: (1) locational information is probably encoded automatically by young children (under 8 years of age), even though their ability to use location in strategic memorizing is minimal; (2) young children have sufficient knowledge of their natural surroundings to develop schematic internal representations for common scenes (which can be used in memorizing), even though they are unable to apply schema in remembering unfamiliar scenes. In remembering, then, young children can make effective use of spatially organized internal representations when the target items and their spatial layout are fairly simple (as in horizontally arrayed items where the left-most item serves as an anchor or "landmark") or when items and their layout are very familiar. Only older children have the ability to integrate or reorganize complex or abstract to-be-remembered information into an understandable representation containing spatial information.

SPATIAL INFERENCES

Memory representations are often characterized as constructive in nature—they are not exact copies of original input. Rather, stored information is changed by omissions, elaborations, blending, inferences, and other transformations that facilitate the integration of ideas (Paris & Lindauer, 1977). Thus, stored memories contain more information and different information than that available in the separate inputs. The process of constructing and synthesizing information is assumed to be internally consistent with the structural knowledge of the child; that is, the child's knowledge and comprehension of relationships influences what is retained.

Research on constructive memory has included a variety of research paradigms including logical inference and semantic integration tasks that emphasize different, but interrelated mechanisms of constructive comprehension and memory. Most constructive memory tasks deal with linguistic materials rather than the concrete stimuli used in typical studies on spatial cognition. Yet, an analysis of the processes underlying performance on these tasks reveals that spatial cognition plays a role in transitive inferences and in the integration of spatial information presented in prose or pictorial form. In this section, we explore the role that spatial cognition plays in these constructive memory tasks.

Logical Inferences

One major method to assess children's ability to derive logical inferences is to present them with premise statements that give information about comparative relationships among objects (e.g., "Tom is taller than John; Jim is shorter than John"), and then test their ability to derive inferences from these premises ("Who is the tallest?"). An important aspect of this paradigm is that rote recall of the premises does not give the information asked for in the inference question. Rather, inferences are derived through transformation of the representations of the premises in memory. Information from the premises must be interpreted semantically and held in memory while transformations are performed. These transformations include construction of relationships among stimuli that are not explicitly stated in the premises (Trabasso, 1977).

Two major theoretical views exist for how children use constructive processes in transforming information and solving inference problems—Piagetian and information processing. Piaget describes the child as progressing from a categorical to a relativistic conception of logical relations (Brainerd, 1978). Preoperational children operate according to a categorical conception, regarding relations as absolute properties or attributes of things. For example, "larger" and "smaller" are understood to be two mutually exclusive attributes. Preoperational children are unable to solve inference problems from the premises, "B is taller than A" and "B is smaller than C," as they do not understand that an object can be both larger than some things and smaller than others. Concrete operational children, however, have acquired a relativistic conception of asymmetrical relations. They understand that the term "B" holds a position relative to the other terms "A" and "C," thus solving the transitive inference problem by combining the two premises (Breslow, 1981).

Thus, the Piagetian view holds that inferencing ability is closely related to the child's operative schemes. Performance on transitive inference tasks is determined by the development of certain grouping structures (cf. Flavell, 1963). Piagetians assert that the logical operations required for solving transitive inferences are acquired by middle childhood. Facility in concrete operations is necessary and sufficient for competency on simple transitive inference problems; dealing with conditional statements in more abstract problems requires formal operations.

A serious challenge to the Piagetian account of transitive reasoning has been brought by Trabasso and his colleagues (Bryant & Trabasso, 1971; Trabasso, 1977). Trabasso (1977) reported that children as young as 4 can perform transitive inferences as well as adults when premise memory is ensured by training. He argues that young children's poor performance on transitive inference tasks is due to deficits in memory rather than in logical structures. Support for this claim is derived from findings by Bryant and Trabasso (1971) that children in the preoperational stage, 4 to 7 years of age, can correctly solve inference problems. During a training phase, children learned color codes to relate differences in lengths between adjacent pairs of sticks. Four pairs of sticks (*AB, BC, CD,* and *DE*) were presented successively with the colors visible. After the children learned which color indicated the longer or shorter member of each pair, they were able to infer size relationships between the nonadjacent pairs. Thus, they could infer that $A > C$, $B > D$, and $D > E$. Trabasso (1977) interpreted this finding as demonstrating that the conceptual understanding underlying transitive reasoning does not develop with age as Piaget suggested; rather, children can reason like adults provided that memory and comprehension are ensured.

An empirical challenge to Trabasso's claim that memory for premises is necessary for inferencing comes from a series of studies which demonstrated that children may make incorrect inferences even though they are able to recall the premises correctly (Halford & Galloway, 1977; Smedslund, 1964). In a review of the literature, Breslow (1981) asserted that differences in memory ability do not account for the developmental trends in inference performance that have been found by Piaget. Rather, Breslow argues that Trabasso's procedures (intended as controls for language comprehension and memory) may, in fact, enable the child to discover a nontransitive solution to the problem.

Trabasso further claims that seriation underlies solution of transitive inference tasks and not other logical operations noted by Piaget (cf. Brainerd, 1978).

Trabasso asserted that individuals form serial images of the objects involved in transitive inference problems, and then make comparisons directly between the objects rather than drawing inferences from separate premises. Thus, Trabasso and others maintain that spatial imagery is used in the solution of transitive inference problems such as linear syllogisms (Huttenlocher, 1968; Huttenlocher & Higgins, 1971; Sternberg & Weil, 1980; Trabasso, 1977). Premises are encoded linguistically and transformed into internal representations, such as an internal array having spatial properties. Manipulation of this imaged spatial array leads to solution of the transitive inference problem. For example, the child is assumed to take premises such as "Tom is taller than John; Jim is shorter than John" and arrange the information mentally, into an ordered spatial array. The child first locates the ordinal position of the stimuli in the spatial array using the comparative labels of taller, shorter, and so on, then inspects the visual image to answer questions requiring an inference such as "Who is the tallest?" Comparisons are made on the basis of the serial internal representations formed by subjects rather than on the basis of the inferences they derive from separate premises (Trabasso, 1977).

Building on this, Huttenlocher and Higgins (1971) suggested that the exact form of the imagined array will depend on the adjective in the premises. Certain adjectives, such as "taller," are more likely to lead to imagery of vertical arrays whereas other adjectives, such as "faster," are more likely to result in horizontal arrays. In addition, high imagery nouns tend to be more "visible" in the array, and more visible arrays are easier to solve.

Semantic Integration

Closely related to children's ability to derive logical inferences is their ability to construct relationships in memory by integrating information presented in different sentences or pictures. Paris and his colleagues demonstrated that children use constructive processes in remembering related sentences (Paris & Carter, 1973; Paris & Lindauer, 1976; Paris & Mahoney, 1974; Paris & Upton, 1976). The integration of semantic information is assessed typically by presenting children with premise statements from which inferences may be drawn. In a subsequent recognition memory test children are asked to judge whether an inference derived from the premises (but not directly presented) was heard earlier. Typical findings demonstrate the strong tendency for children to recognize semantically congruent true inferences as if they were sentences originally heard in the stories. Children, like adults, cannot tell the difference between sentences that actually appear in the original premises and those that are correct inferences from the premises.

Although most of the research on constructive memory employs verbal material and deals with the construction of semantic relationships, the premises used by Paris and Carter (1973) involved implied spatial relationships among objects. Using the constructive memory paradigm described above, Paris and Carter presented sets of sentences containing spatial relationships such as "The bird is inside the cage" and "The cage is under the table" to second- and fifth-grade children. Children reported consistently that they had heard the true-inference statements. That is, both groups of children tended to recognize spatially congruent true inferences such as "The bird is under the table" as if they were premises given during acquisition.

In a later study, Paris and Mahoney (1974) demonstrated that children exhibit constructive integration in their memory for spatial relationships when given either pictures or sentences. The study examined recognition (using verbal or pictorial items) of the same spatial relationships when they were presented verbally or pictorially. The 8- and 10-year-old children falsely recognized new pictures and sentences that were consistent with the original premise items. This finding suggested that the children derived inferred relationships about the spatial aspects of both the pictures and sentences. Construction of these derived spatial relationships could not be explained by rote rehearsal of the sentences or by eidetic storage of the pictures. Paris and Mahoney (1974) suggested that children incorporated the sequential pictorial or semantic relationships into unified representations from which they achieved an understanding of a set of related events. The point of interest here is that the children derived inferred spatial relationships among the objects, whether presented linguistically or pictorially, and integrated the relationships in memory.

Summary

Although this discussion of the role of spatial representation in solving inferencing problems is not exhaustive, it highlights the need for greater attention to the interrelationship between spatial thinking and inferencing ability. By using spatial representations, individuals are able to conceptualize linguistically presented objects in arrays, that is, to mentally arrange objects in configurations. Thus, they use imagery to give spatial orientations of sequence and order to verbal arrangements of objects. This use of spatial representation results in increased ability to solve transitive inference problems, in addition to facilitating the integration and comprehension of implied spatial relationships.

ACADEMIC TASKS

Although the importance of spatial cognition to the development of higher level mathematical and scientific concepts is generally recognized, its contribution to the acquisition of basic academic skills has not been examined carefully. The purpose of this section is to discuss the influence of spatial cognition on the academic tasks of mathematics, science, and reading.

Mathematics

There is a substantial literature in which the relationships between spatial ability, mental imagery, and mathematical performance have been investigated (Bishop, 1980; Fennema, 1974, 1979; Guay & McDaniel, 1977; Lin, 1979; Sherman, 1980; Smith, 1964). Some of these studies have suggested a strong correlation between spatial skills and performance on mathematical tasks, but others have not (cf. Lean & Clements, 1981). These discrepancies may be due, in part, to the fact that there is little consistency among studies in measures used for spatial abilities. Jahoda (1979) argued that spatial ability is not a single homogeneous entity capable of being assessed equally well by means of different tests or tasks.

In assessing spatial skills, Bishop (1980) stated that a distinction should be made between spatial visualization and spatial orientation. Spatial visualization involves imagining the rotations of objects in space whereas spatial orientation involves recognition and comparison of the relationships between various parts of a configuration and one's position. Bishop also made a distinction between low-level spatial abilities, which require the visualization of two-dimensional configurations but no mental transformations of those visual images, and high-level spatial abilities, which require the visualization of three-dimensional configurations and the mental manipulation of these images.

In examining the role of spatial abilities in the development of math skills, Smith (1964) concluded that although spatial ability is related positively to high-level mathematical conceptualization, it may have little to do with the acquisition of low-level mathematical concepts and skills such as those requiring simple calculations. However, other studies (Guay & McDaniel, 1977; Sherman, 1980) have presented evidence suggesting that mathematical and spatial thinking are highly correlated among elementary school children, and that this relationship exists for both low- and high-level spatial abilities.

Despite the lack of conclusive evidence regarding the influence of specific spatial abilities upon various math tasks, there is growing interest in identifying cultural and environmental factors (for example: formal schooling; an urban vs. rural environment; sex role constraints) that may affect the development of spatial ability (Norman, 1980; Sherman, 1980). In addition, educators have made more use of the spatial metaphor in the classroom in an effort to aid children in mastering math concepts. Math teaching methods that incorporate spatial thinking have included the following: requiring the student to build simple geometric figures and to construct more complex forms from these figures; using puzzles relating spatial and number concepts; using spatial tasks such as having the student make as many shapes as possible with toothpicks and then drawing a picture of each shape; constructing mobiles from various cardboard shapes to increase awareness of the influence of various perspectives; and using soma cubes (Zjawin, 1980). Little research, however, has investigated spatial skill training and its transfer to math performance. Investigations of this nature are imperative (cf. Bishop, 1980).

Science

Spatial thinking has not received as much attention among science educators as among math educators. However, it is generally recognized that good spatial conceptualization is an asset and often a necessity for understanding certain scientific concepts. Several studies have found a relationship between spatial thinking and scientific ability. Roe (1950), for example, studied 64 eminent scientists and found that they all tended to depend upon visual imagery in their thinking. Math and science teachers also tended to be more successful on the spatial reasoning scale of the Differential Aptitude Test than those in the humanities or social sciences (Martin, 1967-68). A study of science, math, and art majors in college revealed that they performed significantly better on spatial visualization tasks than did students majoring in other fields, such as English, foreign languages, and business administration (Siemankowski & MacKnight, 1971). Successful college physics majors were found to have excellent three-dimensional conceptualization—better than majors of any other science, math, or art group—but nonscience students demonstrated less proficiency in this area.

Since spatial visualization is useful in and important to scientific reasoning, specific teaching recommendations are made with this in mind. Teachers are encouraged to examine the content of their subjects to see what spatial techniques can be applied to earth sciences, chemistry, and physics classes; for example, manipulation of three-dimensional molecular models has been recommended as a teaching aid for chemistry (Baker & Talley, 1974; Bishop, 1978).

Reading

Reading involves attending to spatial relationships in the process of translating graphic symbols of different shapes and sizes into verbal meaning. In English, these symbols are part of an alphabetic writing system that has unique characteristics. First, the length and pattern of lower case ascending, descending, and small letters define the shape of words (Groff, 1975). Second, the meaning of an individual word depends on the spatial order of the letters that compose the word (Mason, Pilkington, & Brandau, 1981). That is, the spatial sequencing of letters preceded and followed by a blank space determines a word (e.g., rat, tar, art). Words may be stored in memory in the form of images that retain their spatial properties of order and shape. Matching printed words with these images may facilitate word identification (Gibson, 1969). Beginning readers who have not formed images of many words or have incomplete images must rely on decoding each word during reading. In contrast, skilled readers may automatically match visual arrangements of letters with stored images of letter sequences in words, and attach their corresponding verbal labels, enabling them to read words easily and quickly.

Research from various areas has suggested that poor readers have a spatial order deficit that underlies their reading problems. Results from analyses of performance on the Wechsler Intelligence Scale for Children (WISC) suggest that children with reading disabilities have a deficit in sequencing ability, typically scoring low on the Digit Span and Coding tests (Rugel, 1974; Symmes & Rapoport, 1972). However, reading-disabled children score highest overall on spatial visualization tasks such as Block Design and Object Assembly, relative to their performance on the other WISC tasks (Smith, Coleman, Dokecki, & Davis, 1977). Kaufman (1979) suggested that the high Spatial/low Sequencing pattern found in profiles of reading-disabled children may relate to "superior simultaneous/holistic processing coupled with inadequate successive/sequential processing" (p. 74). Additional support for the hypothesis that reading-disabled children have a deficit in sequencing ability comes from studies which have demonstrated that these children have difficulty in arranging items according to their previous order (Mason, Katz, & Wickland, 1975) and in recalling sequentially presented stimuli in serial recall tasks (Torgesen, 1978).

Research on proofreading also provides information on the role that attention to spatial order plays in identification of words. Studies on the effects of misprints have shown that transposed initial pairs of letters are more easily noticed than transposed final ones; medially transposed letter pairs are the most difficult misspellings to detect (Healy, 1980; Sloboda, 1976). An important aspect of misprints is that transposing letters often changes the overall shape of the word so that the pattern of ascending and descending letters is altered. Haber and Schindler (1981) found that misspellings that changed the overall shape of a word were more likely to be detected than ones that did not.

Research on the shapes of words has shown that although a lot of words have the same shape, first-grade readers and beyond use the word shape in conjunction with syntactic and semantic knowledge to facilitate reading performance (Rayner, 1976; Rayner & Hagelberg, 1975). Haber and Haber (1981) suggested that shape information about a word is obtained from peripheral vision and is used to narrow hypotheses about what the word might be. These hypotheses are confirmed or rejected by the more specific information gained when a person fixates directly on the word.

It is possible to read print in which familiar word shape information is deleted, as in text printed in all capital type that scales all letters to the same size and location on the line, thus removing the shape pattern except for length (cf. Haber & Haber, 1981). However, removing shape information decreases reading speed (Rayner, 1978). Fisher (1975), for example, found that adults experienced a small reduction in reading speed when words normally printed in lower case were printed in all upper-case letters. Reading speed became significantly slower when the information gained from segmentation was lost by removing the spaces between words (Fisher, 1975), inserting an X between words (Spragins, Lefton, & Fisher, 1976), or by inserting meaningless numbers printed in letters between words (Wilkinson, Guminski, Stanovich, & West, 1981). These findings suggest that the order and the shape of letters in words are important in reading and that changes in these spatial information sources disrupt normal reading rates.

Summary

In general, internal representations of spatial information and the inferences based upon these representations affect performance in mathematics, science, and reading. The research suggests that a student who demonstrates limited ability to use spatial information might be expected to do poorly in mastering certain academic tasks. Accordingly, teachers are encouraged to spatialize academic concepts in order to foster understanding in their students. However, few studies have investigated the factors in academic tasks that lend themselves to spatial thinking. For example, most of the research relating spatial abilities and mathematics performance has been correlational. It does not identify particular strategies involving spatial cognition that might be productive in problem solution. Perhaps individual approaches to math problem solving should be examined to identify effective strategies based on spatial information. In addition, research investigating the effectiveness of spatial skill training and its transfer to academic tasks appears necessary in order to clarify the role of spatial cognition in academic achievement. For example, with regard to reading, answers to the following questions should be sought: What is the most effective way to foster sequencing skills in preschoolers and first graders? Does this result in a lower incidence of reading problems among these children in later grades? Do training programs that focus on remediation of the hypothesized deficits in sequencing ability among older children result in improved reading skills?

CONCLUSIONS

One important theme in this book is the interrelationship between spatial cognition and cognition in general. Unlike the other chapters, which focus on cognitive processes as revealed in studies investigating spatial knowledge, this one focused on spatial knowledge as revealed in studies investigating other cognitive abilities. The research reviewed here clearly indicates that spatial knowledge can affect performance on a broad spectrum of cognitive tasks. In fact, the spatial metaphor has considerable heuristic value, as it enhances our understanding of empirical evidence from a variety of research domains.

The theme unifying this research is the role of spatial representation in cognition, and the need for studying spatial representation in its broader context. To the extent that internal pictures are used in cognitive processing, whether they are organized schemas for typical real-world scenes, or mental images occurring during reading or encoding, these pictures are very likely to be spatially organized. And they are very likely to reflect one's knowledge about spatial relationships among objects in the world. To the extent that spatial information occurs in task stimuli—whether they are geometry problems, written descriptions of a scene, or items in an array—the ability to encode spatial information as cues, to make a mental picture, and to transform that picture will enhance performance on the task.

Spatial cognition needs to be viewed in this broader sense, not only to increase our knowledge about children's sense of space, but also to expand our knowledge about cognitive development. There is circumstantial evidence suggesting that young children, in particular, are disadvantaged when research fails to consider spatial information: spatial proximity enhances young children's memory performance (e.g., Baumeister & Smith, 1979); spatial arrangements have a profound impact on conservation performance (e.g., Miller, Heldmyer, & Miller, 1975) and classification performance in young children (e.g., Markman, Cox, & Machida, 1981); young children's tendencies to focus on positional information in discrimination learning problems are well documented (e.g., Gholson, Levine, & Phillips, 1972); and spatially organized imagery may be more accessible to young children than abstract propositional representations (e.g., Kosslyn, 1978b). If it is true that spatial attributes are encoded automatically (von Wright et al., 1975) or that they are one of the first attributes abstracted in stimuli by young children (Underwood, 1969), it may be that young children's capabilities have been underestimated by using cognitive tasks that lack spatial information (e.g., the typical memory paradigm with serial presentation) and by ignoring the spatial aspects of tasks that do contain such information (e.g., the probe-type serial recall task). Clearly, there needs to be more investigation of the spatial knowledge of young children in an attempt to access and build on that knowledge to improve performance on a variety of tasks.

Many of the following techniques, often recommended by others, could be used more often in teaching and research with children: examples conveyed through the use of diagrams, graphs, and spatially organized configurations rather than verbal information; concrete stimuli; presentation techniques in which all items are arrayed before the child simultaneously; encouragement and training to use visual imagery; emphasis on the strategic use of spatial cues and spatial organization strategies; tests in which stimuli are embedded in real-world scenes. The relationship between the development of mathematics and spatial abilities needs to be further explored, including investigations to determine if training in one area will generalize to the other. More objective measures of imagery are needed (perhaps children could reconstruct their images using concrete stimuli). Systematic research is needed to examine the relationship between children's developing spatial abilities and performance on tasks that have been regarded heretofore as nonspatial, in particular to investigate the effects of manipulations that change the spatial characteristics of the stimulus materials.

It is apparent to us that this research will probably uncover developmental trends parallel to those observed in the spatial cognition literature. For example, landmark and route learning occur earlier than configurational knowledge, which involves integrating spatially separated information into an organized view of the environment. In this chapter there was repeated evidence for age-related improvements in this kind of integration. Furthermore, it appears that there are similarities between the development of route learning and the development of sequential memory strategies, or there may be similarities between the development of configurational knowledge and transitive inferencing ability. We leave it to others to elaborate on the precise nature of these parallel trends as the research progresses.

The arrays and pictured scenes that children have to memorize, the imaginal representations or schemata for objects and relationships among objects, the prose descriptions of scenes that need to be understood—all of these can be viewed as tiny environments. Children often have to conceptualize and ''learn their way around'' these tiny environments, just as they have to learn their way around the larger environments in which they live. A broader conception of spatial knowledge should lead to an understanding of the developmental processes involved in learning to represent spatial information in a microcosm, as well as in rooms, on playgrounds, and in neighborhoods. Together with research on children's spatial thinking in large-scale environments, a new focus on other kinds of cognitive tasks will expand knowledge about spatial cognition and its relationship to general cognitive development.

REFERENCES

Altom, M. W., & Weil, J. Young children's use of temporal and spatial order information in short-term memory. *Journal of Experimental Child Psychology*, 1977, *24*, 147–163.

Anderson, J. R., & Bower, G. H. *Human Associative Memory*. New York: Wiley, 1973.

Atkinson, R. C., Hansen, D. N., & Bernbach, H. A. Short-term memory with young children. *Psychonomic Science*, 1964, *1*, 255–256.

Baker, S., & Talley, L. Visualization skills as a component of aptitude for chemistry. *Journal of Research in Science Teaching*, 1974, *11*, 95–98.

Baumeister, A. A., & Smith, S. Thematic elaboration and proximity in children's recall, organization, and long-term retention of pictorial materials. *Journal of Experimental Child Psychology*, 1979, *28*, 132–148.

Berch, D. B. The role of spatial cues in the probe-type serial memory task. *Child Development*, 1978, *49*, 749–754.

Berch, D. B. Coding of spatial and temporal information in episodic memory. In H. W. Reese & L. P. Lipsitt (Eds.), *Advances in child development and behavior* (Vol. 13). New York: Academic Press, 1979.

Bishop, A. J. Spatial abilities and mathematics education: A review. *Educational Studies in Mathematics*, 1980, *11*, 257–269.

Bishop, J. E. Developing students' spatial ability. *The Science Teacher*, 1978, *45*, 20–23.

Bower, G. H. Analysis of a mnemonic device. *American Scientist*, 1970, *58*, 496–510.

Brainerd, C. J. *Piaget's theory of intelligence*. Englewood Cliffs, NJ: Prentice-Hall, 1978.

Bransford, J. D., & Johnson, M. K. Considerations of some problems of comprehension. In W. Chase (Ed.), *Visual information processing*. New York: Academic Press, 1973.

Breslow, L. Re-evaluation of the literature on the development of transitive inference. *Psychological Bulletin*, 1981, *89*, 325–351.

Brody, G. H., Mattson, S. L., & Zuckerwise, B. L. Imagery induction in preschool children: An examination of subject and experimenter generated interactions. *Journal of Genetic Psychology,* 1978, *132,* 307–311.

Brown, A. L. The construction of temporal succession by preoperational children. In A. D. Pick (Ed.), *Minnesota Symposium on Child Psychology* (Vol. 10). Minneapolis: University of Minnesota Press, 1976.

Brown, R. M., Brown, N. L., & Caci, M. Serial position effects in young children: Temporal or spatial? *Child Development,* 1981, *52,* 1191–1201.

Bryant, P. E., & Trabasso, T. Transitive inferences and memory in young children. *Nature,* 1971, *232,* 456–458.

Ceci, S. J., Lea, S. E. G., & Howe, M. J. A. Structural analysis of memory traces in children from 4 to 10 years of age. *Developmental Psychology,* 1980, *16,* 203–212.

Childs, M., & Polich, J. Developmental differences in mental rotation. *Journal of Experimental Child Psychology,* 1979, *27,* 339–351.

Collins, A. M., & Loftus, E. F. A spreading-activation theory of semantic processing. *Psychological Review,* 1975, *82,* 407–428.

Conroy, R. L., & Weener, P. The development of visual and auditory selective attention using the central-incidental paradigm. *Journal of Experimental Child Psychology,* 1976, *22,* 400–407.

Cooper, L., & Shepard, R. Chronometric studies of the rotation of mental images. In W. Chase (Ed.), *Visual Information Processing.* New York: Academic Press, 1973.

Danner, F. W., & Taylor, A. M. Integrated pictures and relational imagery training in children's learning. *Journal of Experimental Child Psychology,* 1973, *16,* 47–54.

Davidson, R. E., & Adams, J. F. Verbal and imagery processes in children's paired-associate learning. *Journal of Experimental Child Psychology,* 1970, *9,* 429–435.

Dempster, F. N., & Rohwer, W. D. J. A component analysis of the elaborative encoding effect in paired-associate learning. *Journal of Experimental Psychology,* 1974, *103,* 400–408.

Druker, J., & Hagen, J. Development trends in the processing of task-relevant and task-irrelevant information. *Child Development,* 1969, *40,* 371–382.

Fennema, E. Mathematics learning and the sexes: A review. *Journal for Research in Mathematics Education,* 1974, *5,* 126–139.

Fisher, D. F. Reading and visual search. *Memory & Cognition,* 1975, *3,* 188–196.

Flavell, J. H. *The developmental psychology of Jean Piaget.* Princeton, NJ: D. Van Nostrand, 1963.

Forbes, E. J., & Reese, H. W. Pictorial elaboration and recall of multi-list paired associates. *Journal of Experimental Psychology,* 1974, *102,* 836–840.

Furth, H. G., & Milgram, N. A. Labeling and grouping effects in the recall of pictures by children. *Child Development,* 1973, *44,* 511–518.

Geis, M. F., & Lange, G. Children's cue utilization in a memory-for-location task. *Child Development,* 1976, *47,* 759–766.

Gholson, B., Levine, M., & Phillips, S. Hypotheses, strategies, and stereotypes in discrimination learning. *Journal of Experimental Child Psychology,* 1972, *13,* 423–446.

Gibson, E. J. *Principles of perceptual learning and development.* Englewood Cliffs, NJ: Prentice-Hall, 1969.

Groff, P. Research in brief: Shapes as cues to word recognition. *Visible Language,* 1975, *9,* 67–71.

Guay, R., & McDaniel, E. The relationship between math achievement and spatial abilities among elementary school children. *Journal of Research in Mathematics Education,* 1977, *7,* 211–215.

Guttman, J., Levin, J. R., & Pressley, M. Pictures, partial pictures, and young children's oral prose learning. *Journal of Educational Psychology,* 1977, *69,* 473–480.

Haber, R. N., & Haber, L. R. The shape of a word can specify its meaning. *Reading Research Quarterly,* 1981, *16,* 334–345.

Haber, R. N., & Schindler, R. Errors in proofreading: Evidence of syntactic control of letter processing? *Journal of Experimental Psychology: Human Perception and Performance,* 1981, *7,* 573–579.

Hagen, J. W., Jongeward, R. H., & Kail, R. V. Cognitive perspectives on the development of memory. In H. W. Reese (Ed.), *Advances in child development and behavior* (Vol. 10). New York: Academic Press, 1975.

Hagen, J. W., & Kail, R. V. Facilitation and distraction in short-term memory. *Child Development,* 1973, *44*, 831–836.

Hagen, J. W. & Stanovich, K. G. Memory: Strategies of acquisition. In R. V. Kail, Jr., & J. W. Hagen (Eds.), *Perspectives on the development of memory and cognition.* Hillsdale, NJ: Lawrence Erlbaum Associates, 1977.

Halford, G., & Galloway, W. Children who fail to make transitive inferences can remember comparisons. *Australian Journal of Psychology,* 1977, *29*, 1–5.

Hart, R. A., & Moore, G. T. The development of spatial cognition: A review. In R. M. Downs & D. Stea (Eds.), *Image and environment.* Chicago: Aldine, 1973.

Healy, A. F. Proofreading errors on the word *the:* New evidence on reading units. *Journal of Experimental Psychology: Human Perception and Performance,* 1980, *6*, 45–57.

Henek, T., & Miller, L. K. The effects of display conditions upon developmental trends in incidental learning. *Child Development,* 1976, *47*, 1214–1218.

Hock, H. S., Romanski, L., Galie, A., & Williams, C. S. Real-world schemata and scene recognition in adults and children. *Memory & Cognition,* 1978, *6*, 423–431.

Hollenberg, C. K. Functions of visual imagery in the learning and concept formation of children. *Child Development,* 1970, *41*, 1003–1015.

Holyoak, K., Hogeterp, H., & Yuille, J. C. A developmental comparison of verbal and pictorial mnemonics in paired-associate learning. *Journal of Experimental Child Psychology,* 1972, *14*, 53–65.

Horowitz, L. M., Lampel, A. K., & Takanishi, R. N. The child's memory for unitized scenes. *Journal of Experimental Child Psychology,* 1969, *8*, 375–388.

Huttenlocher, J. Constructing spatial images: A strategy in reasoning. *Psychological Review,* 1968, *75*, 550–560.

Huttenlocher, J., & Higgins, E. T. Adjectives, comparatives and syllogisms. *Psychological Review, 1971, 78*, 487–504.

Jahoda, G. On the nature of difficulties in spatial-perceptual tasks: Ethnic and sex differences. *British Journal of Psychology,* 1979, *70*, 351–363.

Kaufman, A. S. *Intelligent testing with the WISC-R.* New York: Wiley, 1979.

Kosslyn, S. M. Scanning visual images: Some structural implications. *Perception & Psychophysics,* 1973, *14*, 90–94.

Kosslyn, S. M. Information representation in visual images. *Cognitive Psychology,* 1975, *7*, 341–370.

Kosslyn, S. M. Can imagery be distinguished from other forms of internal representation? Evidence from studies of information retrieval time. *Memory & Cognition,* 1976, *4*, 291–297.

Kosslyn, S. M. The angle of the mind's eye. *Cognitive Psychology,* 1978, *10*, 356–389. (a)

Kosslyn, S. M. Imagery and cognitive development: A teleological approach. In R. Siegler (Ed.), *Children's thinking: What develops?* Hillsdale, NJ: Lawrence Erlbaum Associates, 1978. (b)

Kosslyn, S. M. The medium and the message in mental imagery: A theory. *Psychological Review,* 1981, *88*, 46–66.

Kosslyn, S. M., Ball, T., & Reiser, B. Visual images preserve metric spatial information: Evidence from studies of image scanning. *Journal of Experimental Psychology: Human Perception and Performance,* 1978, *4*, 47–60.

Lampel, A. K. The child's memory for actional, locational, and serial scenes. *Journal of Experimental Child Psychology,* 1973, *15*, 266–277.

Lean, G., & Clements, M. A. Spatial ability, visual imagery, and mathematical performance. *Educational Studies in Mathematics,* 1981, *12*, 267–299.

Levin, J. R., Divine-Hawkins, P., Kerst, S. M., & Guttmann, J. Individual differences in learning from pictures and words: The development and application of an instrument. *Journal of Educational Psychology*, 1974, *66*, 296–303.

Liben, L. S. Spatial representation and behavior: Multiple perspectives. In L. S. Liben, A. H. Patterson, & N. Newcombe (Eds.), *Spatial representation and behavior across the life span.* New York: Academic Press, 1981.

Lin, C. Imagery in mathematical thinking and learning. *International Journal of Mathematics Education in Science and Technology*, 1979, *10*, 107–111.

Mandler, J. M., & Johnson, N. S. Some of the thousand words a picture is worth. *Journal of Experimental Psychology: Human Learning and Memory*, 1976, *2*, 529–540.

Mandler, J. M., & Parker, R. E. Memory for descriptive and spatial information in complex pictures. *Journal of Experimental Psychology: Human Learning and Memory*, 1976, *2*, 38–48.

Mandler, J. M., & Ritchey, G. H. Long-term memory for pictures. *Journal of Experimental Psychology: Human Learning and Memory*, 1977, *3*, 386–396.

Mandler, J. M., & Robinson, C. A. Developmental changes in picture recognition. *Journal of Experimental Child Psychology*, 1978, *26*, 122–136.

Mandler, J. M., Seegmiller, D., & Day, J. On the coding of spatial information. *Memory & Cognition*, 1977, *5*, 10–16.

Mandler, J. M., & Stein, N. L. Recall and recognition of pictures by children as a function of organization and distractor similarity. *Journal of Experimental Psychology*, 1974, *102*, 657–669.

Markman, E. M., Cox, B., & Machida, S. The standard object-sorting task as a measure of conceptual organization. *Developmental Psychology*, 1981, *17*, 115–117.

Martin, B. Spatial visualization abilities of prospective mathematics teachers. *Journal of Research in Science Teaching*, 1967-68, *5*, 11–19.

Mason, M., Katz, L., & Wickland, D. A. Immediate spatial order memory and item memory in sixth-grade children as a function of reader ability. *Journal of Educational Psychology*, 1975, *67*, 610–616.

Mason, M., Pilkington, C., & Brandau, R. From print to sound: Reading ability and order information. *Journal of Experimental Psychology: Human Perception and Performance*, 1981, *7*, 580–591.

Miller, P. H., Heldmyer, K. H., & Miller, S. A. Facilitation of conservation of number in young children. *Developmental Psychology*, 1975, *11*, 253.

Norman, D. K. A comparison of children's spatial reasoning: Rural Appalachia, suburban and urban New England. *Child Development*, 1980, *51*, 288–291.

Paivio, A. Mental imagery in associative learning and memory. *Psychological Review*, 1969, *76*, 241–263.

Paris, S. G., & Carter, A. Y. Semantic and constructive aspects of sentence memory in children. *Developmental Psychology*, 1973, *9*, 109–113.

Paris, S. G., & Lindauer, B. K. The role of inference in children's comprehension and memory for sentences. *Cognitive Psychology*, 1976, *8*, 217–227.

Paris, S. G., & Lindauer, B. K. Constructive aspects of children's comprehension and memory. In R. V. Kail, Jr., & J. W. Hagen (Eds.), *Perspectives on the development of memory and cognition.* Hillsdale, NJ: Lawrence Erlbaum Associates, 1977.

Paris, S. G., & Mahoney, G. J. Cognitive integration in children's memory for sentences and pictures. *Child Development*, 1974, *45*, 633–642.

Paris, S. G., & Upton, L. R. Children's memory for inferential relationships in prose. *Child Development*, 1976, *47*, 660–668.

Piaget, J., & Inhelder, B. *Memory and intelligence* (A. Pomerans, trans.). New York: Basic Books, 1973.

Pressley, G. M., & Levin, J. R. Developmental differences in subjects' associative learning strategies and performance. *Journal of Experimental Child Psychology*, 1977, *24*, 431–439.

Pressley, M. Imagery and children's learning: Putting the picture in developmental perspective. *Review of Educational Research*, 1977, *47*, 585–622.

Pylyshyn, Z. W. What the mind's eye tells the mind's brain: A critique of mental imagery. *Psychological Bulletin*, 1973, *80*, 1–24.

Pylyshyn, Z. W. The imagery debate. *Psychological Review*, 1981, *88*, 16–45.

Rayner, K. Developmental changes in word recognition strategies. *Journal of Educational Psychology*, 1976, *68*, 323–329.

Rayner, K. Eye movements in reading and information processing. *Psychological Bulletin*, 1978, *85*, 618–660.

Rayner, K., & Hagelberg, E. M. Word recognition cues for beginning and skilled readers. *Journal of Experimental Child Psychology*, 1975, *20*, 444–455.

Reese, H. W. Imagery in children's paired-associate learning. *Journal of Experimental Child Psychology*, 1970, *9*, 174–178.

Reese, H. W. Imagery and multiple list paired associate learning in young children. *Journal of Experimental Child Psychology*, 1972, *13*, 310–323.

Roe, A. A psychologist examines 64 eminent scientists. *Scientific American*, 1950, *187*, 21–25.

Rosner, S. R. Primacy in preschoolers' short-term memory: The effects of repeated tests and shift-trials. *Journal of Experimental Child Psychology*, 1972, *13*, 220–230.

Rugel, R. P. The factor structure of the WISC in two populations of disabled readers. *Journal of Learning Disabilities*, 1974, *7*, 581–585.

Samuels, M., Hiscock, M., & Kinsbourne, M. Development of strategies for recalling letter sequences. *Journal of Experimental Child Psychology*, 1978, *25*, 298–314.

Schulman, A. I. Recognition memory and the recall of spatial location. *Memory & Cognition*, 1973, *1*, 256–260.

Shepard, R. N. The mental image. *American Psychologist*, 1978, *33*, 125–139.

Shepard, R. N., & Metzler, J. Mental rotation of three-dimensional objects. *Science*, 1971, *171*, 701–703.

Sherman, J. A. Mathematics, spatial visualization, and related factors: Changes in girls and boys grades 8–11. *Journal of Educational Psychology*, 1980, *72*, 476–482.

Shimron, J. Imagery and comprehension of prose by elementary school children. (Doctoral dissertation, University of Pittsburgh, 1974.) *Dissertation Abstracts International*, 1975, *36*, 795-A. (University Microfilms No. 75-18, 254).

Siegel, A. W., Allik, J. P., & Herman, J. F. The primacy effect in young children: Verbal fact or spatial artifact? *Child Development*, 1976, *47*, 242–247.

Siegel, A. W., & White, S. H. The development of spatial representations of large-scale environments. In H. W. Reese (Ed.), *Advances in child development and behavior* (Vol. 10). New York: Academic Press, 1975.

Siemankowski, F. T., & MacKnight, F. C. Spatial cognition: Success prognosticator in college science courses. *Journal of College Science Teaching*, 1971, *1*, 56–59.

Sloboda, J. The effect of item position on the likelihood of identification by inference in prose reading and music reading. *Canadian Journal of Psychology*, 1976, *30*, 228–237.

Smedslund, J. Concrete reasoning: A study of intellectual development. *Monographs of the Society for Research in Child Development*, 1964, *29*, (2, Serial No. 93).

Smith, I. *Spatial ability*. London: University of London Press, 1964.

Smith, M. D., Coleman, J. M., Dokecki, P. R., & Davis, E. E. Recategorized WISC-R scores of learning disabled children. *Journal of Learning Disabilities*, 1977, *10*, 444–449.

Spragins, A. B., Lefton, L. A., & Fisher, D. F. Eye-movements while reading and searching spatially transformed text: A developmental examination. *Memory & Cognition*, 1976, *4*, 36–42.

Sternberg, R. J., & Weil, E. M. An aptitude X strategy interaction in linear syllogistic reasoning. *Journal of Educational Psychology*, 1980, *72*, 226–236.

Symmes, J. S., & Rapoport, J. L. Unexpected reading failure. *American Journal of Orthopsychiatry*, 1972, *42*, 82–91.

Torgesen, J. K. Performance of reading disabled children on serial memory tasks: A review. *Reading Research Quarterly*, 1978, *19*, 57–87.

Trabasso, T. The role of memory as a system in making transitive inferences. In R. V. Kail, Jr., & J. W. Hagen (Eds.), *Perspectives on the development of memory and cognition*. Hillsdale, NJ: Lawrence Erlbaum Associates, 1977.

Underwood, B. J. Attributes of memory. *Psychological Review*, 1969, *76*, 559–573.

Varley, W. H., Levin, J. R., Severson, R. A., & Wolff, P. Training imagery production in young children through motor involvement. *Journal of Educational Psychology*, 1974, *66*, 262–266.

von Wright, J. M., Gebhard, P., & Karttunen, M. A developmental study of the recall of spatial location. *Journal of Experimental Child Psychology*, 1975, *20*, 181–190.

von Wright, J. M., Loikkanen, P., & Reijonen, P. A note on the development of recall of spatial location. *British Journal of Psychology*, 1978, *69*, 213–216.

West, R. L. *The effects of category salience and strategy control on the development of memory organization*. Unpublished doctoral dissertation. Vanderbilt University, 1980.

Wheeler, R. J., & Dusek, J. B. The effects of attentional and cognitive factors on children's incidental learning. *Child Development*, 1973, *44*, 253–258.

Wilkinson, A. C., Guminski, M., Stanovich, K. E., & West, R. F. Variable interaction between visual recognition and memory in oral reading. *Journal of Experimental Psychology: Human Learning and Memory*, 1981, *7*, 111–119.

Wolff, P., & Levin, J. R. The role of overt activity in children's imagery production. *Child Development*, 1972, *43*, 537–547.

Yuille, J. C., & Catchpole, M. J. Associative learning and imagery training in children. *Journal of Experimental Child Psychology*, 1973, *16*, 403–412.

Zjawin, D. Open-ended math for open-minded kids. *Instructor*, 1980, *89*, 52–53.

3 Representing and Manipulating Spatial Information from Different Environments: Models to Neighborhoods

David L. Weatherford
Vanderbilt University

The environments that have been used in spatial cognition research are quite varied. Some researchers have employed table-top model spaces with small objects to create a sort of "mini-environment" (e.g., Nigl & Fishbein, 1974; Piaget & Inhelder, 1967). Others have used environmental spaces ranging from classrooms (e.g., Siegel & Schadler, 1977), to neighborhoods (e.g., Ladd, 1970), to cities (e.g., Appleyard, 1970), to geographic regions as large as the United States (e.g., Evans & Pezdek, 1980) and North and Central America (Stevens & Coupe, 1978). Clearly, there is reason to wonder to what extent we can generalize the findings on spatial behaviors from one type of environment to those with another. Are the same cognitive processes required in interaction with the various types of environments or spaces, and if so, are they applied in similar fashion? This is the basic issue addressed in this chapter.

The many naturalistic and experimental environments that have been used in spatial cognition research have varied on many factors, including content, shape, utility, artificiality, and familiarity. In this chapter, I am concerned primarily with two structural features that differ across spatial studies: size and scale. The use of small-size model spaces has been popular for many years. However, subsequent to some consideration of possible differences between cognition applied to tabletop model spaces and cognition applied to larger, full-size spaces, researchers became sensitive to the distinction between "microspatial" and "macrospatial" layouts. The physical distinction between micro- or small-size space and macro- or full-size space is fairly obvious. The concept of "scale" has been less clearly delineated. Environments often have been referred to as being "large" or "small" in scale without explicit definitions. Many researchers have used the term in a way suggesting synonomy between the terms "scale" and "size."

Coupled with the growing attention to differences between microspace and macrospace, Siegel and White's (1975) important paper on large-scale environments served as an impetus for a shift from the use of model spaces to what were termed large-scale spaces or environments (e.g., Acredolo, 1977; Acredolo, Pick, & Olsen, 1975; Hardwick, McIntyre, & Pick, 1976; Herman & Siegel, 1978; Weatherford & Cohen, 1980). The implied criterion for being large-scale seemed to be that the space involved was big, relative to the ubiquitous model spaces. This conceptualization of scale proved awkward due not only to its obvious covariation with size, but also to its subjectivity. This probably becomes most obvious in making cross-discipline comparisons. For example, whereas a standard classroom might qualify as a large-scale space for an experimental child psychologist, an urban planner, geographer, or environmental psychologist would likely view it as small-scale.

Recent efforts have been made to define the term scale. The following criteria have evolved: (a) an individual can move around within the space, and (b) multiple vantage points must be occupied in order for the space to be visually apprehended in its entirety (Acredolo, 1981; Hazen, Lockman, & Pick, 1978; Siegel, 1981; Weatherford & Cohen, 1981). In spite of this general agreement on what is meant by the term "large-scale," there is still inconsistency in its application. For example, Acredolo (1981) and Herman (1980) referred to barrier-free spaces the size of an average classroom or smaller as large-scale spaces. Weatherford and Cohen (1981), on the other hand, have labeled very similar classroom environments small-scale, maintaining that they were large in size, but not in scale. It seems, then, that there is still some tendency to confuse scale and size. In a recent publication (Weatherford, 1982), I offered the following categorization of spaces: (1) model/small-scale—this category includes tabletop model spaces or "mini-environments" that can only be observed or manipulated from the outside; (2) navigable/small-scale—includes spaces that are large enough in size to permit travel within, but still can be viewed in their entirety from a single vantage point; and (3) large-scale—as noted above, these are spaces in which an observer can move around, and for which an observer must occupy multiple viewing locations in order to visually extract all of the spatial information needed to generate an overall spatial representation.

In the present chapter, research conducted in these three spatial contexts is selectively reviewed for four spatial processes: perspective taking, mental rotation, cognitive mapping, and orientation. In a perspective-taking situation, an individual mentally must determine the spatial transformations in self-environment relationships that would occur as a result of an imagined movement of self. Mental rotation requires a logically similar mental transformation but based on an imagined movement of the environment. In both cases, the environment typically is visible to the individual during the mental manipulation. The same generally is not true of cognitive-mapping tasks. Here, an individual is usually required to recall spatial information stored in memory as a result of an earlier encounter with an environment. Finally, orientation requires that one mentally transform information about one's spatial relations to objects in the environment in accordance with one's actual physical movements in or around that environment. Research that directly compared performance as a function of environmental scale follows this review. In the final section of this chapter, conclusions and implications are drawn.

MODEL/SMALL-SCALE SPACE

Model spaces have been used in spatial cognition research in two ways. First, they are employed for reasons of convenience to serve as small "environments" to be mentally represented or manipulated according to particular task demands. Cognitive processing of the spatial information contained in the mini-environment often is assumed to be isomorphic to that which occurs in similar types of interaction with spatial aspects of the "real-world" environment. Second, model spaces often have been used as a means for allowing the subject to externalize spatial knowledge. For example, a subject may construct a model array to demonstrate how well he or she recalls the appearance of an environment previously encountered. The focus in this chapter is on research using model spaces in the first way described—that is, models as analogues to study environmental cognition. The means by which the subject is asked to demonstrate spatial knowledge of the model space is not of primary interest here. Let us begin by reviewing some of the studies on perspective taking and mental rotation using model spaces. These two spatial abilities are discussed together because the small number of studies on mental rotation typically have been comparison studies looking at both mental rotation and perspective taking.

Perspective Taking and Mental Rotation

Model spaces have been used more for the study of perspective taking than for any other spatial ability. The original study of this ability, conducted by Piaget and Inhelder (1967), employed a tabletop model environment, and the majority of subsequent studies on this subject have followed that example. In the traditional perspective-taking situation, a subject is asked to infer the view that another observer has of an object or array of objects. Assuming that they occupy different viewing positions, the subject must determine how the objects and their spatial interrelationships appear to the second observer. If a subject can do this for numerous viewpoints held by the other observer, it is assumed that the subject is able to coordinate the various perspectives of the spatial array (Piaget & Inhelder, 1967).

Piaget and Inhelder's model environment consisted of a miniature replica of three mountains, varying in height and further differentiated by color and landmarks (e.g., cross, house). The children tested ranged in age from 4 to 12 years. Piaget reported that the younger children (4 to 6) were typically egocentric in that they tended to attribute their own view to the other observer (a doll) regardless of the latter's viewing position. This was followed by a period of transition (7 to 8 or 9) during which this egocentric inclination diminished and a limited understanding of the observer-array relationship evolved. Finally, in the final stage of the developmental process (9 or 10), children fully comprehended the relativity of perspectives. They were able to understand the specific spatial transformations in object relations that accompany any change of perspective or viewpoint.

Piaget's finding of improved perspective-taking ability with development has been consistently replicated (e.g., Coie, Costanzo, & Farnill, 1973; Cox, 1978; Dodwell, 1963; Flavell, Botkin, Fry, Wright, & Jarvis, 1968; Knudson & Kagan, 1977; Minnigerode & Carey, 1974; Salatas & Flavell, 1976; Schachter & Gollin, 1979). However, the age of mastery for this skill remains in question. Several studies support Piaget and Inhelder's (1967) finding that consistently accurate perspective taking does not occur until late childhood. For example, Nigl and Fishbein (1974) assessed the perspective-taking ability of children ranging from 4 to 12 years of age. In the first two experiments, a standard picture-choosing task was employed. In this task, children were asked to select from a group of photographs of a spatial array the one depicting the other observer's view of the display. The oldest children (fifth graders in Experiment 1 and sixth graders in Experiment 2) performed significantly better than the younger age groups, with the greatest improvement in performance occurring between the ages of 9 and 11. In addition to these age trends, Nigl and Fishbein found that the number of objects (3, 5, or 7) did not affect perspective taking. Their analysis of errors suggested that children of all ages had the most difficulty with left-right relations, followed by front-back relations, then up-down relations. In fact, very few children committed up-down relation errors. In a third experiment, the use of three-dimensional choice arrays made the percept-inference judgements easier than the use of pictures for fifth graders, but not for kindergartners.

Miller (1967) used a position-designation task to investigate the perspective-taking ability of children in kindergarten and first, second, third, fourth, and sixth grades. A three-dimensional map of a fictitious group of islands was placed on a circular table. Standing at different locations around the table, the children were instructed to look at a number of slides and, for each one, to indicate where a camera had to be positioned to take that picture. Miller reported that kindergartners and first graders had considerable difficulty in making inferential assessments, third and fourth graders demonstrated some success, and sixth graders were most accurate and performed near adult levels.

Flavell et al. (1968) used a reconstruction task in which children from the 2nd to the 11th grade were required to arrange objects to represent an observer's perspective. In the most demanding of a series of tests, the stimulus display consisted of three red and white cylinders of varying heights (2, 4, and 6 inches).

This task required the subjects to consider both the left-right and before-behind relations of objects in reference to the observer's position. In addition, the task required subjects to orient each object correctly so that, for example, if the observer saw the red half of the 6-inch object, this was depicted similarly in the reconstructed scene. Again, perspective-taking performance was shown to be age dependent; however, even adolescents had some difficulty on this difficult task. A number of other investigations have reported that consistently successful perspective-taking performance is not found until late middle childhood or adolescence (e.g., Brodzinsky, Jackson, & Overton, 1972; Cox, 1978; Dodwell, 1963; Laurendeau & Pinard, 1970).

A number of researchers have designed less demanding perspectives tasks in order to demonstrate that younger children can in fact ignore their own view and successfully make simple judgments about another observer's perspective. Fishbein, Lewis, and Keiffer (1972) varied age, stimulus complexity, and mode of response with preschoolers, first graders, and third graders. The experiment involved two perspectives tasks. One was a traditional picture-choosing task. The second was an array-turning task in which children were asked to turn the model display so that the experimenter could see specified views of the array. All children performed on both tasks, and an array of either one or three differentiable objects was used with both. Performance on the turning task was excellent and very similar for all age levels under both the one-object and the three-object conditions. Across all age groups and conditions, correct responses ranged from 91% to 100%. The picture selection task proved more difficult. For the three-object array and four-choice photographs, preschoolers and first graders made 80% correct judgments. In addition, increasing the number of objects caused a decrease in performance on the pictures task, which did not occur for the turning task. Fishbein et al. pointed out that unlike the findings of earlier studies, such as those described above, children as young as 3½ years of age can be extremely accurate in coordinating perspectives under certain experimental conditions.

Borke (1975) administered an array-turning perspectives task to a group of 3- and 4-year-old children. Children were instructed to turn a revolving array so that they had a view of it identical to an observer's (doll) view of a duplicate display. All children were presented this task three times, with each presentation involving a different model space. Display 1 was a scene involving small objects such as a house, cow, horse, boat, and lake. Display 2 was a papier-maché replica of the Piaget and Inhelder (1967) three-mountain scene. Display 3 contained a wide variety of miniature people and animals in natural settings. Results showed that for Display 1 and Display 3, perspective judgments were quite accurate. Both 3- and 4-year-olds were correct over 80% of the time for the first scene. For Display 3, the 3-year-olds predicted the doll's view accurately over 79% of the time, and the 4-year-olds were correct over 93% of the time. In contrast, the younger group gave only 42% correct judgments and the older group 67% correct for the three-mountain scene. Thus, the nature of the spatial array is important on the perspectives task. The scenes involving small toy figures offered more differentiable cues, which could be used to better visualize the other observer's view. Other researchers have produced evidence to suggest that very young children can overcome the impact of their own view and make accurate inferences about the perceptual viewpoints of others (e.g., Flavell, Everett, Croft, & Flavell, 1981; Knudson & Kagan, 1977; Liben, 1978; Masangkay et al., 1974; Walker & Gollin, 1977).

In a number of perspective-taking studies, the roles of various stimulus features such as number of objects, arrangement of objects, or differentiability of the spatial scene were investigated. Hoy (1974) used seven types of spatial layouts, which varied in terms of the relative positions of three stimulus objects. The positions of these objects were manipulated such that the other observer's view would differ from the subject's along a before-behind, right-left, change-of-shape dimension, or all possible combinations of these. This model array was used in both a picture-choosing and a reconstruction task to assess perspective ability in 6-, 8-, and 10-year-old children. Hoy found that accuracy declined from the change-of-shape to the before-behind/change-of-shape to right-left stimulus types. The change-of-shape was more often considered by subjects in the perspective-taking situation than the before-behind or right-left dimensions. Generally, performance was better for reconstruction than for picture choosing, and it improved with age. Hoy concluded that children's ability to infer perspectives was dependent on the type and number of dimensions that must be mentally transformed and on the mode of response used.

Eliot and Dayton (1976) examined the effect of board shape, block arrangement, and block shape on children's ability to determine the viewing position that corresponded to a slide representation of the array. Investigating perspective ability in first graders, fifth graders, and college students, they found that if the stimulus arrangement was "symmetrical" to the board shape (e.g., triangular object arrangement on a triangular board), children were most accurate in identifying various perspectives when the contrast in object height and shape was greatest. In addition, performance improved with age. Hoy (1974) and Eliot and Dayton (1976) are only two of many studies that demonstrate that features of the model spatial array play an influential role in the perspective-taking situation (e.g., Borke, 1975; Flavell et al., 1968; Finlay, 1977; Liben, 1978; Phinney & Nummedal, 1979; Schlechter, 1977; Schlechter & Salkind, 1979).

Not only can perceptual cues contained within the spatial array affect performance on a perspectives task, but cues external to the actual array can also influence perspective taking. The role of such external cues, or landmarks, were investigated by Fehr (1980) using children from Grades 1, 3, and 6. The results of a standard picture-choosing task indicated that children of all three age levels were able to make more accurate spatial inferences when a landmark was present. This study confirmed the findings of Fehr and Fishbein (1976), which demonstrated that the presence of a microspatial landmark can facilitate perspective taking. More support was offered by Lapsley, Fehr, and Enright (1981), who made the results somewhat more generalizable by testing kindergartners, children in Grades 2, 4, and 6, and college students. Improved performance was found as a function of landmark presence and age. Furthermore, the presence of the landmark facilitated correct perspective inferences for all ages except the college group. Consider the implications of these findings for perspective taking with model layouts. Such miniature arrays are frequently set up in a room filled with distinctive features that can be used as a reference against which to code spatial information contained in the model. Huttenlocher and Presson (1979) have noted that children facing a perspective-taking model task tend to code objects in the array in relation to landmarks in the larger spatial field (e.g., doors or windows of the experimental room). Research evidence has suggested that the use of the containing room as a frame of reference may in fact significantly affect perspective judgments either in a positive fashion (e.g., Acredolo, 1977), as the studies described above would lead one to expect, or in some cases in a negative fashion (see Presson, 1980).

There is considerable evidence, then, for the impact of both model array features and the relation of display objects to external cues. Several investigations also have shown that the removal of all stimulus display features can have interesting effects on perspective taking. This is typically done by placing a shield in front of the model array after the subject has had a chance to learn the layout of the display. Brodzinsky, Jackson, and Overton (1972) looked at the influence of this procedure on perspective-taking performance of 6-, 8-, and 10-year-old children. Each child was administered a picture-choosing task with two single-object arrays and two multiple-object arrays (farm scenes). A 12-inch high piece of posterboard was used as the shield for half of the children. Perspective taking improved with age, and was enhanced in the shielded condition for the two older groups. Shielding as an aid occurred only for the multiple-object arrays.

Walker and Gollin (1977) asked children of ages 4, 5, 6, and 7 to indicate the photograph showing a puppet's view of a model-size dollhouse. For half the children, a shield masked the dollhouse during the perspective judgments. Although shielding the model display did not significantly increase correct choices, it did diminish the production of egocentric errors in the 4-year-olds. The ability to differentiate one's own view from that of another observer was found to improve with age. Huttenlocher and Presson (1973), testing third- and fifth-grade children, similarly reported that while the ratio of egocentric to miscellaneous errors was 10:1 for the standard perspective-taking situation, it was only 4:1 when the spatial array of small blocks was shielded.

The Huttenlocher and Presson study (1973) was also one of the first to systematically compare perspective taking and mental rotation ability. Under the mental rotation instructions, children were required to mentally rotate the spatial array around its central axis in order to anticipate what view thay would have, given a specified rotation. The stimulus array consisted of three small colored blocks in a row. The perspectives task required children to select from a group of four answer cards the one that represented how the blocks would look to a second observer (a small wooden horse). For the rotation problem, the horse was attached to the array so that when it was moved to another location around the table, the entire display moved with it. The children were instructed to determine how the array would look to them if the horse was turned to a new specified position around the table. The rotation task was significantly easier than the perspectives task at each grade level, and for both a shielded array and a visible array. In addition, fifth graders made fewer errors than third graders on both tasks. Finlay (1977) replicated this work with children between the ages of 7 and 10. The perspectives task proved more difficult than the rotation task for both visible- and hidden-array conditions. Furthermore, the 9- to 10-year-old group generally demonstrated better performance than the 7- to 8-year-old group. Harris and Bassett (1976) also did a follow-up study to Huttenlocher and Presson (1973). Children 6 and 8 years of age participated in a reconstruction task. They were directed to construct an array of small cubes to represent a second layout of cubes as viewed from a perspective other than their own (perspectives task), or as viewed from their current position given a specified rotation of the second array (rotation task). Again, the perspectives task was found to be more difficult than the rotation task. This was especially true for the younger children. Improved performance with age was also found for both tasks.

Summary.   Model spaces, then, have been used in numerous experimental investigations of the ability to infer a visual percept different from one's own. Although this line of research has established that perspective-taking ability is age-related, there is considerable disagreement about the course of its development and age of mastery. Some research findings have suggested that young children are incapable of comprehending how another observer's percept of a spatial array is determined by viewing position, and that perspective-taking ability is not well developed until around or after middle childhood (e.g., Dodwell, 1963; Flavell et al., 1968; Laurendeau & Pinard, 1970; Miller, 1967; Piaget & Inhelder, 1967). However, other research employing less demanding perspectives tasks has demonstrated that it would be wrong to think that young children between 3 and 7 years of age are not able to make accurate inferences about the visual perspectives of others (e.g., Borke, 1975; Fishbein, Lewis & Keiffer, 1972; Liben, 1978; Masangkay et al., 1974). Yet it would be a mistake as well to suggest that because a child can perform successfully on a very simplified perspective-taking task the child has a well-developed comprehension of perspective and can understand all dimensions of projective relations and how they are systematically transformed with positional change of self or others. Research seems to indicate that various perspective-taking tasks may tap different levels of a general ability (e.g., Coie et al., 1973; Cox, 1978; Flavell, 1974; Flavell et al., 1968).

A child's performance on a perspectives task may depend upon the specific demands made on the child's knowledge of perspective. For example, does the child only have to report what object or objects are being viewed by the other observer or must the child infer *how* the object or objects appear to that observer (see Masangkay et al., 1974)? If the child must determine appearance of the display, must he or she merely judge the orientation of a single object or must the child assess the spatial interrelationships among various objects (see Coie et al., 1973)? If interrelationships must be considered, do they involve up-down, before-behind, right-left relations, or some combination of these (see Hoy, 1974; Nigl & Fishbein, 1974)? Children under 5 years of age may be able to recognize that another observer sees a toy doll's face, or they might even be able to turn a display so that the other observer sees a specified view such as a view of the doll's back. But it is much later before children can accurately coordinate numerous perspectives of a spatial array in a situation demanding that they consider the orientation of each object and all of the spatial interrelationships as viewed from various stationpoints. In fact, it appears that perspective ability continues to develop after late middle childhood, with only the most rudimentary elements of the ability appearing at the preschool and kindergarten level. The difficulty of any given perspective-taking task will be dependent upon a complex interaction of response demands, stimulus display features, and procedural variables (see Fehr, 1978; Shantz, 1975).

Very few model space studies of mental rotation have been conducted to date, and those that have been carried out have typically been designed to compare this spatial ability with that of perspective-taking ability. Like the latter, mental rotation seems to be an age-related ability. However, it seems to be easier than perspective taking and has produced different error patterns, suggesting that perhaps different mental operations or strategies underlie these two distinct skills (Huttenlocher & Presson, 1973).

Cognitive Mapping

As noted, a cognitive-mapping task is a spatial memory task in which an individual must demonstrate ability to recall the spatial layout of a given environment. Very few such studies have been conducted involving a model layout or mini-environment as the space to be reproduced. Anooshian and Wilson (1977) investigated the influence of route extensity. Kindergarten and adult subjects were trained to remember the locations of four small objects. During this training, experimental subjects observed objects connected by indirect, circuitous train tracks and direct train tracks. Control subjects saw a layout of objects connected only by direct train tracks. Subjects were told to place the four objects on a response board (no tracks included) to show how they had been arranged on the original display board. Analyses based on the actual interobject distances revealed that children, but not adults, tended to overestimate distances between objects connected by indirect routes.

Bullinger and Pailhous (1980) compared the influence of two sensorimotor modalities on the ability of subjects to reconstruct a model village. The age groups tested were 4.5–5.5 years, 7–8 years, 10–11 years, and adults. Subjects observed the miniature village for 2 minutes through a TV camera equipped with a viewfinder. The structural composition of the village in conjunction with the camera's angle of view made it possible for the subjects to visually experience the village layout in each of two ways: (1) a given view of the layout included a single element, such that to relate this element to another required a movement of the camera (this modality is termed "vision + displacement"); and (2) a given view contained several elements such that a set of spatial relations was observed simultaneously ("direct vision"). Bullinger and Pailhous were able to compare each subject's reconstruction to the original model environment and determine how much of the resemblance could be attributed to "direct vision" experience and how much to the "vision + displacement" modality. Improvement in reconstruction was especially marked between the 7–8-year level and the 10–11-year level—similar to other findings of a significant increase in spatial ability during this period (e.g., Kurdek & Rodgon, 1975; Nigl & Fishbein, 1974). At the two youngest age levels, 4.5–5.5 and 7–8 years, there was a significant difference between the influence of the two sensorimotor modalities, in that "direct vision" facilitated more accurate reproductions. This difference was not found at the two older age levels. Finally, the investigators noted that the subjects' reconstructions revealed disparity between the modalities at the two younger age levels based on differences in the nature of the spatial relations conserved in their reproductions. At the 7–8-year age level the "direct vision" modality led to a conservation of alignment and angles, and thus proportionate distances, whereas in the "vision + displacement" modality only one type of conservation was observed, that being the topological relation of "next to." Thus, it seems that the cognitive processes brought into play in representing a spatial layout experienced through "direct vision" are applied effectively at an earlier developmental point than those brought to bear when spatial relations must be represented on the basis of multiple percepts connected by camera movements.

Orientation

Successful maintenance of orientation during locomotion requires that one mentally process the accompanying transformations in the network of spatial relationships between self and environmental features. It is not surprising that this ability has not been examined much with the use of small-scale model spaces, given that such spaces are not themselves navigable. In fact, few, if any, such studies have been conducted for the expressed intention of investigating maintenance of orientation. However, there have been model studies that examined orientation ability while not labeling it as such. Three such studies are described here. In each of these, the standard perspective-taking task was modified so that the subject actually moved to the station point corresponding to the view that had to be inferred. The array was hidden, of course, to preclude the subject from simply experiencing the visual percept directly. Clearly, what is required here is that the subject determine how the spatial relations of self to the model array features change as a function of the particular set of movements involved. That is, the individual must orient self with respect to the miniature environment during movement from one side of the display to another.

Shantz and Watson (1971) administered to children between 3½ and 6½ years of age a standard perspective-taking task and a second task which they called the "box task." In the latter, a box contained a spatial display including a miniature house, a tree, and a streetlight. After the children learned the arrangement of objects, the array was covered with a lid and the children were moved to various station points around the display. The task was to point out the location of each object as it would be viewed from newly occupied perspectives. Thus, the children had to mentally transform or update spatial information in accordance with movements around the nonvisible array. Doing so would permit one to know, for example, that if one moved 180° from the starting position, the streetlight that had been observed in the right-front corner of the box would now be located in the left-back portion of the box. Performance on the box task was related to that on the standard perspective-taking task, but the box task was much easier. In fact, half of the children performed perfectly on this measure of orientation ability, including 7 of the 16 children in the youngest group (from 3 years-8 months to 5 years). Another 25% of the children made only 1 to 3 errors (out of a possible 15).

A similar task was included in the Huttenlocher and Presson (1973) study of perspective ability. In a modification of their perspective-taking task (described above), fourth graders were directed to infer the appearance of the hidden block array after walking around the model display to a new station point. Performance on this movement or orientation task was compared to that on the standard perspectives task. The movement task proved much easier with the children in this group making about 88% correct judgments, whereas children in the perspectives tasks made only 64% correct responses.

Using a similar methodology, Schatzow, Kahane, and Youniss (1980) assessed orientation ability in children, although, like the studies above, their expressed intention was to examine perspective ability. Third- and fifth-grade children were presented a standard perspective-taking task and a movement task. Percentage of correct judgements were 44% and 83% respectively for perspective taking and actual movement at the third-grade level. For Grade 5, the imagined movement yielded 56% correct and the actual movement or orientation task resulted in 83% correct.

These studies are very similar in their investigation of how children can mentally compensate for their movements and the accompanying changes in spatial relationships of self to the objects in the miniature environment. They demonstrate that young children can maintain their orientation with respect to a model space during the course of a short, simple locomotor movement. Thus, successful performance on both orientation tasks and on mental rotation tasks precedes, developmentally, successful performance on perspective-taking tasks. It seems that children can mentally manipulate spatial relations of a model space in accordance with movement of self or imagined movement of the model, prior to manipulating these relations with respect to another observer.

NAVIGABLE/SMALL-SCALE SPACE

The environments used in the studies described in this section meet the criteria for navigable/small-scale as defined earlier. However, the experimenters who constructed them referred to them as being large-scale. It seems that this is because of the once traditional use of the term large-scale to denote a big space relative to the small model spaces so prevalent in spatial cognition research. The spaces used in these studies are large enough to permit travel, but they can be visually experienced in full from a single vantage point and thus considered here as small-scale spaces.

Perspective Taking and Mental Rotation

Most studies of perspective taking have involved a model space. However, there have been a few experiments recently that have extended the study of this spatial ability into a new and perhaps more ecologically valid kind of spatial context. Weatherford and Cohen (1980) used a spatial area of 1.5 × 2.5 m containing seven landmark objects. Although this was a rather small area, it did move the traditional perspective-taking task into a space that one could enter and experience locomotively. The locomotor activity of third graders was systematically varied prior to a standard picture-choosing perspectives task. Children walked along one of two routes of observation: either inside or outside the delineated environment. In addition, one of two types of movement/interaction was included. Children either moved nonstop about the space, labeling each object sequentially, or stopped periodically along the route and labeled all objects in a systematic fashion. For males, perspective taking was facilitated in the "stop-look" movement/interaction groups. Also, for both sexes, the "stop-look" experience coupled with an outside route of observation led to fewer egocentric responses.

Hardwick, McIntyre, and Pick (1976) tested first- and fifth-grade children along with college students in a familiar library. Four objects defined the spatial layout with which the subjects interacted. Both a perspective-taking task and a mental rotation task were administered to all subjects. Both tasks involved pointing a "sighting tube." Under perspective-taking instructions, subjects were directed to align the tube toward each target "as if" standing at a specified station point other than that actually occupied. That is, they were to imagine that they had moved to a second viewing location in the room and now had to sight the target object through the tube. Under mental rotation instructions, the subjects were told to point the sighting tube toward a target "as if" the room had been rotated. Half the subjects had a large screen blocking their view of the spatial array of landmarks, but the other half could freely observe the array at all times. A dramatic improvement in performance occurred with age, with the age of mastery occurring sometime after the fifth grade. The children were more accurate on the mental rotation task than on the perspective-taking task with adults performing equally well on both tasks. Interestingly, egocentric responding on the perspective-taking task by first graders was much higher when the screen was absent.

Herman and Coyne (1980) examined perspective taking and mental rotation in a classroom using subjects who were 20, 60, and 70 years of age. Their tasks were patterned after those of Hardwick et al. (1976). Subjects received one of two experiences in the room prior to testing. In the "single experience" condition, they were taken to the center of the room and the target objects were pointed to and named by the experimenter. In the "multiple experience" condition, the subjects were taken to each of the target objects and their attention was directed to the other target objects in the room. The 20-year-old subjects were more successful in making perspective judgements than were the older subjects, whereas the three age groups performed equivalently on the mental rotation task. In addition, subjects in the multiple experience condition were more accurate at perspective taking than subjects who were in the single experience condition. This experience variable had no effect on mental rotation. Finally, mental rotation performance was superior to perspective-taking performance in the single experience condition, but accuracy was equivalent for the two tasks in the multiple experience condition.

Cognitive Mapping

The few studies of spatial representation ability that have been done using navigable/small-scale spaces have typically been done in large rooms (e.g., classrooms). With investigators taking advantage of the size of such spaces, the role of locomotion has been a popular variable for study. This issue is considered in detail in the chapter by Cohen and Cohen in this book. Herman and Siegel (1978) had kindergartners, second graders, and fifth graders observe a mock town set up in a 4.9 × 6.1 m space easily viewed in its entirety from any location on the perimeter. In one experiment, the town was set up in a classroom and in a second experiment in the center of a large gymnasium. The children were required to reconstruct the small town after the objects were removed. Comparing performance across the two contexts, it was found that young children's accuracy in the bounded space (classroom) was far more accurate than their performance in the unbounded space (gymnasium), while older children's accuracy was relatively unaffected by this variable. The role of travel was assessed, as well. In one experiment, half the children at each grade level walked through the town three times and the other half stood at the starting point on the perimeter and watched the experimenter walk through the town. Walking through the spatial layout did not facilitate reconstruction relative to the looking-only experience.

Cohen, Weatherford, and Byrd (1980) did a similar study in an average size classroom. Children either walked through the environment or only viewed it from a stationary position on the periphery. However, there were two important differences from the Herman and Siegel (1978) study. First, the walking experience here allowed considerably more travel among the landmarks in the environment. Second, the response measure was a distance estimation task for which subjects estimated all pairwise interpoint distances among landmark locations. Findings here also indicated that a no-movement experience could lead to performance equivalent to that following a travel experience. However, this was only true when the distance estimation task was congruent to the acquisition experience, that is, involved no locomotor movement on the part of the subject.

Herman (1980) tested kindergartners and third graders using the same mock town and reconstruction task of Herman and Siegel (1978). Children who walked within the environment ("within" condition) later reproduced the layout better than those who had only walked around the perimeter ("around" condition). Even better performance was demonstrated by children whose attention was directed to spatial relationships among the parts of the town as they walked within the environment ("within-relational" condition). In all three of these conditions, third graders were more accurate than kindergartners. In addition, reconstruction accuracy improved with repeated walks and repeated reconstructions.

Orientation

Navigable/small-scale spaces have been used in several studies of the ability to maintain spatial orientation during positional changes. Acredolo (1978) tested a group of infants at three ages (6, 11, and 16 months) on their ability to compensate for displacement in a 3.2 × 3.2 m space. Infants were placed at the starting position in the room and trained to expect an interesting event at a window on the left or the right. Next, they were moved to the opposite side of the room where they now had the reverse perspective. The ability of the infants to track their event's occurrence was given. Acredolo surmised that repetition of the same head movement used to observe the event during training (e.g., turn head to the right if the event had originally appeared at right-side window) would indicate an infant's reliance on an egocentric frame of reference. However, an infant who compensated for the change of perspective and looked at the actual location of the event was felt to be capable of tracking the changing relation of self to the location during the forced movement. The results indicated a developmental improvement in the ability to maintain spatial orientation during this simple movement. Whereas at 6 months of age the infants were largely unable to take into account their movement, at 16 months they were quite successful. Performance at the intermediate age level was very similar to that at the younger level when the event location was not associated with a salient landmark. When such a landmark was present, the 11-month-old infants demonstrated the ability to update the crucial spatial relation, although they still did not approach the success seen at 16 months of age.

Acredolo and Evans (1980) replicated this study with the addition of a more perceptually salient stimulus serving as the landmark associated with the event location. The infants participating were 6, 9, and 11 months of age. Few of the infants in any age group were observed to consistently track their relation to the event site and compensate for their change of position when no landmark was available. However, when a very salient stimulus was associated with the event location, 80% of the 9- and 11-month-old infants were successful on the task, whereas only 17% of the youngest infants were consistently successful. Thus, the finding of an age-related improvement in orientation ability reported in the previous study was supported.

Rieser (1979) tested 6-month-old infants on their ability to maintain spatial orientation during a simple 90° rotation. He compared their reliance upon three different kinds of reference information during the orientation task: movement, gravity, and landmark cues. The test was conducted in a round experimental chamber. Children faced a set of four small, identical doors on the wall of the chamber. They were trained to anticipate an interesting display at one of the four doors. When an anticipatory response was well learned, the infants were rotated 90°. Then they were observed to see which door they looked at when the interesting display was signaled to occur. If they looked at the correct or "geocentric" door, Rieser presumed that they had been able to take into account their changed relationship to the location of that door. If they looked to an irrelevant door by making the same physical response as required during the training phase, they were thought to be relying on an egocentric code and failing to compensate for the rotation. Subjects were divided into six experimental conditions varying the type of reference information available. When the 6-month-old infants were forced to keep track of the designated door solely on the basis of movement-derived cues, they had great difficulty. Much like their same-age counterparts in Acredolo (1978), these infants did not mentally update their spatial relationship to the event location, but rather relied upon egocentric cues in making their response. The availability of gravitational cues, however, did seem to facilitate infants' ability to compensate for the positional change. Landmark cues were associated with different combinations of doors across several conditions. Only when the correct door and the one diametrically opposite to it were marked by distinctive patterns did the infants successfully use this landmark information to monitor their changing relation to the correct door. Rieser posited the following developmental sequence: (1) infants first base their search for a target location on gravity as reference information; (2) next, they probably rely on landmark information to maintain spatial orientation; (3) finally, they develop the ability to glean useful orientation information from their own movements, which enables them to mentally update the spatial relation of self to a given target location.

Rieser and Heiman (1982) tested spatial orientation ability in 18-month-old toddlers in a round experimental chamber. Equally spaced along the wall of the chamber were eight identical opaque windows. One window was rigged to open automatically when touched, to reveal an interesting display. The window when closed, however, was indistinguishable from all of the others. Children were first trained to walk to the target window from a designated start position. For one group, the target window was straight ahead, for a second group 45° to the left or right, and for a third group 90° to the left or right. After the search response was well learned, children were again located at the start position. Now, however, they were turned so that they had a new facing direction or orientation. The movements into this test position were always in the direction of and then past the target window. Half of the movements were 135° and half were 180°. The children then had to search for the target window, with a correct response requiring that they compensate for the rotational movement. During the test phase, subjects were always turned in the same direction in which they themselves had turned during training in order to walk to the target window. Since this test movement was always past the target window, the most efficient test response was opposite of the training search response. Rieser and Heiman surmised that spatially egocentric children would fail to compensate for the test movement and would repeat the originally learned search response. However, the children moved in this egocentric fashion on only 17% of their initial test responses. Results also indicated that the toddlers took into account the magnitude of the test rotation. When turned 180°, toddlers tended to move a greater distance as they turned in search of the target than when they had been moved only 135°. Rieser and Heiman concluded that even at this young age, children are able to mentally update their spatial relation to a designated environmental feature in accordance with the direction and magnitude of their physical movement. The research on the spatial abilities of infants is discussed at length in Acredolo's chapter in this book.

LARGE-SCALE SPACE

The use of large-scale space has been primarily restricted to the study of cognitive mapping. There is a strong need for experimental developmental research that examines perspective taking, mental rotation, and orientation using large-scale environments. The present section, then, is limited to discussion of re-search on cognitive mapping.

Piaget, Inhelder, and Szeminska (1960) and Shemyakin (1962) were among the first to investigate children's ability to represent large-scale space. They had children draw a sketch of a familiar spatial terrain, and in addition Piaget instructed them to construct a model based on the sketch. Similar methodology became popular with the many urban planners and geographers who studied children's and adults' ability to represent naturalistic settings such as neighborhoods and cities (e.g., Appleyard, 1970; Ladd, 1970; Lynch, 1960).

In the mid-1970s, experimental child psychologists began to heed arguments that more spatial research should be conducted in full-size spaces or environments. In response to this impetus, there was a move toward the use of large-scale as well as navigable/small-scale spaces. In the last several years, there have been numerous representational-mapping studies employing both naturalistic and experimental large-scale spaces. Perhaps the first study to construct an experimental large-scale space was by Kosslyn, Pick, and Fariello (1974). Theirs was a 17-foot square area divided into four quadrants by two opaque and two transparent barriers. Preschoolers and adults learned the locations of 10 landmarks placed throughout the space. Based on analyses of the rank orderings of the distances among objects, it was found that preschoolers tended to overestimate the distance between objects separated by either type of barrier relative to estimates of distance between objects with no intervening barrier. Similar distortions in adults' judgments occurred only for landmarks separated by opaque barriers. Kosslyn et al. concluded that the young children's judgments were greatly influenced by functional distance considerations—that is, the physical effort required to move from one location to another. Visible distance, however, seemed to be an important factor for the adults. Being able to see one location from the position of another provided sufficient information for the adults to accurately represent the physical distance between them. The chapters by Cohen and Cohen and by Liben and Newcombe in this volume explore the effects of barriers in environments on spatial cognition.

Hazen, Lockman, and Pick (1978) constructed two large-scale environments for their mapping study of 3- to 6-year-old children. One environment consisted of four collapsible rooms and the other, six rooms (each 5½ × 5½ × 6 feet), each room containing a distinctive landmark. Children walked through the arrangement of small rooms along either a U-shaped or a Z-shaped route. Several tests were then administered to assess children's route knowledge and configurational knowledge of the layout of landmarks and rooms. Hazen et al. concluded that the cognitive maps of the younger children were route-like and not well integrated into an overall representation, in comparison to the older children. They noted a failure of the younger children to coordinate the various types of spatial knowledge needed to generate such an integrated representation—knowledge of route, knowledge of landmark sequence, and knowledge of overall shape of the space. In addition, 5-year-old children had more difficulty on a reconstruction task if they had traveled the Z-route than if they had walked along the U-route. The 6-year-old children did not show such a difference as a function of route pattern. This influence of activity experience when learning an environment has also been demonstrated in other studies using large-scale experimental spaces (Cohen & Weatherford, 1981; Hazen, 1982).

There also have been a number of cognitive-mapping studies conducted in naturalistic large-scale environments. Curtis, Siegel, and Furlong (1981) assessed the representations of a familiar space by first-, fifth-, and eighth-grade children. The environment was a school with an L-shaped structure. Children were taken to three sighting locations in the school and asked to make bearing and distance estimates to six nonvisible targets located at various points throughout the school. Route knowledge was well represented by all the age levels. However, a measure of configurational accuracy produced developmental differences, with improvement from the first- to the fifth-grade level, and from the fifth- to the eighth-grade level.

Anooshian and Young (1981) also found developmental improvement in representational mapping of a familiar neighborhood using a similar methodology based on bearing estimates from various sighting locations. Other studies have used large-scale naturalistic settings to study how cognitive mapping is influenced by various factors such as type of activity experience (Feldman & Acredolo, 1979), barriers and functional distance (Cohen, Baldwin, & Sherman, 1978), and familiarity (Acredolo, Pick, & Olsen, 1975; Siegel & Schadler, 1977).

COMPARISON STUDIES

Obviously, the most useful kind of study to consider in our efforts to address the central question raised in this chapter is one that systematically compares spatial behavior across the different kinds of spaces. Unfortunately, not many studies of this type have been conducted to date. Three such comparison studies are described here.

Acredolo (1977) compared children's interactions with a small-scale model space and a navigable/small-scale space. Her spatial task required children to maintain their orientation during the course of a simple movement. The large space was a 12 × 12-foot room with no barriers to block one's view of the room. Three-, 4-, and 5-year-old children were trained to find a trinket hidden on one side of the room. Next, the children were walked straight to the other end of the room, turned, and told to find the trinket from the new station point. An analogous situation was designed using a 2 × 2-foot tabletop model board with 3- and 4-year-old children. The change of position here involved moving from a chair at one end of the table to a chair at the other end. A variable manipulated for both spaces was that of landmark differentiation: no landmarks, landmarks at the two viewing locations, and landmarks at the two possible locations for the hidden trinket. Performance of the 3- and 4-year-old children was better with the model space than with the full-size space when no landmarks were available. In the larger space, these children showed greater success in compensating for the movement when differentiating landmarks were present. However, with the model space, landmarks did not have the same facilitative effect, overall performance being very good even without the aid of landmarks. Acredolo offered two hypotheses regarding this discrepancy in performance for the two types of spaces. First, with the model space there was a possible advantage of relating the small spatial layout to features of the larger environment (i.e., the room). Second, the ability to visually apprehend the entire model space in a single glance may have reduced memory demands. The findings of this study support the importance and usefulness of the distinction made in this chapter between model/small-scale space and navigable/small-scale space.

Siegel, Herman, Allen, and Kirasic (1979) compared spatial representation skills applied to a navigable/small-scale and a model/small-scale space. The full-size space was an area of 4.6 × 6.1 m containing a small, mock town. An identical spatial layout was arranged on an 81.3 × 101.6-cm model board, with small color photos representing the buildings. After encountering one of the two environments, children reconstructed the town layout in either the model space or the navigable/small-scale space. Thus, kindergartners, second-, and fifth-grade children participated in four conditions: (1) expose large–construct large; (2) expose small–construct small; (3) expose large–construct small; (4) expose small–construct large. Performance on the spatial recall task was best when children reconstructed the layout in the spatial area whose dimensions were similar to those of the environment originally encountered. Accuracy was significantly reduced in the expose small–construct large condition. Hence, given congruence between the learned space and the response space, there was no difference in reconstruction accuracy for the model layout and the larger layout. Siegel et al. concluded that "one may with caution generalize research findings from small-size models to actual real-world spaces" (p. 584).

Weatherford and Cohen (1981) examined the ability of third- and fifth-grade children to mentally represent spatial relations observed in either a navigable/small-scale or a large-scale environment. The same 8.1 × 6.2 m space containing six landmarks was used for both environments. The difference in scale was achieved by strategic placement of three opaque barriers, which precluded viewing the entire layout of landmarks from a single vantage point. In conjunction with scale of environment, type of acquisition experience was varied. Children either observed the layout of landmarks during a walk through the environment, or viewed it from four stationary viewing positions on the perimeter of the environment. For the large-scale environment, walking through the space facilitated interpoint distance estimates by the younger children, relative to the "look-only" experience. Type of acquisition experience did not have a differential effect on their recall of distances in the small-scale space. Fifth graders were equally accurate in all conditions.

Investigations such as these can be especially valuable in our endeavors to answer the kinds of questions being raised in this chapter. Future research should include more efforts to compare spatial abilities as they are applied to different types of environments. In addition, a useful tactic for such comparison studies would be to use multiple response measures designed to tap the same general spatial ability in order to reveal possible interactions between the type of space and task demands. For example, we can only wonder if Siegel et al. (1979) might have found performance differences for the model space and the navigable/small-scale space had they employed a different cognitive-mapping task. Liben, Patterson, and Newcombe (1981), as well as various chapters in this book, provide testimony to the important influence of task demands on spatial performance.

CONCLUSIONS

As the above review indicates, there has been a considerable amount of spatial cognition research conducted in the three types of spaces defined. Of course, not all spatial research fits these three structure-of-environment categories. For example, other research has presented spatial information in such forms as slides (e.g., Allen, Kirasic, Siegel, & Herman, 1979; Cohen & Schuepfer, 1980), sketch maps (e.g., Thorndyke, 1981), and computer simulation (e.g., Clayton & Woodyard, 1981). Yet the majority of research investigating mental representation and/or transformation of spatial relations has involved a spatial setting that falls into one of the three categories. Accepting the differences that constitute the bases of this three-category conceptualization, we are faced with several related questions. Do the different types of spaces make similar demands on the mental processes of the individual interacting with them? Are the same processes tapped by spatial cognition studies designed to look at the same ability even though different types of spaces are used? How generalizable are the findings from one kind of space to another kind? Although it is probably too soon to answer these questions with any certainty, we can at least ponder the questions and consider the modicum of relevant evidence that is currently available.

Let us begin by considering the most obvious comparison—cognitive/behavioral interaction with a microspace (i.e., model/small-scale) versus that with a large, full-size space (i.e., navigable/small-scale and large-scale). The model space differs structurally from the navigable/small-scale space in terms of size and from the large-scale space in terms of both size and scale. Various theorists and researchers have attempted to direct attention to possible differences between processing spatial information contained in mini-environments and processing spatial information derived from full-size environments (e.g., Acredolo, 1981;

Ittelson, 1973). This is a matter of some importance considering the great number of studies that have employed model spaces in order to learn about the macrospatial cognition that we apply to our everyday environments. Investigators have expressed their concern over the artificiality of model environments and the question of generalizability of findings obtained with them. There have been at least two responses to this concern about microspaces. First, recognition of their potential limitations led various researchers to use full-size spaces where model layouts had been used before (e.g., Hardwick et al., 1976; Weatherford & Cohen, 1980). Second, researchers and theorists became interested in fundamental similarities and differences between microspatial and macrospatial cognition (e.g., Acredolo, 1977; Gold, 1980; Moore, 1979).

Clearly, model spaces differ from the two kinds of full-sized spaces in terms of structure. As a result, they may under some circumstances make different demands on the observer's cognitive processes (e.g., Acredolo, 1977). Yet considerable research has been conducted using the microspaces largely under the assumption that the knowledge about spatial cognition would be applicable to our everyday interactions with full-size environments. How valid is this assumption? One way to begin to address this question is to examine the similarity of findings from model studies with those from full-size space studies. Differences would be less interesting because they may be just as easily attributable to one of the many other factors (or interaction of factors) that vary along with type of space. However, similarities or congruences that exist in spite of such differences would seem to be useful in evaluating the utility and validity of model spaces.

A finding that has been common to all three types of spaces is that perspective-taking ability is a developmental phenomenon. Model studies demonstrating developmental improvement in this ability have been numerous (e.g., Fishbein et al., 1972; Nigl & Fishbein, 1974; Piaget & Inhelder, 1967), and have been supported by studies conducted in navigable/small-scale space (Hardwick et al., 1976), and large-scale space (Anooshian & Young, 1981). Related to this is the finding that egocentric responding declines with age. This has been demonstrated in many model space studies (e.g., Hoy, 1974; Piaget & Inhelder, 1967) as well as in navigable/small-scale space (Hardwick et al., 1976). Egocentric responding has been reduced in a perspectives task by using a shield to preclude the subject from viewing the spatial layout during the judgments. This has been shown with model arrays (e.g., Huttenlocher & Presson, 1973; Walker & Gollin, 1977) and in a navigable/small-scale space as well (Hardwick et al., 1976). Different spaces also have been used in looking at how the nature of one's experience during exposure to the spatial layout influences performance on a perspectives task. Different types of exposure have led to different levels of performance with both microspace (Eiser, 1974) and with navigable/small-scale space (Herman, 1980; Weatherford & Cohen, 1980). Finally, male superiority over their female counterparts has been reported in the perspective-taking situations for both model space (Kurdek & Rodgon, 1975) and large-scale space (Anooshian & Young, 1981).

Research comparing mental rotation to perspective taking has produced two findings common to both microspaces and macrospaces. First, mental rotation has been shown to be a developmentally related ability in model space (Finlay, 1977; Harris & Bassett, 1976; Huttenlocher & Presson, 1973) and in navigable/small-scale space (Hardwick et al., 1976). Second, mental rotation has consistently been found to be easier than perspective taking in both microspace (Finlay, 1977; Harris & Bassett, 1976; Huttenlocher & Presson, 1973) and navigable/small-scale space (Hardwick et al., 1976; Herman & Coyne, 1980).

As noted earlier, few cognitive-mapping studies have been done in the model spaces. Yet, there is some evidence that the representational mapping of spatial relations in a miniature layout may be influenced by some factors in the same way as mapping of the full-size spaces. For example, a microspace has been used to show that certain patterns of movement (of a model train) can affect the representation one constructs of the layout of landmarks in the space (Anooshian & Wilson, 1977). This is roughly similar to the finding that different kinds of movement-based learning experiences differentially influence representation of navigable/small-scale space (e.g., Herman, 1980) and large-scale space (e.g., Cohen & Weatherford, 1981; Hazen et al., 1978). Also the developmental level of the cognitive-mapper influences the accuracy of representation of model space (Bullinger & Pailhous, 1980; Watkins & Schadler, 1980), navigable/small-scale space (Cohen et al., 1980; Herman & Siegel, 1978), and large-scale space (Anooshian & Young, 1981; Curtis et al., 1981).

Finally, there are cross-space similarities for orientation skills. The finding that landmarks can be used to facilitate performance on an orientation task has been produced with both model space (Huttenlocher & Presson, 1973) and navigable/small-scale space (Acredolo, 1977; Acredolo & Evans, 1980). Also, evidence suggesting that maintaining orientation during actual movement is easier than mentally transforming the changes that would accompany an imagined movement (perspective taking) has come from both model space research (Huttenlocher & Presson, 1973; Schatzow et al., 1980; Shantz & Watson, 1971) and navigable/small-scale space (e.g., Rieser, Guth, & Hill, 1982).

The above comparisons were of studies on a given spatial ability conducted in different types of spaces. One also can find similarities in microspatial and macrospatial cognition across different kinds of spatial skills or abilities. For example, the greater accuracy of males relative to females has been found on cognitive-mapping tasks in navigable/small-scale space (Cohen et al., 1980; Herman & Siegel, 1978) and large-scale space (Siegel & Schadler, 1977), and on a perspective-taking task using a model space (Kurdek & Rodgon, 1975). A finding common to all three types of spaces has been a developmental decline in reliance on topological cues during a spatial task. This has been found for cognitive mapping in both navigable/small-scale space (Cohen, Weatherford,

Lomenick, & Koeller, 1979; Herman & Siegel, 1978) and large-scale space (Acredolo et al., 1975), for perspective taking on microspace (Lapsley et al., 1981), and for orientation in navigable/small-scale space (Acredolo, 1977). Thus, certain variables appear to influence some spatial abilities in model spaces in the same way that they affect other spatial skills in full-size spaces.

These similarities are encouraging and suggest that various spatial interactions with model arrays and full-size spaces possess underlying processing commonalities. At least we can present some evidence that models are useful as a convenient means of learning about spatio-cognitive interaction with real-world environments. The degree of isomorphism that exists between microspatial operations and macrospatial operations is still open to question. Given the limits of knowledge on this matter, and the findings of at least one comparison study suggesting differences under certain conditions (see Acredolo, 1977), we must continue to be tentative about generalizing from model spaces to full-size spaces.

Even if we find that the cognitive processes applied to microspaces are generally isomorphic to those applied to macrospaces, there are nevertheless a number of inherent differences that limit what we can learn about the larger spaces from the smaller, model spaces. Let us consider five limitations that restrict the usefulness of the model spaces.

One must always remain outside of the model space, never experiencing the space from within as a participant. The importance of this inside/outside distinction to environmental cognition has been presented in both theory (see Ittelson, 1973) and research (e.g., Herman, 1980; Weatherford & Cohen 1980). As a related limitation, one cannot *locomote* within a tabletop model space. We learn about environments primarily by observing spatial relations as we move, integrating the information derived during travel from one spatial point to another. The ability of direct locomotor experience to facilitate cognitive mapping has been stressed in theory (see Siegel & White, 1975) and empirically supported in numerous studies (e.g., Cohen & Cohen, this volume; Hazen, 1982; Herman, Kolker, & Shaw, 1982). There are also certain features that are part of our everyday living environments, for example, barriers, whose effects can only be fully studied in spaces in which movement is possible. In addition, since active movement within models is precluded, it is difficult to use them to make inferences about spatial cognition based on real behaviors in space—that is, one cannot easily conduct a microspace study that assesses spatial knowledge by observing some naturally occurring behavior such as returning to the location of a particular event (see Acredolo et al., 1975).

A third limitation of model spaces is that they do not lend themselves to the study of such psychological variables as familiarity, meaningfulness, or the socio-emotional quality of the environment, due to their contrived and artificial nature. Many full-size spaces, such as classrooms, homes, and playgrounds, possess a certain meaning for the individual as well as an emotional or motivational dimension (see Gold, 1980; Ittelson, 1973). Model environments, such as those typically employed in spatial research, fail to capture this qualitative essence in spite of empirical findings suggesting its potential impact (see Acredolo, 1979).

Fourth, miniature spaces differ from the larger spaces not only qualitatively, but in a quantitative sense as well. Ittelson (1973) has indicated that full-size environments provide much more information than an observer can possibly process. It is questionable whether a model can adequately simulate the complexity of the spatial information found in such macrospaces as schools, neighborhoods, or cities.

Finally, there are frames of reference differences between microspaces and the macrospaces. In many cases, model layout features may be coded against cues in the larger environment that contains the mini-environment (Pick, 1976, labels these container cues). This advantage is generally not available in the same way in macrospace studies. This problem has received the attention of various investigators (e.g., Acredolo, 1977, 1981; Presson, 1980).

These points illustrate the fact that many features and aspects of our real-world environments are not easily (and sometimes not possibly) portrayed in the model spaces. Thus, the generalizability of microspace findings is limited not only by the extent to which such obvious features as size and contents are simulated (see Siegel, Kirasic, & Kail, 1978), but also by the extent to which the mini-environments permit the observer to encounter the variety of physical and psychological experiences that are part of our everyday interactions with real-world, full-size environments.

Thus far, this section has been concerned only with the distinction between microspace and the two kinds of macrospaces. This has been because it is especially important to question the ecological validity of the mini-environment and the similarity of microspatial cognition to macrospatial cognition. The distinction between navigable/small-scale space and large-scale space is also worthy of consideration. This was demonstrated in the Weatherford and Cohen (1981) comparison study, which showed that such factors as age and type of acquisition experience may influence cognitive mapping in one scale of environment and not another. These findings warn us against lumping all full-size spaces together as though one were just like another in terms of spatio-cognitive demands. It illustrates the inadequacy of the small-size/full-size dichotomy that has frequently been used to categorize environments.

But the scale distinction implemented to compensate for this shortcoming is not without its own problems. This type of labeling implies that there is something purely structural about the space that makes it inherently small-scale or large-scale, something largely permanent given that all environmental features remain constant. But this is not the case. Whether the entire set of spatial relations contained in a given layout can or cannot be perceived from a single vantage point depends not only on the structural makeup of the environment, but also on the observer's position. To borrow an example from Siegel (1981), the city of Pittsburgh clearly cannot be visually apprehended in its entirety from any single position at ground level, but may in fact be termed small-scale given a vantage point atop the U.S. Steel Building. To eliminate this problem, I have based my definition of large-scale space on the assumption that the imaginary observer stands on the same plane as the spatial layout itself (Weatherford, 1982). Similarly, Blaut and Stea (1974) defined a macro-environment as a region which is too large to be perceived as a whole from a single "earthbound" vantage point (p. 5).

However, even this type of qualification does not entirely eliminate the problem associated with the observer's viewing position. Even on the plane of the environment the observer's position may determine whether or not a layout can be seen entirely from one station point. A navigable/small-scale space may be observed in a single percept from the perimeter or it may be seen from the center of the area with the observer turning a full 360° to visually extract all of the available spatial information. The latter circumstance, of course, requires an integration process not required in the perimeter-viewing situation. Does this central station point experience make representing the navigable/small-scale space similar to the large-scale space that also requires an integration of multiple percepts? Environments differ in scale and it is useful to consider this dimension of the space we use in any given research project. One should be careful to describe how the scale of a space, in interaction with an observer's particular experience with the space, determines the processing demands made when representing or manipulating spatial information contained in the area.

Perhaps, then, such structural features as size and scale should be described by indicating the processing demands made on an individual operating on a given layout of spatial information. Thus, a given environment would not simply be described in terms of a few simple labels or categorical terms, but instead would be depicted in terms of the demands made on the observer's spatio-cognitive processes given that observer's particular exposure to the space. A model space, a navigable/small-scale space, and a large-scale space would differ not simply in terms of size and/or scale, but more importantly, along continua of processing demands.

The model space would seem to make the least demands in that the spatial array can be perceptually captured in a single glance. A navigable/small-scale space might be distinguished from the model space in that greater effort is required to extract all of the available spatial information. Generally, more eye, head, and neck movements are required to survey the entire set of spatial relations. There is often more information to be processed and it typically is not given in a single percept, even though it is all gathered from a single vantage point. In addition, the processing requirements will depend on whether the spatial information is gathered through a sweeping glance from a station point on the perimeter, or from a 360° turn in the center of the environment. The latter would seem to make even greater demands in that successive percepts must be coordinated across time and positional change (rotation).

Time and positional changes are also part of the acquisition experience with large-scale spaces. The change of position, however, involves movement from one spatial point in the environment to another. Thus, very distinct, successively experienced percepts must be integrated across broader movements and greater lengths of time. In fact, it may be that the demands made by large-scale spaces make certain experiences such as locomotion (Weatherford & Cohen, 1981) and repeated exposure (Cohen & Weatherford, 1981) especially important for the construction of cognitive representations of these spaces.

The study of spatial cognition has involved a wide variety of environments as sources of stimulus information to be cognitively represented and/or manipulated. This chapter has attempted to stimulate thinking about the comparability of processing demands that accompany cognitive interaction with these various types of spaces. The brief review of the literature in four spatial subareas offers evidence that there are apparent similarities in how different kinds of spaces affect processing of the layout information. At the same time, however, the differences found in comparison studies (Acredolo, 1977; Weatherford & Cohen, 1981) illustrate that under some circumstances different cognitive demands are created by the different kinds of spaces. Hence, it is important to learn as much as possible about how various environmental features influence the spatio-cognitive processes that are applied to them. For example, we have seen here the value of specifying not only size but scale of an environment in order to anticipate the physical (e.g., locomotion, head movements, etc.) and accompanying cognitive (e.g., integration of distinct percepts) activities required to extract and organize the necessary spatial information. There are, of course, many other features that dictate processing demands, including not only structural features, but also such aspects of the environment-observer system as experiential factors (e.g., pattern of movement) and psychological dimensions (e.g., meaningfulness, function, familiarity). For example, a classroom is clearly associated with a different meaning and function than a playground. Ittelson (1973) has noted that environments have particular qualities that call forth or elicit certain actions. This is important in that the observer's actions can influence how the spatial information is represented (see Cohen & Cohen, 1982; Moore, 1979; Pick, 1976).

Future efforts should be made to identify the features having the greatest influence on spatial processing and the nature of this influence. This knowledge should then be used to guide us in our environment descriptions. It is insufficient, for example, to note that the space used in a given study of environmental cognition is a large room of such and such dimensions. The description should be expanded to tell the reader all the environmental features known to increase or decrease processing requirements given the observer's experience with the space and the demands of the task involved.

REFERENCES

Acredolo, L. P. Developmental changes in the ability to coordinate perspectives of a large-scale space. *Developmental Psychology*, 1977, *13*, 1–8.

Acredolo, L. P. Development of spatial orientation in infancy. *Developmental Psychology*, 1978, *14*, 224–234.

Acredolo, L. P. Laboratory versus home: The effect of environment on the nine-month-old infant's choice of spatial reference system. *Developmental Psychology*, 1979, *15*, 666–667.

Acredolo, L. P. Small- and large-scale spatial concepts in infancy and childhood. In L. Liben, A. Patterson, & N. Newcombe (Eds.), *Spatial representation and behavior across the life span*. New York: Academic Press, 1981.

Acredolo, L. P., & Evans, D. Developmental changes in the effects of landmarks on infant spatial behavior. *Developmental Psychology*, 1980, *16*, 312–318.

Acredolo, L. P., Pick, H. L., & Olsen, M. G. Environmental differentiation and familiarity as determinants of children's memory for spatial location. *Developmental Psychology*, 1975, *11*, 495–501.

Allen, G. L., Kirasic, K. C., Siegel, A. W., & Herman, J. F. Developmental issues in cognitive mapping: The selection and utilization of environmental landmarks. *Child Development*, 1979, *50*, 1062–1070.

Anooshian, L. J., & Wilson, K. L. Distance distortions in memory for spatial locations. *Child Development*, 1977, *48*, 1704–1707.

Anooshian, L. J., & Young, D. Developmental changes in cognitive maps of a familiar neighborhood. *Child Development*, 1981, *52*, 341–348.

Appleyard, D. Styles and methods of structuring a city. *Environment and Behavior*, 1970, *2*, 100–118.

Blaut, J. M., & Stea D. Mapping at the age of three. *Journal of Geography*, 1974, *73*, 5–9.

Borke, H. Piaget's mountains revisited: Changes in the egocentric landscape. *Developmental Psychology*, 1975, *11*, 240–243.

Brodzinsky, D., Jackson, J., & Overton, W. Effects of perceptual shielding in the development of spatial perspectives. *Child Development*, 1972, *43*, 1041–1046.

Bullinger, A., & Pailhous, J. The influence of two sensorimotor modalities on the construction of spatial relations. *Communication and Cognition*, 1980, *13*, 25–36.

Clayton, K., & Woodyard, M. The acquisition and utilization of spatial knowledge. In J. Harvey (Ed.), *Cognition, social behavior, and the environment*. Hillsdale, NJ: Lawrence Erlbaum Associates, 1981.

Cohen, R., Baldwin, L. M., & Sherman, R. C. Cognitive maps of a naturalistic setting. *Child Development*, 1978, *49*, 1216–1218.

Cohen, R., & Schuepfer, T. The representation of landmarks and routes. *Child Development*, 1980, *51*, 1065–1071.

Cohen, R., & Weatherford, D. L. The effect of barriers on spatial representations. *Child Development*, 1981, *52*, 1087–1090.

Cohen, R., Weatherford, D. L., & Byrd, D. Distance estimates of children as a function of acquisition and response activities. *Journal of Experimental Child Psychology*, 1980, *30*, 464–472.

Cohen, R., Weatherford, D. L., Lomenick, T., & Koeller, K. Development of spatial representations: Role of task demands and familiarity with the environment. *Child Development*, 1979, *50*, 1257–1260.

Cohen, S., & Cohen, R. Distance estimates of children as a function of type of activity in the environment. *Child Development*, 1982, *53*, 834–837.

Coie, J., Costanzo, P., & Farnill, D. Specific transition in the development of spatial perspective-taking ability. *Developmental Psychology*, 1973, *9*, 167–177.

Cox, M. V. Order of the acquisition of perspective-taking skills. *Developmental Psychology*, 1978, *14*, 421–422.

Curtis, L. E., Siegel, A. W., & Furlong, N. E. Developmental differences in cognitive mapping: Configurational knowledge of familiar large-scale environments. *Journal of Experimental Child Psychology*, 1981, *31*, 456–469.

Dodwell, P. Children's understanding of spatial concepts. *Canadian Journal of Psychology*, 1963, *17*, 141–161.

Eiser, C. Recognition and inference in the coordination of perspectives. *British Journal of Educational Psychology*, 1974, *44*, 309–312.

Eliot, J., & Dayton, C. Factors affecting accuracy of perception on a task requiring the ability to identify viewpoints. *Journal of Genetic Psychology*, 1976, *128*, 201–214.

Evans, G. W., & Pezdek, K. Cognitive mapping: Knowledge of real-world distance and location information. *Journal of Experimental Psychology: Human Learning And Memory*, 1980, *6*, 13–24.

Fehr, L. A. Methodological inconsistencies in the measurement of spatial perspective-taking ability: A cause for concern. *Human Development*, 1978, *21*, 302–315.

Fehr, L. A. Spatial landmarks revisited: Are they useful? *Journal of Genetic Psychology*, 1980, *136*, 299–300.

Fehr, L. A., & Fishbein, H. D. The effects of an explicit landmark on spatial judgements. In P. Suedfeld, & J. Russell (Eds.), *The behavioral basis of design* (pp. 86–93). Stroudsburg, PA: Dowden, Hutchinson, & Ross, 1976.

Feldman, A., & Acredolo, L. P. The effect of active versus passive exploration on memory for spatial location in children. *Child Development*, 1979, *50*, 698–704.

Finlay, D. C. Rotation and perspective tasks in 7–8 and 9–10-year-old children. *Perceptual and Motor Skills*, 1977, *44*, 1216–1218.

Fishbein, H. D., Lewis, S., & Keiffer, K. Children's understanding of spatial relations: Coordination of perspectives. *Developmental Psychology*, 1972, *7*, 21–33.

Flavell, J. H. The development of inferences about others. In T. Mischel (Ed.), *Understanding other persons*. Oxford: Blackwell, Basil, & Mott, 1974.

Flavell, J. H., Botkin, P. T., Fry, C. L., Wright, J. W., & Jarvis, P. E. *The development of role-taking and communication skills in children*. New York: Wiley, 1968.

Flavell, J. H., Everett, B. A., Croft, K., & Flavell, E. R. Young children's knowledge about visual perception: Further evidence for the Level 1—Level 2 distinction. *Developmental Psychology*, 1981, *17*, 99–103.

Gold, J. R. *An introduction to behavioral geography*. New York: Oxford University Press, 1980.

Hardwick, D. A., McIntyre, C. W., & Pick, H. L. The content and manipulation of cognitive maps in children and adults. *Monographs of the Society for Research in Child Development*, 1976, *41*, (3, Serial no. 166).

Harris, P., & Bassett, E. Reconstruction from the mental image. *Journal of Experimental Child Psychology*, 1976, *21*, 514–523.

Hazen, N. L. Spatial exploration and spatial knowledge: Individual and developmental differences in very young children. *Child Development*, 1982, *53*, 826–833.

Hazen, N. L., Lockman, J. J., & Pick, H. L. The development of children's representations of large-scale environments. *Child Development*, 1978, *49*, 623–636.

Herman, J. F. Children's cognitive maps of large-scale spaces: Effects of exploration, direction, and repeated experience. *Journal of Experimental Child Psychology*, 1980, *29*, 126–143.

Herman, J. F., Kolker, R. G., & Shaw, M. L. Effects of motor activity on children's intentional and incidental memory for spatial locations. *Child Development*, 1982, *53*, 239–244.

Herman, J. F., & Coyne, A. C. Mental manipulation of spatial information in young and elderly adults. *Developmental Psychology*, 1980, *16*, 537–538.

Herman, J. F., & Siegel, A. W. The development of cognitive-mapping of the large-scale environment. *Journal of Experimental Child Psychology*, 1978, *26*, 389–406.

Hoy, E. Predicting another's visual perspective: A unitary skill? *Developmental Psychology*, 1974, *10*, 462.

Huttenlocher, J., & Presson, C. Mental rotation and the perspective problem. *Cognitive Psychology*, 1973, *4*, 277–299.

Huttenlocher, J., & Presson, C. The coding and transformation of spatial information. *Cognitive Psychology*, 1979, *11*, 375–394.

Ittelson, W. H. Environment perception and contemporary perceptual theory. In W. H. Ittelson (Ed.), *Environment and cognition*. New York: Seminar Press, 1973.

Knudson, K., & Kagan, S. Visual perspective role-taking and field-independence among Anglo-American and Mexican-American children of two ages. *Journal of Genetic Psychology*, 1977, *131*, 243–253.

Kosslyn, S. M., Pick, H. L., & Fariello, G. R. Cognitive maps in children and men. *Child Development*, 1974, *45*, 707–716.

Kurdek, L., & Rodgon, M. Perceptual, cognitive, and affective perspective-taking in kindergarten through sixth-grade children. *Developmental Psychology*, 1975, *11*, 643–650.

Ladd, F. C. Black youths view their environment: Neighborhood maps. *Environment and Behavior*, 1970, *2*, 64–79.

Lapsley, D. K., Fehr, L. A., & Enright, R. D. Coordination of perspectives: The comparability of results. *Journal of Genetic Psychology*, 1981, *138*, 311–312.

Laurendeau, M., & Pinard, A. *The development of the concept of space in the child*. New York: International University Press, 1970.

Liben, L. S. Perspective-taking skills in young children: Seeing the world through rose-colored glasses. *Developmental Psychology*, 1978, *14*, 87–92.

Liben, L. S., Patterson, A. H., & Newcombe, N. (Eds.). *Spatial representation and behavior across the life span*. New York: Academic Press, 1981.

Lynch, K. *The image of the city*. Cambridge, MA.: MIT Press, 1960.

Masangkay, Z. S., McCluskey, K. A., McIntyre, C. W., Sims-Knight, J., Vaughn, B. E., & Flavell, J. H. The early development of inferences about the visual percepts of others. *Child Development*, 1974, *45*, 357–366.

Miller, J. Measuring perspective ability. *Journal of Geography*, 1967, *66*, 167–171.

Minnigerode, F., & Carey, R. Development of mechanisms underlying spatial perspectives. *Child Development*, 1974, *45*, 496–498.

Moore, G. T. Knowing about environmental knowing: The current state of theory and research on environmental cognition. *Environment and Behavior*, 1979, *11*, 33–70.

Nigl, A. J., & Fishbein, H. D. Perception and conception in coordination of perspectives. *Developmental Psychology*, 1974, *10*, 858–866.

Phinney, J. S., & Nummedal, S. G. Effects of left-right orientation and position reversals on spatial perspective-taking in young children. *Perceptual and Motor Skills*, 1979, *48*, 223–227.

Piaget, J., & Inhelder, B. *The child's conception of space*. New York: Norton, 1967.

Piaget, J., Inhelder, B., & Szeminska, A. *The child's conception of geometry*. New York: Basic Books, 1960.

Pick, H. L. Transactional-constructivist approach to environmental knowing: A commentary. In G. Moore, & R. Golledge (Eds.), *Environmental knowing*. Stroudsburg, PA: Dowden, Hutchinson, & Ross, 1976.

Presson, C. C. Spatial egocentrism and the effect of an alternate frame of reference. *Journal of Experimental Child Psychology*, 1980, *29*, 391–402.

Rieser, J. J. Reference systems and the spatial orientation of six-month-old infants. *Child Development*, 1979, *50*, 1078–1087.

Rieser, J. J., Guth, D. A., & Hill, E. W. Mental processes mediating independent travel: Implications for orientation and mobility. *Journal of Visual Impairment and Blindness*, 1982, *76*, 213–218.

Rieser, J. J., & Heiman, M. L. Spatial self-reference systems and shortest-route behavior in toddlers. *Child Development*, 1982, *53*, 524–533.

Salatas, H., & Flavell, J. H. Perspective-taking: The development of two components of knowledge. *Child Development*, 1976, *47*, 103–109.

Schachter, D., & Gollin, E. S. Spatial perspective-taking in young children. *Journal of Experimental Child Psychology*, 1979, *27*, 467–478.

Schatzow, M., Kahane, D., & Youniss, J. Effects of movement on perspective-taking and the coordination of perspectives. *Developmental Psychology*, 1980, *16*, 582–587.

Shantz, C. U. The development of social cognition. In E. M. Hetherington (Ed.), *Review of child development research* (Vol. 5). Chicago: University of Chicago Press, 1975.

Shantz, C. U., & Watson, J. S. Spatial abilities and spatial egocentrism in the young child. *Child Development*, 1971, *42*, 171–181.

Shemyakin, F. N. Orientation in space. In B. G. Ananyev et al. (Eds.), *Psychological science in the USSR* (Vol. 1, Part 1). U. S. Office of Technical Reports (#11466), 1962, 186–255.

Shlechter, T. M. *Children's spatial coordination and the influences of environmental differentiation.* Paper presented at the Biennial Meeting of the Society for Research in Child Development, New Orleans, 1977.

Shlechter, T. M., & Salkind, N. J. Influences of environmental differentation and conceptual tempo on young children's spatial coordination. *Perceptual and Motor Skills*, 1979, *48*, 1091–1097.

Siegel, A. W. The externalization of cognitive maps by children and adults: In search of ways to ask better questions. In L. Liben, A. Patterson, & N. Newcombe (Eds.), *Spatial representation and behavior across the life span.* New York: Academic Press, 1981.

Siegel, A. W., Herman, J. F., Allen, G. L., & Kirasic, K. C. The development of cognitive maps of large- and small-scale space. *Child Development*, 1979, *50*, 582–585.

Siegel, A. W., Kirasic, K. C., & Kail, R. V. Stalking the elusive cognitive map: The development of children's representations of geographic space. In I. Altman & J. F. Wohlwill (Eds.), *Human behavior and environment* (Vol. 3). New York: Plenum Press, 1978.

Siegel, A. W., & Schadler, M. Young children's cognitive maps of their classroom. *Child Development*, 1977, *48*, 388–394.

Siegel, A. W., & White, S. H. The development of spatial representations of large-scale environments. In H. W. Reese (Ed.), *Advances in child development and behavior* (Vol. 10). New York: Academic Press, 1975.

Stevens, A., & Coupe, P. Distortions in judged spatial relations. *Cognitive Psychology*, 1978, *10*, 422–437.

Thorndyke, P. W. Distance estimation from cognitive maps. *Cognitive Psychology*, 1981, *13*, 526–550.

Walker, L., & Gollin, E. Perspective role-taking in young children. *Journal of Experimental Child Psychology*, 1977, *24*, 343–357.

Watkins, B., & Schadler, M. The development of strategy use in a spatial task. *Journal of Genetic Psychology*, 1980, *137*, 109–117.

Weatherford, D. L. Spatial cognition as a function of size and scale of the environment. In R. Cohen (Ed.), *New directions for child development: Vol. 15. Children's conceptions of spatial relationships.* San Francisco: Jossey-Bass, 1982.

Weatherford, D. L., & Cohen, R. Influence of prior activity on perspective-taking. *Developmental Psychology*, 1980, *16*, 239–240.

Weatherford, D. L., & Cohen, R. *Influence of locomotor activity on spatial representations of large-scale environments.* Paper presented at the Biennial Meeting of the Society for Research in Child Development, Boston, April 1981.

4 The Environments of Children: From Home to School

Chloee K. Poag
Judith A. Goodnight
Robert Cohen
Memphis State University

The study of environmental psychology, while embracing a conceptualization of the intimate transactional nature of people and space, has a number of different focal points. Many researchers examine covert psychological processes important for understanding space, which are presumed to be relatively independent of any particular setting. Certainly much of the research on spatial cognition that examines the acquisition, representation, and manipulation of spatial information follows this reasoning.

Other research in environmental psychology focuses on the settings themselves. For these investigators, the structural, functional, and interpersonal characteristics of particular environments interact with the personal characteristics of participants in the space in important ways. This is not to imply a total uniqueness of every behavior setting; rather it emphasizes the examination of the constellation of environmental and personal factors that influence behavior and development.

The present chapter offers a review of some environments in which children frequently participate. We have chosen to review a variety of features associated with home, neighborhood, and school settings. The choice of these settings as important arenas for children requires little justification. The omission of other, perhaps equally important settings reflects simply a narrowing of scope and not any statement about potential significance. The home, neighborhood, and school settings certainly have received the greatest attention by social scientists and offer perhaps the best vehicle for evaluating our knowledge about children in everyday settings.

71

THE HOME

Although children are spending ever increasing amounts of time in day-care centers, preschools, elementary schools, and other settings, the home environment remains the primary setting in which the child's early social, emotional, and cognitive development occurs. The physical features of the home environment and the physical context in which the home is embedded, including the neighborhood and community, have an enduring effect on the child's socioemotional and cognitive development (Parke, 1978). Research on the effects of home environments on children is presented under five headings. The first two, noise and organization of the home, are general factors associated with the home milieu. The next two, crowding and privacy, relate to interpersonal aspects of the home. The final section contains a review of research on specific environmental features of homes: inanimate objects such as toys and television.

NOISE

Cohen, Glass, and Singer (1973) studied second, third, fourth, and fifth graders living in high-rise apartment buildings near a busy highway. The higher the floor on which the children lived, the less noisy their homes. For those children living in an apartment 4 or more years, the lower, and consequently the noisier, the apartment, the poorer their auditory discrimination and reading test scores. Although the magnitude of the relation between apartment floor level and reading deficits was reduced somewhat when social class was partialed out, analyses indicated that the auditory discrimination effects could not be explained in terms of social class or physiological damage. The experimenter suggested that auditory discrimination may mediate the association between noise and reading deficits. Although the tendency of children from noisy environments to block out sounds indiscriminately in an attempt to cope with the noise may be a useful way to deal with the situation, these children apparently ignored relevant speech cues as well, thus making learning to read more difficult.

Also studying children from homes with differing levels of background noise, Heft (1979) found that kindergartners from relatively noisy homes were less responsive to extraneous sounds in general, reflecting their adaptation to the noise in their homes. Yet these children were less efficient than children from quieter homes in performing a task designed to assess their attentional skills. The relationship between home noise levels and perceptual and cognitive development was attributed in part to attentional deficits. However, rather than actually measuring the home noise level, Heft assessed it through parent interviews concerning the intensity and frequency in occurrence of noise from various sources, e.g., television and family activities. Furthermore, because the children were from urban, suburban, and rural families with somewhat different incomes, other mediating factors, such as household crowding, might have influenced the findings.

In a longitudinal study, Wachs (1976, 1978, 1979) found that too much stimulation, as from high home noise, may be detrimental to the intellectual development of the young child. Noise level in the home was negatively related to children's scores on the Infant Psychological Development Scale during the second year of life and on the Stanford-Binet at 2½ years. Sex of child and ability to control excess noise appeared to be major factors in determining the degree to which the home's noise level affected cognitive development. For males, the relationship between noise in the home and development was strongly negative, whereas for females, home noise appeared to be either unrelated or even positively related to intellectual development. Furthermore, the opportunity for the child to control high noise levels temporarily by escaping to a stimulus shelter, such as a quiet room, was a good predictor of positive cognitive development.

Together, these studies strongly suggest that too much noise in the home environment is negatively related to early cognitive and motivational development, particularly for boys. As noted by Heft (1979) the child's adaptation to potential environmental stressors, such as noise, may be merely a partial process, temporarily reducing but not completely ameliorating their long-term effect on the individual.

ORGANIZATION

Using the Home Observation for Measurement of the Environment (Caldwell, Heider, & Kaplan, 1966), a systematic measure of home stimulation and emotional support, Elardo, Bradley, and Caldwell (1975) and Bradley and Caldwell (1976a, 1976b) evaluated the homes of infants at 6 months and later at 12 months of age on a number of factors, including the home's organization of the physical and temporal environment. High scores on this scale were given to homes in which objects (e.g., furniture and toys) had typical locations and in which family activities (e.g., meals) occurred according to a predictable schedule. Untidy, messy homes in which daily activities took place haphazardly were given low scores. When these children were 3 and 4½ years old, they were tested with the Stanford-Binet. Those from homes that had been given high ratings on the organization measure had significantly higher IQ scores than children from low-scoring, messy homes. Although both boys and girls appeared to benefit from a highly organized home environment, the impact tended to be greater on boys (Bradley & Caldwell, 1980).

The influence of the home's organization on the cognitive development of its young occupants was also suggested by the research of Greenberg and Davidson (1972) and Wachs (1976, 1978, 1979). An examination of the school records and an evaluation of the homes of economically disadvantaged New York City fifth graders indicated that 90% of the homes of high-achieving children were clean and orderly, while 62% of the low achievers had such homes (Greenberg & Davidson, 1972). Wachs (1976, 1978, 1979) reported a significant positive correlation between the regularity of children's home routines and their performance on the Infant Psychological Development Scale during the second year of life and on the Stanford-Binet at 2½ years.

To explain the relationship between mental development and the organization of the home, Maccoby (1975) noted that young children tend to prefer furniture to remain in the same place and family members to sit in the same chair during meals. Perhaps when the physical and social environments are stable and predictable, children are better able to concentrate on understanding a few crucial events. Although the home's organization may affect the cognitive development of its young occupants, other possible covarying influences also must be considered. For example, brighter, better educated parents may tend to prefer more highly organized homes than less bright, less educated parents.

CROWDING

Crowding in home environments appears to influence children's behavior and their intellectual and physical development. Third graders (Walder, Abelson, Eron, Banta, & Laulicht, 1961) and fourth and fifth graders (Murray, 1974) from crowded homes were rated by their peers as more aggressive than children from less crowded homes. Murray (1974) suggested that punitive child-rearing practices may be an inevitable outcome of crowded homes in which interpersonal encounters are more frequent and the opportunities for mutual interference are greater than in less crowded residences. Because parents in crowded homes tend to use more punitive child-rearing tactics and because such practices have been correlated with increased aggression (Martin, 1975), the high levels of aggression in children from crowded environments may be partially attributed to parental discipline practices.

Household crowding may affect not only children's behavior but also their cognitive and physical development. Based on the findings of a longitudinal study, Wachs (1979) reported a positive correlation between young boys' cognitive development and adequate personal space, defined as the lack of overcrowding and the presence of a stimulus shelter in the home, such as a room to which the child could go to be alone. However, the intellectual development of girls appeared unrelated to household crowding. Taking family income differences into consideration, 3-year-old Israeli boys from crowded homes performed significantly poorer on tasks measuring physical development and mental competence than did boys from homes with medium or low crowding, with the latter two groups differing little from each other (Shapiro, 1974). Again, home crowding had minimal effects on girls' performance. In contrast, a study of children from working-class families (Booth & Johnson, 1975) reported that although crowded homes tended to be associated with small negative influences on the physical and intellectual development of both male and female elementary school children, the health of boys and the school performance of girls were particularly affected by a crowded home environment. However, parental health and socioeconomic status, rather than household crowding, appeared to be more strongly related to child health and school performance.

Perhaps the relationship between the degree of crowding in the home and performance on intellectual tasks can be partially explained in terms of a sense of helplessness. Rodin (1976) found that children from crowded residences performed more poorly on puzzles than those from less crowded ones. Furthermore, children living in a high density home were less likely to assume control of outcomes when given the opportunity than those from less dense homes. Crowded home environments may influence the child's ability to regulate social control and consequently contribute to feelings of helplessness, which in turn interfere with intellectual performance.

Together these studies support the view that children, especially boys, are vulnerable to the impact of household crowding. When compared to children from uncrowded homes, those living in crowded settings were reported to be more aggressive (Murray, 1974; Walder et al., 1961) and the intellectual development of young boys was found to be negatively affected (Shapiro, 1974; Wachs, 1979). Some research has assessed the effects of crowding using controlled experimental procedures and is included in the section on school environments. This study of the short-term influence of crowding offers mixed support for the negative impact of crowding reported here and conceptual clarifications are offered in the later section.

PRIVACY

Closely linked to household crowding is the issue of privacy in the home. Wolfe and Laufer (1974) interviewed 5- to 17-year-olds concerning their conceptions of privacy. Four major definitions of privacy were identified: aloneness, information management, lack of disturbance, and control of space. Aloneness was the most frequently used definition of privacy for all age groups and increased in prevalence with age. Controlling access also was an important component as described by 8- to 12-year-olds, while 13- to 17-year-olds frequently mentioned the managing of information.

Using a behavioral questionnaire and data obtained in the Fels Research Institute's longitudinal study, Parke and Sawin (1979) examined privacy regulation in the homes of children aged 2 to 17 years. As children grew older, they made greater use of privacy mechanisms, such as closed doors and knocking rules. The greatest increase in privacy control behaviors took place in early adolescence. Physical maturity, rather than chronological age, correlated with this increase. The sex of the child and of the other person involved also influenced privacy regulation. For example, fathers tended to knock on their daughters' bedroom doors more frequently than on their sons' doors. Mothers knocked on the bedroom doors of sons and daughters equally often but knocked on the bathroom doors of sons more frequently than on those of daughters.

Although a child's privacy reflects the individual's personal characteristics, the impact of the physical environment also must be considered. Parke and Sawin (1979) noted that the square footage of the home was not consistently related to privacy variations. However, the number of bedrooms and bathrooms was significant in determining children's privacy in their homes. A positive correlation was found between the number of rooms in the house and the proportion of children reporting that they kept their bedroom and bathroom doors closed. Thus, children living in homes with a larger number of rooms had greater privacy.

No relationship between family size and children's privacy was found by Parke and Sawin (1979), although a significant correlation between family density within the home and privacy variations was noted. Both low-density (small families in large homes) and high-density (large families in small homes) situations resulted in greater bathroom privacy for the child than did moderately dense conditions (small families in small homes, large families in large homes). This finding suggests that both the amount of space available in the home and the psychological need for privacy in very dense conditions are related to increased use of privacy mechanisms by children (Parke, 1978).

The research reported on children's privacy in the home demonstrates the importance of considering the interrelationship among environmental, developmental, and personal variables in the analysis of children's behavior. The physical setting and characteristics of the child interact with parental practices to determine a child's experience of privacy. We turn next to a discussion of the effects of certain inanimate objects found in the home. The most studied of these have been toys and television.

INANIMATE OBJECTS

Toys

The variety of inanimate objects, especially toys, appears to be a factor strongly related to cognitive development. By observing the homes of 5-month-old black infants, Yarrow, Rubenstein, and Pedersen (1975) identified three dimensions of the infants' inanimate home environment: the responsiveness, the complexity, and the variety of toys and household objects available to the infants. Although none of these dimensions related to language or social development, the variety of inanimate objects available to the infants was positively related to general mental, psychomotor, and cognitive/motivational development.

Wachs' (1976) longitudinal study of the physical environment correlates of intellectual development identified major classes of experiences relevant to early cognitive development. Among these was the adequacy of inanimate stimulation offered the child, including the availability of a variety of inanimate objects such as toys. Long-term variety in stimulation appeared to relate more to girls' cognitive development than to boys' (Wachs, 1979). However, Bradley and Caldwell (1980) found that the variety of appropriate play material in the home was associated with IQ scores for both boys and girls. Consistent with a Piagetian view of cognitive development, when a young child is exposed to variety in the environment, both motivation and capacity to assimilate new information increase (Yarrow et al., 1975).

Although much of the research on the relation of inanimate play objects to cognitive development is correlational in nature, the studies focusing on the association between toys and social development tend to be experimental. Vandell, Wilson, and Buchanan (1980) observed pairs of infants at 6, 9, and 12 months of age in both toys-present and toys-absent conditions. For all ages, more and longer social interaction occurred in the absence of toys. With the exception of object-related social acts, every social act was more frequent when no toys were present. However, the social use of objects increased toward the end of the first year. Similar findings of reduced peer interaction in the presence of toys were obtained with 5-month-olds (Ramey, Finkelstein, & O'Brien, 1976), 10- to 12-month-olds, and 22- to 24-month-olds (Eckerman & Whatley, 1977).

Toys apparently reduce the young child's reliance on the mother in unfamiliar settings. Corter, Rheingold, and Eckerman (1972) observed 10-month-olds and their mothers in a novel room in either a toy-present or a toy-absent condition. When the mothers left the room, the infants with a toy followed them less quickly than those without one. Furthermore, when the toy was novel rather than familiar, the following was more delayed. Those with the unfamiliar toy exhibited the least amount of distress when their mothers left. Similarly, Rheingold and Eckerman (1969) found that although 10-month-old infants left their mothers and entered a new environment with no distress whether or not toys were present, they spent more time away from their mothers when a toy was available in the unfamiliar room. The more toys present (one versus three), the longer the infant voluntarily remained separated from the mother.

Considering the specific characteristics of toys, a toy's contingent responsiveness tends to influence not only how long an infant will play with it but also its impact on the child's development. McCall (1974) found that 7- to 11-month-old infants preferred to play with less rigid and noisier toys than with rigid, noiseless ones. The more responsive the toy, the more the infant manipulated it. Wachs (1976) observed that the number of toys in the home that produced auditory and visual feedback was positively related to the cognitive development of the young child. Yarrow et al. (1975) also noted a positive correlation between the responsiveness of toys available in the home and infants' gross and fine motor, and cognitive/motivational development.

Experimental studies support these correlational findings. Watson and Ramey (1972) exposed infants to a mobile under one of three conditions: the movement of the mobile was contingent on the infant's behavior, the movement was non-contingent, or the mobile was motionless. After the presentation of these conditions for 14 days, all of the infants were tested in a situation where they could control the mobile's movement. Only those who had been exposed to the mobile with contingent movement exercised control over the mobile's turning. Six weeks later, with no additional contact with the mobiles, the same results were obtained. In a related study (Finkelstein & Ramey, 1977), infants' prior experience with contingent stimulation subsequently improved their performance of another response to control a different stimulus. Together, the findings of these correlational and experimental studies indicate the importance of toys with contingent responsiveness. Being able to exert some control over the physical environment appears to promote the infant's cognitive, motivational, and motor development.

Content analyses of the bedrooms of middle-class 1- to 6-year-old children revealed that boys had significantly more sports equipment, vehicles, animal furnishings, and spatial-temporal toys (e.g., clocks and shape-sorting toys), while girls were provided more dolls, domestic toys, and floral and lacy furnishings (Rheingold & Cook, 1975). Essentially, boys were given objects that encouraged active involvement in activities outside the home, and girls received objects that promoted activities directed toward more passive activities within the home. Furthermore, sex differences tend to exist not only in the toys provided but also in parents' attitude toward their children's style of play (Fagot, 1978). Parents allowed 20- to 24-month-old sons to explore objects and to learn about the physical world with less criticism than daughters, and girls received more positive reactions than did boys if they sought their parents' help while playing.

Maternal marital status and employment influence the selection of inanimate objects. MacKinnon, Brody, & Stoneman (1982) applied the Home Observation for the Measurement of the Environment Inventory Preschool Scale (Bradley & Caldwell, 1979) and the checklist used by Rheingold and Cook (1975) to the environments of 3- to 6-year-old middle-class children whose mothers were married/working, married/nonworking, or divorced/working. Taking family income differences into consideration, the homes of divorced mothers had fewer toys, games, and reading materials than the homes of the two groups of married mothers, which did not differ statistically from one another on these measures. From the previous section, one could speculate that the home environments of children from homes with divorced/working mothers were less cognitively stimulating than the home environments of children with married mothers.

Also, children with working mothers (either married or divorced) had less sex-typed rooms. Boys from married/nonworking households had more sex-typed items in their rooms than boys and girls from homes with employed mothers. Perhaps women who hold more traditional views of women's roles choose not to work. The mother's perceptions of the woman's role may influence her consideration of appropriate male and female behaviors and room furnishings.

Television

In the past 30 years the television has become an almost universal aspect of the home environment in the United States. By high school graduation, the average person has devoted 15,000 hours to television (Coppola, 1978). Television can be conceptualized as having a direct impact on the child through the content of its programs and as exerting an indirect influence through its effects on social interactions (Parke, 1978).

Much of the research related to TV has investigated the direct influence of different types of programming on the social and cognitive development of children. Violent and high-action programs have been found to be positively related to children's aggression (Bandura, Ross, & Ross, 1963; Feshback & Singer, 1971; Greer, Potts, Wright, & Huston, 1982; Huston-Stein, Fox, Greer, Watkins, & Whitaker, 1981; Liebert & Baron, 1973; Murray, 1973). So potent is the effect of televised violence that some evidence suggests that high exposure to such programming may influence aggressive behavior after a 10-year period. Eron (1980) reported a positive relationship between the amount of TV violence boys saw at 8 years of age and their interpersonal aggressiveness at the age of 19.

Not only does TV violence appear to influence children's aggressive behavior, it also may affect their attitudes toward real-life violence. Drabman and Thomas (1975, 1976) found that third graders who had viewed a violent TV program were more indifferent to another individual's distress than were third graders who had watched a baseball game.

In television programs, males and females often are depicted in sex-stereotyped ways. Males tend to be portrayed as rational, powerful, and professionally competent, whereas females are usually presented as unemployed or household caretakers, emotional and warm (Sternglanz & Serbin, 1974). The potentially far-reaching influence of these portrayals is suggested by the findings of Davidson, Yasuna, and Tower (1979). Five- to 6-year-old girls viewed TV cartoons that were high or low sex role stereotyped, or neutral. Later, when all of the girls were tested, those girls who had watched the low stereotyped program received much lower sex role stereotype scores than the girls in the other conditions. Furthermore, Frueh and McGhee (1975) reported that children who watched much TV tended to have stereotypical views of sex roles and to conform to culturally appropriate sex role preferences.

The content of TV programs does not necessarily have a negative impact on children. As noted below, certain shows, e.g., Sesame Street and Mister Rogers' Neighborhood, have a positive influence on children's cognitive skills, imaginative play, and prosocial behavior.

Regardless of the child's sex or social class (middle class or disadvantaged) and regardless of the setting of the TV viewing (home or preschool), preschoolers who watched Sesame Street were reported to show a marked improvement in a number of cognitive skills. In fact, the greater the frequency of viewing this program, the greater the amount of improvement (Ball & Bogatz, 1972). A reanalysis of these data by Cook, Appleton, Conner, Shaffer, Tamkin, and Weber (1975), however, indicated that gains in cognitive skills were overestimated in general and were greater for viewers from advantaged homes than for those from economically disadvantaged ones.

Television programs also can increase a child's imaginative play (Huston-Stein et al., 1981; Singer & Singer, 1976; Tower, Singer, Singer, & Biggs, 1979). Preschoolers watched Mister Rogers' Neighborhood, Sesame Street, or a control series of animal and nature films in a study by Tower et al., (1979). The format of Mister Rogers produced positive changes in fantasy play, especially for less imaginative children.

In terms of prosocial behavior, TV programs with a prosocial content appeared to have a moderating effect on antisocial behavior exhibited by preschoolers in free play (Bankart & Anderson, 1979). Friedrich and Stein (1973, 1975) examined the effect of viewing Mister Rogers' Neighborhood, a program that emphasizes helping and understanding the feelings of others. For 4 days, 5- and 6-year-olds watched either this program or a neutral one. Those who viewed Mister Rogers learned the prosocial content of the program and were able to apply this knowledge to other situations involving children. Two procedures, verbal labeling and role playing, were investigated in order to determine whether they, in combination with the program, might increase the learning and performance of prosocial behavior. Verbal labeling training, which included listening to a story and rehearsing the labels, strongly affected verbal measures of prosocial behavior learning, particularly for girls. Role playing increased prosocial behavior for both boys and girls, with the boys being especially influenced by this procedure. Exposure to prosocial TV programs, particularly when combined with verbal labeling and role playing, increased children's helping behavior.

Together, these studies suggest that the content of television programs strongly affects the social and cognitive development of children. Depending on the type of program, television can influence young viewers' aggressiveness, attitudes toward violence, sex role stereotyping, fantasy play, prosocial behavior, and cognitive skills.

Although much research has focused on the direct impact of television programming, TV also can be conceptualized as a physical environment event that influences social interactions and thus indirectly affects the child (Parke, 1978).

Maccoby (1951) noted that the availability of TV increased the amount of time family members spent together, but it decreased the amount of time they spent on non-TV-related family activities. In spite of this greater contact, true social interaction within the family did not increase; when the TV was on, family social life was more parallel than interactive, with the television dominating family life. Brody, Stoneman, and Sanders (1980) observed families watching TV and during a family play session. While watching TV, fathers oriented toward their children less and talked less. Children oriented toward their parents less, talked less, and were less active. Mothers, however, showed few differences in behavior in the two situations.

What the child watches, not merely the act of viewing TV, may also indirectly affect the quality of parent-child interactions. Stoneman and Brody (1981) reported that children who watched a TV program with embedded food advertisements attempted to influence their mothers' selections while grocery shopping more than those who did not view the food commercials. The mothers whose children viewed the programs with food advertisements reciprocated by displaying more control strategies and more power assertion when grocery shopping than mothers of children not exposed to the commercials.

In a national survey, Steiner (1963) found that nearly one third of the parents queried cited babysitting as a major advantage of TV. The use of television for this purpose varied with parental education. Among college-educated parents, 21% of the mothers and 19% of the fathers mentioned using the TV as a babysitter, whereas among those with a grade-school education, 53% of the mothers and 44% of the fathers referred to this function. For some parents, the presence of the television lessened their need to interact with their children.

Although stress in the family may be positively related to the availability of TV (Maccoby, 1951), Rosenblatt and Cunningham (1976) found this relationship to be true only for high-density homes. Rather than being the cause of tension, TV viewing may be used to control the stress caused by the crowded conditions (Gillis, 1979). Families with great tension may avoid conflict by focusing on the TV instead of on each other.

Social interactions with nonfamily members are reduced by the availability of television. Hamilton and Lawless (1956) reported that not only did TV families visit friends less often than did non-TV families, there was less conversation among visitors to the TV home. For children, spending a great deal of time in front of the TV was related to social adjustment problems (Murray, 1973). These problems often appeared when the child was 3 years old. However, TV watching may have been a symptom rather than a cause of poor social adjustment.

In summary, television appears to have a major impact on its young viewers both directly through the content of its programs and indirectly through its influence on social interactions inside and outside the home. Considering the fact that the vast majority of homes in the United States have television, the importance of this inanimate object can hardly be overrated.

THE NEIGHBORHOOD

The home, of course, is physically, socially, and culturally embedded within the neighborhood. As in the home setting, the physical context of the neighborhood has a major impact on its residents. A general review of urban, suburban, and rural environments is presented. Following this is a review of the literature on children and adolescents in these settings, with particular emphasis on their outdoor activities. In contemporary urbanized countries, such as the United States, even those residing in rural areas are undergoing a process of pseudo-urbanization because information, goods, and services are controlled and disseminated from cities to other consumers (Porteous, 1977). Although urban, suburban, and rural settings are becoming increasingly similar in the American society, the urban/suburban/rural distinction remains relevant.

GENERAL REVIEW

Based upon both common opinion and research (Milgram, 1970), city residents appear to be less helpful, less polite, and more suspicious than people from smaller communities. Investigations attempting to understand the influence of the urban environment tend to focus on the physical, mental, and social pathology exhibited by some city dwellers. In Philadelphia, McHarg (1969) found that the incidence of physical diseases such as diabetes, heart disease, tuberculosis, and cirrhosis of the liver was highest in the center city, with a gradual reduction in the rate of occurrence toward the suburban periphery. Social pathology, including suicide, homicide, rape, robbery, and juvenile delinquency, also showed a higher rate of occurrence in the center city than in the outlying areas.

To explain urban social behavior, theorists have offered a number of suggestions. Perhaps some of the behavior of city dwellers can be understood in terms of the diffusion of responsibility created by the large numbers of people (Kamman, Thomson, & Irwin, 1979; Latané & Darley, 1969). Another explanation hypothesizes that the relative anonymity provided by urban life releases city residents from social controls that usually influence social interaction (Zimbardo, 1969). Additional interpretations assert that some urban behavior can be understood in terms of reactions to generalized urban stresses, such as noise (Glass & Singer, 1972), size (Sadalla, 1978), and overcrowding caused by density (Kirmeyer, 1978). Milgram (1970) suggested that when individuals are subjected to levels of environmental input that exceed their ability to deal effectively with them, they adopt tactics to reduce the pressure of these to a more acceptable level. To adapt to this overload, urban dwellers tend to ignore some sources of stimulation, to pay less attention to each input, and to decrease involvement with other people. Thus, some urban social behavior can be viewed as an adaptation to an overload of environmental stimuli, such as noise, sights, events, or demands.

However, the high incidence of physical, mental, and social pathology reported in inner-city areas may not be due solely to the urban environment itself. Perhaps the urban environment attracts people who already have pathological tendencies, or rural communities may simply keep poorer records (Cappon, 1971). Possibly the fact that the center city is often occupied by the lowest socioeconomic group accounts for the high rate of pathology (Hollingshead & Redlich, 1958; Martin, 1967).

An environment unique to the urban setting is the inner-city slum. Although life in such places may appear intolerable to an outsider, Yancey (1971) reported that 74% of the residents of a St. Louis slum were satisfied with the neighborhood, and Fried and Gleicher (1961) found that 75% of the inhabitants of Boston's West End liked the area. Two possible factors involved in this high satisfaction are the vast informal network of social ties and the tendency to view the area around the dwelling unit as an integral part of the home.

The value of ecologically local networks of relatives and friends to lower class city dwellers is strikingly illustrated by the example of the Pruitt-Igoe Housing Project in St. Louis (Yancey, 1971). When first designed, this project of high-rise apartments was praised for having so little "wasted" space between dwelling units; but soon after the first residents moved in, the importance of this "wasted" space for neighboring relations became apparent. Slum dwellers tend to socialize outside their homes. Where the slum's streets, sidewalks, and stores provided numerous semiprivate meeting areas, the housing project offered few. Because the physical characteristics of the buildings did not facilitate social interaction among the residents or normal family activities, such as children's play, undesirable behavior (e.g., assaults, robbery, vandalism) became rampant.

In contrast, an inner-city public housing project designed with its working and lower class tenants in mind can be successful. San Francisco's St. Francis Square contains low-rise apartment buildings built around interior landscaped courtyards. The exterior areas of the project were used frequently by residents for casual, recreational activities (Marcus, 1974). In addition, public housing in Baltimore has shown that an architectural design that provides common space and facilities encourages interpersonal interaction among people moving from a slum into a project (Wilner, Walkley, Pinkerton, & Tayback, 1962).

The suburban environment is widely thought to be very different from the urban one. Suburbia is commonly considered to combine the best of two worlds, country living with easy access to the city. For the modern nuclear family, it is often seen as the favored place to raise a family (Michelson, 1970). The essence of the suburb is homogeneous land use; residential, commercial, and industrial areas are strictly separated.

Privacy appears to vary in urban, suburban, and rural settings (Laufer, Proshansky, & Wolfe, 1976). Because urban, suburban, and rural areas differ greatly in population density, physical privacy is much easier to achieve in a rural environment than in an urban one. However, psychological accessibility, and therefore privacy, are easier to regulate in the urban setting, where life's activities are more segmented. For example, city dwellers neither expect nor appreciate a grocery store clerk asking about other aspects of their lives, such as inquiring about the health of a child. In summary, urban, suburban, and rural areas have features that may facilitate or inhibit different forms and patterns of privacy.

Outdoor recreation necessarily reflects the various settings. Whereas parks and playgrounds provide recreation spots for middle-income urban families, and streets and sidewalks often are used by lower income city residents for informal socializing with neighbors (Brower & Williamson, 1974), the private backyard is frequently the location of recreation in the suburbs. In small, culturally homogeneous towns, the recreation group often includes nearly the entire community. In large, urban areas, recreation may be a neighborhood affair, particularly if the neighborhoods are culturally homogeneous (Klausner, 1971).

When comparing urban, suburban, and rural dwellers' satisfaction with their environments, researchers must consider that suburbs and rural areas tend to contain single-family dwellings, while large urban areas often have high-rise multiple-family dwellings. The single-family home repeatedly has been shown to be the preferred place of residence, regardless of the respondent's race, nationality, or religion (Cooper, 1972; Ladd, 1972). This preference, along with the general dissatisfaction of families with high-rise living, could account for some of the criticism concerning the urban environment. Furthermore, the urban studies of people living in multiple-family housing often are carried out in public housing projects where the occupant's socioeconomic level is likely to be lower than that of the suburbanite (Heimstra & McFarling, 1974).

The architecture of apartment buildings affects children directly by influencing their opportunities for outside activities and indirectly by affecting interaction patterns with their families (Parke, 1978). High-rise apartment buildings tend to be oriented to adult needs, such as placing a priority on parking spaces over playgrounds (Williamson, 1978). In a survey of British residents of high-rise buildings, Bromley (1979) found that 21% of the households with one or two adults and no children were unhappy with their homes, while 46% of those with children were dissatisfied. Similar findings were obtained in California by Marcus (1974). Although 73% of the parents living in low-rise apartments believed their buildings were a good place to raise children, only 39% of those residing in high-rise apartments felt this way.

A major source of parents' dissatisfaction with high-rise housing is the difficulty in supervising their children when they are outdoors (Becker, 1976; Marcus, 1974; Williamson, 1978; Yancey, 1971). Among Marcus's (1974) California mothers, more than twice as many residents of low-rise buildings (75%) permitted their children to play outside alone than did residents of high-rise buildings (35%). While the ease of supervision allowed children residing in low-rise apartments to play actively outdoors (e.g., riding bicycles and sliding on hills), children living in high-rise buildings tended to engage in more passive activities (e.g., sitting, watching, and talking), as reported in Becker (1976).

According to Parke (1978), the restrictive play schedule of children who reside in high-rise buildings may have several negative effects. Insufficient sunshine and exercise may affect their health (Fanning, 1967). The forced and continued contact between parents and their children may contribute to family tension, which, in turn, may adversely influence the child. Limited interactions with peers may have a negative impact on the child's social development (Hartup, 1975, 1978). Finally, the inability of parents to supervise their children's outdoor play activities tends to create opportunities for the children to become involved with crime (Rouse & Rubenstein, 1978).

Although the aversion to high-rise buildings as child-rearing environments is widespread, economic and demographic factors may make multistory housing the only option for many families. The mean sales price of new single-family dwellings rose from $26,600 in 1968 to $78,300 in 1980 (U.S. Bureau of the Census, 1980a). Furthermore, the number of families with mothers employed outside the home is steadily increasing. Between 1960 and 1979 the percentage of working mothers with children under 6 more than tripled to 43.2% (U.S. Bureau of the Census, 1980b). With both parents employed outside the home, the convenience of living in an apartment close to work may outweigh the desire to live in a house farther away. Van Vliet (1983) suggested that the stereotypic notion of the negative effects of high-rise apartment living on children may be overstated. Attention to specific factors, e.g., architectural design and setting of high-rises, may make apartments an acceptable form of family housing.

In summary, the physical environments provided by urban, suburban, and rural settings appear to be conducive to varying lifestyles. Those individuals with lifestyles oriented toward careers and consumerism are likely to value the city's convenience and accessibility to services and facilities. Child-oriented individuals may prefer the greater physical space associated with suburban or rural areas.

NEIGHBORHOODS: CHILDREN AND ADOLESCENTS

Young people lead very different indoor/outdoor life-styles. "Indoors is a private domain, the source of physical shelter, social security, and psychic support—and also the locus of adult dominance...Outdoors is a necessary counterbalance, an explorable public domain providing engagement with living systems and the prevailing culture" (Moore & Young, 1978, p. 88). The outdoors has special emotional importance for children. When youngsters were asked to name their favorite place to play and what they liked about where they lived, they were likely to refer to the outdoors (Moore & Young, 1978). However, there was an apparent contradiciton between the affective significance children placed upon the outdoors and their actual use of it. The outdoors seemed to figure more in their minds and emotions than in their activities.

Urban/Suburban/Rural Neighborhoods

According to Hart (1979), suburbia's spacious landscapes allow better auditory and visual contact between the parent and child and fewer perceived dangers of crime and traffic. Therefore, suburban parents allow their children more spatial freedom than those in busier, more built-up environments. Yet, the spaciousness of the suburban setting presents its young occupants fewer opportunities to develop their environmental competence. Compared to the "loose" environment and play equipment of many rural and urban children, the highly prescriptive toys and equipment often provided suburban youngsters further convinced Hart (1979) that on balance, suburban living is detrimental to the development of post-kindergarten children. Similarly, Wohlwill (1981) suggested that the single-family suburban house may be more advantageous to the young child than an urban high-rise apartment. However, as the child's territorial range expands and opportunities for exploration of the area beyond the home increase, the complex urban setting may be more favorable, particularly for the adolescent.

Advocating high-density environments with heterogeneous land use for children of all ages, Jacobs (1961) noted that the opportunity to grow up in a daily world composed of both men and women is possible for children living in an area where working places, commerce, and residences are mingled together. This mixed land use is especially important for adolescents who, lacking personal mobility, find the homogeneous land use of the suburbs provides them little to do.

In opposition to the advocates of urban life for young people, Gump and Adelberg (1978) concluded that although the absolute number of things to do is greater in cities than in small towns, the presence of many people lessens the urban child's chance to participate. For the small town's children, repeated exposure to fewer behavior settings allows them to learn more about the places, people, and activities of their community than city children.

The beneficial nature of urban neighborhoods for young residents is noted in several recent studies. Taking neighborhood social and economic differences into account, Garbarino, Burston, Raber, Russell, and Crouter (1978) found that although rural sixth graders reported their social networks (excluding family members) as including more people (16.8) than did the urban children (12.2) or the suburban ones (11.1), the urban sixth graders listed a higher proportion of adults in these networks (33.3%) than did the suburban students (22.3%) or the rural ones (19.1%). Thus, the urban sixth graders had the benefit of much more adult involvement than the children in the other settings.

By observing 11- and 12-year-olds in four different neighborhoods, Berg and Medrich (1980) investigated the ways in which neighborhoods as physical environments influence play and play patterns. The neighborhoods included a suburb with houses far apart, a suburb of small houses with small yards, a densely populated neighborhood next to an industrial site, and an inner-city setting. The preadolescents in the low-density neighborhood (i.e., suburb with houses far apart) felt isolated. Those in the densely populated neighborhoods lacked the area for play of the other groups, but they were more mobile, had less formal friendship patterns, and created their own play spaces in vacant lots and parking lots. Although the parents of these children favored low density and the separation of residential and commercial areas, the preadolescents preferred the density and the independence from adults for transportation provided by the more urban settings.

In an extensive survey of children from many countries, including the United States, Russia, Italy, Japan, France, and India, urban dwellers between the ages of 7 and 17 were found to exceed their rural peers in standing height and body weight during the period 1950 to 1980 (Meredith, 1982). However, caution must be used in assuming that the urban environment promotes physical growth. Social and financial factors may be major sources of these differences.

Outdoor Activities

What young people do outdoors is influenced both by the environmental context and by the characteristics of the individual. For example, playgrounds with swings tend to encourage parallel play among the users, who are likely to be young children. Such playgrounds are usually avoided by adolescents. The outdoor activities of young people is examined in terms of home range, i.e., how far children range from home, and in terms of outdoor recreation.

Home Range.   Home range expands from a fairly small and continuous territory known by young children to a relatively diffuse and discontinuous set of activity nodes covering large areas for adults (Andrews, 1973). The limits of home range are negotiated between children and their parents (Hart, 1979). Controlling factors on range extension include age and sex of child, neighborhood context (urban/suburban/rural), environmental fears of both children and parents, and the "pull" of the landscape (Moore & Young, 1978).

Not surprisingly, the distance children travel away from home increases with age (Andrews, 1973; Coates & Bussard, 1974; Hart, 1979). Consistent sex differences emerge between the ages of 8 and 10, with boys ranging farther from home than girls (Hart, 1979). Although both sexes were sent on errands, girls were more likely to be assigned domestic chores involving staying close to home (Hart, 1979). Boys were allowed to explore the physical world, but girls were more restricted in their movements (Fagot, 1978; Hart, 1979; Marcus, 1974).

This greater freedom for boys was due not only to the protection of girls but also to the maxim that "boys will be boys" and need to have this freedom to develop properly into men (Hart, 1979; Saegert & Hart, 1978).

Controlling for sex and age, Anderson and Tindall (1972) noted that the home range of suburban children was consistently larger than that of inner-city children. However, rural, suburban, and urban neighborhood contexts interact with the child's age and sex to determine range experience. A comparison of findings of Anderson and Tindall (1972) for urban and suburban children and those of Hart (1979) for rural children indicates that across neighborhood contexts, boys range farther than girls, with the difference between boys' and girls' ranges being less for younger children than for older. Among the older groups, suburban boys and girls were the most similar in range distance, followed closely in terms of similarity by the urban group. The rural older group had the greatest inequality between the distances boys and girls traveled.

Environmental fears of both parents and children tend to limit range experience, especially for girls. Some of these fears, such as busy streets and rivers, were realistic but others, such as haunted houses, were not (Hart, 1979). In spite of being feared, some places, like woods, often hold much attraction for children. "Wild" areas were highly valued, particularly by boys (Coates & Bussard, 1974).

In summary, the combination of age, sex, environmental context, and parental control affect children's home range experience. In turn, these differences in contact with the world outside the home may influence the child's social and cognitive development. According to Saegart and Hart (1978), limiting children's ability to determine where they range may result in reduced competence and numerous handicaps in dealing with the world. However, Moore and Young (1978) suggested that although limited home range may produce particular handicaps, it is possible that children with less extensive ranges may compensate by gaining experience through extended involvement in fewer places.

Outdoor Recreation.   The outdoor recreation of young people takes place in both planned (e.g., playgrounds) and unplanned (e.g., vacant lots) settings. Haywood, Rothenberg, and Beasley (1974) identified three general types of playgrounds, called traditional, contemporary, and adventure, which differed in terms of the type of equipment available, the form of the play in which the children engaged, and the ages of the users. The traditional playground contained swings, slides, and climbing bars, while the contemporary playground featured mounds and tunnels. Instead of pieces of play equipment, the adventure playground provided materials (e.g., wood, nails, tires, and rope) that could be used in a variety of ways.

At the traditional and contemporary settings, preschoolers and their adult caretakers were the primary occupants. Play tended to be parallel in nature, such as swinging. In contrast, school-aged children and young teenagers were the principal users of the adventure playground. Activities focused on a self-built clubhouse where the young people met to talk, listen to music, and eat. Thus, a playground's equipment and materials appeared to influence what age group chose to use it and the type of activities that took place. Because children's play behavior changes as they age and acquire new interests, their playground needs also change. Different types of playgrounds are suitable at various times in the child's development (Haywood et al., 1974; Wuellner, 1979).

Of course, not all outdoor recreation occurs in settings designated for play. Sidewalks, lawns, undeveloped areas, and other "found" play areas are often preferred by children (Becker, 1976; Hart, 1979; Ittelson, Proshansky, Rivlin, & Winkel, 1974; Marcus, 1974). For example, parking lots were considered good places to ride bicycles, and child-made paths were more valued than those created by engineers. It has been suggested that unplanned recreation settings may be more beneficial to their users than isolated playgrounds. Jacobs (1961) stressed the use of city sidewalks as play sites allowing children to interact with people of different ages. Furthermore, a greater variety of play behaviors may occur in ambiguous play settings than in those designated for play (Coates & Sanoff, 1972). The use of "found" recreation areas sometimes is a source of conflict with adults, however (Becker, 1976). Children who played on a lawn and adolescents who "hung out" around stairwells or parking lots were often labeled "trouble."

In summary, the type of housing and type of neighborhood interact to provide a range of cognitive and social experiences for children and their families. This interaction is quite complex: the needs and desires of residents can take on different forms depending on the physical setting. Importantly, it should be reiterated that the features that make an environment attractive to architects or city planners may not be viewed as attractive by adult or child residents. Further, favorable features as perceived by adults may not be valued similarly by their children. Finally, the needs, desires, and perceptions of children concerning the attractiveness of homes, neighborhoods, and play areas will change with development.

THE SCHOOL

To this point we have reviewed the literature on environments most frequented by children and their families. While these environments continue to have a strong influence on development beyond the preschool years, a great deal of time and energy is spent in the classroom setting. In fact, by the time an average child has completed the twelfth grade, he or she will have spent almost 14,000 waking hours in a classroom. This figure reaches 20,000 hours when preschool and college years are added. As Gump (1978) pointed out, this awesome amount of time is not devoted exclusively to learning of a curriculum, but to living in school. The school as an institution is critically involved with many aspects of socialization. This is the arena for the formation of many peer relationships and for encounters with adults as societal authority figures. As such, the school's effect on social and cognitive development is of vital importance to educators, parents, and other concerned citizens, as well as to social scientists.

The material to be discussed concerning schools is presented in two sections. In the first section on preschool environments, research is presented on (1) school structure variables, (i.e., program, size, and density), and (2) classroom design and activity settings. Discussion in the second section on the elementary school is based on research of (1) school program (specifically open versus traditional classrooms), and (2) intraclassroom factors such as size and density, design and management, classroom distractions, and seating arrangements. Also discussed is the child's experience of the transition from home or preschool to elementary school.

THE PRESCHOOL

The issue of the quality of early childhood care has gained increasing importance in our current socioeconomic climate. According to the 1980 Statistical Abstract of the United States, the number of married women with the husband present in the family and children under the age of 6 has increased from 2.5 million to 4.8 million in the years from 1960 to 1979. The corresponding labor participation rate of these women has also increased from 18.6% in 1960 to 43.2% in 1979. Whether women enter the work force by choice or by economic necessity, one byproduct of this movement is an increased demand for quality day-care arrangements for children. For many families, placing their child in a preschool has been the best available alternative.

The term "preschool" is used in a generic sense in this chapter to refer to any day-care center, nursery school, or organized child care outside of a home. One goal of many preschools is to promote the child's cognitive and social development. It has been recognized that the years from 2 to 5 are important for the child's development of peer relations. Children at this age become more responsive to peers as their opportunities to interact with peers increase. The peer group becomes a significant source of social reinforcement as well as providing the child with an index by which he or she can compare self-achievements.

Early research examined the effects of the preschool environment on the development of intelligence and subsequent public school performance in terms of the presence or absence of prior preschool experience. Overall, the results of this research (Horowitz & Paden, 1973; Swift, 1964) neither support nor refute claims made for long-term benefits from preschool attendance. Currently, rather than relying on global descriptions such as whether a child has or has not attended preschool, interest has focused on what the child actually experiences in the nursery school and on the development of a set of measurable dimensions with which to assess the preschool environment.

School Structure

Program. The term "program" refers to the underlying pedagogical model and goals of the educators as they are realized in the curriculum and schedule of activities in the school. Program also influences the design of the school in terms of spatial arrangements. In turn, the physical factors of the school (size, shape of rooms) influence the program of that school. Preschool educators who believe in structuring the child's environment to optimally match the child's capabilities may divide the room physically into distinct play areas, allowing child choice of activity, while the teacher limits the density or number of children in any particular area. A program guided by a more laissez-faire attitude may physically structure the school space in less restrictive ways still allowing child choice of activity but with fewer controls imposed by the teacher.

Early studies of program were based on classifying types of schools and did not examine explicitly how the program was mediated by the physical setting of the school. Berk (1971) compared a Montessori and a traditional university school in terms of Schoggen's (1963) Environmental Force Units (EFUs), i.e., the relation between what the environment demands of the child and what the child is trying to do. In the Montessori school, most conflicts occurred between the child's desires and the teacher's expectations. Since the child's usual response to these conflicts was compliance, twice as many dependent-compliant behaviors were observed at the Montessori school than at the traditional school. In the traditional school, conflicts arose between the child's desires and his/her own capacity to meet environmental challenges, which resulted in the display of more persistent behavior. These differences in behavior were consistent with differences in program emphasis. The Montessori program presented carefully graded environmental challenges matched to the child's abilities, whereas the traditional nursery school program allowed the child to decide whether to engage the challenge or not regardless of its difficulty. Variations in the program requirements produced variations in the conflict EFUs, which were, in turn, reflected in variations in the children's responses.

Reuter and Yunik (1973) compared rates of social interaction in three types of nursery schools: (1) a Montessori school, (2) a university laboratory preschool based on behavior modification principles, and (3) a parent cooperative preschool. The Montessori setting produced the lowest rate of child-adult interactions and the highest rate of child-child interactions.

Prescott (1978) investigated the differences between four types of child care arrangements: (1) home care with half-day nursery school attendance, (2) day care in another person's home, (3) open day-care centers, and (4) closed day-care centers. The primary dimension by which Prescott defined centers as open or closed was the number of the child's activities that were child-chosen (open) relative to teacher-chosen. The percentage of adult-initiated activities was 58% in closed day-care centers, 20% in open day-care centers, 13% at another's home, and 9% at the child's own home. The proportion of time spent in transition (i.e., moving from one activity to another), was highest in closed day care (26%), followed by open day care (14%), other homes (7%), and the child's own home (8%).

The picture of a closed center that emerged was one that is highly regimented. These centers were also likely to group children according to age, and unlikely to have "soft" items such as cozy furniture, rugs, furry pets, water and sand to play in, or available adult laps. Closed activities, ones that inherently discourage creative and exploratory behaviors, such as copying tasks or puzzles, tended to predominate in closed centers. A factor that seemed to be most important in determining whether a center was open or closed was the size of the enrollment. All the closed centers found by Prescott were large (more than 60 children) while no small centers (less than 30 children) exhibited closed structures.

Johnson, Ershler, and Bell (1980) examined the effects of program differences on children's play behavior. Two adjacent classrooms in a university preschool were selected for study. The first classroom followed a formal education program that emphasized the role of preschool education to provide knowledge and enhance skills through direct teaching. The program of the second classroom was discovery-based, that is, an emphasis on the process of thinking, rather than skill acquisition. These rooms were equivalent in amount and types of physical materials at hand, but they differed in the organization and scheduling of the day. The formal education program focused on small group goal-directed learning activities rather than free play. The two free-play periods were considered central to the discovery-based program, which stressed the child's spontaneous interactions with class materials, peers, and teachers.

Observations of the amount of constructive (goal-directed) play, functional (manipulative) play, and symbolic play revealed striking differences. Children in the formal classroom engaged in more constructive play than children in the discovery classroom. Children in the discovery classroom engaged in more functional play and more nonplay behaviors than the children in the formal program. There were no differences in the amount of symbolic play or the amount of social interaction between programs. Thus, the theoretical foundations of the program as realized in the organization and scheduling of the child's environment influenced the type of children's play behaviors exhibited in the preschool.

Density.   Little research has been concerned with preschool size due, perhaps, to a basic ambiguity in the term. Is size meant to refer to the number of children attending the school or to the actual physical dimensions of the school? Many researchers have turned instead to the examination of density or the amount of available space. Several studies have found that high-density conditions are related to increased difficulties in social interaction including increased aggression (Hutt & Vaizey, 1966; Jersild & Markey, 1935). However, some evidence has shown that children often adapt well to high-density conditions without exhibiting social difficulties (Swift, 1964).

The source of this inconsistency may be attributable to a problem in defining density. McGrew (1972) suggested that, in fact, there are two kinds of density: social and spatial. Social density refers to variations in the number of people occupying a given amount of space and spatial density refers to variations in the amount of physical space per a given number of people. For example, a gymnasium occupied by 100 people, while retaining an adequate space per person, has high social density. If that same number of people were then compressed into one half of the gymnasium, there would be high spatial density as well. In observations of the effect of density on the rate of preschool children's running behavior, changes in spatial density, i.e., increasing or decreasing the available space, produced corresponding changes in the frequency of running. No differences in frequency of running were reported for changes in social density, i.e., increasing or decreasing the number of children while holding the amount of space constant (McGrew, 1972). However, Loo and Kennelly (1980) reported that increased group size in the same space (i.e., social density increase) led to an increase in children's aggressive behaviors. Thus, changes in the amount of space affected a physical behavior—running—while changes in the number of people affected social behavior.

In a study of preschoolers' interpersonal distance during free-play periods, it was reported that under high spatial density conditions, children maintained interpersonal distances of approximately 3 feet and played in groups more than singly (McGrew, 1970). In another study of preschoolers during free play, Loo (1972) found that children showed less social interaction and less aggression under high spatial density conditions than under low spatial density conditions. Loo (1972) hypothesized that the increase in solitary play by the children indicated that it was used as a psychological coping mechanism to alleviate the crowded high spatial density conditions.

This discrepancy in results can perhaps be explained by Shapiro (1975) who discovered a curvilinear relationship between the amount of noninvolved solitary behavior and level of spatial density. Noninvolved behavior of preschoolers occurred most often both in very high spatial density and in low spatial density conditions. At moderate levels of spatial density, noninvolved behaviors were relatively infrequent.

It has been proposed that spatial density is actually a particular instance of a more basic type of density, that of the amount of physical resources available per person. Smith (1974) found that a decrease in resources—the available toys, games, and large play equipment—had both positive and negative effects on 3- and 4-year-old children's social interactions. Children played together in larger groups including children who were usually isolated in the habitual play patterns.

However, there was also an increase in aggression from conflicts over the available scarce resources. Similar findings were obtained by Johnson (1935) for a reduction in the amount of preschool playground equipment. This reduction prompted more imaginative social play as well as more conflict-related responses from the children. In a second experiment, Smith (1974) removed all the toys and games from the classroom but left items such as tables and chairs. An increase in the children's sociality and inventiveness was observed compared to the observed levels prior to removal. For example, the children lined up the chairs and pretended that it was a "train." Interestingly, when the toys were returned and the tables and chairs removed, the children returned to more solitary play patterns.

From a series of experiments on the effects of group size, spatial density, and amount of resources on social and aggressive behaviors, Smith and Connolly (1977) concluded that either high spatial density or low resources could lead to an increase in aggressive responses. However, Rohe and Patterson (1974) found that when high spatial density was held constant, increased aggression took place only when resources were low. It appears, then, that the provision of plentiful resources can act to reduce aggression under high spatial density conditions.

Besides toys, games, and play equipment, one other important resource in the preschool environment is the number of adults available to respond to the child's needs. O'Connor (1975) examined the effects of different teacher-child ratios on the children's social interactions. Two preschools were used that were similar in all respects except for the teacher-child ratios. With fewer children per adult (3.5:1), the children tended to interact more with those adults than with their peers. With seven children per adult, only the children who had been identified independently as dependent tended to seek out adults frequently.

The effects of spatial density also have been examined with respect to other individual differences between children. Loo (1978) assessed 5-year-olds from regular preschool classrooms on measures of hyperactivity-distractibility, hostility-aggressiveness, anxiety, and behavior disturbance using the Preschool Behavior Questionnaire. Children scoring below the median on each scale were designated the "low" scorers while children scoring above the median were the "high" scorers. The high-scoring children did not comprise a severely disturbed population. They did show some evidence of behavioral disturbance in that they were consistently rated more distractible, inattentive, anxious, aggressive, and so forth than the low-scoring children. Groups of six children each spent an hour in free play in both high and low spatial density conditions counterbalanced across groups. For certain dependent variables, the density conditions differentially affected the low- and high-scoring children on the hyperactivity, anxiety, and behavior disturbance scales. For instance, children scoring high on hyperactivity (especially boys) were much more active, restless, and less likely to sit under high-density conditions than low-density. Children who scored high on anxiety expressed three times as much negative affect, primarily anger and distress, under high spatial density conditions as compared to under low spatial density conditions. They also expressed significantly more negative affect than low-scoring children in either density condition. Interestingly, the density conditions had no significant effect on the frequency of aggressive behavior for either the low- or high-scoring children. Loo suggested that the low-scoring children were able to adjust better to the high density conditions through the use of strategies that increased interpersonal distance thus reducing stress (e.g., avoidance behaviors) and that the high-scoring children's failure to use such strategies increased their susceptibility to the stress engendered by the high spatial density conditions.

Few studies have assessed the effects of restructuring the preschool environment. One notable exception is Rohe and Nuffer (1977). In their initial observations, they noted that high-density conditions discouraged activities that required a high level of concentration. They also reported a significant decrease in children's cooperative behavior along with a trend of increased aggression compared to lower density conditions. The second phase of their study involved the insertion of partitions into the preschool classroom. These partitions functioned to shelter and bound specific activity areas such as blocks, art, and housekeeping. After the insertion of the partitions, a marked increase in constructive behavior and in cooperative behavior occurred. It appears, then, that the action of clearly delimiting the work/play area can act to reduce the negative impact of high spatial density conditions.

Classroom Design and Activity Settings

The research in this section offers a more concrete, applied view of the preschool environment in terms of scheduling, ambient factors, type of storage, and room arrangement. As such, it has clear implications for the design and management of preschool classrooms.

Efficient functioning in the preschool revolves around daily scheduling, which imparts an order to both the teacher's and the child's activities. In an optimal schedule, activities flow smoothly into one another with a minimal time spent in transition. LeLaurin and Risley (1972) found that transition time could be cut in half by using a "zone" staff assignment where a teacher was in charge of one particular area to which the children came in groups, rather than "man-to-man" assignment where one teacher led an entire group of children through each activity setting. With regard to the temporal ordering of activities, children showed more attentiveness when storytime followed a rest period rather than following highly physical activities (Krantz & Risley, 1972). Kindergarten children also are more attentive to the teacher's reading or demonstrations when they are spread out in a semicircle instead of crowding around the teacher.

In terms of classroom design, Twardosz, Cataldo, and Risley (1974) found that differing illuminations had no effect on preschoolers during naptime.

Whether napping in dark closed rooms, light open rooms, or in an open play area, there were no differences in the mean amount of time that the group slept or in the sleep patterns of the individual children.

Montes and Risley (1975) varied the type of storage (shelves versus toy boxes) within three activity areas (manipulative toys, housekeeping, and blocks) to assess effects on the use of materials and amount of cleanup time in those areas. When manipulative toys were stored in toy boxes instead of arranged on shelves, children spent significantly more time selecting the toys, which reduced their actual play time with the toys. In the housekeeping area, there was less clean-up time with the toy box compared to the shelves and no difference in playing time. In the block area, box versus shelf storage produced no use or cleanup time differences.

The term "activity setting" refers to a spatially and/or temporally bounded section of the preschool classroom, which is defined by the type of play materials and activities that occur there. For example, the housekeeping area is usually a relatively permanent space that serves no other regular function. A large free space may, on the other hand, be several different activity settings throughout the day such as a group meeting area, directed large motor movement area, or free-play space. In observations of children's preferences measured by the number of different children appearing in an area and the total number of appearances by all children in an area, the block and art areas were the most popular activity settings and the book/reading area was the least popular (Shure, 1963). There are at least two components to this popularity (Rosenthal, 1974). These activity settings can be described according to their attraction and holding power. Attraction power refers to the number of children who enter a particular play area, and holding power refers to the length of time a child stays in that area. The art and block areas had the most attraction power, but the greatest holding power was for role play and art.

Children's social interactions are related to activity setting. With toys that require only one person's participation (e.g., puzzles), social play occurs only 16% of the time. As might be expected, with toys that necessitate two or more people's participation (e.g., games), social play occurs 78% of the time (Quilitch & Risley, 1973). In within-subject comparisons of preschoolers' play across activity settings, Vandenberg (1981) found more social play occurring in the "big muscle" room designed for climbing, running, and so on, while more solitary or parallel play was associated with the fine motor room, which consisted primarily of art activities. High sociality is associated with preparation and clean-up times, role play, and large muscle multiple-person activities such as block and climber play (Doyle, 1975). Not surprisingly, as in the studies reviewed in the section on density, more frequent but short-lived conflicts are related to these settings as well as with small-toy play (e.g., Lego building sets). Houseman (1972) has suggested that three factors are responsible for these conflicts. The presence of interchangeable toy parts, along with a common floor space for playing, makes it difficult for the child to bound his or her own activity from that of surrounding others. Thus, frequent squabbles erupt over the possession of a particular playing piece. Also, a common feature of large block play that prompts conflict is the central issue of "insiders," or those building the house, fort, and so forth versus the "outsiders," those who wish to participate but cannot gain entrance.

Kinsman and Berk (1979) introduced a design modification into a preschool classroom. Prior to the change in the environment, children spent most of their time playing with same-sex peers. By joining the block and housekeeping areas, Kinsman and Berk were able to produce more mixed play across sexes. The social play of the older girls and of the younger boys and girls was greatly enhanced. Mixed-age grouping rather than same-age grouping was itself found to have a facilitative effect on children's social participation in the preschool (Goldman, 1981). Children in mixed-age groups spent significantly less time in parallel play than same-age grouped children.

Structured activities are those that have clearly delineated rules or guidelines imposed on them through either teacher feedback or the availability of adult models. Carpenter and Huston-Stein (1980) found that compliance was greater in highly structured activities whereas novel use of materials was greater in low-structure activities. Girls tended to participate more in high-structure activities; boys more often in low-structure activities. However, with structure held constant, there were no differences attributable to sex of child on either compliance or the novel use of materials.

Summary

In summary, the program, size and density of the center, and classroom design factors have been shown to have an effect on the behavior of the preschool child. Researchers have attempted to partial out the separate effects of each, although these variables mesh together in mutual influence. For example, the size and density of the school and the classroom design factors influence the type of program and the extent of its implementation and vice versa.

THE ELEMENTARY SCHOOL

The rapid increase in preschool attendance is a fairly recent phenomenon. In contrast, elementary school attendance has a much longer history in the United States and is regarded as a fact of childhood. Yet, just in the last century, many changes have taken place in the elementary school. Increasing urbanization and compulsory education turned the one-room schoolhouse into the single grade, multiclassroom buildings with which we are so familiar.

Getzels (1974) postulated that the changes in physical style of the elementary classroom (e.g., from desks bolted to the floor to movable desks to no desks at all) reflect changes in educators' views of the child as a learning organism. At the beginning of the 20th century, the child was regarded as an "empty learner" responding only to input stimuli. This view reflected the S-R psychology predominant in that period. The classroom in turn was teacher-centered. The teacher was positioned at the front and center of the room while the pupils sat in desks bolted to the floor, which forced them to face forward.

Over time, the vision of the child changed to that of an "active learner"—not just an organism that responds, but one that processes and synthesizes information. In the learner-centered classroom, the teacher's desk was moved off to the side and students now sat at desks that could be moved as the need arose. The next change in point of view characterized the child as a "social learner." With an emphasis on social interaction and learning from others, the group-centered classroom contained circular arrangements of students' desks. The final change in classroom form was associated with the conception of the child as a stimulus-seeking organism—one who was innately curious and driven to explore. The open classroom, characterized by spatially bounded interest areas, no desks, and freedom of movement, was regarded as the optimal arrangement by which to encourage the child to explore his or her own interests. The open classroom represented a major break with traditional conceptions of the school and, as such, has been the object of numerous research investigations. In the next section, we examine research findings that contrast the open classroom with the traditional classroom.

Program

Recent research on elementary school programs has focused for the most part on the comparison of "open" schools with traditional schools. There are problems with research of this type due to confusion in the distinction between open space and open education (Ellsworth, 1979). Open space refers to those schools that lack self-contained classrooms. Instead, the interior walls are removed facilitating flow from one room to another. Open education denotes child-directed choice of activity, freedom to explore areas of interest, and shared responsibility for learning where the teacher functions as a guide. Open education was intended to enhance the child's school experience resulting in increased achievement, more satisfaction, greater creativity, and greater curiosity. The open education teaching strategy implies open space to some extent. For instance, it emphasizes the use of the child's immediate environment as a basis for learning, the child's freedom to move unrestrained around the classroom, and a more flexible scheduling of activities.

In addition to this often confused distinction between teaching strategy and architectural space, Marshall (1981) pointed out that there are implementation differences in the degree and area of openness across schools. Marshall suggested that research in this area consider the degrees of openness in the classroom, rather than regarding openness as an all-or-none phenomenon. This suggestion concurs with a point made by Proshansky and Wolfe (1974). They noted that the philosophy of education (program) and the school design are not always congruent in actual practice. For example, in an open-space school where the absence of intervening walls was intended to promote movement across three class areas, the three teachers maintained their traditional strategies and taught as if walls were, in fact, in place. On the other hand, a self-contained classroom does not prohibit the teacher's employment of open education strategies. Actually, one might expect greater difficulties for the teachers and students in the first incongruent situation than in the second because of increased noise and distractions due to the lack of architectural boundaries.

In comparisons of open and traditional school programs, one of the claims for open classrooms is an increase in academic achievement, curiosity, and creativity. Klein (1975) found that, for third graders, children with low-anxiety levels were more creative in open schools than in traditional schools. There were no differences between schools for children with high-anxiety levels. Students in open schools also have higher overall curiosity test scores shown primarily in subtests of preference for novelty and change (Elias & Elias, 1976). It appears then that open schools do, to some extent, foster greater creativity and curiosity than traditional schools.

With regard to academic achievement, Reiss and Dydhalo (1975) compared second-grade students from open-space and conventional schools on their persistence with a difficult task and their standardized achievement test scores. Children from the open-space schools showed more persistence than the conventional school children. In terms of achievement, nonpersistent boys from open-space schools had significantly lower achievement test scores than nonpersistent boys from conventional schools. This result suggests that open-space schools may not be beneficial to all students. Krasner and Richards (1976) implemented an open education program called the Open Corridor, which was combined with a planned environmental design. On standard achievement tests there were no differences between the Open Corridor classes and traditional classes. However, several studies (Horwitz, 1979; Lukasevich & Gray, 1978; Stallings, 1975) have suggested that traditional schools produce greater achievement in reading and math than open schools.

Despite the reading and math gains, these same studies found that the open school students overall were more satisfied with themselves and their school experience than the traditional school students. For Krasner and Richards' (1976) Open Corridor program, the evaluations by students, teachers, and parents were very positive. They liked the program, preferred it to the traditional school program, and thought it was educationally sound. Individual differences also have an effect on the degree of satisfaction with the type of school. Arlin (1975) reported that children with an internal locus of control were more satisfied in open school classrooms than in traditional classrooms.

Hallinan (1976) examined the friendship patterns in open education and traditional classrooms. Although students in the traditional classrooms tended to have more friends, there were fewer isolates in the open classrooms and more even distributions of popularity. It was suggested that this less hierarchic structure was due to increased opportunities for student interactions in the open classrooms.

In summary, open school programs do seem to produce increases in children's creativity, curiosity, and satisfaction with school. However, the expected increase in academic achievement scores compared to traditional program schools has not materialized. In order to probe beyond these findings with regard to open and traditional schools, a consideration and assessment of the actual program differences and methods of implementation are necessary.

Intraclassroom Factors

Size and Density.   Although the issue of size and density has been examined for the preschool and for the high school (Barker & Gump, 1964; Wicker, 1968), surprisingly we found little research on these variables in the elementary classroom. Dawe (1934) reported that group size had no effect on story recall performance of kindergarten groups of 15 to 46 children, but that amount of discussion was greater in small groups than in large groups. More recently, Cassidy and Vukelich (1977) compared three different teacher-child ratios: 1:1, 1:8, 1:15. Group size was found to have a significant effect on children's listening comprehension, with the greatest gains in comprehension made by the 1:1 group. Drawing any conclusions about size and density issues in the elementary school appears unwarranted given the severely limited amount of research.

Design and Management.   As stated previously, educational program is mediated through classroom design. Classroom design has an effect on various child behaviors including the use of space. Damico (1975) examined the use of physical space in self-contained classrooms of 8-, 9-, and 10-year-olds who did not have regularly assigned seats. Girsl were more likely to habitually work in particular corners of the room while boys tended to be more wide-ranging.

Rivlin and Rothenberg (1976) noted that teachers tend not to take advantage of the ability to vary their open classrooms. In eight classes from two schools, the location of furniture was stable over the school year, even though behavioral mapping of patterns of use indicated that particular areas of the room were subject to continual heavy use while other areas were underutilized.

Zifferblatt (1972) compared two third-grade classrooms, which were similar in terms of teaching style, curricula, and activities but which differed in the physical arrangement of the room. In the first room, the desks were arranged in small groups and placed in less accessible areas affording some degree of privacy for the students. Barriers in the room clearly bounded areas of specific activity. In the second room, a large number of desks were grouped together and activity areas were unbounded. From behavior observations of the children, Zifferblatt noted shorter attention spans, more off-task behavior, and more loud conversation in the second room than in the first.

In a design modification study, Evans and Lovell (1979) intervened at an open-plan school that was experiencing problems with pupil distraction, noise, and poor traffic flow. After the insertion of partitions to delineate various areas of the school, they noted a decrease in the number of class interruptions and an increase in the number of content questions asked by the students, which was considered indicative of greater attention being paid to the subject matter.

Weinstein (1977) implemented a well-planned modification in a self-contained, open classroom of second- and third-grade students. Over a 3-month period, seven areas were identified in the classroom: five subject matter areas, a file area including the teacher's desk, and a set of table and chairs placed in a corner. There were no assigned seats and activities were not confined to any particular area. After 2 weeks of formal data collection, Weinstein conducted individual interviews with the teacher and students regarding the room arrangement. Five problems were identified: (1) an uneven distribution of students across the room, (2) avoidance of the games and science areas by the girls, (3) little variety or creativity in the use of materials in the games and science areas, (4) little use of manipulative materials, and (5) a disruptive reading area that had to be large enough for the entire group to meet, while remaining quiet and cozy. Modifications were made by adding shelving and storage, providing work surfaces in the science and games areas, placing carrels and a raised platform in the reading area, and building a "house" in the corner for a quiet, private place. Two weeks of post-change observation were done after a 4-day waiting period. Following the change, there was a more even distribution of students across the room. This was due primarily to a decrease of students in the math area accompanied by a greater move to the games and science areas, especially by the girls. There was also an increase in the use of manipulative materials.

Both Evans and Lovell (1979) and Weinstein (1977) illustrate the potential practical value in applications of research on the physical environment. Interestingly, these modifications closely parallel those studies done in the preschool environment in terms of both the intervention and the resultant changes in child activity.

Classroom Distractions.   Noise is frequently cited as the primary source of distraction in the classroom and is assumed to have a detrimental effect on student performance. Yet, by and large, the empirical evidence has been mixed. As previously reported, Evans and Lovell (1979) found that prior to intervention, an open-space school was experiencing loud noise, poor traffic flow, and high student distractibility. Attention increased after the school design was modified.

Studies that look at performance measures other than attention provide contradictory findings on the effects of noise. Ollila and Chamberlain (1975) reported that under high-noise conditions kindergarten girls' performance in acquisition of sight vocabulary was depressed by the presence of classroom noise. Differential effects according to sex were also reported by Christie and Glickman (1980). Under low-noise conditions, girls performed better than boys on a Standard Progressive Matrices task. However, under high-noise conditions, boys outperformed girls. Slater (1968), using seventh-grade students in three different noise conditions, found no effects either detrimental or facilitative on either speed or accuracy of performance on a standardized reading test. Weinstein and Weinstein (1979) obtained similar results with fourth graders on a reading test. There was a nonsignificant tendency to work slower under the noisy condition. Weinstein and Weinstein suggested that noise is considered more of a problem by the teacher than by the students.

All of the studies cited thus far in this section were concerned with the short-term effects of noise. In a study of long-term effects, Bronzaft and McCarthy (1975) reported a decrement in performance at an elementary school located near an elevated train. The reading scores of children on the noisy side of the school were significantly lower than those on the quieter side. Also, Cohen, Evans, Krantz, and Stokols (1980) cómpared third and fourth graders whose homes and schools were located under the air corridor of a busy airport with a group whose homes and schools were in relatively quiet neighborhoods. The two groups of children were similar in age, social class, and hearing ability. Children in the noisy environment had higher blood pressure and were more likely to fail on a cognitive task and to give up before time to complete the task had elapsed. During the next year, architectural changes were made in 43% of the noisy classrooms to make them quieter. The effects of the classroom noise abatement were minimal (Cohen, Evans, Krantz, Stokols, & Kelley, 1981), suggesting a stability of the influence of noise on cognitive, motivational, and physiological mechanisms. As the investigators noted, perhaps the children were still exposed to a high-noise level at home or perhaps more than 1 year in a quieter classroom was necessary for the children to return to more normal levels of behavior and health. The findings of these studies are supported by laboratory reports on the stressful impact of noise on the individual (Glass & Singer, 1972). Thus, the long-term effects of noise in the school appear to be just as detrimental as the effects of interior and exterior noise in the home.

Another potential distractor is the presence of windows in the classroom. The relevance of windows in the classroom to psychological functioning is ambiguous at best. Karmel (1965), testing ninth- and tenth-grade adolescents, found that those from windowless classrooms put windows in their drawings more often than students from classrooms with windows. Karmel interpreted this as a negative effect produced by windowless rooms, demonstrating fewer positive feelings about the school. In a review of the literature, Collins (1975) concluded that there is no evidence to support any position concerning the importance of windows in the classroom.

Seating Arrangement. Besides studying the size of kindergarten groups, Dawe (1934) also found an effect of position of the child in the classroom. As the child's distance from the teacher increased, his or her discussion participation decreased.

An "action zone" in the classroom was first identified by Adams (1969). Across grade level, sex or age of the teacher, and the subject being taught, the front center section of the classroom was the location of maximal teacher-student interaction. Although failing to obtain the identical action zone, Delefes and Jackson (1972) found that teachers were more likely to initiate talks with students in the front center of the room. However, students sitting in the middle back of the room were more likely to initiate communication with the teacher than students sitting in other areas.

Schwebel and Cherlin (1972) observed and rated students in kindergarten through fifth grade at two schools. Students assigned to front row seats were rated more attentive and showed more on-task behavior. When students were reassigned seats on a random basis, those who had been moved forward showed the greatest mean increase in on-task behavior and the greatest mean decrease in the amount of time spent in inactivity. Teachers' ratings of the students' likableness and attention also increased.

This research suggests the possibility of long-term effects of classroom-assigned seating arrangements. The child who sits regularly in the "action zone" benefits from the teacher interaction in terms of doing more work and paying more attention. In turn, the teacher is likely to form high-positive expectations, which may follow the child through later school years. Similarly, it seems entirely possible that a child consistently relegated to the back of the room will have less positive expectations, which could affect his or her attitudes toward school and school performance in later years.

Consistent with the trend toward open education, many teachers have begun to use table or clustered seating with the children as an alternative to the traditional row seat arrangement. In a direct comparison of these two arrangements, it was found that the average amount of study behavior for students in a second-grade classroom increased from 62% of the time with the table clusters to 82% with desks in rows (Axelrod, Hall, & Tams, 1979). Similarly, with a seventh-grade classroom, the number of times students talked out loud without permission decreased from an average of 58 incidents during a single class period with table clusters to an average of 30 incidents with the row arrangement. It is possible that the optimal classroom seating arrangement depends on the classroom activity involved. Flexible seating that can form clusters for activities involving group interaction and be replaced into rows for individual work may be the most efficient compromise for the open classroom teacher.

Summary

Whereas the effects of the preschool setting were examined mainly in terms of social behaviors, the focus for the elementary school setting has been its effects on academically related behaviors. Studies of elementary school program have primarily contrasted traditional and "open" schools. Keeping in mind the much-needed distinction between open-space schools and open education schools, the consensus of the reviewed research is that although open education schools can increase the child's satisfaction and enjoyment of school, open education has not yet consistently produced academic gains beyond the traditional approach.

While a great deal of research remains to be done on the implementation of various educational programs, and the effects of environmental factors such as noise, size and density, and seating arrangements, the research reviewed offers useful suggestions for structuring the classroom for the individual teacher. An awareness of the effects of variables such as noise, density, and so forth along with a willingness to alter the physical arrangement of the classroom in response to changing spatial needs should allow the teacher to structure an environment that not only meets the needs of students and teacher but furthers the goals of education as well.

CONCLUSIONS

We have provided a general review of an extensive literature on the influence of various home, neighborhood, playground, and school settings. This literature highlights an examination of physical setting as more than simply a backdrop for behavior; the structure, organization, and functions of a setting are intimately related to the psychological status and behavior of the participants. Our purpose in this final section is not to provide a summary of the preceding pages but to offer some general conclusions and implications of this work.

Although some environmental effects are direct (e.g., deficits in auditory discrimination as a function of home noise; mobility as a function of urban/rural/suburban setting), the vast majority of effects due to the physical environment are indirect. Small spaces do not lead to aggressive behavior because they are small; they promote aggressive behavior due to the increased opportunities for interpersonal conflicts over activities. In short, a variety of intrapersonal and interpersonal mediators influence the ultimate effect of an environmental setting.

As a step toward identifying some of these mediational factors, a number of individual differences in behavior were noted in the review. Numerous sex differences were uncovered, for example, in the composition of toys in a child's room. Some children (i.e., those high in internal locus of control; those low in anxiety) were shown to do better in open classroom settings while others (i.e., boys who tend not to persevere on tasks) performed better in more traditional classrooms. Children who tend toward being distractible and aggressive show more negative influences in high-density settings. Rural versus urban versus suburban environments provide different social opportunities to children versus adolescents. Thus different types of children as well as different-aged children respond differently to different settings. A great deal more research is needed to identify individual differences, which are important mediators of environmental influence.

Much of the research reported was correlational in nature and thus prohibits making general causal statements. In addition, some results may be due to Hawthorne-type effects in which the act of changing the environment rather than the particular aspects being changed results in differences in the subjects' behavior. A more important limiting issue, however, concerns the various definitions of environments used by researchers. A great deal of variance exists on how to categorize settings; for example, how high does a building have to be to be considered a high rise? What are the defining parameters of the rural/urban/ suburban distinction? How does one best define a school program? Perhaps it is time for researchers to spend less time defining settings as categories and instead investigate the important dimensions of environments that encompass structural and organizational as well as social factors. Not only would comparisons across different neighborhood, home, or school settings be more meaningful, but also comparisons and evaluations across home/neighborhood/school settings would become possible.

The applied implications of this research are quite numerous, and indeed many are quite elegant in their simplicity. The use of partitions, arranging of desks, and the organization of materials in the classroom offer teachers quite easy means to generate both academic and social interactions. Parents need to become aware of the importance of privacy issues at home, particularly the issue of being able to escape, psychologically and/or physically. Another issue for parents to consider involves the neighborhood setting and the importance of peer contacts and freedom of movement.

A number of factors have been studied in each of the environments reviewed, for example, the effects of noise, density, and privacy. Very little research, however, has examined the interactive roles among environments. Homes, neighborhoods, and schools are closely enmeshed and, of course, are strongly related to particular family socioeconomic and cultural characteristics. It would be very interesting to assess the environmental transitions of children. What is it like to enter a particular school as a function of coming from particular home and neighborhood environments? Conversely, how do the child's home and neighborhood interactions change when the child enters elementary school and high school?

This issue of transitions, of course, relates to the conceptual point above about the definition of important environmental parameters. It also relates to the point above concerning important mediators of environmental effects. In short, we are suggesting a more comprehensive approach to the study of physical settings. A constellation of factors leads to a particular child's participation in a particular setting. This child carries with him or her a past history of prior environmental interactions and a host of cognitive and interpersonal skills and knowledge. This past history and current abilities come into play in the current setting and are influenced by the current participation. Thus the present performance of a child may be directly influenced by the nature of the present setting and may be indirectly influenced by past experiences in other settings. And it is assumed that these influences will be related to the developmental status of the child.

In conclusion, the study of the environments of children can lead to a rich understanding of important factors influencing behavior and development. This chapter highlights a literature that documents many of the important variables for some important environments. Future research that helps clarify the important physical and social parameters of settings and that analyzes the developmental and other individual differences of participants can help to extend our knowledge, and ultimately our applications, of this work.

REFERENCES

Adams, R. S. Location as a feature of instructional interaction. *Merrill-Palmer Quarterly*, 1969, *15*, 309–321.

Anderson, J., & Tindall, M. The concept of home range: New data for the study of territorial behavior. In W. J. Mitchell (Ed.), *Environmental design: Research and practice*. Los Angeles: University of California Press, 1972.

Andrews, H. F. Home range and urban knowledge of school-age children. *Environment and Behavior*, 1973, *5*, 73–86.

Arlin, M. The interaction of locus of control, classroom structure, and pupil satisfaction. *Psychology in the Schools*, 1975, *12*, 279–286.

Axelrod, S., Hall, R. V., & Tams, A. Comparison of two common classroom seating arrangements. *Academic Therapy*, 1979, *15*, 29–36.

Ball, S., & Bogatz, G. Summative research of Sesame Street: Implications for the study of preschool children. In A. D. Pick (Ed.), *Minnesota Symposium on Child Psychology* (Vol. 6). Minneapolis: University of Minnesota Press, 1972.

Bandura, A., Ross, D., & Ross, S. Imitation of film-mediated aggressive models. *Journal of Abnormal and Social Psychology*, 1963, *66*, 3–11.

Bankart, C. P., & Anderson, C. C. Short-term effects of prosocial television viewing on play of preschool boys and girls. *Psychological Reports*, 1979, *44*, 935–941.

Barker, R. G., & Gump, P. V. *Big school, small school*. Stanford, CA: Stanford University Press, 1964.

Becker, F. D. Children's play in multifamily housing. *Environment and Behavior*, 1976, *8*, 545–574.

Berg, M., & Medrich, E. A. Children in four neighborhoods: The physical environment and its effect on play and play patterns. *Environment and Behavior*, 1980, *12*, 320–348.

Berk, L. E. Effects of variations in the nursery school setting on environmental constraints and children's modes of adaptation. *Child Development*, 1971, *42*, 839–869.

Booth, A., & Johnson, D. R. The effects of crowding on child health and development. *American Behavioral Scientist*, 1975, *18*, 736–749.

Bradley, R. H., & Caldwell, B. M. Early home environment and changes in mental test performance in children from 6 to 36 months. *Developmental Psychology*, 1976, *12*, 93–97. (a)

Bradley, R. H., & Caldwell, B. M. The relation of infants' home environments to mental test performance at fifty-four months: A follow-up study. *Child Development*, 1976, *47*, 1172–1174. (b)

Bradley, R. H., & Caldwell, B. M. Home observation for measurement of the environment: A revision of the preschool scale. *American Journal of Mental Deficiency*, 1979, *84*, 235–244.

Bradley, R. H., & Caldwell, B. M. The relation of home environment, cognitive competence, and IQ among males and females. *Child Development*, 1980, *51*, 1140–1148.

Brody, G. H., Stoneman, Z., & Sanders, A. K. Effects of television viewing on family interactions: An observational study. *Family Relations*, 1980, *29*, 216–220.

Bromley, R. Households suited to high flats. *Town and Country Planning*, 1979, *48*, 116–118.

Bronzaft, A. L., & McCarthy, D. P. The effect of elevated train noise on reading ability. *Environment and Behavior*, 1975, *7*, 517–527.

Brower, S. N., & Williamson, P. Outdoor recreation as a function of the urban housing environment. *Environment and Behavior*, 1974, *6*, 295–345.

Caldwell, B., Heider, J., & Kaplan, B. *The inventory of home stimulation.* Paper presented at the annual meeting of the American Psychological Association, New York, 1966.

Cappon, D. Health, malaise and the promise of the cities. *Ekistics*, 1971, *32*, 48–50.

Carpenter, C. J., & Huston-Stein, A. Activity structure and sex-typed behavior in preschool children. *Child Development*, 1980, *51*, 862–872.

Cassidy, A. M., & Vukelich, C. The effects of group size on kindergarten children's listening comprehension performance. *Psychology in the Schools*, 1977, *14*, 449–455.

Christie, D. J., & Glickman, G. D. The effects of classroom noise on children: Evidence for sex differences. *Psychology in the Schools*, 1980, *17*, 405–408.

Coates, G., & Bussard, E. Patterns of children's spatial behavior in a moderate-density housing development. In R. C. Moore (Ed.), *Childhood city, man-environment interactions* (Vol. 12). Milwaukee: EDRA, 1974.

Coates, G., & Sanoff, H. Behavioral mapping: The ecology of child behavior in a planned residential setting. In W. J. Mitchell (Ed.), *Environmental design: Research and practice.* Proceedings of EDRA-3/AR-8 Conference, Washington, DC: American Institute of Architects, 1972.

Cohen, S., Evans, G. W., Krantz, D. S., & Stokols, D. Physiological, motivational, and cognitive effects of aircraft noise on children: Moving from the laboratory to the field. *American Psychologist*, 1980, *35*, 231–243.

Cohen, S., Evans, G. W., Krantz, D. S., Stokols, D., & Kelley, S. Aircraft noise and children: Longitudinal and cross-sectional evidence on adaptation to noise and the effectiveness of noise abatement. *Journal of Personality and Social Psychology*, 1981, *40*, 331–345.

Cohen, S., Glass, D. C., & Singer, J. E. Apartment noise, auditory discrimination, and reading ability in children. *Journal of Experimental Social Psychology*, 1973, *9*, 407–422.

Collins, B. L. Windows and people: A literature survey. In *Psychological reaction to environments with and without windows* (National Bureau of Standards Building Science Series, No. 70). Washington, DC: Institute for Applied Technology, 1975.

Cook, T. D., Appleton, H., Conner, R. F., Shaffer, A., Tamkin, G., & Weber, S. J. *"Sesame Street" revisited.* New York: Russell Sage Foundation, 1975.

Cooper, C. The house as symbol. *Design and Environment*, 1972, *3*, 30–37.

Coppola, R. *Successful children.* New York: Walker, 1978.

Corter, C. M., Rheingold, H. L., & Eckerman, C. O. Toys delay the infant's following of his mother. *Child Development*, 1972, *6*, 138–145.

Damico, S. B. Sexual differences in the responses of elementary pupils to their classroom. *Psychology in the Schools*, 1975, *12*, 462–467.

Davidson, E. S., Yasuna, A., & Tower, A. The effects of television cartoons on sex-role stereotypes in young girls. *Child Development*, 1979, *50*, 597–600.

Dawe, H. C. Influence of size of kindergarten group on performance. *Child Development*, 1934, *5*, 295–303.

Delefes, P., & Jackson, B. Teacher-pupil interaction as a function of location in the classroom. *Psychology in the Schools*, 1972, *9*, 119–123.

Doyle, P. A. *The efficacy of the ecological model: A study of the impact of activity settings on the social behavior of preschool children.* Doctoral dissertation, Wayne State University, 1975.

Drabman, R. S., & Thomas, M. H. Does TV violence breed indifference? *Journal of Communication*, 1975, *25*, 86–89.

Drabman, R. S., & Thomas, M. H. Does watching violence on television cause apathy? *Pediatrics*, 1976, *57*, 329–331.

Eckerman, C. O., & Whatley, J. L. Toys and social interaction between infant peers. *Child Development*, 1977, *48*, 1645–1656.

Elardo, L., Bradley, R., & Caldwell, B. M. The relation of infants home environments to mental test performance from six to thirty-six months: A longitudinal analysis. *Child Development*, 1975, *46*, 71–76.

Elias, S. F., & Elias, J. W. Curiosity and openmindedness in open and traditional classrooms. *Psychology in the Schools*, 1976, *13*, 226–232.

Ellsworth, R. Research on open-education: Do we need a moratorium? *Education*, 1979, *100*, 149–152.

Eron, L. D. Prescription for reduction of aggression. *American Psychologist*, 1980, *35*, 244–252.

Evans, G. W., & Lovell, B. Design modification in an open-plan school. *Journal of Educational Psychology*, 1979, *71*, 41–49.

Fagot, B. J. The influence of sex of child on parental reactions to toddler children. *Child Development*, 1978, *49*, 459–465.

Fanning, D. M. Families in flats. *British Medical Journal*, 1967, *18*, 382–386.

Feshbach, S., & Singer, R. D. *Television and aggression.* San Francisco: Jossey-Bass, 1971.

Finkelstein, N. W., & Ramey, C. T. Learning to control the environment in infancy. *Child Development*, 1977, *48*, 806–820.

Fried, M., & Gleicher, P. Some sources of residential satisfaction in an urban slum. *Journal of the American Institute of Planners*, 1961, *27*, 305–315.

Friedrich, L., & Stein, A. Aggressive and prosocial television programs and the natural behavior of preschool children. *Monographs of the Society for Research in Child Development*, 1973, *38*, No. 151.

Friedrich, L., & Stein, A. Prosocial television and young children: The effects of verbal labeling and role playing on learning and behavior. *Child Development*, 1975, *46*, 27–38.

Frueh, T., & McGhee, P. Traditional sex role development and the amount of time spent watching TV. *Developmental Psychology*, 1975, *11*, 109.

Garbarino, J., Burston, N., Raber, S., Russell, R., & Crouter, A. The social maps of children approaching adolescence: Studying the ecology of youth development. *Journal of Youth and Adolescence*, 1978, *7*, 417–428.

Getzels, J. W. Images of the classroom and visions of the learner. *School Review*, 1974, *82*, 527–540.

Gillis, A. R. Coping with crowding: TV, patterns of activity, and adaptation to high density environments. *Sociological Quarterly*, 1979, *20*, 267–278.

Glass, D. C., & Singer, J. E. *Urban stress.* New York: Academic Press, 1972.

Goldman, J. A. Social participation of preschool children in same- vs. mixed-age groups. *Child Development*, 1981, *52*, 644–650.

Greenberg, J. W., & Davidson, H. H. Home background and school achievement of black urban ghetto children. *American Journal of Orthopsychiatry*, 1972, *42*, 802–810.

Greer, D., Potts, R., Wright, J. C., & Huston, A. C. The effects of television commercial form and commercial placement on children's social behavior and attention. *Child Development,* 1982, *53,* 611–619.

Gump, P. V. School environments. In I. Altman & J. Wohlwill (Eds.), *Children in the environment.* New York: Plenum Press, 1978.

Gump, P. V., & Adelberg, B. Urbanism from the perspective of ecological psychologists. *Environment and Behavior,* 1978, *10,* 171–191.

Hallinan, M. T. Friendship patterns in open and traditional classrooms. *Sociology of Education,* 1976, *49,* 254–265.

Hamilton, R. V., & Lawless, R. H. Television within the social matrix. *Public Opinion Quarterly,* 1956, *20,* 393–403.

Hart, R. *Children's experience of place.* New York: Irvington Publishers, 1979.

Hartup, W. W. The origins of friendships. In M. Lewis & L. A. Rosenblum (Eds.), *Friendship and peer relations.* New York: Wiley, 1975.

Hartup, W. W. Children and their friends. In H. McGurk (Ed.), *Child social development.* London: Methuen, 1978.

Haywood, D. G., Rothenberg, M., & Beasley, R. R. Children's play and urban playground environments: A comparison of traditional, contemporary, and adventure playground types. *Environment and Behavior,* 1974, *6,* 131–168.

Heft, H. Background and focal environmental conditions of the home and attention in young children. *Journal of Applied Social Psychology,* 1979, *9,* 47–69.

Heimstra, N. W., & McFarling, L. H. *Environmental psychology.* Monterey, CA: Brooks/Cole, 1974.

Hollingshead, A. B., & Redlich, F. C. *Social class and mental illness.* New York: Wiley, 1958.

Horowitz, F. D., & Paden, L. Y. The effectiveness of environmental intervention programs. In B. M. Caldwell & H. N. Ricciute (Eds.), *Review of child development research* (Vol. 3). Chicago: University of Chicago Press, 1973.

Horwitz, R. A. Psychological effects of the open-classroom. *Review of Educational Research,* 1979, *49,* 71–85.

Houseman, J. *An ecological study of interpersonal conflict among preschool children.* Unpublished dissertation, Wayne State University, 1972.

Huston-Stein, A., Fox, S., Greer, D., Watkins, B. A., & Whitaker, J. The effects of action and violence in television programs on the social behavior and imaginative play of preschool children. *Journal of Genetic Psychology,* 1981, *138,* 183–191.

Hutt, C., & Vaizey, M. J. Differential effects of group density on social behavior. *Nature,* 1966, *209,* 1371–1372.

Ittelson, W. H., Proshansky, H. M., Rivlin, L. G., & Winkel, G. H. *An introduction to environmental psychology.* New York: Holt, Rinehart & Winston, 1974.

Jacobs, J. *The death and life of great American cities.* New York: Random House, 1961.

Jersild, A. T., & Markey, F. V. Conflicts between preschool children. *Child Development Monographs,* No. 21, 1935.

Johnson, J. E., Ershler, J., & Bell, C. Play behavior in a discovery-based and a formal-education preschool program. *Child Development,* 1980, *51,* 271–274.

Johnson, M. W. The effect on behavior of variation in the amount of play equipment. *Child Development,* 1935, *6,* 56–68.

Kammann, R., Thomson, R., & Irwin, R. Unhelpful behavior in the street: City size or immediate pedestrian density? *Environment and Behavior,* 1979, *11,* 245–250.

Karmel, L. J. Effects of windowless classroom environments on high school students. *Perceptual and Motor Skills,* 1965, *20,* 277–278.

Kinsman, C. A., & Berk, L. E. Joining the block and housekeeping areas: Changes in play and social behavior. *Young Children,* 1979, *35,* 66–75.

Kirmeyer, S. L. Urban density and pathology: A review of research. *Environment and Behavior,* 1978, *10,* 247–269.

Klausner, S. Z. *On man in his environment.* San Francisco: Jossey-Bass, 1971.

Klein, P. S. Effects of open vs. structured teacher-student interaction on creativity of children with different levels of anxiety. *Psychology in the Schools,* 1975, *12,* 286–288.

Krantz, P., & Risley, T. *The organization of group care environments: Behavioral ecology in the classroom.* Lawrence: Kansas State University, 1972. (ERIC Document Reproduction Service No. ED 078 915)

Krasner, L., & Richards, C. S. Issues in open education and environmental design. *Psychology in the Schools,* 1976, *13,* 77–81.

Ladd, F. Black youths view their environments: Some views on housing. *Journal of the American Institute of Planners,* 1972, *38,* 108–115.

Latané, B., & Darley, J. M. Bystander apathy. *American Scientist,* 1969, *57,* 244–268.

Laufer, R. S., Proshansky, H. M., & Wolfe, M. Some analytic dimensions of privacy. In H. M. Proshansky, W. H. Ittelson, & L. G. Rivlin (Eds.), *Environmental psychology: People and their physical settings.* New York: Holt, Rinehart & Winston, 1976.

LeLaurin, K., & Risley, T. R. The organization of day care environments: "Zone" versus "man-to-man" staff assignments. *Journal of Applied Behavioral Analysis,* 1972, 5, 225–232.

Liebert, R., & Baron, R. Some immediate effects of television violence on children's behavior. In F. Rebelsky & L. Dorman (Eds.), *Child development and behavior.* New York: Knopf, 1973.

Loo, C. M. The effects of spatial density on the social behavior of children. *Journal of Applied Social Psychology,* 1972, *2,* 372–381.

Loo, C. M. Behavior problem indices: The differential effects of spatial density on low and high scorers. *Environment and Behavior,* 1978, *10,* 489–510.

Loo, C. M., & Kennelly, D. Social density: Its effects on behaviors and perceptions of preschoolers. *Environmental Psychology,* 1980, *3,* 131–146.

Lukasevich, A., & Gray, R. F. Open space, open education, and pupil performance. *Elementary School Journal,* 1978, *79,* 108–114.

Maccoby, E. E. Television: Its impact on school children. *Public Opinion Quarterly,* 1951, *15,* 421–444.

Maccoby, E. E. *Socialization theory: Where do we go from here?* Presidential Address, Western Psychological Association, Sacramento, 1975.

MacKinnon, C. E., Brody, G. H., & Stoneman, Z. The effects of divorce and maternal employment on the home environments of preschool children. *Child Development,* 1982, *53,* 1392–1399.

Marcus, C. Children's play behavior in a low-rise, inner-city housing development. In R. C. Moore (Ed.), *Childhood city, man-environment interactions* (Vol. 12). D. Carson (General Ed.). Milwaukee: EDRA, 1974.

Marshall, H. H. Open classroom: Has the term outlived its usefulness? *Review of Educational Research,* 1981, *51,* 181–192.

Martin, A. E. Environment, housing, and health. *Urban Studies,* 1967, *4,* 1–21.

Martin, B. Parent-child relations. In F. D. Horowitz (Ed.), *Review of child development research* (Vol. 4). Chicago: University of Chicago Press, 1975.

McCall, R. B. Exploratory manipulation and play in the human infant. *Monographs of the Society for Research in Child Development,* 1974, *39,* No. 155.

McGrew, P. L. Social and spatial density effects on spacing behaviour in preschool children. *Journal of Child Psychology and Psychiatry,* 1970, *11,* 197–205.

McGrew, W. C. Interpersonal spacing of preschool children. In J. S. Bruner & K. J. Connolly (Eds.), *The development of competence in early childhood.* London: Academic Press, 1972.

McHarg, I. *Design with nature.* Garden City, NY: Natural History Press, 1969.

Meredith, H. V. Research between 1950 and 1980 on urban-rural differences in body size and growth rate of children and youths. In H. W. Reese (Ed.), *Advances in child development and behavior* (Vol. 17). New York: Academic Press, 1982.

Michelson, W. *Man and his urban environment: A sociological approach.* Reading, MA: Addison-Wesley, 1970.

Milgram, S. The experience of living in cities. *Science,* 1970, *167,* 1461–1468.

Montes, F., & Risley, T. R. Evaluating traditional day care practices: An empirical approach. *Child Care Quarterly,* 1975, *4,* 208–215.

Moore, R., & Young, D. Childhood outdoors: Toward a social ecology of the landscape. In I. Altman & J. F. Wohlwill (Eds.), *Children and the environment.* New York: Plenum, 1978.

Murray, J. Television and violence. *American Psychologist,* 1973, *28,* 472–478.

Murray, R. The influence of crowding on children's behavior. In D. Canter & T. Lee (Eds.), *Psychology and the built environment.* New York: Wiley, 1974.

O'Connor, M. The nursery school environment. *Developmental Psychology,* 1975, *11,* 556–561.

Ollila, L. O., & Chamberlain, L. A. The effect of noise and object on acquisition of a sight vocabulary in kindergarten children. *The Alberta Journal of Educational Research,* 1975, *21,* 213–219.

Parke, R. D. Children's home environments: Social and cognitive effects. In I. Altman & J. F. Wohlwill (Eds.), *Children and the environment.* New York: Plenum, 1978.

Parke, R. D. & Sawin, D. B. Children's privacy in the home: Developmental, ecological, and child-rearing determinants. *Environment and Behavior,* 1979, *11,* 87–104.

Porteous, J. D. *Environment and behavior.* Reading, MA: Addison-Wesley, 1977.

Prescott, E. Is day care as good as a good home? *Young Children,* 1978, *33,* 13–19.

Proshansky, E., & Wolfe, M. The physical setting and open education. *School Review,* 1974, *82,* 557–574.

Quilitch, H. R., & Risley, T. R. The effects of play materials on social play. *Journal of Applied Behavior Analysis,* 1973, *6,* 573–578.

Ramey, C. T., Finkelstein, N. W., & O'Brien, C. Toys and infant behavior in the first year of life. *Journal of Genetic Psychology,* 1976, *129,* 341–342.

Reiss, S., & Dydhalo, N. Persistence, achievement and open space environments. *Journal of Educational Psychology,* 1975, *67,* 506–513.

Reuter, J., & Yunik, G. Social interaction in nursery schools. *Developmental Psychology,* 1973, *9,* 319–325.

Rheingold, H. L., & Cook, K. V. The contents of boys and girls room as an index of parents' behavior. *Child Development,* 1975, *46,* 459–464.

Rheingold, H. L., & Eckerman, C. O. The infant's free entry into a new environment. *Journal of Experimental Child Psychology,* 1969, *8,* 271–283.

Rivlin, L. G., & Rothenberg, M. The use of space in open classrooms. In H. M. Proshansky, W. H. Ittelson, & L. G. Rivlin (Eds.), *Environmental psychology: People and their physical settings.* New York: Holt, Rinehart & Winston, 1976.

Rodin, J. Density, perceived choice, and response to controllable and uncontrollable outcomes. *Journal of Experimental Social Psychology,* 1976, *12,* 564–578.

Rohe, W. M., & Nuffer, E. L. *The effects of density and partitioning on children's behavior.* Paper presented at the annual meeting of the American Psychological Association, San Francisco, 1977.

Rohe, W., & Patterson, A. J. The effects of varied levels of resources and density on behavior in a day care center. In D. H. Carson (Ed.), *Man-environment interactions: Evaluations and applications.* Stroudsburg, PA: Dowden, Hutchinson, & Ross, 1974.

Rosenblatt, P. C., & Cunningham, M. R. Television watching and family tensions. *Journal of Marriage and Family,* 1976, *38,* 105–110.

Rosenthal, B. A. An ecological study of free play in the nursery school. *Dissertation Abstracts International,* 1974, *34,* 4004–4005.

Rouse, W. V., & Rubenstein, H. *Crime in public housing: Vol 1, A review of major issues and selected crime reduction strategies.* Washington, DC: U.S. Department of Housing and Urban Development, 1978.

Sadalla, E. K. Population size, structural differentiation, and human behavior. *Environment and Behavior,* 1978, *10,* 271–291.

Saegart, S., & Hart, R. The development of sex differences in the environmental competence in girls and boys. In P. Stevens, Jr. (Ed.), *Studies in the anthropology of play: Papers in memory of B. Allan Tindall.* Cornwall, NY: Leisure Press, 1978.

Schoggen, P. Environmental forces in the everyday lives of children. In R. Barker (Ed.), *The stream of behavior.* New York: Appleton-Century-Crofts, 1963.

Schwebel, A. I., & Cherlin, D. L. Physical and social distancing in teacher-pupil relationships. *Journal of Educational Psychology,* 1972, *63,* 543–550.

Shapiro, A. H. Effects of family density and mothers' education on preschoolers' motor skills. *Perceptual and Motor Skills,* 1974, *38,* 79–86.

Shapiro, S. Preschool ecology: A study of three environmental variables. *Reading Improvement,* 1975, *12,* 236–241.

Shure, M. B. Psychological ecology of a nursery school. *Child Development,* 1963, *34,* 979–992.

Singer, D., & Singer, J. American television viewing habits and the spontaneous play of preschool children. *American Journal of Orthopsychiatry,* 1976, *46,* 496–502.

Slater, B. Effects of noise on pupil performance. *Journal of Educational Psychology,* 1968, *59,* 239–243.

Smith, P. Aspects of the playgroup environment. In D. Canter & T. Lee (Eds.), *Psychology and the built environment.* London: Architectural Press, 1974.

Smith, P. K., & Connolly, K. J. Social and aggressive behavior in preschool children as a function of crowding. *Social Science Information,* 1977, *16,* 601–620.

Stallings, J. Implementation and child effects of teaching practices in Follow-Through classrooms. *Monographs of the Society for Research in Child Development,* 1975, *40.*

Steiner, G. *The people look at television.* New York: Knopf, 1963.

Sternglanz, S. H., & Serbin, L. A. Sex-role sterotyping in children's television programs. *Developmental Psychology,* 1974, *10,* 710–715.

Stoneman, Z., & Brody, G. H. The indirect impact of child-oriented advertisements on mother-child interactions. *Journal of Applied Developmental Psychology,* 1981, *2,* 369–376.

Swift, J. W. Effects of early group experience: The nursery school and day nursery. In M. Hoffman & I. Hoffman (Eds.), *Child development research* (Vol. 1). New York: Russell Sage Foundation, 1964.

Tower, R. B., Singer, D. G., Singer, J. L., & Biggs, A. Differential effects of TV programming on preschoolers' cognition, imagination, and social play. *American Journal of Orthopsychiatry,* 1979, *49,* 265–281.

Twardosz, S., Cataldo, M. F., & Risley, T. R. Open environment design for infant and toddler day care. *Journal of Applied Behavior Analysis,* 1974, *7,* 529–546.

U. S. Bureau of the Census. *Construction reports: Characteristics of new one-family homes.* Washington, DC: U.S. Government Printing Office, 1980. (a)

U. S. Bureau of the Census. *Statistical abstract of the United States.* Washington, DC: U.S. Government Printing Office, 1980. (b)

Vandell, D. L., Wilson, K. S., & Buchanan, N. R. Peer interaction in the first year of life: An examination of its structure, content, and sensitivity to toys. *Child Development,* 1980, *51,* 481–488.

Vandenberg, B. Environmental and cognitive factors in social play. *Journal of Experimental Child Psychology,* 1981, *31,* 169–175.

Van Vliet, W. Families in apartment buildings: Sad storeys for children? *Environment and Behavior,* 1983, *15,* 211–234.

Wachs, T. Utilization of a Piagetian approach in the investigation of early experience effects: A research strategy and some illustrative data. *Merrill-Palmer Quarterly,* 1976, *22,* 11–30.

Wachs, T. D. The relationship of infants' physical environment to their Binet performance at 2½ years. *International Journal of Behavioral Development,* 1978, *1,* 51–56.

Wachs, T. D. Proximal experience and early cognitive intellectual development: The physical environment. *Merrill-Palmer Quarterly,* 1979, *25,* 3–41.

Walder, L. O., Abelson, R. P., Eron, L. D., Banta, T. J., & Laulicht, J. H. Development of a peer rating measure of aggression. *Psychological Reports,* 1961, *9,* 497–556.

Watson, J. S., & Ramey, C. Reactions to response-contingent stimulation in early infancy. *Merrill-Palmer Quarterly,* 1972, *18,* 219–227.

Weinstein, C. S. Modifying student behavior in an open classroom through changes in physical design. *American Educational Research Journal,* 1977, *14,* 249–262.

Weinstein, C. S., & Weinstein, N. D. Noise and reading performance in an open space school. *Journal of Educational Research,* 1979, *72,* 210–213.

Wicker, A. W. Undermanning, performances, and students' subjective experiences in behavior settings of large and small high schools. *Journal of Personality and Social Psychology,* 1968, *10,* 255–261.

Williamson, R. C. Socialization in the high-rise: A cross-national comparison. *Ekistics,* 1978, *45,* 122–130.

Wilner, D. M., Walkley, R. P., Pinkerton, T. C., & Tayback, M. *The housing environment and family life.* Baltimore: Johns Hopkins University Press, 1962.

Wohlwill, J. F. Experimental, developmental, differential: Which way the royal road to knowledge about spatial cognition? In L. S. Liben, A. H. Patterson, & N. Newcombe (Eds.), *Spatial representation and behavior across the life span.* New York: Academic Press, 1981.

Wolfe, M., & Laufer, R. The concept of privacy in childhood and adolescence. In S. T. Margulis (Ed.), *Privacy, man-environment interactions* (Vol. 6). D. Carson (General Ed.). Milwaukee: EDRA, 1974.

Wuellner, L. H. Forty guidelines for playground design. *Journal of Leisure Research,* 1979, *11,* 4–14.

Yancey, W. L. Architecture, interaction, and social control: The case of a large-scale public housing project. *Environment and Behavior,* 1971, *3,* 3–21.

Yarrow, L. J., Rubenstein J. L., & Pedersen, F. A. *Infant and environment: Early cognitive and motivational development.* New York: Wiley, 1975.

Zifferblatt, S. M. Architecture and human behavior: Toward increased understanding of a functional relationship. *Educational Technology,* 1972, *12,* 54–57.

Zimbardo, P. G. The human choice: Individuation, reason, and order versus deindividuation, impulse, and chaos. In W. J. Arnold & D. Levine (Eds.), *Nebraska Symposium on Motivation* (Vol. 17). Lincoln: Univeristy of Nebraska Press, 1969.

III SPECIFIC AGE GROUPS

5 Coordinating Perspectives on Infant Spatial Orientation

Linda P. Acredolo
University of California, Davis

A strong resurgence of interest in the development of spatial representation occurred in the decade of the 1970s. The result has been a multitude of studies focusing on a great range of topics, from search strategies to map reading to memory for spatial layout. Up until 1977, however, these studies were almost exclusively devoted to the study of the strides made during the preoperational and concrete operational stages of development, i.e., the years 3 to 11. Since then, the search for early foundations of spatial representations during infancy has grabbed the attention and enthusiasm of a growing number of researchers. As a consequence, there are already nearly two dozen studies devoted to spatial development during the first 2 years of life. What I propose to do in the present chapter is to organize this burgeoning literature into a cohesive framework, to evaluate the contributions made, and to sketch a portrait of the child's spatial abilities during each phase of this early period of development.

PIAGET'S CONTRIBUTION

The quest for understanding infant spatial abilities inevitably begins with consideration of Piaget's thoughts on the subject. Based upon careful observation of his own three children, particularly during their search for hidden objects, Piaget concluded that infants pass through a sequence of three types of spatial knowledge during the sensorimotor period: practical, subjective, and objective. These three developmental phases are linked in general to the six substages of sensorimotor intelligence and in particular to his description of the development of object permanence. For Piaget, any discussion of spatial knowledge is mean-

115

ingless without simultaneous consideration of the child's understanding of the things that space contains. As a result, many of the paradigms used to assess object constancy also have been applied to the study of developing awareness of spatial relations. As Piaget stated, "only the degree of objectification that the child attributes to things informs us of the degree of externality he accords to space" (Piaget, 1971, p. 110).

During the first two substages of the sensorimotor period, from approximately birth to 4 months of age, the infant's interactions with space are practical in nature. Although the infant does make movements in space and does act on objects, Piaget suggests that these behaviors are done without any notion of a separateness between self and objects in the environment. All experience is global in nature. Consequently, when the infant manages to do something that looks sophisticated, such as reversing a visual tracking behavior to return to the point of origin, Piaget describes the infant's experience as an impression of effort resulting in a general feeling of recovery without any knowledge of the nature of his specific behavior as a causative factor. In other words, to the extent that it exists, reversibility at this point is a simple sensory accommodation accomplished without knowledge of action distinguished from object. It follows from this conceptualization that the infant has no notion of locations in space, for to understand location one must first understand that there are objects in the world to occupy those locations.

The third substage of the sensorimotor period, from approximately 4 to 10 months, is characterized by the advent of subjective concepts of space in place of the earlier practical concepts. No longer is experience undifferentiated; the infant is now aware of self as distinguished from object. This awareness, however, is "subjective" in nature. This descriptor is used by Piaget to reflect his belief that the infant still harbors a major misconception about objects and their properties. During this stage, infants consider objects, and particularly the displacements of objects in space, to be products of their own actions. From being at one with the world of objects the infant now moves to being an all-powerful causative agent. Consequently, conception of an object's location in space is tied to the infant's knowledge of the action taken to encounter that object. The term "egocentric" is used to describe this self-centered referencing system.

> Therein is manifest undeniable memory of position, which seems at first to attest to the presence of stable objective groups. But . . . that which the child rediscovers is still only his own initial position related to the object and not yet that of the objects themselves in relation to each other. (Piaget, 1971, p. 135)

These subjective notions of space are not easily overcome. In fact, the fourth stage of the sensorimotor period, from approximately 10 to 12 months, is only a transitional phase between subjective knowledge and the next step, objective concepts of space. During this transition period the infant is able to relate objects to one another independent of their relation to him in some but not all situations. The gains made by the infant are particularly noticeable in that occluded objects are now easily uncovered, a form of reversibility not possible in substage 3. However, these objective notions of space are still restricted to very simple situations. When spatial displacements or relations between objects are complex, as in the substage 4 A$\bar{\text{B}}$ object permanence error, the infant is still incapable of behaving objectively. Subjective tendencies hold sway over spatial decisions, and the infant once again makes himself and his actions the center of the universe.

> The group of reversible operations is, on the contrary, an objective group, but limited to elementary relationships of subject and object. But, if he thus emerges from his solipsism, the subject at this stage remains egocentric, geometrically speaking; he does not yet recognize positions and displacements as being relative to one another, but only as relative to himself. He therefore still does not locate his whole body in a stationary field that includes other bodies as well as his own. (Piaget, 1971, p. 206)

The child establishes truly objective notions of space and the relationship among objects by substage 5 (12 to 18 months). Displacements of objects in space are now coded in relation to other objects rather than in relation to self. The properties of objects themselves become salient and the infant takes great pleasure exploring what objects can and cannot do to each other as well as to self. Objects are put in and taken out of containers, balanced on one another, and used as tools. Spatial behavior, however, is still limited in one very important way. Piaget suggests that the substage 5 child is still restricted to immediate perception; spatial problems cannot be mentally represented and solved. Consequently, although detours can be achieved, the paths must be available through direct perception. Trial and error behavior is still the order of the day.

> Furthermore, the subject becomes aware of his own displacements and thus locates them in relation to others. But the intellectual construction which made possible this elaboration of spatial perceptions does not yet transcend perception itself, to give rise to true representation of displacements. On the one hand, the child does not take account of the displacements which occur outside the visual field. On the other, the subject does not represent to himself his own total movements, outside his direct perception of them. (Piaget, 1971, p. 229)

As with other dimensions of sensorimotor behavior, substage 6 (18 to 24 months) of spatial development heralds the onset of mental representation. Infants finally consider space as a motionless container in which they are located and through which they can move imaginally. Detour paths can be contemplated mentally without necessarily having direct perceptional experiences. True spatial orientation is now possible and the child reacts by exploring the world at greater and greater distances.

In summary, Piaget's view of the development of spatial knowledge proposed a trend toward increasing differentiation of self and environment. The practical space of the earliest months in which neither self nor objects are discerned is replaced by an overemphasis on self as a creator and controller of objects, a misconception Piaget labels "subjective" or "egocentric." Such notions, however, eventually give way to truly objective knowledge of space allowing a child to acknowledge his or her position as just one object among many. The advent of mental representation puts the icing on the cake by finally freeing the child from direct perception and allowing spatial problems to be solved mentally.

> At the moment when sensorimotor intelligence has sufficiently elaborated understanding to make language and reflective thought possible, the universe is, on the contrary, formed into a structure at once substantial and spatial, causal and temporal. This organization of reality occurs, as we shall see, to the extent that the self is freed from itself by finding itself and so assigns itself a place as a thing among things, an event among events. (Piaget, 1971, p. xi)

RECENT EMPIRICAL INVESTIGATION: THE SEARCH FOR HIDDEN OBJECTS

Piaget's theory as outlined above was based on fairly casual observations of his own three children. He was interested particularly in how they searched for hidden objects, and to this end he created situations in which objects were covered or removed, or people ducked behind curtains or doors. Although this emphasis on search for hidden objects as a clue to the infant's conceptions of objects and space has been criticized (e.g., Ninio, 1979), it still remains the primary strategy used by recent researchers in their attempts to evaluate Piaget's theory.

Such studies can be divided into two main categories. In one case the question being posed is at what age spatial relations are understood to an extent that enables an infant to retrieve an object whose location behind an occluder is already known. In other words, when do infants deal effectively with spatial barriers that require detour behavior? Piaget addressed this question, but recent studies have approached the topic more systematically and with perhaps even greater ingenuity. Unfortunately, space limitations prevent me from reviewing the studies in this second major category. For readers interested in pursuing the question on their own, the most relevant studies to date include Heth and Cornell (1980), Lockman (1980), and Rieser, Doxsey, McCarrell, and Brooks (1982).

The questions being asked in the second major category of hidden object studies concern the nature of the infant's hypotheses about the location of objects in space. For example, does the infant know where to look for an object when the container in which it is hidden is moved, or when the infant is moved after the object is hidden? Is the infant in fact as subjective, as egocentric, in his or her conceptions of spatial location as Piaget argued? As indicated by the questions just posed, the research within this category can be divided into two groups based on whether the object is displaced after it is hidden or whether the infant is moved to a new location before search is allowed. Studies in both categories are reviewed.

Following brief review of the studies in this second category, an attempt is made to integrate the findings into a cohesive picture of spatial location knowledge as it develops across the first 2 years of life.

Understanding Object Location: Effects of Changing Vantage Points

Piaget (1971) contended that a good portion of infancy is spent with subjective notions of space in which the infant assumes that an object's existence and location are contingent upon the accommodations (actions) the infant has made in initially encountering that object. If this is indeed the case, then during substages 3 and 4 of the sensorimotor period (approximately 4 to 12 months) an infant should be fairly oblivious to the impact of bodily movement through space on the location of objects in that space. Quite simply, if an item has been encountered by a glance to the left, it should continue to be expected to appear on the left despite the infant's movement to a new location.

This hypothesis has been explored systematically in more than a dozen studies since 1977. The studies fall into three categories differing in the dependent variable used to infer the infant's decision about location. The group to be discussed first focuses on visual fixation as an index and includes studies by Acredolo (1978), Acredolo and Evans (1980), Cornell and Heth (1979), and Rieser (1979). The second, more frequently used approach depends upon the infant's reaching behavior and therefore involves locations quite close to the infant's body. This category includes studies by Acredolo (1979, 1982), Benson and Uzgiriz (1981), Braine and Eder (1981), Bremner (1978a,b), Bremner and Bryant (1977), and Goldfield and Dickerson (1981). The third approach requires the child to walk to the correct location and to this point is represented by only one study, Rieser and Heiman (1982).

Visual Fixation.   The use of visual fixation as an index of location knowledge has at least two advantages over the use of reaching or walking. First, it allows testing of younger infants since the ability to manually uncover a hidden object and the ability to walk are fairly late developments. Thus, the youngest age tested with reaching as the dependent variable is 8 months, compared to 4 months with fixation. The second advantage is that visual fixation allows the testing of knowledge of spatial locations in a space that extends well beyond the infant's reach.

In one of my own first attempts to assess Piaget's theory (Acredolo, 1978), I took advantage of both these factors in a series of studies with 6-, 11-, and 16-month-old infants. In each study the infants were seated in the middle of one side of a 10 × 10 ft (3.2 × 3.2 m) room that was completely bare of distinguishing landmarks except for two identical windows, one in the wall to the infant's right, the other in the wall to the infant's left. During training trials a buzzer was sounded in the center of the room followed by the appearance of a friendly adult at one of the two windows, the same window on every trial. Once the infant had learned to anticipate the adult's appearance by turning toward the window as soon as the buzzer sounded, the infant was smoothly rotated to the opposite side of the room, the buzzer was sounded, and observers noted which window the infant turned toward in anticipation of the event. Repetition of the originally correct response from the new vantage point led to the incorrect window and was interpreted as evidence of reliance on an egocentric frame of reference to code location. A turn toward the correct window from the new vantage point was interpreted as evidence of reliance on objective spatial relations.

The results strongly supported Piaget's theory. Experiment 1, a longitudinal study, indicated very heavy reliance on egocentric information at 6 months, both in the bare environment described above, and when a yellow star was placed around the target window. When the infants returned at 11 months, egocentric responses still predominated heavily as long as no star was present; but with the star in place, 50% of the infants were able to respond objectively. Finally, at 16 months, objective responding predominated in both conditions. Experiment 2, in which a fresh group of 16-month-olds was tested, indicated that superior performance at 16 months was not due to practice effects, but rather to developmental change. In the last experiment of the series an attempt was made to draw the attention of the infants to the distinctive features of the space, including the yellow star around the target window. To this end, 6- and 11-month-old infants were carried by their mothers on a tour of the room that included two stops at each window. At the target window was the same friendly adult who was to appear during training. The event at the non-target window was the appearance of a squeaking doll. Infants were then seated at the starting position, witnessed both events again, and the traditional training procedures were begun. Despite this additional experience in the space, performance remained identical to that yielded by the earlier studies: egocentric responding by 90% of the 6-month-old infants and 50% of the 11-month-old infants. The conclusion I drew from these results was that infants in the last half of the first year are indeed as stubbornly egocentric in their notions of spatial location as Piaget had contended.

The results of a more recent study using the same basic procedures (Acredolo & Evans, 1980) led me to qualify that conclusion to some extent. In this study, in addition to a landmark-free condition and a star condition, the 6-, 9-, and 11-month-old subjects were tested in two conditions in which blinking lights were placed around one window and bright orange stripes were present on the window's wall. In the Direct Lights condition these presumably very salient cues were located around the target window. In the Indirect Lights condition they marked the incorrect window with the target window free of landmarks. The results indicated that the landmark-free and star conditions replicated the earlier study; egocentricity predominated at all three ages in the absence of cues, and at both 6 and 9 months in the presence of the star. Once again the star enabled about half of the 11-month-olds to respond objectively. In contrast, in the presence of the lights and stripes *directly* marking the target window, egocentric responding practically disappeared at both 9 and 11 months. Infants by 9 months were clearly inclined to give salient landmark information priority over egocentric information. But what of the 6-month-olds? For the first time we found evidence of infants in conflict: the predominating tendency was to turn to *both* windows rather than to one or the other. The infants seemed to us to be showing that they knew something about the objective information provided by the landmark but were still hesitant to totally abandon their egocentric notions. The Indirect Lights condition revealed the same kind of conflict among the 11-month-olds, with both the younger age groups behaving egocentrically. Thus, our more recent study seems to indicate that sensitivity to landmark information is present as early as 6 months, as long as the information is very salient, but that a willingness to rely on that information becomes stronger across the last half of the first year.

Our conclusions were supported in part by the results of a study by Cornell and Heth (1979) in which younger infants were tested. In Experiment 1 of the study, 4-, 8-, and 12-month-olds were seated on their mothers' laps with four screens around them, one to each side, one in back, and one in front. At the start of each trial a visual stimulus appeared on the screen in front, followed by stimuli on each of the side screens. For the experimental group, the stimulus to one side remained the same on every trial while the stimulus on the other side changed. For the infants in the control group, the constant and changing stimuli shifted sides from trial to trial. Infants in the experimental group quickly learned to turn in the direction of the novel stimuli. After 20 trials, the infants and their mothers were rotated 180° so that the screen originally at the front was now behind them. The question was whether the subjects in the experimental group would be able to compensate for their rotation in space.

The answer for the 4-month-olds was clearly no. These infants showed a very strong tendency to simply repeat the response that had worked originally. This tendency was still quite strong at 8 months, although somewhat attenuated. The 12-month-old infants performed most correctly, but even at this age, 5 out of the 12 infants repeated the originally correct response on the first trial from the new position. Experiment 2 of the study revealed that the change across age found in Experiment 1 was due to an increase in the ability to keep track of objective spatial location rather than to any decrease in the ability to remember the originally correct response. The 4-, 8-, and 12-month-old infants in this study were trained under one of three conditions. In the Response condition the infant was turned 180° or 360° on each trial, but the novel stimulus always appeared in the same direction relative to the child's body. Infants were also rotated from trial to trial in the Place condition, but this time the location of the novel stimulus remained unchanged. Finally in the Combined condition, the infants always viewed the array from the same vantage point and the novel stimulus remained in a constant position. Consequently, in this case both response and place cues could be depended upon. The results indicated rapid learning of the location of the novel stimulus in both the Combined and Response conditions. Infants at all three ages found it easy to rely on response cues. Learning was not nearly as good when place cues were all that was available, however. Performance improved with age but was not very good even among the oldest children. Thus, reliance on response cues remained easy throughout the first year while reliance on place cues, admittedly not very salient ones in this case, improved to some extent.

Although these results fit quite well with the results of my own studies described above, two differences should be mentioned. First, the 9- and 11-month-olds in some conditions of our studies appeared to have much less difficulty remembering objective location than the 12-month-olds described by Cornell and Heth. I think the determining factor is the type of landmark information available. Our subjects only did well when very salient landmarks *directly* denoted the correct side. No such salient information was available to the infants in Cornell and Heth's study. A second difference involves the interpretation of the results. In contrast to my inclination to describe the behavior of the infants in Piagetian terms, with particular attention to evidence of ''egocentrism,'' Cornell and Heth (1979) take a learning theory position, arguing that the infants are merely showing their capacity to learn that a particular response is likely to be rewarded. The data are consistent with either view. This distinction is not a trivial one and, as we shall see, reoccurs with regularity in the literature.

A third study using visual fixation to indicate knowledge of location has been reported by Rieser (1979). In this case, 6-month-old infants were placed on their backs with a visual display of four windows over their heads: one 20° to the right of their line of sight, one 20° to the left, one 20° above, and one 20° below. As in my studies, the infants were taught to expect an event at one of the windows, were moved (this time only 90° around their midline), and were observed as they searched for the event from their new position. Each infant was tested in one of six conditions varying in the brightness of the environment, the presence or absence of discriminable landmarks, and the relevance of gravitational cues. The results indicated strong egocentric responding in all but two of the conditions. Specifically, infants fixated the egocentric window first and longest (a) when the environment was so dimly lit that only bodily movement information was available; (b) when texture information was visible as a clue to movement but no landmarks were present; (c) when the target door and the egocentric door were marked by landmarks of different colors; and (d) when the target door was the only door without landmarks. The only cases where responses to the correct door predominated were when the target door but *not* the egocentric door was marked, and when the infants were tilted so that gravity provided a cue to the correct door. These results are not only consistent with those of Acredolo (1978, Acredolo & Evans, 1980), but also help counter the criticism that the failure of Acredolo's infants to maintain their orientation was due to the use of left-right directions in the task—directions notoriously difficult for children to distinguish. Since Rieser included the window above the infant's head as a target window, the egocentric responding that resulted cannot be so easily dismissed.

Reaching.   The results of the studies using visual fixation are consistent in showing a strong tendency from 4 to 12 months to look in the same direction after movement through space that was appropriate before the movement. Offsetting this tendency, however, was an apparent increase in the ability or willingness to use distinctive spatial cues to mark location. What about the studies using reaching as the dependent variable? In general, we find a very similar pattern of results.

In the earliest study reported, Bremner and Bryant (1977) presented 9-month-old infants with an object that was hidden under one of two identical covers, one to the left and the other to the right of midline. The tablecloth beneath the covers was half black and half white, presumably providing some information to help the infants keep track of the object. After the infants had successfully recovered the object on five trials from their initial position at the table, they were rotated to the opposite side and the object was hidden under the same cover. Instead of retrieving it there, however, the infants showed a strong tendency to repeat the action that had led them to the object in initial trials. The contrasting background colors were apparently not being used by the infants. Bremner and Bryant concluded, as I had with the visual fixation studies, that Piaget's description of infants as egocentric had been supported.

Does this mean that infants at 9 months are oblivious to landmark information in the small-scale spaces immediately around them? No, it does not. In a subsequent study by Bremner (1978a) the covers themselves, rather than just the background, were made distinctively different in color. The result was a significant increase in the proportion of 9-month-old infants choosing the correct location despite a change in vantage point. A third study (Bremner, 1978b) resulted in the same pattern. Thus, just as Acredolo and Evans (1980) found for a larger space, the more directly a cue marks a location, the more likely it is that 9-month-old infants will rely on it and ignore information from past actions.

But only 9-month-old infants were tested in these studies. What about younger infants? Might there be a developmental trend toward increased reliance on direct landmarks in near space as had been found in the studies of larger spaces using visual fixation? The only study that has addressed this question is a recent report by Goldfield and Dickerson (1981). In this case both 8½- and 9½-month-old infants were required to find an object hidden in one of two wooden containers. For one group at each age the containers were distinctively different colors (yellow and green); for the other groups they were both white. Following two successful searches, the object was hidden and the child was rotated to the opposite side of the table before being allowed to search. The results, in fact, did indicate a developmental trend toward reliance on cues. When the identical containers were used, response perseveration (egocentrism) in terms of direction characterized performance at both ages. However, when the covers were distinct, response perseveration to a particular place (i.e., container) characterized performance at 9½ months but *not* at 8½ months. The younger age group was still responding as if the egocentric information was the more reliable. Thus, both reaching and visual fixation measures indicate that dependence on direct landmarks after bodily movement becomes increasingly important as the child moves through the last half of the first year.

All of the studies described so far have three things in common: (a) they included repeated practice in finding the object from an initial position; (b) they involved passive movement of the child; and (c) they used no more than two hiding places. Each of these factors has been cited as contributing to response perseveration, the expectation being that if the procedures were changed, the proportion of egocentric responding would decline. In each case recent data indicate some truth to this expectation.

The first of these three is probably the most interesting theoretically since the presence of training trials leaves us with no way to tell whether the egocentrism manifested in these studies is simply the result of a motor habit, as learning theorists like Cornell and Heth (1979) contend, or the result of dependence on a spatial reference system centered on the child's body. Unfortunately, Piaget is somewhat ambiguous on this point. As his emphasis on circular reactions demonstrates, he is not oblivious to the role of motor learning, and he does refer repeatedly to the role played by past actions. However, he also describes repeatedly the infant as tending "to locate things in relation to himself" (1971, p. 196). The ambiguity is particularly apparent in the following description of the substage 4 infant:

> In other words, the child who tries to get an object under a screen understands that the screen is placed "upon" the object but he understands it only to the extent that his relation is, so to speak, *related to himself or to his actions*. (1971, p. 198, emphasis mine)

Is there any way to determine empirically which is the more correct description? Fortunately, Bremner (1978b) came up with the bright idea of simply eliminating the training trials. In this case, 9-month-old infants were rotated to the opposite side of a table as soon as an object was hidden on the first trial. The result was a drop in the proportion of egocentric responders from .88 with training trials to .38 without them, a pattern that suggested strongly that the egocentrism of the earlier studies was really just a motor habit.

In a subsequent study of my own, however (Acredolo, 1979), I discovered that Bremner's results were attributable at least partially to the fact that his infants were tested in their homes. When the task without training trials was repeated in the home, a low level of egocentric responding (15% of subjects) was found once again; however, when the task was repeated in two laboratory environments—a landmark-free enclosure and an unfamiliar office—the levels of egocentrism rose dramatically (76% in each). These results are important for three reasons. First, they stand as a warning to researchers that generalizations from the testing environment to other environments must be made with caution. Second, they indicate that true reliance on an egocentric frame of reference (as opposed to a motor habit) does occur during infancy, at least among 9-month-old infants in unfamiliar environments. Moreover, this is not a trivial finding given the fact that infants no doubt end up spending a good deal of time in such environments. Finally, these results indicate that the familiarity of the home environment is operating in some way to facilitate spatial orientation.

It was this last fact that particularly intrigued me. What exactly was it about the home that was facilitating performance? There seemed to be at least two possibilities. Perhaps greater familiarity with the environment beyond the boundary of the task itself was allowing the infants to use landmark information more effectively. On the other hand, perhaps familiarity was acting to reduce anxiety, thereby enabling the infants to concentrate their attention more directly on the task itself. The possibility that anxiety can affect task performance in infants had recently been suggested by Lingle and Lingle (1981) based on their finding that their two experimenters elicited very different patterns of object permanence behavior from infant subjects. The purpose of the experiment had been to see if hiding an object upon which the child is emotionally dependent would result in better retrieval than an unfamiliar object. They found this was the case with one but not the other experimenter, and concluded that in the first case the experimenter had raised anxiety levels, thereby increasing the infants' motivation to find their attachment objects, but simultaneously distracting them from the task when the emotionally neutral, unfamiliar objects were involved. In contrast, performance with the second experimenter did not vary from object to object.

To see if something similar was happening with our own infants, we again tested 9-month-old infants in the unfamiliar, landmark-free, laboratory environment (Acredolo, 1982). However, in contrast to the original study, which had included a typical, short, "get acquainted" period prior to testing, the present procedure included a 15-minute play period specifically designed to maximize the infant's feelings of security in the experimental space. A shallow wading pool (to keep the child in one place) containing a variety of attractive toys was introduced into the space, and infant, mother, and experimenter interacted with one another for 15 minutes. The pool was then removed, the task materials introduced, and the task completed.

The resulting change in performance from the original study was striking. Of the 16 infants tested, 13 chose one of the two cloths. Of these 13, only 3 (19% of the total N) chose egocentrically. This was a significant drop from the 76% found in the same environment without the extended pretask familiarization period. Since familiarity in this case did not involve increased knowledge of landmarks, the results demonstrated the need to expand the concept of familiarity to include the impact of emotional factors like increased feelings of security. These results, it should be noted, do not negate the value of laboratory research. After all, as mentioned earlier, infants are often placed in totally unfamiliar spaces and it *is* important for us to learn exactly what kinds of spatial behaviors can be expected under such novel circumstances. The results, however, do suggest that the per-formance-competence distinction is an important one to keep in mind as we attempt to describe infant capacities. Nine-month-old infants, it seems, are fully able to keep track of the location of a hidden object when they are moved in space, as long as no motor habits are established prior to that movement and they feel at ease in the situation. Whether the same can be said of younger infants we do not yet know.

A second procedure common to infant rotation studies that has recently been criticized is the total reliance on passive movement of the infant. Perhaps if the infants had moved themselves to the second vantage point they would have been less likely to rely on egocentric information.[1] A recent study from our laboratory has yielded data supporting this hypothesis (Acredolo, Adams, & Goodwyn, in press). Using a modified version of a procedure described initially by Benson and Uzgiris (1981), we first taught 12-month-old infants to retrieve a toy from a large plexiglass box on the floor by crawling around to the open back of the box. Once this had been accomplished, a toy was hidden under one of two identical cloths within the box and the infant was given a series of training trials during which he or she searched from the front of the box. Following the training trials, access at the front was blocked and the infant was either carried passively or allowed to crawl to the other side. Search from this second vantage point was significantly more egocentric (i.e., less accurate) when the infants were carried than when they moved independently, thus indicating that memory for location was indeed facilitated by self-movement. By 18 months when these subjects were retested, the advantage of active over passive movement had disappeared, and all infants searched successfully in this simple task.

---

[1]Despite its ambiguity, the term "egocentric" will continue to be used to refer to any response by the child that maintains the relationship between body and target site that existed before displace-ment.

The final procedural factor to receive attention is the consistent use of two hiding locations. Although their focus was on older children (mean age = 26.5 months), Braine and Eder (1981) found significantly more egocentric responding when subjects were rotated to the other side of a traditional two-choice array than when a 3 × 3 matrix of 9 boxes was used. They suggested that organizing the spatial relations within the 9-box array may have made the children more aware of the relationship between the boxes and the external environment. Whether or not increasing the number of hiding places would also aid younger children to coordinate perspectives after bodily movement is unknown. In view of the fact that Cummings and Bjork (1977) found that increasing the number of sites decreased the proportion of infants making the substage 4 AB̄ object permanence error, we might expect that it would also have an impact on infants whose own vantage point is changed.

Walking.   Coincidentally, the only study so far to use direction of walking as a measure of spatial orientation is also unique in its use of more than two sites from which the child can choose. In this case (Rieser & Heiman, 1982), eight identical windows were evenly spaced at the child's eye level around a circular room. The 18-month-old subjects stood in the center of the room, always facing the same direction. In the training phase of the experiment they were taught to walk from the starting position to a particular window which, when touched, yielded an interesting event. Once the training was complete, the infants were turned away from their initial starting position, sometimes a lot, sometimes a little, before being allowed to search. The results revealed only 17% egocentric responses, i.e., choosing the window from the new position that replicated the original relationship between body and target window. These results are consistent with those of Acredolo (1978) reporting little or no egocentric responding among 16-month-old infants. Of even more interest, however, is Rieser and Heiman's discovery that the infants showed a strong tendency to select the shortest route to the vicinity of the target window from their new position, thus indicating that they were at least crudely maintaining their orientation to the windows.

Summary.   In general, the results of the studies presented in this section have been fairly consistent in showing improvement with age in the ability to compensate for bodily movement, across the three behaviors used as dependent measures. They also are consistent in showing an increasing tendency for landmark information to be relied on as a cue to spatial location in place of established motor habits or egocentric relations. At first such information is useful primarily when it is very salient and in very close proximity to the hidden object. However, as the infant's age increases, so does the range of environmental information of use in keeping track of spatial locations. A more detailed analysis of the factors at work in these change-of-vantage-point tasks follows discussion of the second major category of hidden-object studies, those in which the object moves relative to the subject.

Understanding Object Location: Effects of Object Displacement

Once an object has been hidden and is no longer visible, can an infant keep track of its location as the object moves through space with its occluder? Or does the infant believe the object should continue to be located in the position relative to his body that it was originally encountered? This is the question posed by a number of studies assessing developmental changes in spatial knowledge from 8 months on. The 8-month starting point is necessitated by the need to rely on the ability of the infant to manually uncover a hidden object, a skill not present in younger infants.

The type of object displacement used to challenge the child's knowledge of spatial relations varies from study to study. In a number of cases a desirable toy is hidden in one or two containers. Then, while the child watches, a transposition displacement takes place: The position of the two containers relative to the child is switched, either manually by the experimenter or by rotation of the table. In other cases, a visible rather than invisible displacement is accomplished by simply hiding the object in the second of two containers when the child is accustomed to finding it in the first. This, of course, is the traditional AB̄ object permanence procedure used by Piaget to illustrate the subjective nature of the Stage 4 infant's knowledge of complex spatial relations. In some studies these two types of displacement are combined by both hiding the object under a different container *and* rotating the table. A third type of displacement involves simply moving the container and object laterally relative to the child (Lucas & Uzgiriz, 1977).

Main objectives also differ somewhat from study to study. By far the most popular issue concerns the degree to which distinctive environmental features can serve as cues to the object's location. The result is additional information about the development of landmark usage in infancy. Other questions concern the impact of hiding objects that are especially desirable and the effect of using specific containers with which the child is very familiar. Discussion of this research is presented in terms of these three objectives.

Landmark Information.   The typical way to test the effectiveness of landmark information in helping the infant deal with displacement of an object has been to use containers that vary in shape and/or color, or rest on backgrounds that vary in color. For example, in one of the earliest studies examining this issue, Bremner and Bryant (1977) presented 9-month-old infants with two identical square wells covered with grey cloths. The wells were placed on a table that was half black and half white. In addition to the condition described earlier in which the infants were rotated around the table, Bremner and Bryant also included several conditions in which training trials with the table in one orientation were followed by test trials with the table rotated 180°. The results indicated a strong tendency for the infants to behave as if no rotation had taken place; they continued to reach in the direction that had been appropriate before rotation even though the background colors were now reversed.

Bremner next compared the distinctiveness of background colors versus the distinctiveness of container colors (Bermner, 1978b) with 9-month-old infants. Training trials were eliminated so that no motor habit would be established. In other words, rather than allowing the infant to retrieve the toy several times from an initial location, the object was hidden once and the table immediately rotated. Once again the different background colors failed to facilitate performance. Infants in this condition behaved as though no rotation had occurred. In contrast, the distinctive containers did facilitate performance, at least to the extent of enabling nearly 50% of the infants to keep track of the object through the displacement. Thus, just as was found in the change-of-vantage-point literature, direct landmarks are more likely to be attended to than indirect landmarks at 9 months of age.

How about younger infants? Are distinctive containers equally effective? Two studies report the impact of distinctive containers on 8½-month-old infants. In the earlier of the two (Cornell, 1979),[2] infants in four conditions saw an object hidden in one of two containers, either a red and white box or an inverted green cup, and then saw the containers transposed. The infants' task was to find the object. The conditions varied in terms of which cues, container or left-right position, were reliable indicators of the object's location across trials. In one condition both container and position were constant. In a second condition, position but not container was constant. In a third condition it was container but not position that was constant. Finally, in a fourth condition neither was constant; the infants had to rely completely on their ability to attend to the hiding procedure and track the correct container throughout the transposition maneuver. Analysis of search behavior across 12 trials indicated that 8½-month-olds were sensitive to both position and container cues: Performance was better when one of the two was held constant than when neither was reliable, and was best of all when both could be depended upon. The reliability of the cues also affected the ability of the infants to cope with four subsequent reversal trials. During these trials, within-dimension reversals were presented. Thus, if container had been constant, the object was now hidden in the opposite container, and if position had been constant, the object was now hidden on the opposite side. Not surprisingly, the group that performed the worst on these trials was the group for whom both cues had been constant. These subjects had two habits to unlearn. The subjects

---

[2]Cornell refers to his subjects as 9-month-old infants. However, the mean age given in weeks is 36 weeks, which actually makes his subjects closer to 8½ months of age.

who had the easiest time were those for whom neither cue was constant and who, therefore, had no relearning to do, and those who had experienced a constant position during the original 12 trials. The group for whom the container was constant fell in between. This pattern of results is interesting, indicating as it does that a change of position is a more salient change than a change of container. The infants in the position-constant condition were able more quickly to recognize that the object was now ending up on the opposite side of their body. In contrast, the infants who had learned to reach for a certain container regardless of its position tended to perseverate in that behavior during the reversal trials. Looked at in this way, the results can be interpreted as congruent with Piaget's emphasis on the salience of egocentric spatial relations during this substage of spatial development.

The second study examining the impact of container distinctiveness at 8½ months (Goldfield & Dickerson, 1981) was discussed in some detail in the change-of-vantage-point section. For purposes of the present discussion, the reader will recall that 8½- and 9½-month-old infants saw an object hidden in one of two wooden containers. For half the children at each age the containers were distinctively different in color, but for the other children they were both white. After the infants had successfully retrieved the toy from the same container located on the same site on two successive occasions, the toy was hidden once again in the same container and the table was rotated 180°. The results indicated that the 8½-month-olds were not as capable of retrieving the object following the transposition as the 9½-month-olds were, and that the 9½-month-olds benefited from the use of distinctive containers while 8½-month-olds did not. Thus, Goldfield and Dickerson provide additional evidence that the facilitating effect of landmark information increases with age.

Nature of the Object.   A second issue that has concerned researchers in this area is whether the particular object hidden in the task can make a difference. Perhaps we are dealing with a performance-competence distinction. Perhaps the infants have a level of spatial competence that they fail to show because the objects hidden are not highly valued. Corter, Zucker, and Galligan (1980) assessed this hypothesis using what is probably the most highly valued object of all as the target of search: the infant's mother. Nine-month-old infants and their mothers were taken into a playroom that had two doors, one to the left of the infant, and one to the right. After the infants were happily settled, their mothers left the room through one of the doors while the infants watched. The vast majority of the infants crawled after them without showing much sign of distress. Once they were happily resettled with mother, she left again. This time, for half the infants (the control group) she left through the same door, while for the other half (the experimental group) she left through the opposite door, a procedure analogous to that used in traditional AB̄ object permanence tasks. The results indicated quite clearly that even with Mother as the target object, infants had a tendency to repeat a successful action: The experimental group showed a strong tendency to crawl to the first door rather than the second. In addition, they were much more likely than the control group to show distress at this point, a pattern Corter et al. suggest indicates the presence of feelings of conflict. The infants did not know which information to rely on. Thus, all the spatial errors infants make at 9 months of age cannot be easily dismissed as due to lack of motivation. Nor can they be attributed to a lack of object identity since, as Corter et al. pointed out, the mother's identity was surely known by this age. The problem seems to be in a lack of understanding of object/space relations.

Nature of the Container.   In addition to being concerned about the distinctiveness of objects, researchers are also beginning to notice that the specific container used can make a difference. One container in particular, an upright cup, appears to evoke specific spatial expectations by the time an infant is 9 months old. Freeman, Lloyd, and Sinha (1980) discovered this fact when they compared the ability of 9½-, 10-, 12-, 13- and 15-month-old infants to deal with upright versus inverted cups. In each of five experiments the task of the infants was to retrieve an object hidden either in or behind one of two identical containers. In three of the studies the object was invisibly displaced by transposing the two containers after the infant had successfully retrieved the object from the same container three times in succession. In the other two experiments the object was visibly displaced by hiding it in the previously unused container, a typical AB̄ task procedure. In each case and at each age the results were the same: performance was superior with upright cups. Furthermore, the advantage was specific to cups and not just a function of containers with cavities facing upwards. This was learned by comparing upright and inverted toy houses as the containers; no orientation advantage was found. Freeman et al. label this a "canonicality effect" in that performance seems to be affected by whether or not the cup is used for its canonical purpose, that is, to contain materials that must be transported from place to place. The result is more sophisticated spatial performance with containers whose properties they know well.

The canonicality effect, however, does not always enhance performance, as Lloyd, Sinha, and Freeman (1981) discovered in a subsequent study. In this case, instead of having the cups exchange positions, only one cup was moved. The result was still a change in relative left-right positions because the nonmoving cup was located directly in front of the infant and the moving cup was simply moved from one side to the other. As in the earlier experiments, the transposition occurred after the infant had successfully retrieved the object three times in a row with the cups in their original positions. Also as in the earlier experiment, the infants' attention was drawn away from the target site after the movement. In this way the infants were forced to rely on their memory for position rather than on visual fixation. The results of the study supported the original research by showing that when the object was in the cup that moved, most infants found the object easier to retrieve with upright cups than with inverted cups as the containers. Infants seemed to assume that the upright cup would carry its contents with it as it was moved. However, this knowledge of upright cups apparently tended to lead them astray when the empty cup was the one that moved. In this case, most of the infants did better with inverted cups. Lloyd et al. concluded that for infants at both ages, a moving upright cup is easy to follow when it moves and must be attended to, and is hard to ignore when it is merely a distractor. An inverted cup is hard to follow when it moves and easy to ignore when it is empty. Due to prolonged experience with cups in everyday life, infants apparently consider a moving upright cup to be a reliable cue to the location of a hidden object. The message to researchers is clear. We must no longer assume that any old occluder will do; the infant's developing concepts of the spatial properties of the occluder must be taken into account.

Understanding Object Location: Change of Vantage Point versus Object Displacement

A final question that has received attention in this literature is the direct comparison of the two types of motion described in the previous sections. Is an infant more likely to keep track of an object's location after his or her own movement through space or after movement of the object itself? Unfortunately, the data do not consistently point in one direction or the other. While Bremner (1978b) reported that 9-month-old infants performed better when they were moved than when the table was rotated, Goldfield and Dickerson (1981) report the opposite pattern of results. They suggested that the reason for the apparent contradiction may lie with the specific procedure used in the infant-move conditions of the two studies. In Bremner's study the infant's mother began across from the infant on the same side of the table as the experimenter. As the infant and experimenter changed places, the mother remained stationary, thus providing additional information that movement had occurred. In contrast, the infants in Goldfield and Dickerson's study were seated on their mothers' laps. Since both moved to the opposite side of the table, the mother could not function as a stable landmark.

Two other differences between the studies, however, may also be contributing to the discrepancy. First, in this particular study Bremner eliminated all training trials. Goldfield and Dickerson, in contrast, were still requiring the infant to retrieve the object several times before movement of any kind occurred. Consequently, it may be that development of a motor habit makes it harder for infants to keep track of their motion relative to an object. Finally, the site of testing differed in the two studies. Bremner tested infants in their own homes, but Goldfield and Dickerson tested infants in an unfamiliar laboratory situation. As the results of several of my own studies with 9-month-old infants show (Acredolo, 1979, 1982), the familiarity of the testing environment can make a dramatic difference in the ability of infants to perform in an infant-rotation task.

Thus, there is apparently no easy answer to the question of which is easier, subject movement or object movement. The ability of infants to perform in each case seems to be under the influence of a variety of variables. When even such a presumably straightforward comparison gets bogged down in procedural details, one despairs of ever drawing a meaningful picture of spatial development as a whole. But, forever the optimist, I am going to make the attempt. It is to this admittedly sketchy portrait that we now turn.

THE DEVELOPMENT OF SPATIAL ORIENTATION
IN INFANCY

Despite the wealth of data described in the previous sections, the truth is that we still do not have enough information to present a totally definitive overview of the development of spatial skills in infancy. Consequently, the sequence I am about to outline is just my own "best guess," based on equal parts data interpretation, speculation, and wishful thinking. Such partial flights of fancy are particularly useful, I think, to help identify gaps in our knowledge and to guide us toward appropriate strategies for filling them. So, having created a sufficiently plausible rationalization, I will now indulge myself.

Two indisputable facts provide the foundation for my theory. The first of these is the recognition that infancy is a period of rapid change. The 16-month-old infant differs radically from the 6-month-old infant. Although this fact may seem too obvious to merit discussion, researchers all too frequently ignore this or act as if it were not true. Infants of all ages are too often lumped together under the rubric, "The Infant." Thus, we find "The Infant" described cursorily as egocentric, or nonegocentric, depending on the discussant's perspective, often based upon data from a single age group. One purpose of this section, therefore, is to emphasize the changes I believe are taking place during this period. That way, even if the specific changes I suggest should ultimately prove to be more fiction than fact, at least I will have had the satisfaction of helping to lay to rest further references to our longtime, omni-age friend, "The Infant."

A second indisputable fact to which reference must be made in any developmental history of spatial knowledge is that the motor system undergoes its most extraordinary changes during this period. According to norms established by Shirley (1931), the average infant begins to crawl at about 8½ months, is proficient at creeping and can walk when led by 10½ months, and finally walks alone at 15 months. Clearly, each advancement in the ability to move around space increases the infant's exposure to changes in perspectives. As both Bremner (Bremner & Bryant, 1977; Bremner, 1978a, 1978b) and I have pointed out, the world of the pre-creeping infant is a fairly static one in which long periods of time are spent viewing the world from specific positions to which the infant has been passively carried. And precisely because it is fairly static, the world—at least in terms of spatial relations—is a fairly predictable place where, if the TV is encountered on one's right on Wednesday, chances are good it will also appear there on Thursday. Obviously, then, in a world where vantage points do not often change, some kind of egocentric, body-based reference system is actually fairly practical. Once the infant is mobile, however, vantage points change as often, if not more often, than they stay the same, and new ways of coding location must be found. Thus, we can expect to find different notions of space in the pre-locomotor and post-locomotor infant, with interesting signs of transition in between.

Pre-Locomotor Period

According to Piaget (1971), 4- to 8-month-old infants are in substage 3 of the sensorimotor period. Spatial relations are subjective in nature in that infants rely on their own past actions to specify location, and as a consequence, put themselves at the center of their spatial world. Objects are still not recognized as separate entities existing independently in the "container" of space.

At least three studies described earlier provide data consistent with such a description: Cornell and Heth (1979) with 4-month-old infants and both Acredolo (1978, Acredolo & Evans, 1980) and Rieser (1980) with 6-month-old infants. In each case, infants repeatedly experienced an event in one direction relative to their bodies. When their position in the space subsequently was changed, they showed a strong tendency to repeat a look in the direction that had been appropriate before the move.

Such behavior, however, is actually ambiguous in regard to underlying spatial notions. As was mentioned earlier, it is difficult to tell to what extent the reptition of a previously successful head turn is due to a motor habit established during training trials from the initial position, and to what extent it is due to belief in the validity of an egocentric frame of reference. I would like to suggest that *both* are probably operating at this age. There is no question but that infants of this age are not only capable of learning such motor habit contingencies, but actually enjoy doing so (Papousek, 1969; Watson, 1973). Therefore, it makes sense that in these spatial tasks they may be learning that a particular head turn will result in an interesting event. Obviously, what they have not yet learned is that a movement through space negates the validity of this particular type of contingency.

What about the spatial reference system option? It is my belief that such a phenomenon is also operating at this age, both in general and in these studies in particular. There are two reasons for this conviction. One reason stems from the fact that I have found such a tendency at 9 months under special circumstances. In the study in which I compared performance in different environments (Acredolo, 1979), I found that 9-month-old infants would behave "egocentrically" in unfamiliar laboratory setting even though training trials from the initial position had been eliminated. In the home environment, in contrast, objective responding predominated. Results of a subsequent study (Acredolo, 1982) suggested that it was a feeling of anxiety that was responsible for the egocentric behavior manifested in the unfamiliar environments. Since it is safe to assume that conditions of stress produce less mature rather than more mature behavior, it seems reasonable to suggest that the egocentricity these 9-month-old infants showed was a throwback to an earlier, pre-locomotor tendency to place oneself at the center of spatial coordinates.

My second reason for believing such a frame of reference could be operating stems once again from the fact that infants are sensitive to contingencies. However, in this case what is being evidenced is not a specific motor habit built up through a series of successful action-event trials. Instead, what we are seeing is the result of the infant's having experienced *many* such contingencies between actions and events over the 6 months of life and having abstracted a general rule or set: when in doubt, trust the relationship to your body that existed when the object or event was last seen—even if that view was just a momentary one. As mentioned earlier, such a rule tends to work well as long as the person is stationary. What the 4- and 6-month-old infants have not yet learned is that bodily movement negates such relationships.

In summary, then, both levels of "egocentrisim," the motor habit level and the spatial reference system level, can be viewed as resulting from the infant's sensitivity to contingency relationships. The major difference is that the former results from contingencies established within a particular situation, whereas the latter arises from the accumulated experiences of a lifetime, short though it may have been.

Some of the existing data, however, do not seem to reflect egocentric responding as defined in either way. Specifically, when a very salient landmark is spatially contiguous with a hidden event, such as the flashing lights in Acredolo and Evans (1980) or the array of colored balls in Rieser (1979), even 6-month-old infants turn in that direction in anticipation of the event from their new vantage point. What can we make of this behavior? First, although I do not know how to prove it, it seems likely to me that such a response at this age is an example of learning an association between *action at a landmark* and the occurrence of an event, rather than true recognition of the spatial information the landmark is denoting. In other words, in the Acredolo and Evans (1980) study the infant has learned not only to turn to the right or left as in an egocentric response, but also to the lights: A turn to the lights will succeed in making the event reappear. Thus, the lights are viewed by the infant as important, not because they designate the location in space of the event, but simply because turning toward them for some unknown and uncared-about reason will cause the event to reoccur. If viewed in this way, the infant's knowledge of space is still action-based, and in that sense of the word, actually still egocentric.

What makes me think that landmarks at this age are not functioning in a truly spatial way? First, there is the fact that even through 9 months of age landmarks seem to only affect performance if they are directly contiguous with the hidden object or event. Such a limitation seems more reasonable in a paired-associate scheme than in a situation where a truly spatial notion of "vicinity" is operating. In other words, if a child truly understands the spatial role of landmarks, then he or she should be advanced enough cognitively to understand that less contiguous cues, such as background color, or the *absence* of a landmark, can also be useful.

My second reason for assuming nonspatial knowledge of landmarks at this age is that with this knowledge arises a source of conflict for the infant out of which true landmark knowledge can develop as the infant endeavors to resolve the situation. Specifically, the infant in many instances will be caught between two learned responses: a turn in a certain direction (egocentric) and a turn to a particular "landmark." A perfect example of such conflict occurred in my own study (Acredolo & Evans, 1980) when the flashing lights were used as a cue to the target site. In this case, the 6-month-old infants looked in *both* directions rather than one or the other. Butterworth (cited in Pick, Yonas, & Rieser, 1979) also cites evidence of such conflict at this age. How and when is the conflict resolved? I believe it is resolved once the child becomes mobile, and that takes us to the most frequently studied period of infant spatial development, age 8 to 11 months.

The Newly Mobile Infant

The period from 8 to 11 months is a period of transition in several ways. As I have just indicated, I believe one specific transition involves attempts to resolve the conflict between egocentric and landmark-based response systems. Underlying this transition, in fact making possible the conflict resolution, is another transition, that from stationary to mobile organism. It is during this period that the infant learns to crawl.

As the newly mobile infant begins to change perspectives more frequently, reliance on egocentric information becomes less and less reliable. This no doubt contributes to greater reliance on allocentric or objective information such as landmarks. But I believe something else is also occurring, something that eventually transforms the infant's reliance on landmarks from being stimulus-response based to being a reflection of true "container" knowledge of space. It is during this period, I believe, that visual tracking of spatial locations takes on special importance.

Fortunately, a number of the studies I have described in previous sections also include information about the visual behavior of their infant subjects. Goldfield and Dickerson (1981), for example, found that infants who visually tracked the correct location as they were moved around the table were more likely to show accurate search behavior. Visual tracking was apparently not easily accomplished, however, since the presence of containers of different colors led to more tracking than did identical white containers. The infants appeared to need a distinctive landmark to "hang on to" as they moved. This pattern also gives us some insight into a possible developmental trend. Since the distinctive containers aided the search behavior of the 9½-month-old infants but not the 8½-month-old infants (who continued to search egocentrically), it seems safe to assume that the 9½-month-olds were engaging in more tracking behavior than the younger infants. Such a trend makes sense, given the greater locomotor experience the older infant has had. As an infant crawls, he or she begins to realize that bodily movement negates egocentric relations and that the best procedure to follow to ensure that one can relocate an object after movement is simply to never take one's eyes off it. Thus, I would predict that longitudinal studies would show an increase in visual tracking in rotation situations sometime after crawling has begun. An eventual decline in visual tracking behavior should occur as the infant develops a truly objective notion of space based upon the location data that all the instances of successful tracking have provided. In other words, at some point careful tracking in such simple movement situations becomes unnecessary.

Just such a developmental trend was found in our own study of active versus passive movement described earlier (Acredolo, Adams, & Goodwyn, in press). Recall that infants were tested longitudinally at 12 and 18 months for their ability to search correctly for a toy hidden under one of two cloths in a large plexiglass box on the floor. Infants were either carried or allowed to move on their own to the opposite side of the box once their original access was blocked. In addition to recording search behavior, we also recorded the extent to which infants visually tracked the correct location as they moved. Results at 12 months showed an extremely strong co-occurrence of visual tracking, active movement, and correct search. In fact, a subsequent experiment in which visual tracking was prevented by the use of opaque side walls, indicated that it was the visual tracking and not the active movement per se at 12 months that was most facilitative of search. However, by 18 months, the infants were able to search correctly after either active or passive movement and with or without visual tracking. The visual tracking at earlier ages had served its purpose and infants were now able to automatically coordinate perspectives on this simple spatial task.

If visual tracking is so useful at young ages, why do not 8- to 11-month-old infants always depend upon it in these studies? After all, visual tracking of moving objects has been present in the infant's behavioral repertoire from birth. One would expect them to be fairly proficient at it. The problem, I think, is twofold. First, their successful reliance on egocentric information has operated for a long time as a reasonably successful shortcut. Thus, they are not as well practiced in tracking as one might think. Second, and possibly even more important, visual tracking in these cases is complicated by the fact that the object is itself no longer visible. What the infant must track, therefore, is not the object itself, but rather the occluder. This fact puts an extra burden on the young infant's capacities: The infant must remember the connection between the occluder and the object as well as track the occluder during the move.

That 8- to 9-month-old infants find this rather difficult is indicated in the study by Cornell (1979) in which infants on every trial watched as an object was hidden in one of two containers, which were then transposed before the infants' eyes.

The infants who had the most difficulty finding the object were those for whom no position or container cues were reliable, in other words, those who were completely dependent on visual tracking of the object's location.

Data from other studies suggest that several task and performance variables affect the ability or willingness to track. One task variable already mentioned is the distinctiveness of the location to be tracked. Goldfield and Dickerson (1981) report more tracking with distinctive containers than with identical containers. A second variable that appears to be important is the distance between locations competing for the infant's attention. In a very interesting recent study, Cornell (1981) hid an object in one of two containers while both were far out of the infant's reach. The containers were then moved toward the infant either on paths that brought them close together for most of their movement (narrow trajectory) or on paths that kept them fairly far apart (wide trajectory). Both 9- and 16-month-old infants showed a stronger tendency to restrict their looking to the target container in the wide trajectory condition than in the narrow trajectory condition. The visual tracking, in turn, led to more accurate search in the former condition as well.

A third task variable that apparently affects visual tracking in these tasks is the presence of training trials from the initial position. Data from Experiment 1 of Bremner (1978b) revealed that visual tracking of the correct site as the infants were rotated around the table resulted in more accurate search behavior. Since the accurate searches occurred significantly more frequently in the group for whom training trials were eliminated, it follows that the elimination of the training trials increased visual tracking. But why? I would argue that at this age (9 months), reliance on past actions still is given priority. When initial trials within a task indicate that a certain action can be trusted to yield the object, the infant simply foregoes visual tracking in favor of the less taxing motor habit. This decision also has the advantage of leaving visual attention free for other pursuits.

Certain performance variables may be operating on visual tracking in addition to the task variables already discussed. From my own studies of the effect of different testing environments on search behavior (Acredolo, 1979, 1982) it seems reasonable to suggest that conditions of stress hinder visual tracking and thus favor dependence on egocentric information. It also seems likely that the infant's motivation to find the object would influence visual tracking. A highly valued object might induce the infant to track but a less valued object might not. Of course, the disappearance of a highly valued object might hinder tracking if it results in heightened levels of stress. It may have been an increase in stress, for example, that led to poor visual tracking by the 9-month-old infants in the Corter et al. (1980) study in which it was Mother who disappeared. Also contributing, of course, was the infants' experience of an initial successful search in one direction.

As times passes and infants accumulate both more tracking and more crawling experience, these tasks and performance variables decline in importance. Infants become efficient at following objects as they move in space and, by the time they are ready to walk, have generated the truly objective conceptualization of space that Piaget described as the goal of the sensorimotor period. At this point, landmarks are no longer linked to successful action; instead they are recognized as useful cues existing independent of both the target object and the child. Landmarks, objects, and the child are all accorded equal rank as independent entities in the container of space. The earlier conflict between egocentric and landmark information has been solved; visual tracking has done its job by bringing the infant into a new state of equilibrium with the space around him. And thus ends the saga of the infant's search for spatial knowledge. It is a plausible story; all that is left to do now is to see if it is true.

REFERENCES

Acredolo, L. P. Development of spatial orientation in infancy. *Developmental Psychology*, 1978, *14*, 224–234.

Acredolo, L. P. Laboratory versus home: The effect of environment on the 9-month-old infant's choice of spatial reference system. *Developmental Psychology*, 1979, *15*, 666–667.

Acredolo, L. P. The familiarity factor in spatial research. In R. Cohen (Ed.), *New directions for child development: Vol. 15. Children's conceptions of spatial relationships.* San Francisco: Jossey-Bass, 1982.

Acredolo, L. P., Adams, A., & Goodwyn, S. W. The role of self-produced movement and visual tracking in infant spatial orientation. *Journal of Experimental Child Psychology*, 1984, *38*, 312–327.

Acredolo, L. P., & Evans, D. Developmental changes in the effects of landmarks on infant spatial behavior. *Developmental Psychology*, 1980, *16*, 312–318.

Benson, J. B., & Uzgiris, I. *The role of self-produced movement in spatial understanding.* Paper presented at the Biennial Meetings of the Society for Research in Child Development, Boston, April 1981.

Braine, L. G., & Eder, R. A. *Left-right recall in 2-year-olds.* Paper presented at the Biennial Meetings of the Society for Research in Child Development, Boston, April 1981.

Bremner, J. G. Spatial errors made by infants: Inadequate spatial cues or evidence of egocentrism? *British Journal of Psychology*, 1978, *69*, 77–84. (a)

Bremner, J. G. Egocentric versus allocentric spatial coding in 9-month-old infants: Factors influencing the choice of code. *Developmental Psychology*, 1978, *14*, 346–355. (b)

Bremner, J. G., & Bryant, P. E. Place versus response as the basis of spatial errors made by young infants. *Journal of Experimental Child Psychology*, 1977, *23*, 162–171.

Cornell, E. H. The effects of cue reliability on infants' manual search. *Journal of Experimental Child Psychology*, 1979, *28*, 81–91.

Cornell, E. H. The effects of cue distinctiveness of infants' manual search. *Journal of Experimental Child Psychology*, 1981, *32*, 330–342.

Cornell, E. H., & Heth, C. D. Response versus place learning by human infants. *Journal of Experimental Psychology: Human Learning and Memory*, 1979, *5*, 188–196.

Corter, C. M., Zucker, K. J., & Galligan, R. F. Patterns in the infant's search for mother during brief separation. *Developmental Psychology*, 1980, *10*, 62–69.

Cummings, E. M., & Bjork, E. L. *Piaget's stage IV object concept error: Evidence of perceptual confusion, state change, or failure to assimilate?* Paper presented at the Western Psychological Association, Seattle, April 1977.

Freeman, N. H., Lloyd, S., & Sinha, C. G. Infant search tasks reveal early concepts of containment and canonical usage of objects. *Cognition*, 1980, *8*, 243–262.

Goldfield, E. C., & Dickerson, D. J. Keeping track of locations during movement of 8- to 10-month-old infants. *Journal of Experimental Child Psychology*, 1981, *32*, 48–64.

Heth, C. D., & Cornell, E. H. Three experiences affecting spatial discrimination learning by ambulatory children. *Journal of Experimental Child Psychology*, 1980, *30*, 246–264.

Lingle, K. M., & Lingle, J. M. Effects of selected object characteristics on object-permanence test performance. *Child Development*, 1981, *52*, 367–369.

Lloyd, S. E., Sinha, C. G., & Freeman, N. H. Spatial reference systems and the canonicality effect in infant search. *Journal of Experimental Child Psychology*, 1981, *32*, 1–10.

Lockman, J. The development of detour knowledge during infancy. Doctoral dissertation, University of Minnesota, 1980.

Lucas, T. C., & Uzgiriz, I. Spatial factors in the development of the object concept. *Developmental Psychology*, 1977, *13*, 492–500.

Ninio, A. Piaget's theory of space perception in infancy. *Cognition*, 1979, *7*, 125–144.

Papousek, H. Individual variability in learned responses in human infants. In R. J. Robinson (Ed.), *Brain and early behaviour*. London: Academic Press, 1969.

Piaget, J. *The construction of reality in the child*. New York: Ballantine, 1971.

Pick, H. L., Yonas, A., & Rieser, J. Spatial reference systems in perceptual development. In M. H. Bornstein & W. Kessen (Eds.), *Psychological development from infancy*. Hillsdale, NJ: Lawrence Erlbaum Associates, 1979.

Rieser, J. Spatial orientation of six-month-old infants. *Child Development*, 1979, *50*, 1078–1087.

Rieser, H., Doxsey, P., McCarrell, N., & Brooks, P. Wayfinding and toddlers' use of information from an aerial view of a maze. *Developmental Psychology*, 1982, *18*, 714–720.

Rieser, J. J., & Heiman, M. L. Spatial self-reference systems and shortest route behavior in toddlers. *Child Development*, 1982, *53*, 524–533.

Shirley, M. M. *The first two years: A study of twenty-five babies*. Minneapolis: University of Minnesota Press, 1931.

Watson, J. S. Smiling, cooing and "the game." *Merrill-Palmer Quarterly of Behavior and Development*, 1973, *18*, 323–339.

6

Adults' Memory Representations of the Spatial Properties of their Everyday Physical Environment

Tommy Gärling
Anders Böök
Erik Lindberg
University of Umeå, Umeå, Sweden

That we are able to find our way around in the place where we are is an everyday experience familiar to everyone. This experience is in fact so familiar that we tend to overlook that our accomplishment, and many related accomplishments such as directing newcomers or finding the shortest path to travel, are hardly possible unless we possess a memory representation of the particular place, i.e., a *cognitive map,* to use the more convenient but less precise shorthand term. The relatively rare and sometimes dramatic cases of disorientation have perhaps attracted more interest than they deserve (Binet, 1894; Weisman, 1981; Zimring, 1981).

Research on cognitive maps (the "product") and cognitive mapping (the process of acquisition) is now quite extensive (see Evans, 1980). Although much of the research is developmental, the present chapter focuses on studies of adults. The bulk of these studies have been concerned with the properties of people's memory representations of the large-scale and medium-scale everyday environments, i.e., the neighborhoods, cities, and towns, in which they live. This was actually the concern of the pioneering studies by the nonpsychologists Appleyard (1969, 1970), DeJonge (1962), Gulick (1963), and Lynch (1960). However, these pioneers were more interested in demonstrating the psychological significance of the environment than in analyzing the cognitive map as a cognitive structure serving different adaptive functions.

The main focus of the present chapter is the spatial properties of cognitive maps, although nonspatial properties also need to be considered. Previous research has demonstrated the capability adults possess to cognitively map the spatial layout of the large-scale environment. Furthermore, adults do not seem to differ much from each other in this capability; in fact, few studies have succeeded in showing that there exist important individual differences (Evans, 1980) although a definite statement should perhaps await further, more conclusive evidence (e.g., Bryant, 1982). The question must then be raised how this everyday cognitive skill is accomplished. Other chapters in this volume are concerned with the development of spatial cognition from infancy on. This developmental sequence of basic concepts and skills is of course a necessary prerequisite. The present chapter takes the perspective of environmental psychology and asks: How do people in their everyday lives use their repertoires of basic concepts, skills, and so forth?; How do these repertoires aid them in adjusting to the complexities of man-made environments?; What are the limits of this ability? Tentative answers to these questions are implied by the discussions in the sections to follow.

This chapter is divided into five sections. In the first we present an organizing framework for the chapter. The framework is based on the authors' notions about cognitive mapping and related processes, which they have developed from their own research (Gärling, 1980; Gärling, Böök, & Lindberg, 1979, 1984). It is basically a conceptualization of the real world, which environmental psychologists need to consider in designing their laboratory research. This laboratory research is reviewed in the following sections. In the second section, what is known about the internal structures supporting the representation of information termed the cognitive map is discussed at some length and some ideas of the authors' own are presented. The acquisition process is considered in the third section, followed by a discussion of movement and orientation in the environment. The authors' ongoing studies of other related everyday cognitive skills are presented in the final section.

COGNITIVE MAPPING, ACTION PLANS, ORIENTATION, AND THEIR INTERRELATIONSHIPS: A CONCEPTUAL FRAMEWORK

Background

To explain how people's behavior is interfaced with the social and physical environments in which they live is the most basic theoretical question facing cognitive mapping research from the perspective of environmental psychology (Canter & Craik, 1981; Craik, 1973; Proshansky, Ittelson, & Rivlin, 1970; Stokols, 1978). Behavior in the everyday environment therefore needs to be defined as part of the domain of any general theoretical account of cognitive mapping. This is however at present a difficult task since the research has focused almost exclusively on internal psychological processes.

Our intention here is to present a framework that interrelates the many laboratory studies of different functions, focusing on ways in which these studies bear on the issue of how internal psychological processes and behavior in the everyday environment are interrelated.

Basic Assumptions

The general theoretical frame of reference for the following discussion is the information-processing approach in cognitive psychology (Lindsay & Norman, 1972; Neisser, 1967). The problem then becomes how to explain the interrelationships between internal processing of information from and about the environment (i.e., acquisition, storage, and transformations), and intentional behavior (i.e., actions), in this same environment.

The concept of action plan, proposed by Miller, Galanter, and Pribram (1960), was recently reintroduced by Russell and Ward (1982) as a potentially viable bridge between internal processing of information about large-scale and medium-scale environments and actions carried out in these environments. That action plans influence the way we perceive the environment may be inferred from studies demonstrating effects of cognitive sets (Leff, 1978; Leff & Gordon, 1979; Leff, Gordon, & Ferguson, 1974; Ward & Russell, 1981a, 1981b).

Following this lead, our first basic assumption is: Action plans are important determinants of behavior in the social and physical everyday environments. This assumption mainly serves to set the stage for the following assumptions and is not much further elaborated in this context.

Our second assumption is that travel plans are integrated parts of many action plans executed in large-scale and medium-scale environments. As a familiar example, consider when people need to run a number of errands. In large-scale and medium-scale environments, executing such action plans is likely to require travel to different places, e.g., shops or business offices. According to the second assumption, in such instances travel is carried out in accordance with a plan. That travel sometimes may appear nonrational is beside the point; it is only stated that travel follows a plan.

Many travel plans are likely to be routine, in which case they are retrieved from memory directly. In other cases a travel plan is formed. Our third assumption is that the formation of travel plans is a process consisting of several stages. The first stage entails accessing information about the environment. Although this information may be accessed from the environment by direct observation, it is probably more frequently accessed from the memory representation of the environment and from media such as maps, written texts (brochures, etc.), and face-to-face communications. These stages then follow: Deciding on which places to visit, deciding on the order to visit the places, and, finally, deciding on how to travel.

In general, travel plans are likely to be neither complete nor detailed enough to execute without observing the environment. Therefore, our fourth assumption is that recognition of places and monitoring travel through the environment, as well as anticipating features of the environment (processes subsumed under the function maintenance of orientation in the environment), are nontrivially interrelated with the execution of travel plans.

The fifth assumption is that the formation, execution, and revision (formation and execution interwoven as described below) of travel plans are important controlling factors of the acquisition of cognitive maps of large-scale and medium-scale environments. This assumption does not imply that cognitive maps are not dependent on travel habits (Evans, 1980), but the formation, execution, and so forth, of travel plans entail information-processing operations that are the controlling factors, not the travel itself.

Process Dynamics

The process dynamics implied by the basic assumptions are illustrated in Fig. 6.1. The arrows in the figure denote the flow of control from one process to another (indicated by the boxes drawn by solid lines) as follows.

An action plan necessitates travel to different places in a large-scale or medium-scale environment that may be familiar, partly familiar, or not familiar at all. Following the second assumption above that travel plans are part of action plans, a travel plan fulfilling the goals defined by the action plan may, if the environ-

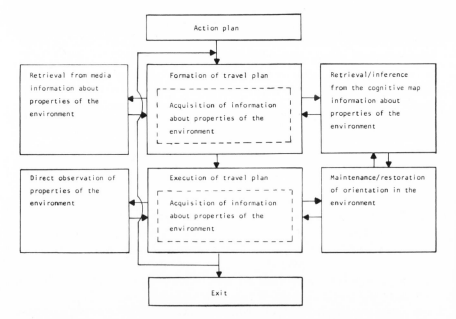

FIG. 6.1.   The process dynamics implied by the conceptual framework. (After Gärling, Böök, & Lindberg, 1982.)

ment is familiar, be directly retrieved from the part of long-term memory that stores information about the particular environment (i.e., the cognitive map). If no travel plan is available (or retrievable), one is formed, and according to the assumptions about how travel plans are formed, information about the environment is accessed from the cognitive map and/or from available media (maps, written texts, people). The accessed information, as well as the travel plan, is with some probability acquired and stored in the cognitive map (as the box in the figure drawn with broken lines is intended to indicate). Note that inferences may be stored; i.e., a travel plan formed from information retrieved from the cognitive map could be considered an inference that is stored. As acquisition proceeds, two things are likely to happen. First, more and more information about the environment becomes retrievable from the cognitive map. Thus accessing information from media becomes superfluous. Second, the number of directly retrievable travel plans increases, thereby reducing the need to form travel plans.

Next, the travel plan that has been formed (or directly retrieved) is executed. According to the assumptions made, it is neither complete nor detailed enough to be executed without the environment being observed during its execution. The execution of the travel plan must not be likened to the automatic execution of motor programs, such as walking or driving. Rather, the travel plan is an incomplete set of instructions for how to travel, which needs to be specified in response to the information received from the environment. A readiness for revising the travel plan may also be preserved, as indicated by the loop in Fig. 6.1. For instance, traffic jams may lead to a revision of the travel plan; the travel plan may also be revised because a hitherto unknown place such as a nice restaurant is observed.

Orientation in the environment must be maintained in the execution of travel plans. Recognizing places and other features of the environment, monitoring movement in relation to points or systems of reference, and anticipating features of the environment during movement are necessary processes. In addition to direct observation, retrieval of information about the environment from the cognitive map and access of information from media are involved. The importance of maintenance of orientation may be assumed to decrease as acquisition proceeds and the environment becomes more familiar. Similarly, the importance of recognition of places and features of the environment may be assumed to increase, while monitoring movement in relation to points or systems of reference diminishes in importance.

The execution of travel plans constitutes another important set of conditions for the acquisition of the cognitive map. Execution relies on direct observation of the environment and requires maintenance of orientation, which in turn entails accessing information from media (e.g., asking people in the street), monitoring movement, and so on. The information acquired during execution may differ in type, quality, and quantity from that acquired in the planning stage. Moreover, information accessed from media is likely to be more important in determining the cognitive map at early stages of acquisition, with information obtained by direct observation of the environment more important at later stages.

Implications

The framework presented here does not provide a general solution to the issue raised in this section (i.e., how people's behavior is interfaced with the social and physical environments in which they live), since it focuses on only one class of behaviors, namely traveling to different places in the environment. Nevertheless, as indicated in the introduction to the chapter, traveling (and movement in general) is one of the main adaptive functions that cognitive maps serve. Moreover, whereas the cognitive mapping literature is concerned almost exclusively with cognitive mapping by direct observation of the physical environment (Evans, 1980), the present framework incorporates the social environment to some extent, as exemplified by the assumption that the environment is learned from media such as maps, other people, and the like. In addition, many of the action plans are also likely to be plans for social actions.

The concept of a travel plan is important because it links movement and travel in the everyday environment to internal information processes such as acquisition and storage, maintenance of orientation (recognition, monitoring movement, anticipation), and planning, which have been studied in the laboratory. At present, the concept as well as the framework lacks an empirical foundation. The time-budgeting studies pursued by geographers (Carlstein, Parkes, & Thrift, 1978), for instance, provide descriptions of people's activities while ignoring their cognitive processing. The laboratory studies of the internal information processes, on the other hand, have with few exceptions not explicitly taken the perspective advocated here.

Before discussing in the following sections the different information processes outlined in the framework, we consider the product of these processes, i.e., the cognitive map. Our framework leads to some definite hypotheses about the cognitive map. These hypotheses are not the only ones possible, are not altogether original, and above all, are incomplete. Theories of the cognitive map are few, and no attempt is made to review those that exist. However, points of communality with these theories are pointed out, and pertinent studies are considered.

THE COGNITIVE MAP

Questions to be Answered

The cognitive map is conceptualized as an internal representation of information about properties of everyday large-scale and medium-scale environments. The basic questions to be answered about the cognitive map are: What properties of the environment are represented; and How are these properties represented? The second question consists of two parts: (1) What internal structures support the representation? (2) In what format is the information represented?

Portions of these issues have been addressed by environmental, developmental, and cognitive psychologists, and by neuroscientists (O'Keefe & Nadel, 1978). Specifically, attempts at theorizing have been directed toward the question of represented properties of the environment (Appleyard, 1969, 1970; Lynch, 1960; Siegel & White, 1975), and drawing on theories of cognitive development, the question involving what internal structures support the representation has been tackled (Hart & Moore, 1973; Moore, 1979; Siegel & White, 1975). In addition, Kuipers' (1978) computer simulation of the cognitive map made use of the information-processing approach in cognitive psychology. For instance, Kuipers makes a distinction between short-term and long-term memory and ascribes different roles to each. In a related major attempt to account for visual imagery, Kosslyn (1980; see also Kosslyn & Schwartz, 1977) introduced the idea that the format of the representation of spatial information is both propositional and analogue.

Our answers to both questions is outlined below. These answers do not differ importantly from those given by the theories mentioned. It may however still be worthwhile to present a coherent set of assumptions that (1) answers the questions raised, (2) is compatible with the framework discussed in the preceding section, (3) is parsimonious, and, finally, (4) is open to falsification.

Properties of the Environment that are Cognitively Mapped

The assumption that travel plans govern the acquisition of information about the environment suggests a variety of information that is cognitively mapped. This information falls into three broad categories. The first refers to "environmental elements" such as those enumerated by Lynch (1960). The elements (or places, which is the term preferred here) are the basic units of the representation and correspond to a number of different components: streets, street crossings, buildings, landmarks (perceptually salient places), districts, and so on. In addition to place units, how these units are interrelated spatially is also represented in the cognitive map. It is these spatial relations (which may be of different types) that give the cognitive map its maplike properties. A third type of information is the travel plans inferred from other types of information, which are closely related to actions and movements.

The assumption, then, is that three interrelated components—places, spatial relations, and travel plans—are the contents of cognitive maps of large-scale and medium-scale environments acquired by people during the course of their daily purposeful interactions with such environments. This is indicated in Fig. 6.2.

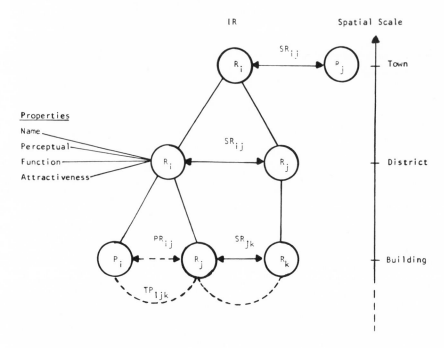

IR   Internal representation
P   Places
R   Reference points
PR   Proximity relations
SR   Spatial relations
TP   Travel plans

FIG. 6.2. The properties of the environment which are cognitively mapped.
(After Gärling, Böök, & Lindberg, 1982.)

Places.   Place is a concept that is rich in meaning and difficult to define
(e.g., Canter, 1977; Russell & Ward, 1982). An understanding of the concept
should be possible by examining the important properties of places that may be
represented in cognitive maps.

One obvious property of places is their spatial scale. The number of "places"
in the environment is practically infinite, and they vary enormously in spatial
scale; places may be very circumscribed spots (e.g., a mailbox, an entrance to a
building); they may also be buildings, plazas, districts, towns, cities. Hence, it is
argued, the taxonomy developed by Lynch (1960) and others (Evans, 1980) is
too narrow in that it is primarily designed to handle elements at the city scale, of
concern to urban planners. It may well be that different types of elements are
represented depending on spatial scale, and that those suggested by Lynch are
only a subset of the psychologically meaningful types.

Another property of many (but not all) places is that they have names. The existence of a name, i.e., a verbal label, for a particular place facilitates communication of information about it, which, by the way, may be one reason why places with names appear to be the most often studied (Evans, 1980). Places also differ from each other with regard to perceptual characteristics and function (e.g., a shop, a restaurant, and so on). These properties have received much less attention in the cognitive mapping research, but recently Pezdek and Evans (1979) showed that they are learned to some extent independently from the locations of places. Milgram, Greenwald, Kessler, McKenna, and Waters (1972) demonstrated that perceptual characteristics of places are fairly accurately remembered.

Much research in environmental psychology also has demonstrated that places have psychological attributes, such as, for instance, attractiveness, affection, and calmness (e.g., Canter, 1977; Lowenthal & Riel, 1972; Ward and Russell, 1981b), and that the attributes of particular places are remembered (Lowenthal & Riel, 1972; Merrill & Baird, 1980). These attributes are referred to in Fig. 6.2 as a single property termed attractiveness, although this property is actually multidimensional. Furthermore, it probably corresponds to a number of different properties of the environment. For instance, a building may be attractive because it is cool, a vista point because it exposes scenic beauty, a district because it is safe, and so on. A still more abstract notion is the concept of affordances (Bell, Fisher, & Loomis, 1978; Gibson, 1966, 1979), which seems to encompass both function and attractiveness.

That cognitive maps contain information about the properties of places is evident from many everyday examples. If someone asks you if you know of, for instance, a good hotel, the answer to such a question may be as follows: "The large brick (perceptual characteristics) building complex (spatial scale) is a rather expensive but very comfortable (attractiveness) hotel (function) called Hilton (name)." The answer is undoubtedly based on information retrieved from the cognitive map, i.e., that part of long-term memory that stores information about particular familiar places. It is unfortunate that so few cognitive mapping studies have been made of memory for the properties of places (rather than places per se). Knowledge is therefore lacking about many important questions. For instance, in making travel plans, are all the different properties equally effective as retrieval cues, and does this hold irrespective of the degree of acquisition? Answers to such questions are important for our understanding of how cognitive maps are used. They are also important for our understanding of how the cognitive map is internally represented.

Spatial Relations.   Spatial relations between places are another class of units that is defined as a property of *pairs* of places. There are minimally three different types of spatial relations that need to be considered: (1) spatial inclusion relations; (2) metric spatial relations; (3) proximity relations (see Evans, Marrero, & Butler, 1981; Hart & Moore, 1973; Kuipers, 1978; Siegel & White, 1975; among others, for related although not identical assumptions).

Stevens and Coupe (1978) and Tversky (1981) have produced evidence congruent with the idea that cities are remembered as spatially nested within the states in which they are located. This principle may hold across the full spatial scale, i.e., any two places at different scales may be spatially nested. For instance, the shop may be remembered as spatially included within the building in which it is located, the building within the district, and so forth. (See Milgram et al., 1972, for further evidence.) The spatial inclusion relation, a property of pairs of places, should not be confused with spatial scale, a property of places. Furthermore, all spatial inclusion relations may not be remembered, and some spatial inclusion relations that do not exist may remain represented in memory. If a shop is moved to another building, the changed spatial inclusion relation is possibly never updated if it does not form part of any travel plan.

Metric spatial relations (direction and distance in polar coordinates from one place to another) are likely to be remembered by adults (see Evans, 1980, for a review). However, it has been argued that cognitive maps are not like maps at all. This argument rests on a particular definition of the concept of a map (Kuipers, 1982) together with the fact that some of the properties of cognitive maps implied by that definition are found empirically to be lacking (Cadwallader, 1979; Lowrey, 1970). That metric spatial relations are represented does not mean, however, that all these relations must be represented, nor does it mean that they all are accurately represented (Byrne, 1979; Canter & Tagg, 1975; Tversky, 1981). The degree of acquisition may simply not have been enough, or the amount of information to be acquired may make it necessary to use simplifying rules for storage in order to overcome capacity limits of the storage systems. The authors, in studies discussed more thoroughly below (Gärling, Böök, & Ergezen, 1982; Gärling, Böök, Lindberg, & Nilsson, 1981), also found that distance estimates requested from the subjects may cause distortions, which are absent when the same subjects perform direction estimates from different vantage points. Thus, the particular methodology used in many studies (e.g., Cadwallader, 1979) may to some extent be responsible for the false conclusion that cognitive maps lack the properties that maps possess. Although attempts at the quantification of cognitive maps (e.g., Baird, 1979; Golledge, 1976, 1977; Golledge, Briggs, & Demko, 1969; Milgram et al., 1972; Sherman, Oliver, & Titus, 1980) are desirable if elusive, the position taken here is that metric spatial relations form part of the cognitive map; no other similarity to a map is necessarily implied.

Sadalla, Burroughs, and Staplin (1980) discussed what they call *reference points*, i.e., places used in defining the locations of other places. For instance, if someone asks where the grocery store is, he or she may receive the answer: "It is near the railway station." In this example, the railway station is the reference point used to direct someone to the grocery store. Metric spatial relations may hold between reference points at the same spatial scale. Other places may be related to reference points at the same spatial scale. Other places may be related to reference points by means of proximity relations (e.g., near to) (Acredolo, Pick, & Olsen, 1975; Sadalla et al., 1980; Sherman, Oliver, & Titus, 1980). Ordinal spatial relations have been suggested to form another class of spatial relations early in the acquisition stage (Evans et al., 1981; Siegel & White, 1975) but these may, as more recent evidence indicates, be distinguished from metric spatial relations in terms of the degree of precision by which the (metric) spatial relations are represented. Gärling et al. (1982) and Gärling et al. (1981) had subjects estimate confidence intervals of direction and distance, in addition to location estimates. Confidence intervals decreased across length of residence in a town in the first study, across tours in an unfamiliar residential neighborhood in the second study. The main change as a function of experience was in both studies that precision increased, whereas accuracy of the point estimates remained approximately the same. Proximity relations, on the other hand, lack ordinal spatial information, and apart from the fact that the Sadalla et al. study demonstrates their existence, proximity relations may have a different representational format than metric (and "ordinal") spatial relations (Kosslyn, 1980; Sherman et al., 1980).

A further reason why the importance of metric spatial relations might have been underplayed is that they are not easily expressed in ordinary language. Take the everyday example alluded to above. If one asks where the hotel is located, this may be the answer: "It is in Berkeley (spatial inclusion) on Shattuck at University (proximity)." If asked for more specific information, the respondent may use metric relations such as cardinal compass directions together with some metric for distance (blocks, miles).

Reference points may be organized as systems of reference. Much discussion has been devoted to the role of systems of reference for spatial orientation (Acredolo, 1976; Hart & Moore, 1973; Kuipers, 1978; Pick, 1976). For instance, streets, compass directions, or one's body axes may function as reference axes. The map metaphor of the cognitive map again is criticized by Kuipers (1982) who argues that systems of reference are local, i.e., "tied" to particular places, rather than global as in a map. That is, metric spatial relations (direction and distance) from one place to other places are remembered relative to a system of reference tied to the first place. The reverse metric spatial relations are, if they are remembered, remembered relative to systems of reference tied to the other places.

Local systems of reference aligned with the streets in a town may be global in a sense if they are laid out in a regular grid pattern. In an unpublished study, Anita Svensson-Gärling and the authors had subjects estimate directions to different places in the average-sized Swedish town Umeå. The subjects were undergraduates who had lived in Umeå for either 2 months or 14 months. The study was essentially a replication of a previous study (Gärling et al., 1982) except that the direction estimates were made relative to absolute reference directions. In one condition the subjects estimated the directions to the places from each other place with reference to the North direction, in another condition they estimated the directions relative to a self-selected reference direction. Whether they had been in the town for 2 or 14 months, the subjects were accurate with respect to the *relative* directions among the places. The self-selected reference directions in most cases coincided with the estimated North, thus suggesting that North may be salient. In downtown Umeå where the streets form a regular grid, the reference directions were aligned with the streets, about 30° to the actual North. In the outskirts where the streets form no regular grid, the reference directions tended to vary from place to place. The results indicated that people may acquire systems of reference that are "more global" but the study does not tell in which way this is achieved. That streets play a role seems certain even though other factors are not ruled out. For instance, rivers, and so forth, may function as reference axes.

Systems of reference are necessary for "keying" the cognitive map to the environment. Recognizing a reference point is insufficient if a local system of reference cannot be inferred. Remembering directions relative to the body axes may be prevalent in infancy (Acredolo, 1977, 1978); to account for the adult's performance, it is more plausible to assume that he or she remembers systems of reference as part of the perceptual characteristics of places. If such reference systems are identified, it would be possible to localize other, perceptually non-available places, irrespective of one's body orientation.

Compass directions are often used to label directions, and may for that reason be learned. However, compass directions may be no more global and accurate than the local systems of reference that they label. The important point is not that this refutes the map metaphor (Kuipers, 1982), but that compass directions play a role that we need to study more carefully.

Travel Plans.   Paths traversed in the environment have been presumed to be learned early in the acquisition of cognitive maps (Siegel & White, 1975). The contention here is that this assumption is based upon an inaccurate conceptualization of the conditions for the acquisition of cognitive maps. To repeat the arguments given above, travel is not executed before it has been preplanned to some degree. The planning process controls the acquisition initially; therefore, information about the environment accessed in connection with planning should be the information acquired early. This information, mainly accessed from media, consists of information about the properties of the environment enumerated above. In addition, the travel plans that are the outcomes of the planning process are remembered. The execution of travel plans, involving revisions and specifications, defines another set of conditions for the acquisition, and in any real situation the acquisition process is bound to be a complex mixture of the cases discussed here. Any straightforward prediction of the order in which different types of properties of the environment are acquired is extremely difficult if it is not based on detailed knowledge about individuals' cognitive activities in relation to their everyday environment.

A travel plan has been assumed to specify (partially) how to get from one place to a number of other places (destinations) or, in the special case, from one place to another, as when, for instance, one travels from home to work. What, then, is the minimal set of properties of the environment that need to be stored? How are these properties related to places and spatial relations?

The assumption is that travel plans are ordered subsets of places and, since some of the places may be reference points, subsets of spatial relations. If paths are defined as ordered subsets of places (Kuipers, 1978), they may either constitute travel plans or parts of travel plans. For instance, the path from home to work may be a travel plan; it may under other circumstances be part of another travel plan, e.g., traveling from work to home, then from home to a restaurant.

Kuipers (1978) assumes that paths are sets of instructions specifying how to travel. These instructions are rather abstract (i.e., specifying directions and distances). It is assumed here that detailed instructions are worked out in connection with the execution of the travel plans. The load on storage capacity should thereby decrease and the travel plan may still be workable. For repeatedly traveled paths, higher-level motor programs may be interfaced with routine travel plans making them executable in a semi-automatic fashion.

Summary. In this section we offered assumptions about the properties of the environment cognitively mapped in connection with the formation and execution of travel plans.

First, as depicted in Fig. 6.2, the basic units (elements) of the cognitive map (the internal representation denoted IR) are sets of places denoted P. Places are defined through a set of properties: their names, perceptual characteristics, functional classes, and attractiveness values. They are also hierarchically organized according to their spatial scale.

Second, within each layer of the spatial scale hierarchy, there exist subsets of places, termed reference points, which are denoted R. The product sets $R \times R$ have the property of being spatially interrelated. The spatial relations (SRs) are defined as polar coordinates in relation to base vector systems defined for each reference point. Information about these vector systems is in some way part of the perceptual characteristics of the reference points. The subsets of places that are not reference points are related to reference points by means of proximity relations (PRs). Probably, each place is related to only one reference point; several places may however be related to the same reference point.

Third, travel plans (TPs) are defined as ordered subsets of places. These subsets also include reference points. One travel plan may include other travel plans, or parts thereof.

Principles of Internal Representation

With the information-processing approach adopted in this chapter, we assume that information from the environment is processed in sequential stages. The information is assumed to be received by the sensory systems, stored for a brief period of time in sensory registers, transformed or recoded, and stored in a unitary short-term memory system, and, finally, more or less permanently stored in a long-term memory system. The distinction between the short-term and long-term memory systems is most useful for our present purposes, even though its validity recently has been questioned (Craik, 1979; Craik & Lockhart, 1972).

According to the original formulations (Atkinson & Shiffrin 1968; Schneider & Shiffrin, 1977; Shiffrin & Schneider, 1977), different memory systems are the structural components of the information-processing system. Atkinson & Shiffrin (1968) also postulated the existence of control processes defined as transient information processes. For instance, forgetting is very pronounced in short-term memory unless it is countereacted by the control process of (maintenance) rehearsal. Information may not be encoded in long-term memory unless it is elaborated, integrated, and so on.

The implicit assumption underlying research on cognitive maps is that the cognitive map is a long-term memory representation. The question must therefore be asked how it is organized. Tulving (1972) made a distinction between episodic and semantic long-term memory. Episodic memory encodes memories for specific events. Such memories usually have an autobiographical reference. They are furthermore assumed to be more susceptible to forgetting. General knowledge shared by many people is classified as semantic memory. The specific encoding contexts are generally not recallable. A prototypical example would be knowledge of language. It is seldom possible to recall when specific word meanings were learned; nevertheless, word meanings are remembered and usually easy to retrieve.

The view adopted here is that the organization of the cognitive map is both episodic and semantic. Visiting a particular place on a vacation may lead to a cognitive map of that place including a number of (pleasant) events. The cognitive map of the town in which we live certainly contains memories of many events, such as meeting a friend in a certain place, visiting a restaurant on a special occasion, and so on. However, the memory of these events probably plays a minor role for the utilization of the cognitive map in our daily commerce with the environment. Rather, we remember more enduring features.

Several models of semantic memory have been proposed, e.g., network, set-theoretic, and semantic-features models (Klatzky, 1980). For instance, in a network model (e.g., Anderson & Bower, 1973; Collins & Loftus, 1975) places should be considered to be the nodes (concepts) hierarchically organized according to their spatial scale. With each node are stored the properties of the places, including their spatial relations, and travel plans.

The cognitive map is not only a long-term memory representation however. There is now empirical evidence supporting that short-term (or working short-term) memory plays a crucial role for the acquisition of cognitive maps (Lindberg & Gärling, 1981a, 1981b, 1982, 1983), for its utilization in connection with orientation in the environment (Böök, 1981; Böök & Gärling, 1980a, 1980b, 1981a, 1981b) and in connection with the formation of travel plans (Gärling, Böök, Lindberg, & Säisä, 1984). This evidence is discussed more thoroughly below.

Information contained in the cognitive map may, as Kuipers (1978) assumes, be represented in short-term memory in connection with operations on this information. For instance, deciding on the shortest path to travel in a familiar environment is a problem-solving task requiring a temporary representation of locations in working short-term memory. The contention here is that in many such cases the short-term memory representation is a spatial image. The spatial relations may be represented in an analog format in short-term memory (rather than propositionally as the models of semantic memory assume). This is exactly what Kosslyn (1980; Kosslyn & Schwartz, 1977) assumes to be the case in many similar problem-solving tasks, e.g., searching for features present. That the spatial image is three-dimensional does not pose a problem because it has been shown that three-dimensional images are possible to form (Cooper & Shepard, 1978).

The short-term memory representation may also be visual, as when the perceptual characteristics of places are represented in short-term memory. In still other cases, the functions, names, and attractiveness values of places are represented in short-term memory. This representation is probably more abstract, resembling the representation of language. Travel plans are likely to be both analog and more abstract.

The conventional conception of short-term memory assumes that the representational format is verbal (auditive-articulatory) (Atkinson & Shiffrin, 1968; Murdock, 1974). This conception is however insufficient to account for the representation in short-term memory of much of the information a cognitive map contains. Recent work on visual and spatial imagery clearly suggests the same thing (Cooper & Shepard, 1978; Finke, 1980; Kosslyn, 1980). Further evidence comes from studies with the short-term memory-scanning paradigm (Sternberg, 1975).

Following Kuipers (1978) and Kosslyn and Schwartz (1977), the long-term memory representation of metric spatial relations may be assumed to be distinct from that of other information in the cognitive map. To account for the spatial imagery character of many short-term memory representations, these authors postulate that the polar coordinates of the locations of ''landmarks'' are stored in long-term memory. This representation is however incomplete or ''skeletal.'' It must be supplemented with other pieces of information, which are retrieved from other parts of the long-term memory store. For instance, proximity relations may, as Sherman, Oliver, and Titus (1980) have argued, be stored in another format.

To summarize, the cognitive map is a representation of information that is supported by several different internal structures. In connection with acquisition and utilization, the information is represented in short-term memory, either in an analog format as a spatial or visual image, or in a more abstract format, as language is represented. Basically, however, the cognitive map is a semantic long-term memory structure organized in the way models of long-term memory assume. It is developed out of episodes or events constituting the commerce with the environment, but these events or episodic memories are either forgotten, or otherwise play a minor role. To account for memory for metric spatial relations (and possibly the perceptual characteristics of places), a distinct long-term memory representation of spatial locations is assumed to exist.

Concluding Comments

This section has reviewed which properties of the environment are cognitively mapped, and how these properties are internally represented. How the properties of the environment become internally represented is treated in the next section. A special emphasis is then given to the acquisition of metric spatial relations, which has been shown to be a unique and important property of the cognitive map.

The views expressed in this section are to some extent intended as suggestions for further research. This holds especially true as far as principles of internal representation are concerned. Too few studies of cognitive mapping have in fact been motivated by explicit hypotheses about how the cognitive map is internally represented. Cross-paradigmatic research, employing, for instance, long-term memory retrieval paradigms (Puff, 1982), may remedy this state of affairs. Some of the studies of acquisition of cognitive maps have made a start by investigating the validity of one of the central postulates of the information processing approach, i.e., if central information processing is a necessary prerequisite for acquisition.

ACQUISITION

Background

There seems to be no current cognitive mapping research dealing explicitly with the acquisition of cognitive maps in connection with the formation and execution of travel plans under real-life conditions. The closest one can come is a field study conducted by Beck and Wood (1976). In that study adolescents who were newcomers to a large city were asked to provide daily reports of their knowledge about the spatial layout of the city. Since the subjects were taken on guided

tourist tours through the city, most of their travel was planned by others. Consequently they had little opportunity to learn about the spatial layout of the city by
forming and executing travel plans of their own.

In this section we selectively review studies of the acquisition of cognitive
maps under laboratory and laboratory-like conditions. The main focus of these
studies is the acquisition of spatial information. Although there are a few studies
of the acquisition of spatial information from media, most of the studies are
concerned with acquisition by direct observation of the environment.

Acquisition of Spatial Information from Media

Graphic media such as visual or tactual maps, floor plans, three-dimensional
drawings, and even scale models, are frequently available for large-scale and
medium-scale environments. Nothing appears, however, to be known about the
frequency with which such media are accessed. They probably vary in attractiveness to different people, depending on what kinds of travel plans are formed
and executed, degree of familiarity with the environment, and, possibly, acquired expertise in using the medium.

Written texts (tour guides, tourist brochures, etc.) and face-to-face communication are other means by which information about the environment is obtained. Face-to-face communication (i.e., asking people) presents special problems. In such cases the "medium" is the cognitive maps possessed by other
people, which they must convey to the enquiring person. The communication is
generally verbal but map sketches, pointing, and guiding also are likely to be
involved. A plausible assumption is that face-to-face communication is by far the
most frequent medium from which knowledge is acquired by lay people. It is
unfortunate, therefore, that map sketches drawn by subjects in cognitive mapping studies typically are not solicited in a communication setting.

The existing research on the acquisition of spatial information from media
(Foos, 1980; Thorndyke & Stasz, 1980) suggests three types of difficulties for
the subjects. The first is that the relevant information must be attended to and
interpreted accurately. Second, the medium itself sometimes imposes memory
requirements. The information may be available only once (as when one looks at
a stationary street map or asks another person for directions), in which case the
relevant information must be focused on and remembered.

The third difficulty for the subject is the need to translate the information
acquired from the medium to the environment. As Blaut, McCleary, and Blaut
(1970) point out, map reading, for instance, involves translating abstract symbols, transforming perspective, and transforming scale. Levine (1982) discusses
how a map user establishes correspondence between the map and the environment. He argues that this requires that the user identify at least two places in the
environment, the locations of which are indicated in the map. A similar analysis
of the acquisition of spatial information from verbal information is unfortunately

lacking. The studies by Sadalla et al. (1980) and Sherman et al. (1980), cited previously, suggest that reference points are important in such cases. Both metric spatial relations and proximity relations may be conveyed by verbal information. Linde and Labov (1975) also found that people describe the layout of their apartments as a guided tour through it. Verbal information may thus provide people with already formed travel plans.

Gärling, Lindberg, and Mäntylä (1983) demonstrated that presenting subjects with a floor plan can facilitate the learning of the spatial layout of a building complex. The subjects were taken on tours through the building by an accompanying experimenter. Some subjects had their sight restricted by means of goggles. The negative effect of restricting the sight was to some extent counteracted by presenting the floor plan before each tour.

Other studies have compared the acquisition of spatial information from maps with direct observation of the environment (Evans & Pezdek, 1980; Hintzman, O'Dell, & Arndt, 1981; Howard & Kerst, 1981; Thorndyke, 1981). The subjects presented the media information were never taken on tours as they were in the study referred to above. The results indicated that spatial information (metric spatial relations) is acquired but also that it may be represented differently depending on the mode of acquisition. When information was acquired from maps, the latency times measured suggested that the representational format is analog. This is in line with the assumption made earlier in this chapter, i.e., that metric spatial relations are represented in an analog format. However, when the environments represented in the maps were observed directly, the latency results were more congruent with a propositional type of representational format (i.e., a list structure). These results are incongruent with what has been assumed earlier.

Lindberg and Gärling (1977a, 1977b) presented subjects with verbal descriptions of paths. The "verbal descriptions" actually consisted of sets of numerical values, e.g., "Go 76 meters straight, turn 53° to the right and continue 34 meters." The numerical values and the length of the descriptions were varied. Verbal reports, latency times of spatial inferences (i.e., inferring the location of the starting point from the end point), and the effect of instructing the subjects to use different methods to represent the information indicated that spatial images were formed from the descriptions. Thus metric spatial relations may be acquired from verbal information, but they probably seldom are, since descriptions of paths in ordinary language are usually different from those used by Lindberg and Gärling in these studies.

Acquisition of Spatial Information by Direct Observation

Large-scale and medium-scale environments completely surround the person and thereby encompass "the world behind the head" (Attneave & Farrar, 1977; Attneave & Pierce, 1978) as well as those parts that are located before one's eyes at any particular moment. As a consequence of that, but also because obstacles block the view, large-scale and medium-scale environments cannot be perceived in their entirety from any single vantage point. Therefore, the acquisition of cognitive maps of such environments by direct observation requires the integration across long time spans of successive perceptions accompanying movements of the eyes, the head, and the body (Gärling, 1980; Kuipers, 1978, 1982; Siegel & White, 1975). An exception of course would be seeing a town from the air or from a vista point on a hill. Similarly, graphic media generally do not require the successive integration of information in the same way; for instance, a map can be seen from one vantage point. Kuipers (1978, 1982), among others, in fact argues that a large-scale environment should be defined as something that cannot be perceived all at once. Size per se is thus not crucial. The problem with this argument is, however, that few things are possible to perceive at a single glance (e.g., Gibson, 1950, 1966, 1979); the important point may be that the integration of information takes place across very long time spans and that eye, head, and body movements (and not only eye and head or only eye movements) must be taken into account in the integration.

Research on the acquisition of cognitive maps by direct observation of the environment has employed two different paradigms. In one, people who have lived for varying amounts of time in the environment are compared to each other. Studies using this paradigm have found that long-term residents produce more accurate and complete sketch maps than newcomers (Appleyard, 1969, 1970). Remarkably accurate localization of important landmarks (reference points) has also been found to be possible after a comparatively short time of residence (Evans et al., 1981; Gärling et al., 1982; Golledge et al., 1969; Herman, Kail, & Siegel, 1979). Furthermore, Evans et al. (1981) and Gärling et al. (1982) found evidence for a faster acquisition of landmark locations than of paths, whereas Herman et al. (1979) did not. Differences in measurement procedures may partly account for the conflicting results.

One of the virtues of the paradigm employing subjects who vary in length of residence should be that it provides knowledge about the degree and rate of acquisition to be expected under real-life conditions. However, the difficulty in sampling environmental properties (e.g., reference points) makes it hazardous to draw any definite conclusions. Furthermore, much supplemental information needs to be collected in order to exert (statistical) control over the conditions of acquisition. For instance, media may play an important role for the short-term residents' acquisition. Moreover, factors affecting acquisition are not easily disentangled. Subjects may, for instance, differ, within and between experimental groups, with respect to the travel plans they execute as well as in other respects (e.g., with respect to personality traits correlated with acquisition strategies; see Bryant, 1983).

To achieve control over the conditions of acquisition, other studies have used a conventional learning paradigm. These studies are not unobtrusive, although some incidental learning studies may be less obtrusive (Brewer & Treyens, 1981; Kozlowski & Bryant, 1977; Lindberg & Gärling, 1983). Another potentially important difference among these studies is that in some of them subjects have been taken on actual tours through an unfamiliar environment (Crane, 1978; Gärling et al., 1981; Gärling et al., 1983; Kozlowski & Bryant, 1977; Lindberg & Gärling, 1981a, 1981b, 1982, 1983; Sadalla & Magel, 1980; Sadalla & Staplin, 1980), but in others such tours have been simulated (Allen, 1981; Allen, Siegel, & Rosinski, 1978; Heft, 1979; Pittenger & Jenkins, 1979).

A general finding of these learning paradigm studies is that acquisition is fast and that the acquired cognitive map appears to be resistant to forgetting, at least for retention intervals up to one month (Bahrick, 1979; Gärling et al., 1981; Gärling et al., 1983). To what extent these findings are generalizable is difficult to tell. Rate of acquisition has also been found to depend on a number of factors, the effects of which may be more generalizable.

The Role of Central Information Processing.   When we move about in a familiar environment we seldom experience disorientation. We also seem to be able to learn new spatial facts with little difficulty. This may be the case in an unfamiliar environment too if we possess a legible map and are skilled at using it. These familiar examples may indicate that the acquisition of a cognitive map by direct observation is an automated process not requiring cognitive resources to any great extent. However, counter-examples are also abundant. Consider that you are engaged in an interesting conversation with an accompanying friend, or that you wander in your thoughts. In an art museum, the pictures may attract your full attention. Disorientation under such conditions is perhaps not infrequent (Binet, 1894); furthermore, not much is likely to be learned about the spatial layout of the place.

The information processing approach within cognitive psychology assumes that the capacity for information processing is limited. One way to account for this limitation is to assume that information processing which is not highly automated cannot proceed efficiently unless what has been termed central processing capacity is allocated (Kahneman, 1973), and that the total amount of this capacity available at any given moment is limited.

The acquisition of information about the perceptual characteristics of places need not be assumed to be different from that of other perceptual scenes. People are believed to possess a substantial ability to encode materials of this kind (Shepard, 1967; Standing, Conezio, & Haber, 1970), and it has been suggested that it does not require much central information processing (Kellogg, 1980). The acquisition of information about the locomotion path presumably requires more processing. The encoding of isolated perceptual scenes in this case is insufficient since a number of such scenes must be remembered in the order in which they were encountered.

Since reference points in large-scale environments are not perceived simultaneously, metric spatial relations as a property of pairs of places must be learned when moving from one reference point to another. Whereas the acquisition of reference points and locomotion paths thus entails the encoding of information about the environment during movement, acquisition of spatial relations should, under many circumstances, require processing of information about the movement per se. The question is: Do the encoding, temporary storage, and spatial inferences that take place require a nontrivial amount of central processing capacity?

One way of finding out whether central information processing is required for efficient performance of a primary task is to compare the performance of that task in a condition in which another central processing demanding task is carried out concurrently, with the performance of the same primary task in another condition with no concurrent task. If the primary task requires central processing capacity, and if the processing demands of both tasks together exceed the available amount, then performance of the primary task should be impaired. On the other hand, if the primary task is one that is highly automated (like walking) and therefore does not require central processing, performance should not be affected by the concurrent task. Another way of investigating the role of central information processing for a given task is to increase the processing demands of the task itself. Performance of tasks already demanding much of the available capacity should then be affected negatively.

In order to investigate the role of central information processing for the acquisition of spatial information by direct observation of the environment, Lindberg and Gärling (1981a, 1981b, 1982, 1983) used both methods outlined above. The environment was a partly subterranean culvert system beneath a large hospital. The pathways were generally featureless and outside views as well as views from one pathway to another were, with few exceptions, blocked. The subjects, who were unfamiliar with the culvert system prior to the experiments, walked a number of times with an experimenter along a circuitous path that was about 600 m long (see Fig. 6.3). They attempted to learn where a number of reference points designated by the experimenter were located. For half the subjects, the amount of available central processing capacity was reduced by giving them a difficult backwards counting task to be performed at maximal speed while walking. The information processing demands of the acquisition task itself were varied by requiring that the subjects learn spatial relations corresponding to a varying number of segments (and direction changes) of the locomotion path, and by varying the number of reference points to be learned. Dependent measures were the constant and variable errors and the latency times of estimates of the directions and crow-flight distances to the designated reference points from stopping points along the locomotion path.

Reducing the amount of available processing capacity by means of the concurrent task negatively affected performance. Locations were estimated less

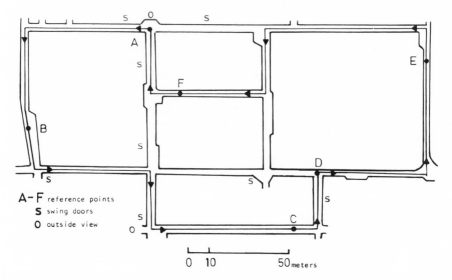

FIG. 6.3.   Path walked by subjects learning the locations of reference points in a culvert system. (From Lindberg & Gärling, 1981a, p. 102.)

accurately and latencies of estimates were longer. Increasing the processing demands of the acquisition task had similar but somewhat less negative effects. Another finding was that acquisition of different types of information represented in the cognitive map require different amounts of processing capacity. As Fig. 6.4 shows, when the concurrent task was performed, the latencies increased with the number of path segments separating the subjects from the reference point locations to be estimated. The interpretation offered was that the subjects were unable to access the spatial relations to be estimated directly but were still able to reconstruct the locomotion path. Thus information about the locomotion path appeared to be acquired despite the fact that the concurrent task was performed, whereas information about the spatial relations did not appear to be acquired. Finally, information about the locomotion path was acquired also when no concurrent task was performed. In this case accuracy of the estimates was higher, indicating that the availability of central processing capacity affects the acquisition of this type of information as well.

The Role of Other Factors.   If the acquisition of spatial relations in the environment requires central information processing, instructions to learn should lead to better acquisition than no instructions. However, this was only partially supported in Lindberg and Gärling (1983). The important role of central information processing is however not ruled out even if instructions to learn are not necessary. The allocation of processing capacity may be automated, but not the

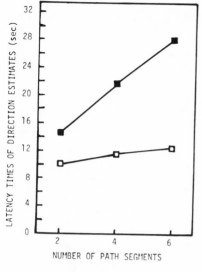

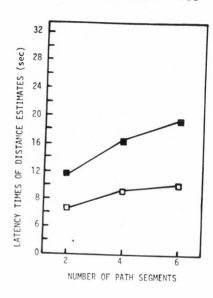

■ Concurrent task

□ No concurrent task

FIG. 6.4. Latency times of estimates of directions and distances to reference points. (After Lindberg & Gärling, 1981a.)

acquisition. For instance, a car driver is not always easy to engage in a conversation, however interesting it may be.

Does acquisition require much time? Two time parameters known to affect acquisition of verbal material are presentation rate and massed versus distributed presentation (Crowder, 1976). The effects of these factors were investigated in a field experiment conducted by the authors (Gärling et al., 1981). Presentation rate was varied by having half the subjects walk through an unfamiliar residential neighborhood accompanied by an experimenter (see Fig. 6.5), the other half were driven on the same path by car. Half of the subjects in each of these conditions were taken on three tours in the same session; the remaining subjects were taken on one tour in each of three sessions separated by one week. The directions and distances obtained from the estimates of the locations of designated targets along the path were regressed on the actual values. The calculated linear correlations averaged across subjects produced only slight, nonsignificant effects. This might have been due to the velocity difference between car riding and walking being too small (about 2 to 1). The fast acquisition and the marginal forgetting effects, which also were observed, probably further precluded a strong effect of massed versus distributed presentation. It also may be speculated that processing time under most ordinary circumstances is sufficient; the difficulty

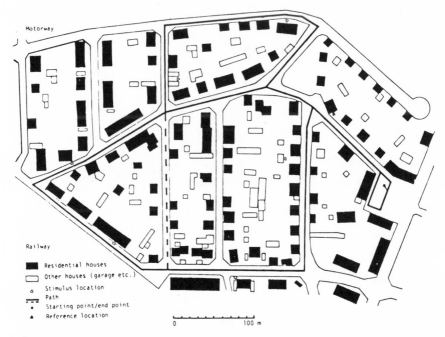

FIG. 6.5.   A residential neighborhood traversed by subjects learning its spatial layout. (From Gärling, Böök, Lindberg, & Nilsson, 1981, p. 266.)

arises when attention is diverted from the locomotion because of other attention-attracting stimuli.

In another similar field experiment subjects were taken on tours through an unfamiliar building complex (Gärling et al., 1983). Subjects whose sight was artificially restricted learned a number of designated target locations less quickly than subjects with unrestricted sight. These subjects could see no more than a few meters in front of them, whereas the building design allowed the remaining subjects to see through the building. The positive effect of "visual access" is substantiated by Evans, Fellows, Zorn, and Doty (1980) who found that way-finding improved if the interior walls in a building were color coded. Perhaps the effect is due to a reduced demand on central information processing capacity. In fact, Gärling, Mäntylä, and Säisä (1978) found that a distraction task affected blindfolded subjects more negatively than sighted subjects.

Individual differences in acquisition rate have been observed (Bryant, 1983; Kozlowski & Bryant, 1977). That subjects themselves are able to predict their performance in advance suggests that one source of these differences may be metacognitive. Subjects knowing that they have a poor "sense of direction" may choose another acquisition strategy than those who know they are good. Anxiety-proneness is another factor that may cause differences in acquisition (Bryant,

1982). Differences in the allocation of processing capacity and susceptibility to distractions are possible mediating factors in such cases.

MOVEMENT AND ORIENTATION

Definitions

The execution of travel plans requires that orientation is maintained in the environment. Orientation also entails a number of other important functions, such as keeping one's balance and localizing important objects, cars, or other people. Most of these functions are subsumed under the general functions of perception and interoception (Gibson, 1966, 1979). Reviews of the related research have been given in Epstein (1977), Howard, (1982), and Howard and Templeton (1966), and are only referred to briefly here.

The main focus in this section is orientation in the environment. The authors previously used the term "environmental orientation" to distinguish it from other classes of spatial orientation (Böök, 1981; Gärling, 1980). We define environmental orientation as the ability to perceive one's position relative to points or systems of reference in the environment. These points or systems of reference may be perceptually available but, for reasons which will be made clear below, this is not a necessary condition.

A hierarchy of orientation functions may tentatively be proposed. Body orientation is defined as the perception of the body axes relative to the line of gravity and of the limbs relative to the body axes (Gibson, 1966, 1979; Howard, 1982; Pick, 1976). At the next level, orientation is maintained in the environment relative to perceptually available reference systems. Visual direction and position constancy (Shebilske, 1977) as well as auditory localization are important here. Geographical orientation poses a special problem. Howard and Templeton (1966) define it as knowledge about the direction faced relative to compass directions. Baker (1980, 1981) assumes that a "magnetic sense" accomplishes this orientation function at a basic level, but the evidence is at best inconclusive (Zusne & Allen, 1981).

At the highest level of the hierarchy, orientation is maintained relative to points and systems of reference that may not be perceptually available. Geographical orientation could be considered a special case. Although compass directions are certainly one of the systems of reference, there are other, perhaps more important ones (the walls in a room, the streets in a town, etc.). Information about the compass directions need not be directly perceptually available as Baker (1980, 1981) have suggested. Other indirect information sources, such as maps, signs, and the sun, are available.

It should be emphasized that orientation is defined as the perception of one's position relative to the environment. For instance, space perception refers to the perception of the locations of objects, surfaces, and so forth in the environment, relative to oneself (Gibson, 1950). The distinction is admittedly somewhat subtle but resembles the distinction made by Sadalla, Burroughs, and Staplin (1980) between points of reference and targets localized in relation to them. The ego is the "target" which in orientation is localized relative to points (or systems) of reference in the environment; in space perception the ego is the reference point in relation to which objects and so on are localized. The contention here is that reference points, in addition to functioning as the spatially organizing elements of the cognitive map, are those properties of the environment in relation to which environmental orientation is maintained. The definition of reference points or systems of reference as not necessarily being perceptually available derives its meaning from this assumption. The reference points are cognitively available, even though they are not perceptually available all the time.

The distinction being made between space perception and environmental orientation does not mean that there are no points of communality. Gibson (1950, 1966, 1979) points out that in space perception we perceive the "visual world" rather than the small segment defined by the momentary field of view. He also discusses the bearing of this fact on our perception of objects and so forth that are concealed by other objects. More recently, Attneave and associates (Attneave & Farrar, 1977; Attneave & Pierce, 1978) empirically demonstrated the validity of Gibson's notion. They found no important differences whether objects to be localized were in view or out of view after having been in view. This similarity is not likely to hold across the full spatial scale however. It is not implied that distant towns are localized in the same way as nearby objects (Ryan & Ryan, 1940). Places in the immediate vicinity (i.e., places that would be possible to perceive had they not been concealed by obstacles) are more likely to comprise the reference points.

The assumed communality between environmental orientation and space perception has an implication that needs to be made explicit. This implication is that the imagined or cognitive space, exactly as the perceptual space, may be metric Euclidean. That is, to perceive one's position relative to, say, points of reference means to perceive the direction and distance to these points of reference. The perception may not under all circumstances be veridical. Moreover, there are exceptions. Maintaining orientation sometimes entails, for instance, knowing in which part of a town one is located. At other occasions, it entails knowing how to get from one place to another. Maintenance of orientation may in itself be a process at different levels, thus adding to the proposed hierarchy of orientation functions. Most research has been carried out at the level of environmental orientation discussed here. The following presentation focuses on this research.

Questions to be Answered

There are two questions that need to be considered in this section. First, how is orientation maintained in the environment? Second, how is maintenance of orientation interfaced with the execution of travel plans? The answer to the first question is presumably different depending on whether the environment is familiar or not. Therefore, these cases are treated separately. The second question has been provisionally answered in one of the preceding sections. After reviewing studies pertinent to the first question, the answer to the second question is elaborated.

Maintenance of Orientation in Unfamiliar Environments

Recognition would seem to serve an important role for orientation. Recognition of places is not possible unless the environment is to some extent familiar. Maps, sign posting, and other media may, however, play an important role for orientation in unfamiliar environments. The use of media in such cases is likely to involve recognition processes. Familiar examples are recognition of places specified by path descriptions, translating symbols in maps to the environment, and so forth.

That maintenance of orientation is a nearly continuous process of monitoring position seems to be less recognized. Although the process may be at work when no movement is executed, for example when waking up in the middle of the night in an unfamiliar hotel room and knowing directly where the window is located, monitoring position while moving is certainly more critical.

Early studies examined the role of the vestibular system for the monitoring of movement (Liebig, 1933; Worchel, 1952), without any definite conclusions (Howard & Templeton, 1966). Monitoring movement is more difficult for divers under water than for people on land (Ross, Dickinson, & Jupp, 1970). A number of other factors affecting performance were investigated in a study that also involved comparisons between sighted, congenitally blind, and accidentally blinded subjects (Juurmaa & Suonio, 1975). Auditory cues were found to be important for orientation, more for the blind than for the sighted subjects. If the path did not contain many direction changes, active locomotion was found to lead to better performance than passive locomotion. Interfering by stopping the subjects during walking had no effect.

Monitoring movement is unlikely to be a completely automated process. Therefore, Böök and Gärling (Böök, 1981; Böök & Gärling, 1980a, 1980b, 1981a, 1981b) raised the question of to what extent central information processing demands account for the above results. That central information processing is important is compatible with the fact that brain disorders appear to impair performance (Byrne, 1982; Potegal, 1971, 1972).

Böök and Gärling (1980a, 1980b, 1981a, 1981b) assumed that monitoring movement requires recurrent central processing of information received through different sensory systems about locomotion distances and direction changes. The subject encodes the sensory information in short-term working memory as unitary codes corresponding to the distances and direction changes, further processes the information by computationlike operations (coordination of the memory codes) resulting in information about position of self relative to reference points and, finally, decodes this information as a perception of position relative to the reference points.

In order to study the type of central information processing assumed to take place, Böök, Gärling, and Lindberg (1975) presented subjects numerical values corresponding to simple locomotion paths and required the subjects to infer the location of the starting point from the end point. The results suggested that spatial imagery processes played a crucial role for performance, but Juurmaa and Suonio (1975) argued against that. Gärling, Böök, and Lindberg (1976a, 1976b) subsequently found performance differences depending on whether the subjects only imagined walking or actually walked, and that spatial imagery may play a lesser role in the latter case.

Böök and Gärling (1980a, 1980b, 1981a) had subjects walk pathways laid out on the floor in a large dark room, following a moving line of light as closely as possible. Böök and Gärling (1980a) had subjects walk two straight path segments at an angle to each other. The length of the segments was varied from 5 to about 8 meters, the angle in between was 45°, 90°, or 135°. The walking speed was 1.12 m/sec. When arriving at the end point, the subjects gave numerical estimates of the direction and distance to the starting point. The main finding of the study was that a concurrently performed backwards counting task impaired performance. The latency times of the estimates were longer and the errors in the estimates were larger. The results were interpreted to support the hypothesis that monitoring movement requires central information processing.

The subjects in the study referred to performed at a fairly high level, even though they counted backwards. To account for this, Böök and Gärling (1980b) assumed that the subjects were able to postpone the coordination and decoding operations until they reached the stopping point and were no longer required to count backwards. That the subjects were less accurate than those subjects not counting backwards was explained by the effect of forgetting the codes of distance and direction that needed to be retained in short-term memory. The difference between actual walking and a condition in which walking is imagined may at least partly be due to the fact that in the former condition the processing is recurrent; in the latter it is postponed exactly as when subjects are prevented from recurrent processing when actually walking.

If subjects update their position relative to reference points recurrently while walking, there should be marginal negative effects of forgetting. Subjects still make errors however. Böök (1981) suggested that each coordination and decoding takes a nontrivial amount of time, that during coordination and decoding, subjects are prevented from encoding information about how far they have walked and, finally, that the process is outcome-dependent, i.e., each coordination uses the outcome of the immediately preceding coordination. For simplicity, one can further assume that the coordination/decoding instances take on average an equally long time and that they are evenly distributed along the locomotion path. As Fig. 6.6 is intended to show, these assumptions lead to the prediction that subjects will produce a proportional displacement of the reference point (target) in the same direction as the subject walks.

The results of Böök and Gärling (1981a) verified the prediction illustrated in Fig. 6.6. In this study subjects in a dark room were directed to a starting point, shown a target consisting of a point light on the floor, and required to walk straight at a constant speed following the moving light line. There were several stopping points from which the direction and distance to the target, by then out of sight, were estimated. The data from two experiments are displayed in Fig. 6.7. The experiments differed only with respect to whether the direction or the distance to the target from the starting point was varied. The direction and distance estimates that the subjects made were converted to subjective target locations, and the displacements of these relative to the actual locations were measured. The displacements are, as may be seen, substantial and nearly proportional to the distance walked. The displacements furthermore are in the direction of walking (indicated by positive values of Y in Fig. 6.7) and slightly away from the pathway (positive values of X).

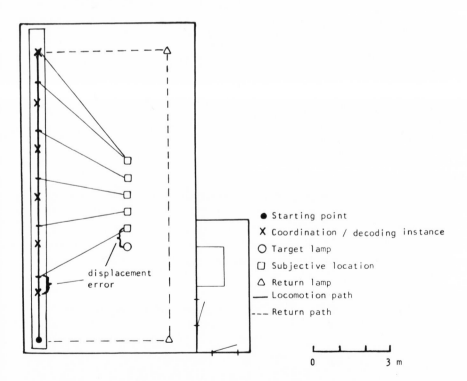

FIG. 6.6.   Predicted errors of displacement in monitoring movement.

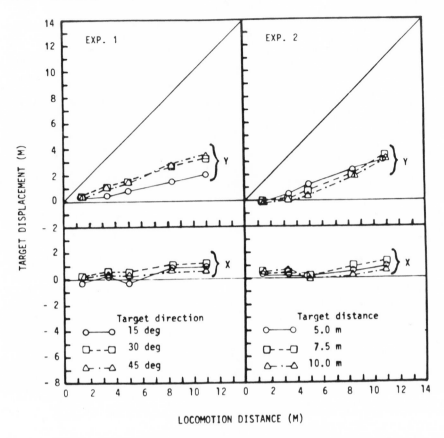

FIG. 6.7.   Displacement errors in monitoring movement observed in two experiments. (From Böök & Gärling, 1981a, p. 1005.)

Böök (1981) reports some further support for his account of the errors the subjects make in monitoring movement. In particular, he found that increasing the speed of walking increased the errors. A paradox should also be mentioned. If subjects postpone the coordination/decoding, forgetting causes errors. However, if they do not, errors still result because of recurrent processing, and, indeed, the more frequent the processing, the larger the errors. The solution to these seemingly paradoxical assumptions is that both factors need to be taken into account. If the frequency of recurrent processing is increased, forgetting is counteracted. Thus there should be an optimal level of recurrent processing that minimizes the errors.

The reviewed research on monitoring movement is certainly limited in scope. In particular, the use of small-scale spaces and the neglect of vision are the most serious limitations. Gärling et al. (1983), in a study already referred to, found that restricting the subjects' sight impaired learning and orientation in a building complex. A hypothesis to account for this result may be offered here. The hypothesis rests on the assumption that one's position relative to reference points can be inferred from transformations of the perspectives of visual scenes. When entering the building, the subjects perceive configurations of objects at a distance. When walking through the building, the same scenes (configurations of objects) may be seen from other perspectives. The perspective transformations carry information about the subjects' changed positions. The situation is very similar to the conditions for visual proprioception (Gibson, 1950, 1966, 1979), although the perspective transformations are noncontinuous since there are concealing objects. Therefore, it seems necessary that the perspective information is retained in memory. A critical factor for accuracy in inferring changed position then appears to be how much information must be retained and for how long.

To summarize, maintenance of orientation in environments that are unfamiliar has been assumed here to depend mainly on monitoring movement. Monitoring movement, in turn, relies on central information processing as well as the reception of different kinds of sensory information, auditory, proprioceptive/tactual, vestibular, and visual. Furthermore, there are three different ways in which the information is processed. First, people may process information about their own movement recurrently, taking into account how far they have walked when inferring the change of position. Second, if recurrent processing is interfered with, people may manage to infer the change of position by reconstructing how they have moved. Third, changes in position can be inferred from transformations of the perspectives of visual scenes. The first and second methods have been carefully studied, which however is not the case with the third method. This method is similar to visual proprioception but differs in that the perspective transformations of the visual array, from which inferences are made, are noncontinuous. Therefore, the inferences rely on temporary and permanent storage of perspective information. The efficiency of the method depends on the limitations imposed by the memory storage systems.

Maintenance of Orientation in Familiar Environments

Most studies of cognitive mapping should bear on the question of how orientation is maintained in familiar environments. Their relevance is, however, in most cases only indirect because in these studies subjects have been interviewed in a neutral setting rather than being requested to demonstrate how they use the cognitive map for navigation and orientation (Evans, 1980).

It is plausible to assume that recognition plays a more important role for orientation in familiar environments. Reference points presumably are recognized so that their spatial relations to other reference points stored in the cognitive map become available. Systems of reference also are likely to be employed more often than single points of reference, because the points of reference are spatially interrelated in the cognitive map. Monitoring movement may still play a role. Few environments are altogether familiar, and there are sometimes extreme conditions, such as darkness, fog, or noise, making monitoring movement necessary.

Lindberg and Gärling (1983) found that subjects distracted by a concurrent task estimated the locations of reference points better after they had been taken on several tours through an environment. Since a concurrent task interferes with monitoring movement, and since a similar effect was found for sighted but not for blindfolded subjects (Lindberg & Gärling, 1981a), recognition of places probably played the important role that has been ascribed to it here.

One problem, mentioned in a preceding section, concerns the "keying" of the cognitive map to features of the environment. It probably entails identifying systems of reference in particular places, which may or may not be coordinated into a more global system. In any case, the identified system of reference should facilitate the use of the spatial relations in the cognitive map for localizing oneself in relation to points or systems of reference not in view.

Maintenance of Orientation and the Execution of Travel Plans

Neisser (1976) favors the term "orienting schema" to cognitive map in order to emphasize "that it is an active, information-seeking structure" (p. 111). An orienting schema not only serves the function of maintaining orientation in the environment but makes possible predictions (or anticipation) of features of the environment.

To predict where one is going is, according to the views advocated here, an important part of monitoring the execution of travel plans. The reference points assumed to be stored in the cognitive map as parts of travel plans may function as retrieval cues for spatial relations. A simple example is that the direction (and distance) from one identified reference point in the environment to another toward which one is heading should be retrievable from the cognitive map. Knowing directions may be all that is needed to work out instructions for how to travel. Monitoring movement when executing the instructions is another necessary condition for the successful execution of the travel plan. If the environment is very familiar, the number of identifiable reference points is likely to help the traveller to the point where monitoring movement is superfluous; the anticipation of the locations of reference points not in view and the formation of travel instructions may be automated to the point where he is no longer consciously aware of these processes being carried out.

Passini (1977, 1980a, 1980b) had subjects walk to a number of destinations in a building and asked them to think aloud when walking. Notwithstanding the methodological problems inherent in the think-aloud technique in this context and the fact that few subjects, understandably, were used, the results were clearly informative. Passini analyzed wayfinding as decision trees focusing on what important information went into decisions at different levels. His main interest was in identifying difficulties people have, such as remembering information accessed from maps. He also provides a valuable conceptual framework by which the formation and execution of travel plans and the accessing of information from the environment, the cognitive map, and media may be analyzed in real-life settings. One conclusion that can be drawn is that, at least in unfamiliar environments, planning and execution of travel plans are interwoven, perhaps to an even larger extent than the present discussion has assumed.

RELATED EVERYDAY COGNITIVE SKILLS

The Spatiotemporal Sequencing of Everyday Actions

Viewed from a macroperspective our daily lives consist of action sequences. As a psychologist, one delimits particular types of actions for study. Actions may then be theoretically described as realizations of hierarchical plans with strategic and tactic components (Miller, Galanter, & Pribram, 1960). When the focus is on single actions some important issues, however, are ignored. One such issue is the *spatiotemporal sequencing* of our everyday activities.

Observations of an individual over a period of time should result in a record of places visited, the type and duration of actions executed in each place, and the temporal ordering of the places and the actions. This action sequence is certainly not the result of a random process but should be viewed from the perspective of a cognitively active, thinking person who tries to make sense of his or her daily life. How physical restrictions, temporal and spatial constraints, and cognitive factors interact in producing action sequences are fundamental questions to pose, particularly for environmental psychologists.

Which are the cognitive skills required for the purposeful execution of action sequences? Actions are here defined as behavior preceded by decisions. Thus the units of analysis are decision-action pairs. Decisions to do something and actually doing it need not however be temporally contiguous events. Execution may be postponed because it is interrupted by other decisions and/or actions. Thus, an important aspect of the decisions is *when* to carry out actions. Moreover, actions can only occur in certain locations. Therefore, a second important aspect is *where* to carry out the action. These decisions must be stored in memory for later realization. The higher-order organization of the sequence of action decisions is likely to be the result of a planning process.

The fundamental cognitive activity in sequencing everyday actions is the planning of a set of decisions with respect to where and when to do what. Goals and physical, spatial, and temporal constraints must be taken into account. As has been argued before, an important class of actions are possible errands. A spatio-temporally integrated action sequence in such cases has been assumed to rely on a completed travel plan. The formation of the travel plan, the cognitive skills it requires, and the required organization of the cognitive skills have been investigated by the authors.

The Formation of Travel Plans

In forming a travel plan, the task is first to decide on a subset of errands given certain constraints. Already at this stage spatial criteria are clearly involved. An errand may be excluded because there is no place known to the planning individual where it can be carried out; a known place may be too far off given the other places to be visited and the present location. Such rejections may rely on information retrieved from the cognitive map, so if they are rational or not depends on the accuracy of the memory representation. The skill in selecting subsets of errands possible to execute for given space-time constraints should be open to experimental investigation. A related skill is to select specific places from optional ones for a given set of errands. A study of this skill may reveal not only inadequacies of the cognitive map people have of their towns, but also difficulties people have in finding the optimal set of places despite the fact that knowledge is independently shown to be accurate.

Knowing which errands to run and which places to visit, one must decide on the order in which to visit the places. The order may be constrained by spatio-temporal criteria but there are also other factors. Some errands must precede others, as, for instance, it may be necessary to cash a check at the bank before going into a shop to buy goods. The cost of traveling may sometimes make spatial criteria dominate temporal. In still other circumstances, spatio-temporal criteria may be of no consequence for the fulfillment of the goal of the travel plan.

A travel plan has been assumed to be fragmented, consisting mainly of an order in which to visit a set of places. How then is this order generated given that distance shall be minimized? In a series of experiments by Jouko Säisä and the authors (Gärling et al., 1984), subjects were requested to solve a "prototypical" planning task. In the Long-Term Memory condition (LTM), this task consisted of presenting the subjects the names of from three to six well-known places in the town in which they lived. A location was defined, and the subjects were asked to report as fast as possible the order in which to visit the places that would minimize travel distance. The results of one experiment suggested that the process proceeded in two stages; first, the order that minimized direct (crowflight) distance was decided on, then, the path in between was decided on. In each stage, information about the environment was accessed from the cognitive map.

The results also indicated, however, that the subjects were not always able to find the order that minimized overall distance. This is indicated in Table 6.1 showing the proportions of cases in which the correct solution was found. Two

TABLE 6.1
Mean Proportions Correct Solutions to a "Prototypical" Travel
Planning Problem (After Gärling, Böök, Lindberg, & Säisä, 1984)

Condition	Set Size (Number of Items)			
	3	4	5	6
Perception (N:12)	.94 (.94[a])	.99 (.82)	.87 (.74)	.83 (.56)
Short-Term Memory (N:12)	.88 (.88)	.88 (.68)	.56 (.47)	.32 (.36)
Long-Term Memory (N:12)	.92 (.92)	.77 (.66)	.51 (.41)	.35 (.22)

[a]The values reported within the parentheses are mean proportions of cases in which the subjects minimized distance locally rather than globally as they were told to do. This "locally-minimizing-distance" heuristic leads to the following proportions of orders between the places that minimize overall distance: 1.00, .83, .83, and .67 in the Perception and Short-Term Memory conditions, 1.00, .67, .50, and .33 in the Long-Term Memory condition.

additional conditions are reported in the table. In the Perception condition (P) the subjects were presented letters in different locations on a computer screen. The same letters were presented in the Short-Term Memory condition (STM) but the subjects were required to retain the information in memory for a short period of time while they figured out the solution. The subjects' task in these conditions was the same as in the Long-Term Memory condition, i.e., to report the order of the locations that would minimize overall distance.

It appeared that the subjects minimized distance locally rather than globally. That is, from each place the subjects selected the nearest one until they found the complete order. This "locally-minimizing-distance" heuristic leads to correct or nearly correct solutions in many cases, and its realization may require less skill than many other methods of solving the problem. Table 6.1 provides partial support for this hypothesis, which was corroborated by the results of two further experiments in the same study.

Another noteworthy finding was that the latency times differed regularly among the conditions, as shown in Fig. 6.8. It was argued that the longer latency times in the Long-Term Memory condition were in part due to the time it takes to retrieve information from the cognitive map, in part due to a different way of realizing the heuristic. In that condition the short-term memory representation of the information about the locations of the places was probably not simultaneous. Therefore, pairwise comparisons of the distances to the different places had to be made. In contrast, in the Perception condition the locations could be perceived directly, while in the Short-Term Memory condition they could be retained simultaneously in short-term memory. This result is another example of differences in the memory representations of information accessed from media as compared to information retrieved from the cognitive map of a real environment

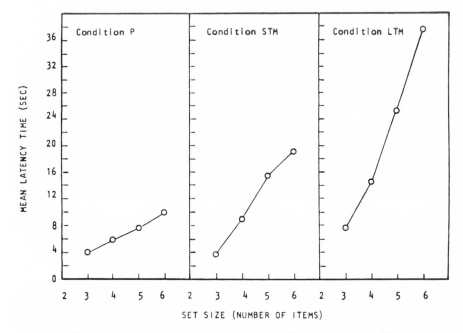

FIG. 6.8.   Latency times obtained in a ''prototypical'' travel planning problem.
(After Gärling, Böök, Lindberg, & Säisä, 1982.)

(Evans & Pezdek, 1980; Hintzman et al., 1981; Howard & Kerst, 1981). The critical factor however, at least in the present case, may not be a qualitative difference (i.e., different formats) but simply a quantitative difference. Because more information needed to be held in short-term memory in the Long-Term Memory condition, the storage capacity may have been exceeded. This overload resulted in a qualitatively different realization of the heuristic used to solve the planning task. Whether the assumption about a quantitative rather than a qualitative difference in the short-term memory representation turns out to be generally true remains to be seen.

The discussion has proceeded as if planning is a unidirectional process. The stages enumerated are ordered according to logical necessity. This does not preclude the possibility for revisions and back-tracking. Multidirectionality may, as Hayes-Roth and Hayes-Roth (1979) have assumed, be the rule rather than an exception. The empirical support for this position, however, is limited. Hayes-Roth and Hayes-Roth provided subjects with a map of a fictitious town, asking them to form a plan for how to run a number of errands. That the subjects made quite a number of discoveries during development of their plans is not surprising. Neither is it surprising that these discoveries were used to revise the plan since no speed requirements were imposed. This process of multidirectional or opportunistic planning may more resemble the execution of travel plans in environments that are only partly known. In this chapter it has been assumed that the execution and planning are interwoven, thus the views expressed by Hayes-Roth and Hayes-Roth (1979) are not necessarily contradicted.

CONCLUSIONS

This chapter has dealt with adults' everyday spatial cognition in relation to the large-scale and medium-scale physical environment. Research on the cognitive maps acquired by people of the place in which they live, how these cognitive maps are acquired, and how they are used in forming travel plans and in maintaining orientation while executing these travel plans have been reviewed. Several hypotheses and suggestions have been offered to fill in gaps in our understanding of these topics. Before drawing any general conclusions from the review, some limitations of the present treatment need to be pointed out.

Beginning with the book by Lynch (1960), quite a number of publications have been issued. However, the area has not been researched extensively for much more than 10 years. Furthermore, because the investigators come from many different fields, such as architecture and urban design, geography, cognitive, developmental, and environmental psychology, zoology, and computer science, there is little cross-referencing. Many studies therefore appear to be unintended replications of each other. Knowledge has thus not accumulated as it should have, given the amount of effort being invested. The present discussion must be viewed in light of this short history of extensive research on cognitive mapping; much of what has been said is by no means as definite as the authors would like it to be. Many statements are no more than suggestions for further research.

Psychologists undoubtedly knew about spatial cognition long before 1960 when Lynch published his book. Tests of spatial ability are in fact part of any standard battery of intelligence tests (Sternberg, 1977). Spatial cognition evidently is involved in many nonspatial reasoning tasks, job performances, and the like. This type of everyday cognition is beyond the scope of the present chapter.

Another limitation is that small-scale space has been largely excluded from consideration. Some references have been made, but the main bulk of studies, primarily concerned with visual attention processes (e.g., Howard, 1982; Shebilske, 1977), have been excluded. There is also interesting work concerned with schemata in such cases (e.g., Brewer & Treyens, 1981; Hochberg, 1970).

In conclusion, a few points should be made. First, a valid conceptualization of the real world is essential for our understanding of the cognitive mapping of large-scale and medium-scale environments. The conceptualization offered here has not been refuted by the few studies that are pertinent. The details still need to be worked out, however, and revisions may need to be made. Second, the information-processing approach appears to be a viable framework for approaching many of the problems raised. In particular, the role of central information processing has been found to be important, and further research may, as has been alluded to, demonstrate an even more important role. Third, and finally, the cognitive map, whether analogous to a map or not, has been found to be a highly dynamic long-term memory representation, which may be both analog and propositional in format. It is also a short-term memory representation of verbal, perceptual, and spatial information. Any attempt to take a more simplistic view of the cognitive map is probably doomed to fail.

REFERENCES

Acredolo, L. P.. Frames of reference used by children for orientation in unfamiliar spaces. In G. T. Moore & R. G. Golledge (Eds.), *Environmental knowing.* Stroudsburg, PA: Dowden, Hutchinson, & Ross, 1976.

Acredolo, L. P. Developmental changes in the ability to coordinate perspectives of a large-scale space. *Developmental Psychology,* 1977, *13,* 1–8.

Acredolo, L. P. Development of spatial orientation in infancy. *Developmental Psychology,* 1978, *14,* 224–234.

Acredolo, L. P., Pick, H. L., & Olsen, M. G. Environmental differentiation and familiarity as determinants of children's memory for spatial location. *Developmental Psychology,* 1975, *11,* 495–501.

Allen, G. L. A developmental perspective on the effects of "subdividing" macrospatial experience. *Journal of Experimental Psychology: Human Learning and Memory,* 1981, *7,* 120–132.

Allen, G. L., Siegel, A. W., & Rosinski, R. R. The role of perceptual context in structuring spatial knowledge. *Journal of Experimental Psychology: Human Learning and Memory,* 1978, *4,* 617–630.

Anderson, J. R., & Bower, G. H. *Human associative memory.* Washington, DC: Winston, 1973.

Appleyard, D. Why buildings are known: A predictive tool for architects. *Environment and Behavior,* 1969, *1,* 131–156.

Appleyard, D. Styles and methods of structuring a city. *Environment and Behavior,* 1970, *2,* 100–117.

Atkinson, R. C., & Shiffrin, R. M. Human memory: A proposed system and its control processes. In K. W. Spence & J. R. Spence (Eds.), *The psychology of learning and motivation: Advances in research and theory* (Vol. 2). New York: Academic Press, 1968.

Attneave, F., & Farrar, P. The visual world behind the head. *American Journal of Psychology,* 1977, *90,* 549–563.

Attneave, F., & Pierce, C. R. Accuracy of extrapolating a pointer into perceived and imagined space. *American Journal of Psychology,* 1978, *91,* 371–387.

Bahrick, H. P. Maintenance of knowledge: Questions about memory we forgot to ask. *Journal of Experimental Psychology: General,* 1979, *108,* 296–308.

Baird, J. C. Studies of the cognitive representation of spatial relation: I. Overview. *Journal of Experimental Psychology: General,* 1979, *108,* 90–91.

Baker, R. R. Goal orientation by blindfolded humans after long-distance displacement; possible involvement of a magnetic sense. *Science,* 1980, *210,* 555–557.

Baker, R. R. *Human navigation and the sixth sense.* London: Hodder & Stoughton, 1981.

Beck, R. J., & Wood, D. Cognitive transformation of information from urban geographic fields to mental maps. *Environment and Behavior,* 1976, *8,* 199–238.

Bell, P. A., Fisher, J. D., & Loomis, R. J. *Environmental psychology.* Philadelphia: Saunders, 1978.

Binet, M. A. Reverse illusions of orientation. *Psychological Review*, 1894, *1*, 337–350.

Blaut, J. M., McCleary, G. F., & Blaut, A. S. Environmental mapping in young children. *Environment and Behavior*, 1970, *2*, 335–349.

Böök, A. Maintenance of environmental orientation during locomotion. (Doctoral Dissertation, Department of Psychology, University of Umeå, Umeå, Sweden, 1981), *Umeå Psychological Reports Supplement Series No. 8*, 1981.

Böök, A., & Gärling, T. Processing of information about location during locomotion: Effects of a concurrent task and locomotion patterns. *Scandinavian Journal of Psychology*, 1980, *21*, 185–192. (a)

Böök, A., & Gärling, T. Processing of information about location during locomotion: Effects of amount of visual information about the locomotor pattern. *Perceptual and Motor Skills*, 1980, *51*, 231–238. (b)

Böök, A., & Gärling, T. Maintenance of orientation during locomotion in unfamiliar environments. *Journal of Experimental Psychology: Human Perception and Performance*, 1981, *7*, 995–1006. (a)

Böök, A., & Gärling, T. Maintenance of environmental orientation during body rotation. *Perceptual and Motor Skills*, 1981, *52*, 583–589. (b)

Böök, A., Gärling, T., & Lindberg, E. Speed and accuracy of orientation performance in verbally presented two-segment route tasks as a function of direction of routes, length of route segments, and angle of turn. *Umeå Psychological Reports No. 92*, 1975.

Brewer, W. F., & Treyens, J. C. Role of schemata in memory for places. *Cognitive Psychology*, 1981, *13*, 207–230.

Bryant, K. J. Personality correlates to geographic orientation. *Journal of Personality and Social Psychology*, 1982, *43*, 1318–1324.

Byrne, R. W. Memory for urban geography. *Quarterly Journal of Experimental Psychology*, 1979, *31*, 147–154.

Byrne, R. W. Geographical knowledge and orientation. In Ellis, A. (Ed.), *Normality and pathology in cognitive functions*. New York: Academic Press, 1982.

Cadwallader, M. Problems in cognitive distance. *Environment and Behavior*, 1979, *11*, 559–576.

Canter, D. V. *The psychology of place.* London: Architectural Press, 1977.

Canter, D. V., & Craik, K. H. Environmental psychology. *Journal of Environmental Psychology*, 1981, *1*, 1–11.

Canter, D. V., & Tagg, S. K. Distance estimation in cities. *Environment and Behavior*, 1975, *7*, 59–80.

Carlstein, T., Parkes, D., & Thrift, N. (Eds.). *Timing space and spacing time* (Vol. 2). London: Arnold, 1978.

Collins, A. M., & Loftus, E. F. A spreading-activation theory of semantic memory. *Psychological Review*, 1975, *82*, 407–428.

Cooper, L. A., & Shepard, R. N. Transformations on representations of objects in space. In E. C. Carterette & M. P. Friedman (Eds.), *Handbook of perception* (Vol. 8). New York: Academic Press, 1978.

Craik, F. I. M. Human memory. *Annual Review of Psychology*, 1979, *30*, 63–102.

Craik, F. I. M., & Lockhart, R. S. Levels of processing: A framework for memory research. *Journal of Verbal Learning and Verbal Behavior*, 1972, *11*, 671–684.

Craik, K. H. Environmental psychology. *Annual Review of Psychology*, 1973, *24*, 402–422.

Crane, P. M. Acquisition of spatial representations for large environments. (Doctoral Dissertation, University of Miami, 1977). *Dissertation Abstracts International*, 1978, *38(B)*, 4501.

Crowder, R. G. *Principles of learning and memory.* Hillsdale, NJ: Lawrence Erlbaum Associates, 1976.

DeJonge, D. Images of urban areas: Their structure and psychological foundations. *Journal of American Institute of Planners*, 1962, *28*, 266–276.

Epstein, W. (Ed.). *Stability and constancy in visual perception*. New York: Wiley, 1977.

Evans, G. W. Environmental cognition. *Psychological Bulletin*, 1980, *88*, 259–287.

Evans, G. W., & Pezdek, K. Cognitive mapping: Knowledge of real-world distance and location information. *Journal of Experimental Psychology: Human Learning and Memory*, 1980, *6*, 13–24.

Evans, G. W., Marrero, D., & Butler, P. Environmental learning and cognitive mapping. *Environment and Behavior*, 1981, *13*, 83–104.

Evans, G. W., Fellows, J., Zorn, M., & Doty, K. Cognitive mapping and architecture. *Journal of Applied Psychology*, 1980, *65*, 474–478.

Finke, R. A. Levels of equivalence in imagery and perception. *Psychological Review*, 1980, *87*, 113–132.

Foos, P. W. Constructing cognitive maps from sentences. *Journal of Experimental Psychology: Human Learning and Memory*, 1980, *6*, 25–38.

Gärling, T. *Environmental orientation during locomotion: Experimental studies of human processing of information about the spatial layout of the environment* (Document D24:1980). Stockholm: The Swedish Council for Building Research, 1980.

Gärling, T., Böök, A., & Ergezen, N. Memory for the spatial layout of the everyday physical environment: Differential rates of acquisition of different types of information. *Scandinavian Journal of Psychology*, 1982, *23*, 23–35.

Gärling, T., Böök, A., & Lindberg, E. Note on speed and accuracy of individual performance in geographical orientation tasks for different modes of presentation. *Umeå Psychological Reports No. 105*, 1976. (a)

Gärling, T., Böök, A., & Lindberg, E. Speed and accuracy of orientation performance in verbally presented two-segment route tasks as a function of route configuration, type and order of presentation of information about route segments. *Umeå Psychological Reports No. 106*, 1976. (b)

Gärling, T., Böök, A., & Lindberg, E. The acquisition and use of an internal representation of the spatial layout of the environment during locomotion. *Man-Environment Systems*, 1979, *9*, 200–208.

Gärling, T., Böök, A., & Lindberg, E. Cognitive mapping of large-scale environment: The interrelationship of action plans, acquisition, and orientation. *Environment and Behavior*, 1984, *16*, 3–34.

Gärling, T., Lindberg, E., & Mäntylä, T. Orientation in buildings: Effects of familiarity, visual access, and orientation aids. *Journal of Applied Psychology*, 1983, *68*, 177–186.

Gärling, T., Mäntylä, T., & Säisä, J. The importance of vision during locomotion for the acquisition of an internal representation of the spatial layout of large-scale environments: Blindfolded and sighted car passengers with and without a distracting task learning to localize invisible targets during a town route. *Umeå Psychological Reports No. 147*, 1978.

Gärling, T., Böök, A., Lindberg, E., & Nilsson, T. Memory for the spatial layout of the everyday physical environment: Factors affecting rate of acquisition. *Journal of Environmental Psychology*, 1981, *1*, 263–277.

Gärling, T., Böök, A., Lindberg, E., & Säisä, J. The spatio-temporal sequencing of everyday activities in large-scale environments. Unpublished manuscript, Department of Psychology, University of Umeå, 1984.

Gibson, J. J. *The perception of the visual world*. Boston: Houghton & Mifflin, 1950.

Gibson, J. J. *The senses considered as perceptual systems*. Boston: Houghton & Mifflin, 1966.

Gibson, J. J. *The ecological approach to visual perception*. Boston: Houghton & Mifflin, 1979.

Golledge, R. G. Methods and methodological issues in environmental cognition research. In G. T. Moore & R. G. Golledge (Eds.), *Environmental knowing*. Stroudsburg, PA: Dowden, Hutchinson & Ross, 1976.

Golledge, R. G. Multidimensional analysis in the study of environmental behavior and environmental design. In I. Altman & J. Wohlwill (Eds.), *Human behavior and environment* (Vol. 2). New York: Plenum Press, 1977.

Golledge, R., Briggs, R., & Demko, D. The configuration of distances in intraurban space. *Proceedings of the Association of American Geographers,* 1969, *1,* 60–65.

Gulick, J. Images of an arab city. *Journal of the American Institute of Planners, 1963, 22,* 179–198.

Hart, R. A., & Moore, G. T. The development of spatial cognition: A review. In R. M. Downs & D. Stea (Eds.), *Image and environment.* London: Arnold, 1973.

Hays-Roth, B., & Hays-Roth, F. A cognitive model of planning. *Cognitive Science,* 1979, *3,* 275–310.

Heft, H. The role of environmental features in route-learning: Two exploratory studies of wayfinding. *Environmental Psychology and Nonverbal Behavior,* 1979, *3,* 172–185.

Herman, J. F., Kail, R. V., & Siegel, A. W. Cognitive maps of a college campus: A new look at freshman orientation. *Bulletin of the Psychonomic Society,* 1979, *13,* 183–186.

Hintzman, D. L., O'Dell, C. S., & Arndt, D. R. Orientation in cognitive maps. *Cognitive Psychology,* 1981, *13,* 149–206.

Hochberg, J. Attention, organization and consciousness. In D. I. Mostofsky (Ed.), *Attention: Contemporary theory and analysis.* New York: Appleton-Century-Crofts, 1970.

Howard, I. P. *Human visual orientation.* New York: Wiley, 1982.

Howard, I. P., & Templeton, W. B. *Human spatial orientation.* New York: Wiley, 1966.

Howard, J. H., & Kerst, S. M. Memory and perception of cartographic information for familiar and unfamiliar environments. *Human Factors,* 1981, *23,* 495–504.

Juurmaa, J., & Suonio, K. The role of audition and motion in the spatial orientation of the blind and the sighted. *Scandinavian Journal of Psychology,* 1975, *16,* 209–216.

Kahneman, D. *Attention and effort.* Englewood Cliffs, NJ: Prentice-Hall, 1973.

Kellogg, R. T. Is conscious attention necessary for long-term storage? *Journal of Experimental Psychology: Human Learning and Memory,* 1980, *6,* 379–390.

Klatzky, R. L. *Human memory* (2nd ed.). San Francisco: Freeman, 1980.

Kosslyn, S. M. *Image and mind.* Cambridge, MA: Harvard University Press, 1980.

Kosslyn, S. M., & Schwartz, S. P. A simulation of visual imagery. *Cognitive Science,* 1977, *1,* 265–295.

Kozlowski, L. T., & Bryant, K. J. Sense of direction, spatial orientation, and cognitive maps. *Journal of Experimental Psychology: Human Perception and Performance,* 1977, *3,* 590–598.

Kuipers, B. Modeling spatial knowledge. *Cognitive Science,* 1978, *2,* 129–153.

Kuipers, B. The ''map in the head'' metaphor. *Environment and Behavior,* 1982, *14,* 202–220.

Leff, H. L. *Experience, environment, and human potentials.* New York: Oxford University Press, 1978.

Leff, H. L., & Gordon, L. R. Environmental cognitive sets: A longitudinal study. *Environment and Behavior,* 1979, *11,* 219–327.

Leff, H. L., Gordon, L. R., & Ferguson, J. G. Cognitive set and awareness. *Environment and Behavior,* 1974, *6,* 395–447.

Levine, M. You-are-here maps: Psychological considerations. *Environment and Behavior,* 1982, *14,* 221–237.

Liebig, F. G. Über unsere Orientierung im Raume bei Ausschluss der Augen. *Zeitschrift Sinnesphysiologi,* 1933, *64,* 251–282.

Lindberg, E., & Gärling, T. Speed and accuracy of performance in geographical orientation tasks for different modes of presentation of information about routes as a function of number of route segments. *Umeå Psychological Reports No. 111,* 1977. (a)

Lindberg, E., & Gärling, T. Performance in verbally presented geographical orientation tasks for different induced information processing strategies as a function of number of route segments. *Umeå Psychological Reports No. 112,* 1977. (b)

Lindberg, E., & Gärling, T. Acquisition of locational information about reference points during blindfolded and sighted locomotion: Effects of a concurrent task and locomotion paths. *Scandinavian Journal of Psychology*, 1981, *22*, 101–108. (a)

Lindberg, E., & Gärling, T. Acquisition of locational information about reference points during locomotion with and without a concurrent task: Effects of number of reference points. *Scandinavian Journal of Psychology*, 1981, *22*, 109–115. (b)

Lindberg, E., & Gärling, T. Acquisition of locational information about reference points during locomotion: The role of central information processing. *Scandinavian Journal of Psychology*, 1982, *23*, 207–218.

Lindberg, E., & Gärling, T. Acquisition of different types of locational information in cognitive maps: Automatic or effortful processing? *Psychological Research*, 1983, *45*, 19–38.

Linde, E., & Labov, W. Spatial networks as a site for the study of language and thought. *Language*, 1975, *51*, 924–939.

Lindsay, P. H., & Norman, D. A. *Human information processing*. New York: Academic Press, 1972.

Lowenthal, D., & Riel, M. The nature of perceived and imagined environments. *Environment and Behavior*, 1972, *4*, 189–207.

Lowrey, R. A. Distance concepts of urban residents. *Environment and Behavior*, 1970, *2*, 52–73.

Lynch, K. *The image of the city*. Cambridge, MA: MIT Press, 1960.

Merril, A. A., & Baird, J. C. Perception and recall of aesthetic quality in a familiar environment. *Psychological Research*, 1980, *42*, 375–390.

Milgram, S., Greenwald, J., Kessler, S., McKenna, W., & Waters, J. A psychological map of New York city. *American Scientist*, 1972, *60*, 194–200.

Miller, G. A., Galanter, E., & Pribram, K. H. *Plans and the structure of behavior*. New York: Holt, Rinehart & Winston, 1960.

Moore, G. T. Knowing about environmental knowing: The current state of theory and research on environmental cognition. *Environment and Behavior*, 1979, *11*, 33–70.

Murdock, B. B., Jr. *Human memory: Theory and data*. New York: Wiley, 1974.

Neisser, U. *Cognitive psychology*. New York: Appleton-Century-Crofts, 1967.

Neisser, U. *Cognition and reality*. San Francisco: Freeman, 1976.

O'Keefe, J., & Nadel, L. *The hippocampus as a cognitive map*. Oxford: Clarendon Press, 1978.

Passini, R. E. *Wayfinding: A study of spatial problem solving with implications for physical design*. Unpublished doctoral dissertation, Department of Man-Environment Relations, Pennsylvania State University, 1977.

Passini, R. E. Wayfinding: A conceptual framework. *Man-Environment Systems*, 1980, *10*, 22–30. (a)

Passini, R. E. Wayfinding in complex buildings: An environmental analysis. *Man-Environment Systems*, 1980, *10*, 31–40. (b)

Pezdek, K., & Evans, G. W. Visual and verbal memory for objects and their spatial relations. *Journal of Experimental Psychology: Human Learning and Memory*, 1979, *5*, 360–373.

Pick, H. L. Transactional-constructivist approach to environmental knowing: A commentary. In G. T. Moore & R. G. Golledge (Eds.), *Environmental knowing*. Stroudsburg, PA: Dowden, Hutchinson & Ross, 1976.

Pittenger, J. B., & Jenkins, J. J. Apprehension of pictorial events: The case of a moving observer in a static environment. *Bulletin of the Psychonomic Society*, 1979, *13*, 117–120.

Potegal, M. A note on spatial motor deficits in patients with Huntington's disease: A test of a hypothesis. *Neuropsychologica*, 1971, *9*, 233–235.

Potegal, M. The caudate nucleus egocentric localization system. *Acta Neurobiologiae Experimentalis*, 1972, *32*, 479–494.

Proshansky, H. M., Ittelson, W. H., & Rivlin, L. G. The influence of the physical environment on behavior: Some basic assumptions. In H. M. Proshansky, W. H. Ittelson, & L. G. Rivlin (Eds.), *Environmental psychology.* New York: Holt, Rinehart & Winston, 1970.

Puff, C. R. (Ed.). *Handbook of research methods in human memory and cognition.* New York: Academic Press, 1982.

Ross, H. E., Dickinson, D. J., & Jupp, B. J. Geographical orientation under water. *Human Factors,* 1970, *12,* 13–24.

Russell, J. A., & Ward, L. M. Environmental psychology. *Annual Review of Psychology,* 1982, *32,* 651–688.

Ryan, T. A., & Ryan, M. S. Geographical orientation. *American Journal of Psychology,* 1940, *53,* 204–215.

Sadalla, E. K., Burroughs, W. J., & Staplin, L. J. Reference points in spatial cognition. *Journal of Experimental Psychology: Human Learning and Memory,* 1980, *6,* 516–528.

Sadalla, E. K., & Magel, S. G. The perception of traversed distance. *Environment and Behavior,* 1980, *12,* 65–79.

Sadalla, E. K., & Staplin, L. J. The perception of traversed distance: Intersections. *Environment and Behavior,* 1980, *12,* 167–182.

Schneider, W., & Shiffrin, R. M. Controlled and automatic human information processing: I. Detection, search, and attention. *Psychological Review,* 1977, *84,* 1–66.

Shebilske, W. Visuomotor coordination in visual direction and position constancies. In W. Epstein (Ed.), *Stability and constancy in visual perception.* New York: Wiley, 1977.

Shepard, R. N. Recognition memory for words, sentences and pictures. *Journal of Verbal Learning and Verbal Behavior,* 1967, *6,* 156–163.

Sherman, R. C., Oliver, C., & Titus, W. Verifying environmental relationships. *Memory and Cognition,* 1980, *8,* 555–562.

Shiffrin, R. M., & Schneider, W. Controlled and automatic human information processing: II. Perceptual learning, automatic attending, and a general theory. *Psychological Review,* 1977, *84,* 127–190.

Siegel, A. W., and White, S. H. The development of spatial representation of large-scale environments. In H. W. Reese (Ed.), *Advances in child development and behavior* (Vol. 10). New York: Academic Press, 1975.

Standing, L., Conezio, J., & Haber, R. N. Perception and memory for pictures: Single-trial learning of 2500 visual stimuli. *Psychonomic Science,* 1970, *19,* 73–74.

Sternberg, R. J. *Intelligence, information processing, and analogical reasoning: The componential analysis of human abilities.* Hillsdale, NJ: Lawrence Erlbaum Associates, 1977.

Sternberg, S. Memory scanning: New findings and current controversies. *Quarterly Journal of Experimental Psychology,* 1975, *27,* 1–32.

Stevens, A., & Coupe, P. Distortions in judged spatial relations. *Cognitive Psychology,* 1978, *10,* 422–437.

Stokols, D. Environmental psychology. *Annual Review of Psychology,* 1978, *29,* 253–295.

Thorndyke, P. W. Distance estimation in cognitive maps. *Cognitive Psychology,* 1981, *13,* 526–550.

Thorndyke, P. W., & Stasz, C. Individual differences in procedures for knowledge acquisition from maps. *Cognitive Psychology,* 1980, *12,* 137–175.

Tulving, E. Episodic and semantic memory. In E. Tulving & W. Donaldson (Eds.), *Organization of memory.* New York: Academic Press, 1972.

Tversky, B. Distortions in memory for maps. *Cognitive Psychology,* 1981, *13,* 407–433.

Ward, L. M., & Russell, J. A. Cognitive set and the perception of place. *Environment and Behavior,* 1981, *13,* 610–632. (a)

Ward, L. M., & Russell, J. A. The psychological representation of molar physical environments. *Journal of Experimental Psychology: General,* 1981, *110,* 121–152. (b)

Weisman, J. Evaluating architectural legibility: Wayfinding in the built environment. *Environment and Behavior*, 1981, *13*, 189–203.

Worchel, P. The role of vestibular organs in space orientation. *Journal of Experimental Psychology*, 1952, *44*, 4–10.

Zimring, C. M. Stress and the designed environment. *Journal of Social Issues*, 1981, *37*, 145–171.

Zusne, L., & Allen, B. Magnetic sense in humans. *Perceptual and Motor Skills*, 1981, *52*, 910.

7

A Roadmap to Research for Spatial Cognition in the Elderly Adult

Kathleen C. Kirasic
Old Dominion University

INTRODUCTION: IS THERE SOME PLACE TO GO?

Spatial cognition and spatial behavior represent an area of inquiry that is of practical and theoretical significance for behavioral scientists. Human beings are an extremely mobile species, and spatial competence is very basic to success as an individual within the species. In consonance with this view, theorists have proposed genetically based propensities for certain spatial cognitive capabilities (Fishbein, 1976; Siegel & White, 1975) and have posited neurological specialization for spatial cognition (Harris, 1975; Luria, 1973). Experimental evidence suggesting that certain spatial aspects of the environment are encoded in memory ''automatically'' (Hasher & Zacks, 1979; Mandler, Seegmiller, & Day, 1977) contribute to the argument that spatial information processing reflects a very basic set of abilities. It is therefore imperative that we understand the nature of any spatial cognitive changes that occur with increasing age because any age-related decline in spatial abilities should have a clear and significant impact on the elderly individual's transactions with his or her spatial environment.

Are elderly adults put at some disadvantage when faced with a new environment or a once-familiar environment that has been changed? Although environmental changes are faced by individuals of every age, there is anecdotal evidence to suggest that the older adult is dramatically affected by such change. To become lost, especially in a once-familiar environment, can create in the older adult, as Lynch (1960) put it, ''much more than simple goegraphic uncertainty: it carries overtones of utter disaster'' (p. 4). A description of being ''lost'' in a familiar environment was recounted recently to me. When the elderly patrons of a popular Memphis supermarket encountered a newly remodeled store, the older shoppers were seen to scan the aisles for items whose location they once knew and then, frustrated, shake their heads and walk on. These shoppers were not only dealing with spatial disorientation; the remodeling obviously had a personal impact on them, as evidenced by a question from one elderly shopper to another, "How could they do this to us?"

This and numerous other incidents point to several important issues concerning the real-world spatial cognitive abilities of older adults. Such issues deal with the extent to which elderly adults are disadvantaged when confronted with new spatial environments, and the extent to which aging reduces the ability of individuals to deal effectively with large-scale spatial information.

Very little research has been done to specifically address the ecologically based concerns just raised. Only very recently have researchers presented reasonable hypotheses regarding the large-scale spatial cognitive abilities of older adults. Previous speculation was based either on nonspatial cognitive data or on laboratory studies of microspatial abilities. Accordingly, the purposes of the present chapter are to (1) summarize much of the early work, (2) provide a review of some of the most promising, ecologically valid research currently being conducted, and (3) provide some focus for future research that will have both scientific and applied ramifications.

WHERE HAVE WE BEEN?

Psychometric Spatiovisual Abilities

Psychometric spatial functions have received a number of psychological interpretations and have been defined in a myriad of psychological tests (Cattell, 1971; French, Ekstrom, & Price, 1963; Guilford & Lacey, 1947; McGee, 1979). A consensus of factor analytic studies has suggested at least three predominant spatial factors. The first factor is a visualization factor, which reflects an individual's ability to imagine spatial displacement or movement. Spatial relations, the second factor, refer to one's ability to recognize an object from different perspectives. Finally, spatial orientation refers to the ability to think about spatial problems in relation to the observer's body and is often presented as a factor independent of spatial relations (Cohen, 1977).

Although the number, content, and meaning of spatial factors are subject to debate among psychometricians, their existence has been well documented in young adults. However, their examination has been relatively neglected in older individuals. The extent of the literature that addresses the maintenance or decline of spatial abilities with increasing age is indeed small. In a review of the research since 1949, Horn (1970) concluded that a clear understanding concerning either the stabilization or the decrement of spatial skills with increasing age was not possible. For example, the cross-sectional findings of Doppelt and Wallace

(1955), Fox and Birren (1949), and Schaie, Rosenthal, and Perlman (1953) have provided evidence for significant decline in the spatial performance of elderly adults, but no such declines were reported by Bilash and Zubeck (1960) and Horn and Cattell (1966, 1967).

Many of these contradictory findings arise from comparisons of cross-sectional versus longitudinal research. In addition, confusions are compounded by (1) the apparent lack of agreement as to how old "elderly" is and (2) the variance in the age of the population tested. For example, consider the difficulty in attempting to reconcile the findings of Schaie and Strother (1968), whose cross-sectional data reflected significant decrements in space and reasoning factors for 25 men and 25 women aged 70–88, with those of Schaie and his colleagues (reported in Nesselroade, Schaie, & Baltes, 1972), whose longitudinal and cross-sequential data on a larger and younger population, aged 20–70, revealed little or no change in these factors.

Unfortunately, evidence from psychometric studies of spatial ability provide a decidedly incomplete picture of the stability of spatial cognitive functioning in old age. At present, this small literature affords only the "non-conclusion" that the spatiovisual abilities of elderly adults either remain stable or decline with increasing years. Ironically, even if this issue were resolved, the implications for spatial behavior would remain unknown.

Spatial Inference Making: Perspective Taking

Research into the elderly individual's problem-solving abilities has almost exclusively focused on problems involving spatial perspective taking. Beginning with the classic developmental work of Piaget and Inhelder (1967), these problems typically require the individual to infer how a spatial array would appear from various viewpoints other than the one perceived. There are many variations of the task. Subjects have chosen how a matrix looked from a different vantage point (Looft & Charles, 1971) or constructed another's view of a stimulus display (Rubin, Attewell, Tierney, & Tumolo, 1973). In another study, subjects were asked to imagine one's self moving to a particular location in a room and then to sight various targets from that imagined position (Herman & Coyne, 1980). Despite the procedural differences among studies, the evidence generally indicates that (1) elderly adults have more difficulty in solving perspective problems than do young adults (e.g., Ohta, Walsh, & Krauss, 1979) and (2) various means used to cognitively manipulate spatial arrays in order to solve perspective problems (e.g., imagining self-movement versus imagining array movement) differentially affect success in solving the problems (Herman & Coyne, 1980; Kirasic, 1979; Krauss & Schaie, 1976).

Although this type of research more closely approximates "real-world" spatial problem solving, the contrived laboratory situations leave much to be desired. In the majority of the research, the spatial problem-solving task involved knowledge of a table-top or room-sized array, which was constructed such that the overall configuration could be perceived from single vantage points. Rarely in daily life do we have the opportunity to organize our knowledge to an area from a single all-encompassing view. Although inference making is undoubtedly required for successful spatial behavior, the present laboratory techniques limit the generalizability of findings. Few statements can be made with confidence regarding the elderly adult's ability to construct an integrated representation of a large-scale space and to successfully navigate in that environment.

Representation In the Elderly Adult

It has been suggested that representations of large-scale space are initially constructed on the basis of landmarks and routes and eventually become configurational in nature (Siegel & White, 1975). There is considerable evidence to substantiate this sequence in young children and adults (e.g., Allen, Siegel, & Rosinski, 1978; Canter & Tagg, 1975; Zannaras, 1973). Krauss and Quayhagen (1977) noted that the nature and structure of spatial representation in older adults are not known. Quite simply, little research has been directed toward the study of these issues.

Because of this lack of research, another way of approaching the issue of representation must be taken. One alternative involves a review of the gerontological studies that explore some of the cognitive mechanisms or processes that may be involved in the representation of large-scale space. The tasks reviewed do not in themselves involve spatial knowledge; however, the conclusions drawn from them may provide insight into macrospatial cognitive processing in older individuals. The landmarks to routes to configurations framework will serve to organize this review.

Landmarks.   Descriptions of environments typically begin with the mention of landmarks (Appleyard, 1970; Downs & Stea, 1973; Gladwin, 1970). Landmarks serve not only as the beginning and end points to and from which we travel, but also as intermediate course-maintaining devices. Underlying landmark knowledge is the process of recognizing a landmark and its appropriate context (Kirasic, Siegel, & Allen, 1980; Siegel, Kirasic, & Kail, 1978). Several studies have reported slight decrements in recognition memory with increasing age (Botwinick & Storandt, 1974; Craik, 1977; Fozard & Waugh, 1969; Gordon & Clark, 1974). Despite this decline, recognition memory remains rather robust in old age (Harwood & Naylor, 1966; Schonfield & Robertson, 1966). In Harwood and Naylor's (1969) study, elderly individual's mean recognition accuracy for line-drawn objects was 87% of that demonstrated by a younger group when both groups were evaluated one month after initial testing. This and other evidence suggest that recognition memory is relatively well preserved in the elderly. Thus, it may be concluded that the ability to recognize the landmarks present in the elderly person's spatial environment is only slightly impaired if at all.

Routes. Although landmarks are important way finding devices, they are insufficient unless they are linked together in the context of effective action. Routes have been defined as sensorimotor routines allowing an individual to proceed from point A to point B (Siegel & White, 1975). Knowledge of routes is to some extent sequence knowledge; while traveling a route, a person knows that a particular succession of landmarks will follow if a certain path is taken. The mechanisms underlying route development are locomotion and concomitant temporal integration. As has been stressed by Beck and Wood (1976), movement through the environment is a necessity for an environmental experience to take place. Accordingly, routes can be conceptualized as those elements that give shape to a spatial representation (Siegel & White, 1975) and represent habitual lines of movement and familiar lines of travel (Lynch, 1960).

An individual's route representation requires the integration of specific, restricted views over a period of time. Thus, a review of the gerontological research on temporal integration, spatial closure, and paired-associated learning may provide some insights into route construction for this age group.

The results of the limited research on temporal integration and spatial closure suggest that elderly individuals would be less successful than younger individuals in the integration of specific components of an environment into a cohesive representation. This conclusion is drawn from the fact that there is a tendency for older adults to fixate on the details of the stimuli, perseverate in their response to stimuli, and to treat individual elements of stimuli as separate entities rather than forming relationships between adjoining elements (Basowitz & Korchin, 1957). Furthermore, Wallace's (1956) findings suggest that older individuals would be less successful in forming route representations, especially as the complexity of the route increases and as the duration and extent of particular views of the route decrease.

Finally, inasmuch as routes are sensorimotor routines in which a serial order of landmarks is temporally integrated (Siegel & White, 1975), paired-associate learning may be said to be involved in route learning. Just as the older adult has exhibited deficits in spatial closure and temporal integration abilities, deficits have been identified in paired-associate learning (Ruch, 1934). However, these findings are explained by Basowitz and Korchin (1957) as reflecting a deficit in the acquisition of *novel* material rather than in the reorganization of previously learned materials. They found that meaningful paired-associate tasks were the least reflective of age decrement. The more meaningful and personally relevant the task is, the higher will be the motivation to successfully complete it (Botwinick, 1973).

It requires substantial inferential leaps to apply these findings to macrospatial cognition. Nonetheless, these leaps lead to the expectation that elderly adults would encounter difficulties in learning new routes in unfamiliar areas.

Configurations. The construction of a representation of large-scale space is an example of the acquisition of configurational knowledge. Configurational representations provide more than a route map of the environment; they provide way-finding information and organize environmental experience into integrated patterns. Characteristic of configurational knowledge is the ability to simultaneously embrace a multitude of details, which permits increasingly flexible ways in which the representation can be used. One might hope that findings from research exploring memory for designs and memory for spatial location could permit inferences regarding the nature and quality of the older adults' configurational representation.

In the investigation of memory for designs, subjects were asked to select previously seen designs from a number of distractors (Bromley, 1958) or to reproduce designs from memory (Davies, 1967; Heron & Chown, 1967). Occasionally, the memory tasks involved an incidental component (Botwinick & Storandt, 1974). These studies along with others (e.g., Adamowicz, 1976; Arenberg, 1978) consistently find poorer memory for designs by older subjects, thus suggesting that the older adult would be less successful in maintaining in memory the design (or configuration) of spatial elements in the environments. Additionally, the poorer incidental memory for the spatial location of designs (Botwinick & Storandt, 1974) suggests that older individuals would have poorer incidental memory for the location of noncentral events in the environment.

However, research relating to configurational knowledge has not been restricted to the use of geometric patterns and designs as stimuli. Attempts have been made to study configurational knowledge using stimuli that approximate real-world situations. There has been research in which subjects studied a map containing landmarks and later were asked to relocate those landmarks on a blank map (Ohta, 1980; Perlmutter, Metzger, Nezworski, & Miller, 1981). Also, in an attempt to more closely approximate the real-world agenda of individuals, Ohta (1980) showed his subjects a model of a nine-block city or a videotaped simulated tour through the model's streets. Afterward, subjects indicated where certain selected landmarks were located in the city using scale models of the landmarks and an outline of the city streets. The results of these studies suggested that the age-related decrement in memory for geometric patterns and designs are also present in memory for landmark location (Ohta & Kirasic, 1983). In short, evidence from the preceding studies appears to point to the existence of a highly reliable and extremely generalized age-related decrement in spatial memory. This may well result in poorer configurational representations of environments, particularly unfamiliar ones.

WHERE ARE WE NOW?

Previous research provides us with a springboard for speculation, but in and of itself it is insufficient to provide a complete (or perhaps even accurate) understanding of the spatial cognitive abilities of the older adult. This cautious approach to the existing data stems from the results of some recent behavioral studies. These studies have suggested an important distinction between elderly adults' ability to process information that has little relevance outside of the psychological laboratory and their ability to process information that has direct relevance to their lives outside of that setting (Demming & Pressey, 1957; Lachman & Lachman, 1979). A growing number of studies report failure to find evidence of declining memory or processing skills in tasks that involve information and situations that are directly related to the experiences of elderly population tested (Lachman & Lachman, 1979; Perlmutter, 1979; Schaie, 1978; Waddell & Rogoff, 1981).

Given the possibility that laboratory tasks may lead to an underestimation of cognitive competence in the elderly adult, it becomes increasingly important to broaden the study of spatial cognition to include the study of spatial behavior and cognition *in situ*. Luckily, since Krauss and Quayhagen's (1977) observation on the dearth of real-world spatial research with elderly adults, several studies have been initiated that have as their primary focus knowledge of a behavior in familiar and novel real-world environments.

In the first of three examples of this type of research, the spatial problem-solving abilities of young, middle-aged, and elderly adults were evaluated in parallel studies using two different environments (Kirasic, 1980). Of primary concern was the subjects' ability to solve problems involving spatial relationships by cognitively manipulating spatial arrays. Subjects were asked to infer various target sites within a novel, laboratory-learned spatial array and within their hometown using two cognitive manipulations referred to as imagined self-movement and imagined array movement (cf. Huttenlocher & Presson, 1979).

In both studies, directional and distance estimates were given for target locations under both sets of cognitive manipulation instructions. In the study involving the novel spatial array, analysis of direction estimates revealed that the elderly adults were less accurate under both manipulation conditions than were middle-aged or young adults, who did not differ from each other. Furthermore, elderly adults performed less accurately under imagined array movement instructions than under self-movement instructions. A corresponding difference was not found for the other age groups. Distance estimation analyses revealed that the elderly adults were less accurate than either the young or middle-aged adults.

These findings could be taken as support for the proposition that perspective-taking and/or mental rotation abilities are diminished in elderly adults (e.g.,

Herman & Coyne, 1980). Had the experimentation stopped here, as many research endeavors do, a general statement of declining spatial competence would have been made. However, a parallel study was conducted involving the same generic procedure and the same subjects as those in the study just described. In this second study, a different spatial array—the subjects' hometown—was used. Analysis of the direction estimates from this study revealed no significant effects or interactions. The same was true for the analysis of distance estimates.

The results of these studies suggest that the accuracy of elderly adults' performance on spatial cognitive tasks is directly affected by the context in which the task is presented. It appears that age-related decrements on some spatial tasks are due to ecologically based performance factors rather than to differences in general cognitive competence per se.

The next example is Ohta's (1981) examination of the common spatial problem of having to deal with a detour situation. In this study, route choice was regarded as a special case of response selection in a problem-solving task.

Botwinick's (1966) hypothetical "life situations" provided the springboard for this study. From their responses on the hypothetical "life situations" test, Botwinick (1966) found that elderly subjects were more likely than young subjects to choose a moderately rewarding alternative with an *assured* outcome rather than a highly rewarding but risky outcome. Ohta's (1981) modified task provided subjects with a hypothetical spatial problem-solving situation similar to Botwinick's tasks except that it was embedded in an actual detour situation.

Upon arriving at the testing site, a university medical center, the subjects were first asked to respond to a *hypothetical spatial detour "life situation."* Subjects were then familiarized with a particular section of the medical complex. Each subject was accompanied by the experimenter on walks along an original route and a return route. Subsequently, the subject was taken to an impasse point along the original route. At that point, the subject was presented with a *real-world detour situation;* it was explained that it was vital to reach a goal (the emergency room) but that the original route was blocked. In this actual spatial problem-solving situation, subjects had the options of (1) backtracking along the original route and then traveling over what was previously the return route, or (2) proceeding along an alternate shorter route, *not previously traversed by the subject.*

The analysis of the hypothetical "life situation" clearly replicated Botwinick's (1966) findings. In contrast to the younger subjects, the elderly subjects chose to avoid an alternate route regardless of its prospect of efficiency. In the real-world problem-solving situation, however, the performance of young and elderly subjects was essentially reversed. The younger subjects tended to select the more conservative path (i.e., backtrack) and the older subjects tended to choose the riskier alternative (i.e., an unexplored route). In short, as in the case of Kirasic's 1980 study of the perspectives problem, the elderly adults' performance in the real-world task could not have been predicted accurately on the basis of their choice in the hypothetical situation.

The final and most ambitious example of research involving real-world macrospatial cognition was conducted by Walsh, Krauss, and Regnier (1981). Their project focused on three central issues. The first concerned the relationship between an individual's knowledge of a neighborhood environment and the degree to which the services and facilities of that environment are used. The second issue concerned the relationship between an individual's spatial-cognitive ability and his or her knowledge of the neighborhood. The third concerned the relationship between an individual's use or exposure to a neighborhood and knowledge of that neighborhood. To obtain this information, a wealth of data was collected from a random sample of elderly individuals regarding their use and perception of their neighborhoods, their knowledge of their neighborhoods, and their ability to acquire information about new environments. The measures gathered in this monumental endeavor are too numerous to list in toto. However, a few examples are given.

To provide data on Environmental Use, subjects reported pedestrian paths, behavioral settings, and use of goods and services, and in addition, kept a diary for a month of all trips outside of their home. To evaluate Environmental Knowledge, time-lapse hand-drawn maps were obtained and evaluated for overall impression, existing schemes, and neighborhood size and content. Also, a landmark recognition memory task was employed to assess relative distance judgments assumed to underly the cognitive representation of the neighborhood. To assess Spatial Abilities in the laboratory, subjects were administered a number of traditional paper and pencil measures of spatial abilities (e.g., an adaptation of the Building Memory test) and were tested for their ability to (1) recognize landmarks from, and (2) solve perspective problems involving, a tabletop model town.

Several basic conclusions emerged for this myriad of data. First, it was found that standardized paper and pencil tests correlated highly with accuracy of locating neighborhood landmarks, indicating that sufficient variation exists in individual spatial ability to predict knowledge of neighborhood layout. Second, analyses showed that the subjects who were more accurate in the laboratory perspective-taking task traveled a longer average distance to retrieve goods and services. There was also a reliable correlation between the accuracy in the laboratory landmark placement task and the total distance subjects traveled per month, with the more accurate subjects traveling greater distances. This suggested that cognitive-spatial ability has a significant effect in determining urban neighborhood use. Finally, it was found that the more neighborhood landmarks the subjects were *unable* to identify, the fewer services they used, indicating that greater knowledge of landmarks in the neighborhood was related to greater use of the available services.

The work of Walsh et al. (1981) not only provides information regarding some very basic spatial abilities but also provides suggestions for service agencies, urban planners, and architects. In the words of these researchers:

This research brings the concerns of Lynch (1960) and other planners a little closer to application by (a) dealing with a subpopulation group who have in some cases limited competence and are therefore more dependent on the clarity of the physical environment; and (b) gathering behavioral data, along with physical design elements, in order to understand better the complex relationship between use, spatial ability, and knowledge of the environment. (p. 356)

WHERE SHOULD WE BE GOING AND HOW DO WE GET THERE?

Stated simply, the experimenter must ask sensible questions in order to obtain valid, interpretable results (Downs & Siegel, 1981; Siegel, 1981). Selection of experimental tasks should either be motivated by a theoretical position or be dictated by ecologically valid research agenda. Otherwise, there is a substantial risk of accumulating isolated, conflicting research findings. The research discussed in the previous section supports this contention (Awad, McCormick, Ohta, & Krauss, 1979; Walsh et al., 1981; Kirasic, 1980; Ohta, 1981). Each of these works indicates that more research must be focused on individuals' spatial behavior in real-world environments. Observational studies would be particularly useful in this regard.

In response to this need for more ecologically valid research, a series of studies have been initiated in my laboratory that explore the interrelationships among psychometric measures of spatial abilities, performance on experimental tasks, and behavior in large-scale spatial environments. From the onset of this project special emphasis was placed on the practical aspects of spatial cognition and behavior. The studies undertaken were concerned with spatial cognition and spatial behavior in the context of a common, real-world task (grocery shopping). The purpose of this ongoing project is to delineate the relationships among psychometric measures of spatial ability (including spatial visualization, spatial orientation, and visual memory factors); behavioral measures in a simulated shopping trip through familiar and unfamiliar supermarkets; and experimental measures involving scene recognition, route planning, and place knowledge within the two supermarket settings.

Since this study is incomplete, only two very general findings found through "data snooping" are pointed out. The early results from the experimental tasks indicated that both young and elderly adults' accuracy in scene recognition, route planning, and item location on supermarket floor plans was lower in the novel supermarket than in the familiar setting. In the unfamiliar setting, a significant age-related decrement was found only on the recognition test, with only slight decrements appearing in the other tests.

Second, behavior during the simulated shopping tasks is being examined in terms of efficiency. Efficiency is determined by how far the subject traveled in order to locate a list of store items compared to the actual minimum possible distance for locating these items. The frequency of four types of behavior is also being examined: standing, walking, standing-scanning, and walking-scanning. Not surprisingly, more efficient travel was accomplished in the familiar store for both age groups. Although no age differences have been observed on the efficiency measure, behavioral differences were apparent during a familiarization period in the novel environment. During this period, subjects quickly explored the novel supermarket prior to the shopping task itself. During the familiarization period, the elderly adults compared to the young adults, exhibited more standing while scanning, and just standing, along with less walking while scanning. These differences appeared again in the shopping task itself in the novel supermarket. During the shopping task in the familiar store, subjects of both age groups spent most of their time walking to the locations, with little time required for scanning that environment.

The results of this study could conceivably indicate that neither psychometric measures nor performance on experimental tasks, either alone or in combination, provides sufficient insight into macrospatial competence in elderly adults. Behavioral measures may be an important missing ingredient in this regard. Thus, future research should be concerned with the relationship between behavior in the environment and the acquisition of spatial knowledge for that environment.

Slowly the profile of environmentally competent elderly adults is emerging. The findings from the work of Kirasic (1980), Ohta (1981), Walsh et al. (1981) and my most recent work point to the need for ecological validity in the determinants of such competence. However, it is important to note that none of these researchers are advocating the abolition of traditional laboratory studies of spatial cognition. Rather, complementing the laboratory approach with studies of spatial cognition and spatial behavior in real environments is recommended. These complementary approaches provide researchers a spatial cognition with a better integrated perspective on age-related changes in these phenomena.

As was stated at the beginning of this chapter, the study of spatial cognition in the elderly adult is not only an issue of empirical concern but is a matter of considerable practical importance. For the elderly adults living in today's urbanized culture, it is highly probable that they will have to face the task of learning a new spatial environment at some time. This learning may result from moving to a retirement community or from having the urban environment change around them. If the elderly individuals face a difficult task in adapting to environmental change, any intervention to aid in the spatial learning of new environments will eventually add to their quality of life. By keeping the focus of spatial cognitive research in elderly adults on the identification and remediation of the potentially negative behavioral consequences of aging, there will be no question as to where we, as researchers, are going.

ACKNOWLEDGMENT

The author's effort in preparing this chapter was sponsored by a grant from the National Science Foundation, DAR 8011000.

REFERENCES

Adamowicz, J. K. Visual short term memory and aging. *Journal of Gerontology*, 1976, *31*, 39–46.

Allen, G. L., Siegel, A. W., & Rosinski, R. R. The role of perceptual context in structuring spatial knowledge. *Journal of Experimental Psychology*, 1978, *4*, 617–630.

Appleyard, D. Styles and methods of structuring a city. *Environment and Behavior*, 1970, *2*, 100–118.

Arenberg, D. Differences and changes with age in the Benton Visual Retention Test. *Journal of Gerontology*, 1978, *33*, 534–540.

Awad, Z. A., McCormick, D. J., Ohta, R. J., & Krauss, I. K. *Neighborhood knowledge of the elderly: Psychological and environmental correlates.* Paper presented at the annual meeting of the Gerontological Society, Washington, D.C., November 1979.

Basowitz, H., & Korchin, S. J. Age differences in the perception of closure. *Journal of Abnormal and Social Psychology*, 1957, *54*, 93–97.

Beck, R. J., & Wood, D. Cognitive transformation from urban geographic fields to mental maps. *Environment and Behavior*, 1976, *8*, 199–237.

Bilash, I., & Zubek, J. P. Effects of age on factorially "pure" mental abilities. *Journal of Gerontology*, 1960, *15*, 175–182.

Botwinick, J. Cautiousness in advanced age. *Journal of Gerontology*, 1966, *21*, 347–353.

Botwinick, J. *Aging and behavior.* New York: Springer, 1973.

Botwinick, J., & Storandt, M. *Memory, related functions and age.* Springfield, IL: Charles C. Thomas, 1974.

Bromley, D. B. Some effects of age on short term learning and remembering. *Journal of Gerontology*, 1958, *13*, 398–406.

Canter, D., & Tagg, S. K. Distance estimation in cities. *Environment and Behavior*, 1975, *7*, 59–80.

Cattell, R. B. *Abilities: Their structure, growth, and action.* Boston: Houghton-Mifflin, 1971.

Cohen, D. Sex differences in spatial preformance in the elderly: A review of the literature and suggestions for research. *Educational Gerontology: An International Quarterly*, 1977, *2*, 59–69.

Craik, F. I. M. Age differences in human memory. In J. E. Birren & K. W. Schaie (Eds.), *Handbook of the psychology of aging.* New York: Van Nostrand Reinhold, 1977.

Davies, A. D. M. Age and the Memory-For-Designs Test. *British Journal of Social and Clinical Psychology*, 1967, *6*, 228–233.

Demming, J. A., & Pressey, S. L. Tests "indigenous" to the adult in older years. *Journal of Counseling Psychology*, 1957, *2*, 144–148.

Doppelt, J. E., & Wallace, W. L. Standardization of the Wechsler Adult Intelligence Scale for older persons. *Journal of Abnormal and Social Psychology*, 1955, *51*, 312–330.

Downs, R. M., & Siegel, A. W. On mapping researchers mapping children mapping space. In L. S. Liben, A. H. Patterson, & N. Newcomb (Eds.), *Spatial representation and behavior across the life span.* New York: Academic Press, 1981.

Downs, R. M., & Stea, D. Cognitive maps and spatial behavior: Process and products. In R. M. Downs & D. Stea (Eds.), *Image and environment: Cognitive mapping and spatial behavior.* Chicago: Aldine, 1973.

Fishbein, H. D. *Evolution, development, and children's learning.* Pacific Palisades, CA: Goodyear, 1976.

Fox, C., & Birren, J. E. Some factors affecting vocabulary size in late maturity: Age, education, and length of institutionalization. *Journal of Gerontology*, 1949, *4*, 19–26.

Fozard, J. L., & Waugh, N. C. Proactive inhibition of prompted items. *Psychonomic Science*, 1969, *17*, 67–68.

French, J. W., Ekstrom, R. B., & Price, L. A. *Kit of reference tests for cognitive factors.* Princeton, NJ: Educational Testing Service, 1963.

Gladwin, T. *East is a big bird.* Cambridge: Harvard University Press, 1970.

Gordon, S. K., & Clark, W. C. Adult age differences in word and nonsense syllable recognition memory and response criterion. *Journal of Gerontology,* 1974, *29,* 659–665.

Guilford, J. P., & Lacey, J. I. *Printed classification tests, A.A.F.* Aviation Psychological Progress Research Report, No. 5. Washington, DC: U.S. Government Printing Office, 1947.

Harris, L. J. Neurophysiological factors in the development of spatial skills. In J. Eliot & N. J. Salkind (Eds.), *Children's spatial development.* Springfield, IL: Charles C. Thomas, 1975.

Harwood, E., & Naylor, G. F. K. Recall and recognition in elderly and young subjects. *Australian Journal of Psychology,* 1969, *21,* 251–257.

Hasher, L., & Zacks, R. T. Automatic and effortful processes in memory. *Journal of Experimental Psychology: General,* 1979, *108,* 356–388.

Herman, J. F., & Coyne, A. C. Mental manipulation of spatial information in young and elderly adults. *Developmental Psychology,* 1980, *16,* 537–538.

Heron, A., & Chown, S. *Age and function.* Boston: Little, Brown, 1967.

Horn, J. L. Organization of data on life span development of human abilities. In L. R. Goulet & Baltes (Eds.), *Life-span developmental psychology: Research and theory.* New York: Academic Press, 1970.

Horn, J. L., & Cattell, R. B. Age differences in primary mental ability factors. *Journal of Gerontology,* 1966, *21,* 277–299.

Horn, J. L., & Cattell, R. B. Age differences in fluid and crystallized intelligence. *Acta Psychologica,* 1967, *26,* 107–129.

Huttenlocher, J., & Presson, C. C. The coding and transformation of spatial information. *Cognitive Psychology,* 1979, *11,* 375–394.

Kirasic, K. C. *Adults' ability to solve spatial perspective problems: A view from the lab and a view from life.* Unpublished doctoral dissertation, Department of Psychology, University of Pittsburgh, 1979.

Kirasic, K. C. *Spatial problem solving in elderly adults: A hometown advantage.* Presented at the meetings of the Gerontological Society, San Diego, 1980.

Kirasic, K. C. *The elusive concept of cognitive competence in aging research: The case of spatial cognition.* Presented at a symposium entitled "New directions in geropsychology" during the meetings of the Midwestern Psychological Association, Detroit, April 1981.

Kirasic, K. C., Siegel, A. W., & Allen, G. L. The development of basic processes in cognitive mapping: Recognition-in-context memory. *Child Development,* 1980, *51,* 302–305.

Krauss, I. K., & Schaie, K. W. *Errors in spatial rotation in the elderly.* Paper presented at the annual meeting of the American Psychological Society, Washington, DC, September 1976.

Krauss, I. K., & Quayhagen, M. *Components of spatial cognition.* Paper presented at the annual meetings of the Gerontological Society, San Francisco, 1977.

Lachman, J. L., & Lachman, R. Age and the actualization of world knowledge. In L. W. Poon, J. L. Fozard, L. S. Cermak, D. Arenberg, & L. W. Thompson (Eds.), *New directions in memory and aging: Proceedings of the George Talland Memorial Conference.* Hillsdale, NJ: Lawrence Erlbaum Associates, 1979.

Looft, W. R., & Charles, D. C. Egocentrism and social interaction in young and old adults. *Aging and Human Development,* 1971, *2,* 21–28.

Luria, A. R. *The working brain.* London: Penquin Press, 1973.

Lynch, K. *The image of the city.* Cambridge: MIT Press, 1960.

Mandler, J. M., Seegmiller, D., & Day, J. On the coding of spatial information. *Memory and Cognition,* 1977, *5,* 10–16.

McGee, M. G. *Human spatial abilities: Sources of sex differences.* New York: Praeger, 1979.

Nesselroade, J. R., Schaie, K. W., & Baltes, P. B. Ontogenetic and generational components of structural and quantitative change in adult cognitive behavior. *Journal of Gerontology,* 1972, *27,* 222–228.

Ohta, R. J. *Spatial cognition and the relative effectiveness of two methods of presenting spatial information in young and elderly adults.* Unpublished doctoral dissertation, Department of Psychology, University of Southern California, 1980.

Ohta, R. J. Spatial problem solving: The response selection tendencies of young and elderly adults. *Experimental Aging Research,* 1981, *8,* 36–39.

Ohta, R. J., & Kirasic, K. C. Learning about environmental learning in the elderly adult. In G. Rowles & R. J. Ohta (Eds.), *Aging and milieu: Environmental perspectives on growing old.* New York: Academic Press, 1983.

Ohta, R. J., Walsh, D. A., & Krauss, D. K. Spatial perspective-taking ability in young and elderly adults. *Experimental Aging Research,* 1981, *7,* 45–63.

Perlmutter, M. An apparent paradox about memory aging. In J. L. Fozard, L. W. Poon, L. S. Cermak, D. Arenberg, & L. W. Thompson (Eds.), *Memory and aging.* Hillsdale, NJ: Lawrence Erlbaum Associates, 1979.

Perlmutter, M., Metzger, R., Nezworski, T., & Miller, K. Spatial and temporal memory in 20 and 60 year olds. *Journal of Gerontology,* 1981, *36,* 59–65.

Piaget, J., & Inhelder, B. *The child's conception of space.* New York: Norton, 1967.

Rubin, K. H., Attewell, P. W., Tierney, M. C., & Tumolo, P. Development of spatial egocentrism and conservation across the life span. *Developmental Psychology,* 1973, *9,* 432.

Ruch, F. L. Adult learning. *Psychological Bulletin,* 1934, *30,* 387–414.

Schaie, K. W. External validity in the assessment of intellectual development in adulthood. *Journal of Gerontology,* 1978, *33,* 695–701.

Schaie, K. W., Rosenthal, F., & Perlman, R. Differential mental deterioration in later maturity. *Journal of Gerontology,* 1953, *8,* 191–196.

Schaie, K. W., & Strother, C. R. Cognitive variables in older college graduates. In G. A. Talland (Ed.), *Human aging and behavior.* New York: Academic Press, 1968.

Schonfield, D., & Robertson, B. A. Memory storage and aging. *Canadian Journal of Psychology,* 1966, *20,* 228–236.

Siegel, A. W. The externalization of cognitive maps by children and adults: In search of ways to ask better questions. In L. S. Liben, A. H. Patterson, & N. Newcomb (Eds.), *Spatial representation and behavior across the life span.* New York: Academic Press, 1981.

Siegel, A. W., Kirasic, K. C., & Kail, R. V. Stalking the elusive cognitive map: The development of children's representations of geographic space. In J. F. Wohlwill & I. Altman (Eds.), *Human behavior and environment: Vol. 3. Children and the environment.* New York: Plenum Press, 1978.

Siegel, A. W., & White, S. H. The development of spatial representations of large-scale environments. In H. W. Reese (Ed.), *Advances in child development and behavior* (Vol. 10). New York: Academic Press, 1975.

Waddell, K. J., & Rogoff, B. Effect of contextual organization on spatial memory of middle-aged and older women. *Developmental Psychology,* 1981, *17,* 878–885.

Wallace, J. G. Some studies of perception in relation to age. *British Journal of Psychology,* 1956, *47,* 283–297.

Walsh, D. A., Krauss, I. K., & Regnier, V. A. Spatial ability, environmental knowledge, and environmental use: The elderly. In L. S. Liben, A. H. Patterson, & N. Newcomb (Eds.), *Spatial representation and behavior across the life span.* New York: Academic Press, 1981.

Zannaras, G. *An analysis of cognitive and objective characteristics of the city: Their influence on movements to the city center.* Unpublished doctoral dissertation, Department of Geography, Ohio State University, 1973.

IV SPECIAL VARIABLES

8 The Role of Activity in Spatial Cognition

Sheila L. Cohen
Robert Cohen
Memphis State University

Historically, much of the experimental research on spatial cognition has involved the use of small-scale or model environments. The primary goal of this work was to assess an individual's ability to mentally manipulate spatial relations among objects. The recent interest among researchers in behavior occurring in large-scale environments has led to a shift both in the type of variables and in the cognitive abilities investigated. Since large-scale spaces surround the individual and demand participation rather than just passive observation (Ittelson, 1973), the person must cognitively integrate multiple views from multiple vantage points. While still interested in the mental manipulation of spatial information, researchers have expanded this interest to the representation and integration of information derived from the successive viewing demanded by large-scale environments. In terms of variables of interest, the move to large-scale environments opens the door for the investigation of the influence of various physical activities that bring the individual into contact with the different views of the space—an influence rarely of interest to researchers using model spaces.

In the present chapter, we review the literature on spatial cognition in terms of the role of activity for acquiring spatial knowledge. We present the research in two major sections. First we discuss research that provides somewhat indirect evidence on the influence of activity—research that often used naturalistic settings. Much of the work cited was not meant to assess activity factors; we have extrapolated the findings for our purposes. Next, we consider research that more systematically assessed the role of activity. It will become clear to the reader that the concept ''activity-in-space'' is often either ambiguously defined or narrowly defined to be synonymous with walking. In the final section of the chapter we present an analysis of previous work and suggest, we hope, a more meaningful conceptualization of activity-in-space.

INDIRECT EVIDENCE ON THE ROLE OF ACTIVITY

In addition to the experimental research with model environments, a great deal of the early research on spatial cognition examined knowledge of "real-world" or naturalistic settings. These settings included college campuses, small towns, and urban areas. The work was conducted in many countries and used a variety of socioeconomic populations. Although the purposes of many of these studies was not to evaluate the role of activity, nonetheless, implications for this influence can be drawn. Since much of this early work was with adults, we first present a discussion of the adult literature followed by a discussion of the research with children. The adult literature is presented under the three headings: length of residence, person variables, and environmental variables.

Adults: Length of Residence

The longer one lives in a particular locale, the greater the number of opportunities to explore and interact within the environment. With few exceptions (e.g., Ladd, 1970), performances on tests of spatial knowledge are positively related to length of residency. This has been found in cross-sectional research evaluating the accuracy of mapping spatial elements by residents of Ciudad Guayana, Venezuela (length of residence less than 6 months, less than 1 year, 1 to 5 years, or greater than 5 years; Appleyard, 1970) and in longitudinal research using wives of naval officers in a small Idaho town (length of residence 3 weeks and 3 months; Devlin, 1976). In addition, Golledge and Spector (1978) found that errors on a paired comparison distance task decreased with length of residence of adults in Columbus, Ohio. Milgram, Greenwald, Kessler, McKenna, and Waters (1972) reported an advantage in landmark usage as a function of length of residence. New York City residents could recognize pictures of locations in their home borough better than pictures of any other borough except Manhattan. The high recognition of Manhattan locations was attributed both to the frequency of visits and to the emotional significance of landmarks there. Finally, Walsh, Krauss, and Regnier (1981) noted a positive correlation between amount of activity and performance on a landmark placement task for elderly residents in Los Angeles.

The research reported above assessed the spatial knowledge only for residents of the locales. Some research has examined the acquisition of spatial knowledge by temporary inhabitants. Beck and Wood (1976) asked 31 adolescents on tour in London to draw maps after 3, 5, and 6 days in residence. There was little improvement in the number of landmarks depicted. The number of routes drawn changed dramatically over the 6 days as did the Euclidean or metric accuracy of the maps; in general, the maps became better integrated over time. These findings were replicated by Evans, Marrero, and Butler (1981), who assessed the maps of junior and senior undergraduates after 2 weeks, then after 10 months in Bordeaux, France. In addition to these longitudinal investigations, and offering a point of comparison with the earlier work cited, Francescato and Mebane (1973) assessed the maps of natives and nonnatives in Rome and Milan. The natives in each city drew more elements and a greater variety of elements than the nonnatives. Interestingly, the maps of the nonnatives contained more surrounding highways of the city than did the maps of the natives.

Three studies assessed the acquisition of spatial knowledge of new arrivals on a college campus. Evans et al. (1981) compared the mapping performance of the students visiting Bordeaux described previously with a group of freshmen entering the University of California, Irvine. Again subjects were tested after 2 weeks and after 10 months. The data across settings were quite similar with one exception. The students at Irvine showed better configuration knowledge earlier in residence and thus showed little improvement. Relevant to the issue of the influence of activity, the authors suggested that the opportunity to view the Irvine campus from single vantage points, which was not available in Bordeaux, led to this difference.

Herman, Kail, and Siegel (1979) tested different groups of entering freshmen at the University of Pittsburgh after 3 weeks, after 3 months, and after 6 months in residence. A variety of tasks was administered (e.g., recall of buildings, recognition of buildings, matching the name of buildings to their pictures, writing directions, and estimating distances between buildings). Although landmark and route knowledge improved between the 3-week and 3-month testings, little additional improvement occurred at 6 months. Some configuration knowledge was demonstrated as early as 3 weeks with a significant amount of "fine tuning" occurring at 6 months. Schouela, Steinberg, Leveton, and Wapner (1980) tested entering freshmen three, five, or six times over a 24-week period. Unlike Herman et al. (1979), these authors reported a continued improvement in landmark and route knowledge over the course of the study.

Summary and Conclusions. Other than Ladd (1970), researchers investigating the effect of increased amounts of activity within a naturalistic environment, defined in terms of length of residence, support the contention that activity within the space improves performance on tests of spatial knowledge. Landmarks and simple routes appear to be learned fairly rapidly—in 3 weeks or less. Slight increase in the number of landmarks and significant improvement in the number of routes and in configuration knowledge occur during the first 3 months of residence. Thus amount of exposure to an environment is an important factor for the construction of spatial representations. The point should be emphasized that time spent in residence is certainly an indirect measure of the activities engaged in by people in environments. The nature and extent of these activities would seem relevant for the acquisition of spatial knowledge.

Adults: Person Variables

Perhaps a more direct set of variables for the assessment of the role of activity falls under the rubric of person variables. We mean here those factors within or attributed to individuals that in part dictate the person's ability to function in the environment. Specifically, under this heading we review the research on variables such as metacognitive awareness of spatial ability, mobility, education, and socioeconomic level.

Kozlowski and Bryant (1977) found that individuals who stated they had a "good sense of direction" were more adept at learning a new environment than those who judged themselves to be poor on such tasks. The congruence of this metacognitive analysis with spatial performance was found on orientation and on mapping tasks. Interestingly, subjects did not differ in performance when they were uninformed about a subsequent spatial task; differences between groups emerged only when subjects were aware that the assessment would follow. This would suggest a conscious control of spatial abilities. As a related finding, Thorndyke and Stasz (1980) assessed visualization abilities and found that subjects who scored better on visualization tasks also more readily learned material from maps than those who scored poorly on visualization tasks.

As Acredolo (1982) in work with infants and Bronzaft, Dobrow, and O'Hanlon (1976) in work with adults have suggested, experience in the environment can give one a sense either of well-being or of insecurity. The awareness of poor directional skills or of poor visualization skills may persuade an individual to avoid situations that necessitate coping with maps or other navigational techniques. Perhaps these are the individuals who are forever asking for directions, thus limiting their opportunities for actively solving spatial dilemmas. Beck and Wood (1976) suggested that general experience in a variety of cities facilitates mastery of a novel city. Furthermore, being active and traveling independently lead to more accurate spatial knowledge than being relatively more passive, such as being one of a traveling group.

Mobility in the environment, as a function of age, health, or social factors, also influences the type of experience one has in an environment. Francescato and Mebane (1973) found that adults in both Rome and Milan who were 30 years of age and under tended to draw more paths in their maps, while older subjects indicated more landmarks. The authors suggested that the older subjects may have been less likely to have learned the city by car than the younger individuals. This interpretation rests on the assumption that landmarks are more salient features to walkers and paths are more salient to drivers/riders.

Walsh et al. (1981) explored the relationship of a number of mobility factors for the spatial knowledge of elderly adults. Healthy males in Long Beach,

California, drew more accurate maps than the other elderly individuals. Good health and higher levels of education also were positively correlated with performances on landmark placements. Finally, as a direct relationship for the issue of mobility, the scope of the neighborhood maps drawn was positively correlated with amount of driving and ability to walk, and the use of facilities in the environment was positively correlated with the amount of exploration of the environment. Karan, Bladen, and Singh (1980) provided additional support for the positive influence of level of education and mobility factors based on maps drawn by slum dwellers and squatters from three areas of Patna, India.

Several studies have noted social and cultural influences on an individual's spatial knowledge. Karan et al. (1980) noted that Hindu subjects emphasized temples in their maps, while Moslem subjects emphasized mosques. Orleans (1973) reported that middle class residents of Los Angeles, relative to lower class residents, had friends in a broader range of locations and drew maps depicting a greater part of the city.

A few studies with adult subjects have examined the effects of specific activity patterns on subsequent tasks of spatial knowledge. Golledge and Spector (1978) had subjects rate their familiarity with 49 locations in Columbus, Ohio, and then give paired comparisons of distance estimates. Those whose home and job required a long travel distance, and thus a more expansive activity pattern, demonstrated a broader knowledge of spatial locations. People who lived in a locale estimated distance between locations in that area more accurately than people who did not live there but traveled to the area. In addition, the closer the sample point was to the activity space of the person, the more accurate the distance estimate.

Summary. It is probable that an individual's mobility affects the type of his or her experiences by modifying the frequency, expansiveness, pleasure, and purpose of the activity. Educational level may provide more experience with such things as maps, and also may influence what the individual comes to feel is important in an environment. Increased travel in a variety of cities may allow one to anticipate the basic layout of a city and more effectively code and store information regarding the routes and landmarks. Sociocultural values as well as socioeconomic status affect types of experiences; for example, religious affiliation will dictate the religious institution one frequents. Also, socioeconomic status determines, in part, the amount and type of travel in a city. A less affluent individual may travel primarily from work to home and within the neighborhood. A person with a greater income may belong to a variety of organizations or attend various social functions that occur throughout a city. Though both may have resided in the city a comparable amount of time, their activity within the space may not be equivalent. Thus, it would appear that person characteristics, such as those reviewed, influence spatial representations through varied types of activity, a consideration obscured in research that only assessed length of residence, and merely implied in research that assessed person variables.

Adults: Environmental Variables

Physical factors of the environment certainly play a major role in the nature of activity that can be performed and consequently the cognitive representation of the space. Environmental factors that have been investigated and are briefly reviewed here are mode of transportation, distances among destinations, physical structures in the environment, means by which the environment was learned, and the weather.

Mode of transportation has been examined by comparing measures of spatial knowledge for people who typically travel through the space in different ways (e.g., car, mass transit, pedestrians). While pedestrians have the most direct sensorimotor experiences, walking limits the amount of space covered. Transit riders are the most physically passive participants of the three and are least involved in navigation decisions. Transit riders have been shown to draw less accurate maps of the environment than the more active travelers (Appleyard, 1970; Beck & wood, 1976), and to make more errors on a paired comparison distance estimation task (Golledge & Spector, 1978). As a final point, Carr and Schissler (1969) reported that although the recall of landmarks along an expressway was not affected as a function of being a driver, commuter, or passenger, all three groups tended to recall landmarks more directly on the road rather than more distant landmarks.

Related to mode of travel, the distance between locations is in itself an important environmental factor. The farther one must travel between home and work, the more accurate and comprehensive are the maps produced (Karan et al., 1980). In addition, the closer a location is to one's activity space between work and home, the more accurate are the distance estimates involving that location (Golledge & Spector, 1978).

The structure of the environment that exists between locations also influences spatial representations. Sadalla and Staplin (1980) found that people at a shopping mall estimated the distance to one location as greater than to another although the two places were in fact physically equidistant from the mall. The location viewed as closer had fewer intervening intersections, less traffic, and less commercial business, and took less time to travel. In a laboratory study also reported, all but the influence of the number of intersections were ruled out.

Lee (1970) reported that distances toward a downtown area were overestimated relative to locations away from the downtown area. This finding was supported by Briggs (1973). Karan et al. (1980) found that on maps of Patna, India, the central or downtown section was exaggerated in area and the outlying residential areas were reduced in relative size. Finally, as a factor peripherally related to the influence of the structure of the environment, several investigators have reported that the functional value of landmarks as foci for activity is highly salient in spatial representations—more so even than perceptually salient landmarks (Golledge & Spector, 1978; Moore, 1979).

The type of activity engaged in while learning an environment is a fourth environmental variable to be considered. Evans and Pezdek (1980) presented subjects slides of states or of buildings on a college campus. Reaction times for recognition increased as a linear relationship to the amount of rotation (i.e., 0°, 60°, 120°, or 180°) for the states but not for the buildings. Presumably the buildings were learned from multiple perspectives but the configuration of states was not. This hypothesis was supported in a second study (Experiment 3) where students at the University of California, Irvine campus, studied maps of the San Bernardino campus. A linear function between response time and degree of rotation of the buildings was found. Furthermore, this explanation is supported by the data reported earlier under length of residence comparing maps after 2 weeks and after 10 months by students at Irvine and at Bordeaux (Evans et al., 1981). The maps of Bordeaux, a city that required multiple views to see the entire space, increased in terms of organization and complexity across testings, whereas the maps of Irvine, which could be viewed in its entirety from single vantage points, showed little additional improvement over time.

As a final environmental influence to be discussed, weather would certainly seem to be an important factor for an individual's activity. Little research has examined this factor. Devlin (1976) assessed changes in maps of navy officers' wives who had moved to Idaho Falls, Idaho, in either September or December. The women were asked to draw maps after residing for 2 to 3 weeks in the city and again after having lived there for 3 months. There was no difference between the two groups in the number of streets drawn on the first map. After 3 months, both groups showed a significant increase in the number of streets depicted. However, the Winter group averaged 20.1 streets and the Fall group showed a mean gain of 8.6 streets. Although the Fall group experienced the weather as increasingly more severe over time, the Winter group experienced relatively constant weather conditions. The Fall group probably curtailed their activity and exploration of the environment whereas the Winter group did not.

Research With Children

Much of the indirect evidence on children relevant to our discussion of the role of activity centers around the notion of home range, or activity space. The physical sphere of activity for children is conceptually parallel to the variable of length of residence for adults. Whereas time is a delimiting factor for how adults interact in their environments, the spatial boundaries placed on children through a home range influence the types of interactions accessible to children.

A general finding in terms of activity space is that with age, children are allowed increasingly broader access to areas away from the home (Andrews, 1973; Hazen, 1982; Matthews, 1980; Mauer & Baxter, 1972). A number of factors influence the determination of activity. Hilly locales, amount of traffic, presence of sidewalks, and distance from home to destination are considerations for parents (Andrews, 1973; Berg & Medrich, 1980). Andrews (1973) asked Grades 9 and 13 adolescents in five schools in west central Toronto, which varied from 1.25 to 16.56 miles from specified landmarks, to identify the location of 20 familiar buildings or areas on an outline map. Grade 13 students overall were more accurate than Grade 9 students, supporting the concept of the development of a broader activity space. In addition, students at the closest schools to the locations were more accurate in their landmark placements than same-grade peers at more distant schools. Interestingly, the Grade 9 students at the most centrally located school were more accurate than the Grade 13 students at the more distant schools. Familiarity with the landmarks was not a determining factor. Rather, the distance from the landmarks and the amount of interactions within the downtown area were the important mediators.

Anooshian and Young (1981) found that groups of first and second graders, fourth and fifth graders, and seventh and eighth graders showed comparable relative accuracy in localizing the positions of landmarks in their own neighborhoods. Although all groups showed a general representation of their neighborhoods, it appeared that, with age, this representation became more coordinated and integrated in terms of such measures as absolute accuracy and consistency of localizations.

Similar to the adult literature, research demonstrates that mode of travel also influences the spatial knowledge of children (Brown & Broadway, 1981; Hart, 1981; Mauer & Baxter, 1972). In general, as would be expected, children who walk to school include natural elements (i.e., trees, grass, etc.) in their maps, while those who are driven by car or bus tend to include roads. Hart (1981) also noted that children under eight years of age who rode to school had less of an idea about the distance between home and school than those who walked. Adolescents who drive draw better maps of neighboring towns than adolescents who do not drive (Andrews, 1973; Brown & Broadway, 1981).

Social class factors influence the activity space of children as well (Berg & Medrich, 1980; Mauer & Baxter, 1972). This influence possibly is mediated by travel experience through such factors as education and amount of travel as mentioned previously in the review of the adult literature.

Nerlove, Munroe, and Munroe (1971) reported that the amount of active exploration of the environment was positively correlated with performance on the spatial tasks of copying block patterns, copying geometric figures, and working mazes for 5- to 8-year-old children in Western Kenya. As a more refined assessment of the effects of exploration, Hazen (1982) first observed children ages 20 to 28 months and 36 to 44 months at a "hands-on" museum and later at a laboratory playhouse. Children who explored actively or independently within the museum did so in the laboratory setting. Amount of exploration was not consistent between settings, but type or style of activity was. Active explorers were better able to find their way when there was a route reversal or a detour in the lab. There was however no difference between groups for learning a new route in the lab.

In another study, Hazen & Durrett (1982) posited that the style of exploration was influenced by interaction with the mother, particularly in terms of the attachment relationship. Children who were judged more securely attached at one year were more active in exploration at 30 to 34 months when compared to children who were classified as anxious/avoidant or anxious/resistant in their attachment relationship. In comparison to the other two groups, the securely attached explorers again were better able to find their way when a detour was demanded. In addition, they tended to be better able to reverse a route ($p < .058$) when compared to the anxious/avoidant group. Finally, active explorers appeared to be better able to manipulate acquired spatial information. Perhaps active explorers have more experience with identifying information necessary for efficient use of a cognitive representation.

DIRECT EVIDENCE FOR THE ROLE OF ACTIVITY

A great number of different spaces and different tasks have been used to assess the role of activity. For example, environments have varied from small enclosures for assessing the abilities of infants (e.g., Reiser, 1979), to classroom size environments (e.g., Cohen & Weatherford, 1980), to environments constructed in gymnasiums (Herman & Siegel, 1978), to hallways (Acredolo, Pick, & Olsen, 1975), to school campuses (Cousins, Siegel, & Maxwell, 1983). Tasks have varied from an orientation task with infants (e.g., Reiser, 1979), to search behavior (e.g., Wellman, Somerville, & Haake, 1979), to distance estimation (e.g., Cohen, Weatherford, Lomenick, & Koeller, 1979), to reconstructing the space onto a model (e..g, Siegel & Schadler, 1977) or back onto the original layout of the environment (e.g., Herman & Siegel, 1978), to what is known as a triangulation procedure (e.g., Cousins et al., 1983).

Our approach for organizing this literature is to focus on the role of movement for the construction of spatial knowledge of children beyond preschool age. However, to provide a more comprehensive background for this work, we first consider briefly the research using orientation tasks with infants and search tasks with infants through school-aged children. Besides being the dominant spatial research paradigms with these young age groups, this work seems to us to be most directly related to the spatial functioning we consider in greater detail later.

Orientation Abilities of Infants

Assessment of the spatial knowledge of the infant has used tasks that require the infant to maintain orientation after a 180° rotation. The infant is conditioned to locate an object (Bremner & Bryant, 1977) or an event (Acredolo, 1978) by looking to the left or to the right. After the training trials to criterion, the infant is rotated 180°. The looking response that follows the movement is assumed to indicate the infant's ability to code spatial information. A variety of factors appear to influence whether the infant responds egocentrically; i.e., after the rotation the infant continues to respond in relation to his or her own body rather than incorporating information about the change of the objects in space relative to the infant's own body.

Initially, in the laboratory, infants 6 to 11 months of age appeared to respond egocentrically (Acredolo, 1978; Bremner & Bryant, 1977; Reiser, 1979). However, further study has indicated that environmental factors such as familiarity, e.g., home versus laboratory setting (Acredolo, 1979), a familiarization period prior to testing (Acredolo, 1982), cues available (Acredolo, 1978; Acredolo & Evans, 1980; Bremner, 1978; Reiser, 1979) and the mother's movement in space (Presson & Ihrig, 1982) modified the infant's style of responding.

Acredolo (1978) demonstrated that 16-month-old infants are better able to maintain orientation than 11- or 6-month-old infants. In addition, the change in orientation ability was much greater between the two older ages than between the 6- and 11-month-olds. The older infants are beginning to walk independently, adding a new dimension to their experiences. It may be that this activity is an important component in the development of orientation.

As an additional study highlighting the role of walking and related to the ability to maintain one's orientation in space, Heth and Cornell (1980) assessed the wayfinding ability of newly walking 1-year-olds versus 3-year-olds in a two-choice maze. Three-year-olds were better able to incorporate feedback following an error and were better able to use information gained from viewing or walking the reversal of the route. However, when observing their mother walk the route, 1-year-olds were able to learn the route as rapidly as 3-year-olds and were better able to use feedback from error trials than in simple trial-and-error experiences. Since the younger infants benefited from watching another walk the route but this experience was unnecessary for facilitating the behavior of the 3-year-olds, the authors suggest that, with development, infants and children become increasingly able to independently glean and use landmark information for wayfinding.

It is understandable that Heth and Cornell (1980) did not want the children to have direct experience with the route. Rather than interpreting the data in terms of the use of landmarks for wayfinding, other processes may be involved. As noted above, research indicates that it is between 11 and 16 months that infants make dramatic gains in the ability to maintain orientation (Acredolo, 1978). Also, mother is often used as an orientation or landmark base (Presson & Ihrig, 1982). Finally, the ability to reverse one's route has been shown to be more difficult for 2-year-olds than for 3-year-olds (Hazen, 1982).

We suggest three projects that would help clarify the role of activity for spatial knowledge in these young children. First, it would be interesting to assess in a novel environment situation the orientation ability of same-aged infants who walk and those who do not. If walking is an important process for the development of orientation skills, those infants with no walking experiences should show low levels of orientation ability. It would also be interesting to extend this procedure down and look at same-aged children who are crawlers versus not crawlers. Second, and similar to the first proposal, it would be interesting to assess the wayfinding ability of same-aged infants who have been walking for different periods of time. Finally, to flesh out the findings from Heth and Cornell (1980), we would like to see how infants do on a wayfinding task, following the model walking the exact route the child must later walk versus the model walking the reverse of that route.

Search Behaviors

An interesting domain of research with young children which is most pertinent to the present chapter concerns search behaviors. The research considered here, relying heavily on the extensive review of Wellman and Somerville (1982), involves a motoric expression of searching rather than just visual scanning or an internal, cognitive search. As noted by Wellman and Somerville, this class of problems involves the recognition of a need to search, an identified object for search, a search space, information about the object, space, and so forth, and strategies for search. There are two basic search strategies, which vary in their efficiency and effectiveness depending on the situation. A comprehensive search strategy involves an exhaustive search of possible locales; a selective search strategy involves sampling a set of locales for search from the entire collection of possible locales.

Wellman and Somerville (1982) document the course of search behaviors in infants through young school-age children. Infant tasks of object permanence satisfy the criteria for search tasks albeit the demands placed on the infant are quite reduced. Piagetian-defined Stage 4 infants (8 to 12 months) will search for a totally hidden object. Although a variety of studies have shown that these infants are sensitive to simple cues, the search behavior remains quite inconsistent. Thus Wellman and Somerville suggest that the infant recognizes that an object is "out there" in some objective way but cannot consistently organize, plan, or execute a successful search.

The Stage 5 infant (12 to 18 months) is quite successful at recovering a viewed object that is hidden. As an additional extension over the younger infant, this aged infant also is quite successful at finding a hidden object that was not in view. For example, if the experimenter covers a desired toy with his or her hand and moves the hand under one of five containers, the infant will most often search under the correct container. However, it is not until the end of infancy, Stage 6 (18 to 24 months), that invisible displacements are mastered. In this task, the object is not only invisibly hidden but also is invisibly moved to another hiding place.

While the research on self-initiated search and on self-defined search spaces is lacking for infants, the research on search behavior of toddlers is more systematic and to the point of the phenomenon. Toddlers have little difficulty performing a selective search when watching an experimenter hide Easter eggs on a playground (Wellman, Haake, & Somerville, 1981); when given verbal instruction to search (Wellman, Somerville, & Haake, 1979); or when the object being searched for has a typical location (e.g., fork in the kitchen; Sophian & Wellman, 1980).

Further work has shown that this selective search is indeed a logical search and not simply due to a strong association by the child. Wellman et al. (1979) and Haake, Somerville, and Wellman (1980) demonstrated that 3- to 5-year-olds would begin their search for a lost object at the last location where the object was seen prior to its absence. Thus a camera used at location 3 and discovered missing at location 7 resulted in the child selectively beginning the search at location 3.

As noted, a comprehensive search is required when no information is available to limit the search space. Children as young as 2 seem to understand this requirement; however, if the task is such that it is difficult to remember which locations were searched previously, 2-year-olds are much less comprehensive in their search than 3-year-olds. A significant majority of 3-year-olds can search comprehensively on this kind of task, even when the array of locations is nonsystematic (Wellman, Revelle, & Sophian, 1982; cited in Wellman & Somerville, 1982). In addition, the 2-year-olds are less efficient in their search behavior. Unlike the 3-year-olds, the younger children repeatedly search those locations they have previously investigated. Thus 2-year-olds are not as successful as 3-year-olds in performing nonredundant, comprehensive searches.

Another aspect of efficiency of comprehensive search is to minimize the amount of distance traveled between locations. Hazen (1982) taught young children a route through three small rooms. When presented with either a novel starting position or a detour in the original route, 3-year-olds minimized the amount of travel distance more than 2-year-olds. Interestingly, children of both ages avoided backtracking.

The 3-year-olds in the above studies showed the ability to derive logical inferences for their search behavior (i.e., they knew to limit a search to a critical area), but inferential abilities are far from fully developed. For example, Drozdal and Flavell (1975) reported that although the majority of 5- to 10-year-olds first searched a critical area, none of the youngest children, and only 50% of the 7-year-olds, recognized that the lost object by necessity had to be in that area and nowhere else.

Another ability to develop beyond the preschool years is in terms of planning. While the literature reported shows that preschoolers can plan ahead to some degree (e.g., no backtracking, little redundant comprehensive searches), Kreutzer, Leonard, and Flavell (1975) noted that fifth graders, more so than kindergartners, were able to generate more alternative plans for a search task, include more indirect steps in the plan, and in general conceive of more complex steps for searching.

In summary, Wellman and Somerville (1982) propose a four-phase sequence for the development of search behaviors from infancy through childhood. One-year-olds will search for an object they see being hidden and are influenced by a number of body and location cues. Following this phase a search for invisibly hidden objects or objects to which they are verbally directed is performed. The preschooler, for whom we have the greatest amount of data, can perform selective and comprehensive searches in a relatively efficient fashion. The school-aged child is considerably more creative and planful and can reflect on the necessity involved in inferences as well as their consistency.

We turn next to an examination of the role of activity beyond the preschool years. Although a great deal of research exists on children's selection and use of landmarks and routes (e.g., Allen, 1981; Allen, 1982; Allen, Kirasic, Siegel, & Herman, 1979; Cohen & Schuepfer, 1980; Hazen, Lockman, & Pick, 1978; Siegel & White, 1975) we limit our discussion to those studies that offer direct evidence for the role of activity. This literature is presented under the headings: familiarity and amount of contact, active versus passive exploration, control of activity, and the functions of activity.

Familiarity and Amount of Contact

Parallel to the adult literature assessing the effect of length of residence in naturalistic settings, some research with children has examined the role of exposure for spatial knowledge of other settings. Siegel and Schadler (1977) had kindergartners create model constructions of their classrooms after 1 month in school, then after 8 months. A measure of absolute accuracy of object placements showed improvement at the second testing. However, on general measures of object location, i.e., local relational accuracy (the accuracy of a placement relative to adjacent items) and global relational accuracy (the accuracy of placement of clusters relative to other clusters of objects), accuracy did not improve over time.

Familiarity with a specific section of a school campus has been found to influence performance on a route scaling task and on bearing estimates. Cousins et al. (1983) examined the spatial knowledge of a school campus of first graders whose activities were primarily on the south side, fourth graders whose activities were on both the south and north sides, and seventh graders whose activities were primarily on the north side. All children had gym and assemblies on the south side and lunch and chapel on the north, thereby assuring some experience with the entire campus. First and fourth graders were more accurate than seventh graders in ordering photographs of scenes from a route on the south side of the campus (route scaling task). When the route was equally divided between the two sides, there was no difference in the performance of the three age groups. When the route was on the north side of the campus, the seventh graders were more accurate than the fourth graders, who in turn were more accurate than the first graders. In addition, on tests of bearing, each grade level was more accurate at pointing from the unfamiliar side of the campus to a target location on the familiar side than the reverse.

The amount of walking in a mock town was controlled by Herman and Siegel (1978). The town was composed of a "road" and "railroad tracks" placed on a 4.9 by 6.1 m area. Eight model buildings were scattered among the four quadrants formed by the intersection of road and railroad tracks. Kindergartners, second graders, and fifth graders walked through the town three times and reconstructed the town either after all three walks or after each walk by replacing the model buildings onto the original layout (Experiment 1). While fifth graders were more accurate than the other age groups on all comparisons, children at each grade level improved as a function of both the number of trips and the number of reconstructions. Interestingly, children were more accurate reconstructing the space for the first time after three walks than they were reconstructing it for the first time after one walk. This influence of repeated trips facilitating the acquisition of spatial knowledge was replicated by Siegel, Herman, Allen, and Kirasic (1979) using the same environment as Herman and Siegel (1978) and varying the scale of acquisition and response environments.

Familiarity with an environment, as measured by amount of exposure, has not always been shown to facilitate spatial knowledge. Using a familiar playground and an unfamiliar hallway, Acredolo et al. (1975) assessed preschoolers' and second graders' memory for the location of an event. During a walk, the experimenter "accidentally" dropped her keys. Later, the children were asked to return to that location. Those forewarned about this task performed significantly better than those not forewarned. Landmarks close to the event also facilitated performance. But familiarity with the environment did not influence performance.

Similarly, Cohen et al. (1979) found that the spatial representation of a familiar environment was not superior to that of a novel space. A comparison of interlocation distance estimates of first and fifth graders for either a novel classroom environment or a familiar school library was made. Although the type of estimation task interacted with the age of the child, both age groups performed better across tasks when estimating distances between locations in the novel space.

In a somewhat different vein, Anooshian and Young (1981) measured familiarity by means of a questionnaire. Results of bearing estimates of the neighborhood indicated that the age differences in accuracy were not due to a difference in familiarity.

Unlike the literature reported earlier on length of residency, the research reviewed here reports equivocal support for the notion that increased contact or activity in an environment results in greater spatial knowledge. Perhaps a more appropriate conclusion as put forth by Cousins et al. (1983) is that some basic amount of experience is necessary. In addition, Cohen et al. (1979) suggested that the amount of activity within the environment may not be as critical for the construction of spatial representations as the specific type of interactions within the space. In short, amount of exposure to an environment is at best a very crude assessment of an individual's activity in that environment.

Active Versus Passive Exporation

From a variety of theoretical perspectives, active locomotor movement within a large-scale environment presumably leads to a more accurate and flexible spatial representation than physically passive experiences (see Siegel & White, 1975). Actively moving through the environment brings the individual into contact with the multiple perspectives of the space and facilitates the integration of views and the coordination of percepts with motor experiences. Although there is little disagreement over this conceptual issue, the research on the role of walking has led to several qualifications on this claim of advantage for active movement.

Herman (1980) assessed the ability of kindergartners and third graders to reconstruct the mock town, previously described, following either a walk through the town or a walk around the periphery of the space. Those who walked through the space reconstructed the environment more accurately than those who walked the perimeter. However, Herman and Siegel (1978) reported that with kindergartners, second graders, and fifth graders, those who merely watched an experimenter walk through the town reconstructed the layout as accurately as those who actively walked through the space (Experiment 2).

Cohen, Weatherford, and Byrd (1980) also examined the effect of walking through an environment versus merely looking at the space. Third and sixth graders either walked through the environment or stood on the periphery while the experimenter directed their attention to objects and distances between locations. Regardless of motor activity, if the response task demanded physical activity congruent with the acquisition experience, children estimated interlocation distances most accurately. The younger children significantly overestimated distances when the acquisition task was passive (viewing only) and the response condition was active (walking to demonstrate distance). Actively walking in the environment during acquisition coupled with a passive response condition (telling the experimenter where to place cards to show distances) led to some overestimation of distances but statistically similar performance to the two congruent conditions. Performances of the older children were equivalent across all experimental groups. Thus, for younger children, actively walking in the environment led to a somewhat more flexible use of spatial knowledge than not walking in the space.

Herman, Kolker, and Shaw (1982) compared the reconstruction of a mock town by kindergartners and third graders following standing and observing the town, riding through the town in a wagon, or walking through the town. Kindergartners who walked or rode were more accurate than those who stood outside and observed. Third graders were more accurate than kindergartners, and there were no significant differences in the performances of the third graders across activity conditions.

Although the above studies assessed the global issue of walking versus simply viewing, two studies have examined the specific effects of the routes walked in an environment. Cohen and Weatherford (1980) assessed the distance estimation ability of second and sixth graders and adults in a novel environment consisting of seven identical stimulus locations and three barriers. The space encountered and the path walked by subjects were designed such that each subject experienced the factorial combination of barriers (present versus absent) and route (traveled versus not traveled) across each of three interlocation distances (4, 6, and 8 feet). For all ages, estimates of traveled routes containing barriers were more accurate than barrier-present routes that had not been traveled. Thus, though other studies have shown that barriers to direct travel lead to distortions in spatial representations when walking is neither controlled nor assessed (Cohen, Baldwin, & Sherman, 1978; Kosslyn, Pick, & Fariello, 1974), walking can help subjects compensate for these potentially distorting effects. These results were replicated using a different environment, first and fifth graders, and a reconstruction response task (Cohen & Weatherford, 1981).

Those studies above reporting no advantage of walking over simply viewing were performed in spaces that were large in size but in fact were small in scale in that the entire space could be viewed from single vantage points (e.g., Cohen et al., 1980; Herman & Siegel, 1978). Cohen and Weatherford (1980, 1981) showed significant benefit attributable to walking when paths were blocked by barriers, i.e., when walking in a large-scale environment. Furthermore, in both of the Cohen and Weatherford studies, estimates for barrier-absent routes were equally accurate whether the route had been directly walked or not.

As a direct test of this relationship between walking and scale of environment, Weatherford and Cohen (1981) had third and sixth graders either walk through a novel experimental environment or view the space from viewing positions on each of the four sides. Screens prevented seeing the environment while moving between viewing positions. In addition to these activity conditions, children were presented either an environment that contained barriers within it, or the same configuration of locations with no barriers. Sixth graders estimated interlocation distances equally accurately whether walking through or simply viewing, for both the small- and large-scale spaces. Third graders were significantly more accurate in their estimates for the large-scale environment when in the walking through condition. These children performed equivalently across activity conditions when the environment was barrier-free (i.e., small-scale). Thus, walking seems to have its greatest influence when an individual is required to integrate multiple views of the space, particularly for young children. This finding is reminiscent of those reported earlier by Evans et al. (1981) comparing the spatial knowledge of new residents to Bordeaux versus the University of California, Irvine. Recall that configuration knowledge was better for the Irvine campus, where the entire space could be viewed from single vantage points.

Control of Activity

Some investigators have examined the influence of the control of activity on spatial knowledge. Feldman and Acredolo (1979) measured the accuracy of memory for the location of an object as a function of either self-directed or experimenter-directed exploration of the environment. Four- and 10-year-old children either walked or were led through a rectangular hallway in search of an object, which they later were asked to relocate. For the younger children, active exploration facilitated memory for spatial location. The older children's memory was not influenced by either control condition. As discussed earlier, this facilitative effect of active exploration is supported by Hazen (1982).

In contrast to these studies, Herman (1980), with kindergarten and third-grade children, found that children with the greater amount of experimenter-directed activity more accurately reconstructed the environment than children in a self-directed activity condition. Children in the self-directed condition were told to remember the location of the buildings of the mock town and were allowed to explore freely. Children in the experimenter-controlled condition were led through the town and directed to look at and label each location.

Feldman and Acredolo (1979) compared child- versus adult-directed movement and left the directing of viewing to the child. Herman (1980) compared child- versus adult-directed movement and viewing. Poag, Cohen, and Weatherford (1983) clarified the contributions of the control of movement versus the control of viewing. Kindergartners and second graders experienced either self-versus adult-directed movement coupled with either self- versus adult-directed viewing in a novel large-scale environment. In terms of interlocation distance estimates, kindergartners who controlled their own movement were able to estimate distances equally well regardless of who controlled the viewing. However, if the experimenter controlled the young child's movement, distance estimates were more accurate if the experimenter also controlled the viewing. Second graders performed equally well across all four experimental conditions. Since all children were forewarned about the estimation task, it seems that the young children based their spatial knowledge primarily on their own self-movements and coordinated their views of the space to those movements regardless of who directed those views. Taking away the control of those movements presumably hindered the kindergartner in this coordination unless the views were directed as well.

Functions of Activity

Moore (1979) reported that for a naturalistic setting, landmarks that have functional value are more salient than landmarks that only have unique physical characteristics. The research reported thus far on the role of activity focused on either the amount of activity in an environment or the movement among locations in the environment. Since landmarks are key organizational features of spatial representations (Siegel & White, 1975), perhaps landmarks that allow for meaningful activity at the locale facilitate the acquisition of spatial knowledge for the space.

This hypothesis was assessed by Cohen and Cohen (1982). First and sixth graders were introduced to a novel environment containing five locations. Children assigned to an interact-linked activity condition were told that they would find what they needed in the space to write and mail a letter. On the first trip through the space the necessary items were pointed out: a pencil at location 1, paper at location 3, envelope and stamp at location 4, and box at location 5. On a second trip through the space, the child performed the activities for writing and mailing a letter. Specifically, the child picked up the pencil at location 1; walked to location 2; walked to location 3 and signed his or her name on the paper; walked to location 4, placed the paper in the envelope and a stamp on the envelope; walked to location 5 and "mailed" the letter in the box; returned the pencil to location 1. Finally, the child was taken on a third trip along the route picking up color cards, which were to be used in the distance estimation task. Note that four of the five locations were functionally linked by the letter-writing activity.

Children in an interact-only activity condition used similar materials as those in the interact-linked group but the activities were not functionally linked. The items were noted on the first trip through the space. On the second trip, the child removed the pencil from its holder and left it at location 1; walked to location 2; walked to location 3 and drew a circle on the paper at location 3; walked to location 4 and placed a blank sheet of paper in the envelope and a sticker on the back of the envelope; walked to location 5 and placed a triangle found there into the box; returned to location 1 and put the pencil back in its holder. Like the interact-linked group, the child in the interact-only group walked the route a third time, picking up color cards.

As a third group, children were assigned to a walk-only group. These children merely walked the designated route three times, performed no other activities, and picked up the color cards on the third trip. Thus, this group experienced the space in much the same manner as many of the groups in the previous studies.

Children estimated all pairwise interlocation distances. Sixth graders were more accurate in their estimates than first graders. Children in the interact-linked group estimated distances more accurately than children in the other two groups, which did not differ statistically from each other. Interestingly, no estimation differences occurred on routes that were directly functionally linked by the letter-writing theme compared to routes not directly linked by the activity. Thus, the facilitative effect of the letter-writing activity was global across the environment and not limited to specific paths.

A recent unpublished study has led us to refine this last conclusion. We replicated Cohen and Cohen (1982) with one critical exception: we included barriers in the space. The results showed that while again the interact-linked group outperformed the other groups, the primary facilitative effect was for the estimation of those paths that contained intervening barriers. Thus, as suggested above for the research on active versus passive exploration, activity plays its greatest role when confronted with large-scale environments. The complexity of these spaces is better comprehended when walking versus merely viewing and when engaged in functional activity versus simply walking or simply performing isolated activities.

CONCLUSION

Children and adults construct their knowledge of environments from their experiences in the environments. In this chapter we reviewed both the indirect and the direct evidence of the parameters of experience that influence this knowledge. In this final section, we offer some tentative conclusions about the role of activity in spatial cognition.

Activity-in-space was proposed as a mediator for many of the effects reported in the first major section. Variables such as socioeconomic class, weather, or home range were shown to be related to spatial knowledge and behavior. Each of these operates, in part, through facilitating and inhibiting a variety of activities in settings. As a general index of activity-in-space, defined as length of residency in naturalistic settings and amount of exposure to novel spaces, the research tends to confirm the expectation that the greater one's experiences in a space, the greater one's spatial knowledge of the space. As we noted, however, this is at best a very crude measure of activity-in-space. Although a certain amount of exposure is of course necessary to glean spatial information, it seems to be far more critical to determine the nature of the individual's activity when assessing the influence of activity.

For the most part, the experimental research has investigated the role of active locomotor movement in space. Given the extant theoretical perspectives on spatial cognition, this was certainly a logical starting point. Yet we would hope that the research presented in the previous section on functional activity will expand the perspectives on activity. Any motor activity in space operates in the service of other cognitive and social concerns. We do not walk (or ride) to a shopping mall in order to walk (or ride). There is a purpose to the activity. This purpose provides a conceptual theme to the activity, which aids not only in the enactment of the theme but also in the use of spatial information in the service of the theme.

From this broader conceptualization, we would urge for the consideration of a variety of variables when investigating the role of activity in spatial cognition. At a molecular level, what cognitive demands are necessitated by various motor activities? How are processes such as attention and integration of multiple views affected by activities? At a more molar level, how do children evaluate the spaces in which they participate? What forms of social interactions are influenced by what types of environmental activity? How do the goals and purposes of activities vary with spaces and with development?

We are not suggesting that spatial cognition is subservient to these other factors, nor are we suggesting an inadequacy to the "pure" research on spatial cognition. Rather, we are suggesting that the ability to encode, comprehend, and manipulate spatial information is an important partner to other cognitive and social abilities. One's behavior in, and knowledge of, space will be determined by the dynamic interplay among one's developmental status, the nature of the setting, how the environment is encountered, the goals of the activity, and the social exchanges in a setting. This position is consistent with what Siegel (1982) terms the social ecology of cognitive mapping.

In terms of developmental status, based on research reported in the first section, it appears that although children are influenced in similar ways as adults, based on mode of travel in the space, the representations of children are less integrated than adults. In addition, children's activities in space are limited by home ranges that are negotiated with parents. Interestingly, exploration was found to be related to attachment relationship with mother (Hazen & Durrett, 1982). In terms of the more direct, experimental research on activity, we know how infants come to rely on cues other than self for orienting in space. We know how toddlers and preschoolers come to be able not only to perform nonredundant comprehensive searches, but eventually to understand and reflect on the logical necessity of their search activities. We know that young children seem to rely more than older children on motor cues when asked to recall environmental information. Movement, practice with the response task, or an organizing theme for the activity leads to better spatial knowledge, in general, than no movement, no practice, or no theme.

It is difficult to make sweeping statements concerning development progressions of the phenomena reviewed. Different age groups were assessed for different forms of spatial knowledge using very different tasks. We can propose the following sequence based largely on the experimental findings. The task of infants is to comprehend the stability of objects in the world and to coordinate, at least in terms of motor responses, the perspectives of self and others in relation to those stable objects. The toddler and preschooler are learning to deal with the world on the conceptual plane. While motor movements are still quite salient, the child is learning to establish spatial plans and goals and to coordinate actions for those plans and goals. The older child comes to demonstrate a great flexibility both in the acquisition and the use of spatial information. This child can reflect on the necessity for certain search patterns, can display spatial knowledge derived from passive as well as active experiences, and can do so across a variety of spatial tasks. Though it is presumably the case that orientation abilities of infants, search behaviors of toddlers, and the memory of spatial layouts of older children are theoretically linked, the empirical sequences of these behaviors remain open to study.

While focusing on the role of activity for spatial cognition, we noted at several points the important interplay of both task demands and structure of the environment. The reader is directed to other chapters in this book (i.e., Newcombe; Weatherford; Poag, Goodnight, & Cohen; Golbeck) for in-depth treatments of these variables. For the purposes of the present chapter it is important to note how these variables interact with various activity experiences.

In terms of task demands, it is clear that different tasks will lead to different performances following identical environmental experiences (e.g., Cohen et al., 1979; Newcombe's chapter, this book; Newcombe & Liben, 1982). Although the cognitive demands of tasks have received some attention, little has been done in terms of the activity demands of tasks. Recall that Cohen et al. (1980) found that young children estimated distances most accurately when the activity of the response task was congruent with the activity of the acquisition experience, whether the two were active (walking) or passive (simply viewing).

The structure of the environment, particularly in terms of barriers to movement and/or viewing, also interacts with the individual's environmental experiences. In our review, it seems to be the case that active movement most facilitates the acquisition of spatial knowledge for large-scale environments, but it presents little advantage when the space can be viewed in its entirety from single vantage points. In addition, Newcombe and Liben (1982) reported that task demands interact with the structure of the space, showing that children's estimates of distance are distorted by the presence of barriers when the task demands are indirect, or derived, estimates of distance, but the barriers have no effect when the task demands a more direct distance estimation.

It should be noted that conceptualizing barriers as obstacles to movement and/or viewing is not the only way to consider these environmental features. Barriers also can be conceptualized as environmental features that physically segment the environment, thus lending immediate cues to aid in the organization and segmentation of the space (i.e., see Allen, 1981, 1982). What may be a hindrance in terms of direct travel may prove to be an important organizational landmark. Viewing activity in the traditional sense of motor movement tends to obscure this other function of these features. A view of activity in terms of goals of the activity in addition to the motor requirements allows for a heuristically more appealing way to consider the experiences an individual has in an environment.

Thus while we have some insights into the interplay of developmental status, environmental structure, task demands, and movement in space, our knowledge is very limited in terms of the goals and functions of activity and the social exchanges in the setting. The section on indirect evidence reporting on naturalistic settings described how sociocultural and socioeconomic factors indirectly influence one's knowledge of space by influencing one's values and one's activity patterns. The section on children's home range points out how children are restricted in their movements in various ways. It would be interesting to know how social and cultural values of neighborhoods and families influence the activity patterns and spatial knowledge of children. In addition, how do these neighborhood and family patterns influence the child's progress in school and other institutions? Assuming that the acquisition of spatial knowledge can lead to feelings of security in an environment (see Acredolo, 1982), and assuming that increased independence and decreased home range restrictions facilitate the ability to glean spatial knowledge, do children who are less protected in their neighborhood settings make smoother transitions to school than those children who are restricted? How are peer interactions affected in other settings based on neighborhood range patterns?

These are a few of the questions that arise when broadening our view of activity-in-space. We urge for the continuation of cognitive research that examines the processes of extraction and manipulation of spatial information. We further urge the beginning of research on the role of activity and spatial cognition for more general cognitive and social concerns.

REFERENCES

Acredolo, L. P. Development of spatial orientation in infancy. *Developmental Psychology*, 1978, *13*, 1–8.

Acredolo, L. P. Laboratory versus home: The effect of environment on the 9-month-old infant's choice of spatial reference system. *Developmental Psychology*, 1979, *15*, 666–667.

Acredolo, L. P. The familiarity factor in spatial research: What does it breed besides contempt? In R. Cohen (Ed.), *New directions for child development: Vol. 15. Children's conceptions of spatial relationships*. San Francisco: Jossey-Bass, 1982.

Acredolo, L. P., & Evans, D. Developmental changes in the effects of landmarks on infant spatial behavior. *Developmental Psychology*, 1980, *16*, 312–318.

Acredolo, L. P., Pick, H. L., & Olsen, M. G. Environmental differentiation and familiarity as determinants of children's memory for spatial location. *Developmental Psychology*, 1975, *11*, 495–501.

Allen, G. L. A developmental perspective on the effects of "subdividing" macro-spatial experience. *Journal of Experimental Psychology: Human Learning and Memory*, 1981, *7*, 120–132.

Allen, G. L. Some things we know about the development of macrospatial cognition now that we didn't know then: The organization of route knowledge. In R. Cohen (Ed.), *New directions for child development: Vol. 15. Children's conceptions of spatial relationships*. San Francisco: Jossey-Bass, 1982.

Allen, G. L., Kirasic, K. C., Siegel, A. W., & Herman, J. F. Developmental issues in cognitive mapping: The selection and utilization of environmental landmarks. *Child Development*, 1979, *50*, 1062–1070.

Andrews, H. F. Home range and urban knowledge of school-age children. *Environment and Behavior*, 1973, *5*, 73–86.

Anooshian, L. J., & Young, D. Developmental changes in cognitive maps in familiar neighborhoods. *Child Development*, 1981, *52*, 341–348.

Appleyard, D. Styles and methods of structuring a city. *Environment and Behavior*, 1970, *2*, 100–118.

Beck, R. J., & Wood, D. Cognitive transformation of information from urban geographic fields to mental maps. *Environment and Behavior*, 1976, *8*, 199–238.

Berg, M., & Medrich, E. A. Children in four neighborhoods: The physical environment and its effect on play and play patterns. *Environment and Behavior*, 1980, *12*, 320–348.

Bremner, J. G. Egocentric versus allocentric spatial coding in nine-month-old infants: Factors influencing the choice of code. *Developmental Psychology,* 1978, *14,* 346–355.

Bremner, J. G., & Bryant, P. E. Place versus response as the basis of spatial errors made by young infants. *Journal of Experimental Child Psychology,* 1977, *23,* 162–171.

Briggs, R. Urban cognitive distance. In R. M. Downs & D. Stea (Eds.), *Image and environment: Cognitive mapping and spatial behavior.* Chicago: Aldine, 1973.

Bronzaft, A. L., Dobrow, S. B., & O'Hanlon, T. J. Spatial orientation in a subway system. *Environment and Behavior,* 1976, *8,* 575–594.

Brown, M. A., & Broadway, M. J. The cognitive maps of adolescents: Confusion about inter-town distances. *Professional Geographer,* 1981, *33,* 315–325.

Carr, S., & Schissler, D. The city as a trip: Perceptual selection and memory in views from the road. *Environment and Behavior,* 1969, *1,* 7–36.

Cohen, R., Baldwin, L. M., & Sherman, R. C. Cognitive maps of a naturalistic setting. *Child Development,* 1978, *49,* 1216–1218.

Cohen, R., & Schuepfer, T. The representation of landmarks and routes. *Child Development,* 1980, *51,* 1065–1071.

Cohen, R., & Weatherford, D. L. Effects of route traveled on the distance estimates of children and adults. *Journal of Experimental Child Psychology,* 1980, *29,* 403–412.

Cohen, R., & Weatherford, D. L. The effect of barriers on spatial representations. *Child Development,* 1981, *52,* 1087–1090.

Cohen, R., Weatherford, D. L., & Byrd, D. Distance estimates of children as a function of acquisition and response activities. *Journal of Experimental Child Psychology,* 1980, *30,* 464–472.

Cohen, R., Weatherford, D. L., Lomenick, T., & Koeller, K. Development of spatial representations: Role of task demands and familiarity with the environment. *Child Development,* 1979, *50,* 1257–1260.

Cohen, S., & Cohen, R. Distance estimates of children as a function of type of activity in the environment. *Child Development,* 1982, *53,* 834–837.

Cousins, J. H., Siegel, A. W., & Maxwell, S. E. Way finding and cognitive mapping in large-scale environments: A test of a developmental model. *Journal of Experimental Child Psychology,* 1983, *35,* 1–20.

Devlin, A. S. The small town cognitive map: Adjusting to a new environment. In G. T. Moore & R. G. Golledge (Eds.), *Environmental knowing: Theories, research, and methods.* Stroudsburg, PA: Dowden, Hutchinson, & Ross, 1976.

Drozdal, J. G., & Flavell, J. H. A developmental study of logical search behavior. *Child Development,* 1975, *46,* 389–393.

Evans, G. W., Marrero, D. G., & Butler, P. A. Environmental learning and cognitive mapping. *Environment and Behavior,* 1981, *13,* 83–104.

Evans, G. W., & Pezdek, K. Cognitive mapping: Knowledge of real-world distance and location information. *Journal of Experimental Psychology: Human Learning and Memory,* 1980, *6,* 13–24.

Feldman, A., & Acredolo, L. P. The effect of active versus passive exploration on memory for spatial location in children. *Child Development,* 1979, *50,* 698–704.

Francescato, D., & Mebane, W. How citizens view two great cities: Milan and Rome. In R. M. Downs & D. Stea (Eds.), *Image and environment: Cognitive mapping and spatial behavior.* Chicago: Aldine, 1973.

Golledge, R. G., & Spector, A. N. Comprehending the urban environment: Theory and practice. *Geographical Analysis,* 1978, *10,* 401–426.

Haake, R. J., Somerville, S. C., & Wellman, H. M. Logical ability of young children in searching a large-scale environment. *Child Development,* 1980, *51,* 1299–1302.

Hart, R. A. Children's spatial representation of the landscape: Lessons and questions from a field study. In L. S. Liben, A. H. Patterson, & N. Newcombe (Eds.), *Spatial representation and behavior across the life span.* New York: Academic Press, 1981.

Hazen, N. L. Spatial exploration and spatial knowledge: Individual and developmental differences in very young children. *Child Development*, 1982, *53*, 826–833.

Hazen, N. L., & Durrett, M. E. Relationship of security of attachment to exploration and cognitive mapping abilities in 2-year-olds. *Developmental Psychology*, 1982, *18*, 751–759.

Hazen, N. L., Lockman, J. J., & Pick, H. L. The development of children's representations of large-scale environments. *Child Development*, 1978, *49*, 623–636.

Herman, J. F. Children's cognitive maps of large-scale spaces: Effects of exploration, direction, and repeated experience. *Journal of Experimental Child Psychology*, 1980, *29*, 126–143.

Herman. J. F., Kail, J. V., & Siegel, A. W. Cognitive maps of a college campus: A new look at freshman orientation. *Bulletin of the Psychonomic Society*, 1979, *13*, 183–186.

Herman, J. F., Kolker, R. G., & Shaw, M. L. Effects of motor activity on children's intentional and incidental memory for spatial locations. *Child Development*, 1982, *53*, 239–244.

Herman, J. F., & Siegel, A. W. The development of cognitive mapping of the large-scale environment. *Journal of Experimental Child Psychology*, 1978, *26*, 289–406.

Heth, C. O., & Cornell, E. H. Three experiences affecting spatial discrimination learning by ambulatory children. *Journal of Experimental Child Psychology*, 1980, *30*, 246–264.

Ittelson, W. H. Environment perception and contemporary perceptual theory. In W. H. Ittelson (Ed.), *Environment and cognition*. New York: Seminar Press, 1973.

Karan, P. P., Bladen, W. A., & Singh, G. Slum dwellers' and squatters' images of a city. *Environment and Behavior*, 1980, *12*, 81–100.

Kosslyn, S. M., Pick, H. L., & Fariello, G. R. Cognitive maps in children and men. *Child Development*, 1974, *45*, 707–716.

Kozlowski, L. T., & Bryant, K. J. Sense of direction, spatial orientation, and cognitive maps. *Journal of Experimental Psychology: Human Perception and Performance*, 1977, *3*, 590–598.

Kreutzer, M. A., Leonard, C., & Flavell, J. H. An interview study of children's knowledge about memory. *Monographs of the Society for Research in Child Development*, 1975, *40*, (1, Serial No. 159).

Ladd, F. C. Black youths view their environment. *Environment and Behavior*, 1970, *2*, 74–99.

Lee, T. Perceived distance as a function of direction in the city. *Environment and Behavior*, 1970, *2*, 40–51.

Matthews, M. H. The mental maps of children. *Geography*, 1980, *65*, 169–178.

Mauer, R., & Baxter, J. C. Images of the neighborhood and city among Black-, Anglo-, and Mexican-American children. *Environment and Behavior*, 1972, *4*, 351–389.

Milgram, S., Greenwald, J., Kessler, S., McKenna, W., & Waters, J. A psychological map of New York City. *American Scientist*, 1972, *60*, 194–200.

Moore, G. T. Knowing about environmental knowing: The current state of theory and research on environmental cognition. *Environment and Behavior*, 1979, *11*, 33–70.

Nerlove, S. B., Munroe, R. H., & Munroe, R. L. Effect of environmental experience on spatial ability: A replication. *Journal of Social Psychology*, 1971, *84*, 3–10.

Newcombe, N., & Liben, L. S. Barrier effects in the cognitive maps of children and adults. *Journal of Experimental Child Psychology*, 1982, *34*, 46–58.

Orleans, P. Differential cognition of urban residents: Effects of social scale on mapping. In R. M. Downs & D. Stea (Eds.), *Image and environment: Cognitive mapping and spatial behavior*. Chicago: Aldine, 1973.

Poag, C. K., Cohen, R., & Weatherford, D. L. Spatial representations of young children: The role of self- versus adult-directed movement and viewing. *Journal of Experimental Child Psychology*, 1983, *35*, 172–179.

Presson, C. C., & Ihrig, L. H. Using mother as a spatial landmark: Evidence against egocentric coding in infancy. *Developmental Psychology*, 1982, *18*, 699–703.

Reiser, J. Spatial orientation of six-month-old infants. *Child Development*, 1979, *50*, 1078–1087.

Sadalla, E. K., & Staplin, L. J. The perception of traversed distance, *Environment and Behavior*, 1980, *12*, 167–182.

Schouela, D. A., Steinberg, L. M., Leveton, L. B., & Wapner, S. Development of the cognitive organization of an environment. *Canadian Journal of Behaviour*, 1980, *12*, 1–16.

Siegel, A. W. Towards a social ecology of cognitive mapping. In R. Cohen (Ed.), *New directions for child development: Vol.15. Children's conceptions of spatial relationships.* San Francisco: Jossey-Bass, 1982.

Siegel, A. W., Herman, J. F., Allen, G. L., & Kirasic, K. C. The development of cognitive maps of large- and small-scale spaces. *Child Development*, 1979, *50*, 582–585.

Siegel, A. W., & Schadler, M. Young children's cognitive maps of their classroom. *Child Development*, 1977, *48*, 388–394.

Siegel, A. W., & White, S. H. The development of spatial representations of large-scale environments. In H. W. Reese (Ed.), *Advances in child development and behavior* (Vol. 10). New York: Academic Press, 1975.

Sophian, C., & Wellman, H. M. Selective information use in the development of search behavior. *Developmental Psychology*, 1980, *16*, 323–332.

Thorndyke, P. W., & Stasz, C. Individual differences for knowledge acquisition from maps. *Cognitive Psychology*, 1980, *12*, 137–175.

Walsh, D. A., Krauss, I. K., & Regnier, V. A. Spatial ability, environmental knowledge, and environmental use: The elderly. In L. S. Liben, A. H. Patterson, & N. Newcombe (Eds.), *Spatial representation and behavior across the life span.* New York: Academic Press, 1981.

Weatherford, D. L., & Cohen, R. *The influence of locomotor activity on spatial representations.* Paper presented at the biennial meeting of the Society for Research in Child Development, Boston, April 1981.

Wellman, H. M., Haake, R., & Somerville, S. C. *An Easter egg hunt: Young children's developing abilities in searching for missing objects.* Paper presented at the biennial meeting of the Society for Research in Child Development, Boston, 1981.

Wellman, H. M., & Somerville, S. C. The development of human search ability. In M. E. Lamb & A. L. Brown (Eds.), *Advances in developmental psychology* (Vol. 2). Hillsdale, NJ: Lawrence Erlbaum Associates, 1982.

Wellman, H. M., Somerville, S. C., & Haake, R. J. Development of search procedures in real-life spatial environments. *Developmental Psychology*, 1979, *15*, 530–542.

9 Spatial Cognition as a Function of Environmental Characteristics

Susan L. Golbeck
Rutgers University

The study of spatial representation has intrigued scholars for decades. Developmental psychologists have examined age-related changes in emergent spatial representation. Geographers, architects, and planners also have studied representations of the environment in an effort to understand behavior in the environment. Missing from both these approaches has been a systematic examination of the reciprocal relationships between the physical environment itself and the representation of the environment. Representation not only influences behavior in the environment (Walsh, Krauss, & Regnier, 1981), but characteristics of the environment also influence the representation (Lynch, 1960). In this chapter a framework for articulating the reciprocal relationships between the characteristics of the environment and large-scale spatial cognition is presented.

Theory and research in large-scale spatial cognition incorporate perspectives from cognitive, developmental, and environmental psychology (Altman & Wohlwill, 1978; Baird & Lutkus, 1982; Liben, Patterson, & Newcombe, 1981). Cognitive and developmental psychologists have been interested primarily in cognitive processes within the individual and the emergence of abstract spatial concepts. Although memory and representation of environmental arrangements such as rooms, neighborhoods, and cities have been studied, spatial concepts and spatial representations per se have been the concern (e.g., Acredolo, 1981; Weatherford, 1982). In contrast, environmental psychologists (e.g., Ittelson, 1973) studying large-scale spatial cognition have been concerned with knowledge of specific spaces or places rather than abstract spatial concepts (see Liben, 1981, for further discussion of this distinction). While cognitive developmental psychologists are concerned with general characteristics of spatial representation but not the specific characteristics of the spatial referent, environmental psychologists are concerned with particular kinds of settings, such as schools, playgrounds, hospitals, or the out-of-doors (for example, Moore & Young, 1978; Runyon, 1976; Wohlwill, 1973) but not the general features cutting across these places. These differing interests have resulted in a failure to consider how environmental characteristics themselves influence spatial representation.

Exploration of the reciprocal relationships between the physical environment and spatial cognition calls for further clarification of general features cutting across specific settings. The approach presented here draws upon work from a variety of psychological orientations and employs data from a variety of cognitive tasks to identify a taxonomy of general environmental characteristics relevant to large-scale spatial cognition. This taxonomy provides a language for describing the environment in its own right and a means for discussing cognition across a range of specific spaces or places. In short, the taxonomy provides an important conceptual tool for clarifying relationships between characteristics of the environment and spatial knowledge.

The first portion of the chapter is a presentation of the environmental features included in the taxonomy. Each feature exists in a variety of specific places or settings and is viewed as a potential independent variable influencing spatial representation. However, since spatial representational competence changes as a function of development, features may take on different meanings for individuals at different developmental levels.

The second portion of the chapter applies the taxonomy to one real-world environment, the early childhood classroom. The purpose of this application is twofold. First, it shows how the general taxonomy may be applied to a specific setting. Second, and more important, it illustrates how representation helps explain behavior in a setting, particularly when the effects of the environmental features themselves upon spatial representation are considered.

TAXONOMY OF ENVIRONMENTAL FEATURES

Two broad categories of environmental characteristics are included in the taxonomy presented here; structural features and organizational features. Structural features include the presence of landmarks, the proximity of containing features, and the presence of barriers. All are highly objective, easily measureable, discrete elements in the environment. In contrast, organizational features refer to relationships between elements; they include the clustering, orientation, and saliency of objects in the environment. All of these features refer to aspects of the physical setting. No attempt is made here to deal with social and affective variables (Parke, 1978) or ecological variables (Gump, 1978).

In the following discussion, each structural and organizational feature is defined. An overview of the relationship between each feature and the development of spatial representation is offered, when there are sufficient data to do so. For some features, such as boundaries and saliency, it is difficult to identify developmental trends because so little data are available. However, the relationship between these features and spatial representation is discussed.

It is important to note that this taxonomy does not include all possible structural and organizational features of the environment. Other elements could be added to both superordinate categories. This discussion is restricted to environmental features which have received some study by cognitive developmental psychologists with the availability of empirical evidence determining their inclusion.

Structural Features

Structural features refer here to physical characteristics of space that are highly objective and easily measurable. Three classes of structural features are considered: degree of differentiation, containing features, and barrier-like features. Unlike organizational features, structural features are discrete elements in the setting. Landmarks, walls, paths, and roads are all structural features. The features described here are not intended to be a comprehensive list of all possible structural features in the environment. All, however, appear to influence spatial representation of the environment. Also, there is reason to believe that each potentially interacts with age or developmental status of the individual in affecting representation. Research in children's memory and spatial representation is presented to demonstrate the importance of each of the structural features included in the taxonomy.

Degree of Differentiation: The Presence of Landmarks.   Landmarks are the basic structural features of any environment. Settings can be evaluated in terms of the availability of perceptually salient objects that differentiate the environment. Also, settings vary in degree of differentiation as the number and variety of landmarks change. In this section, the function of landmarks in spatial cognition is briefly overviewed and some developmental changes in the use of landmarks in spatial representation are identified.

Landmarks facilitate the encoding and retrieval of information about spatial location. Information such as next to, near, or in between may be encoded in terms of the relationships between two objects in the environment. Siegel and Schadler (1977) asked kindergarten children to reconstruct the arrangement of their classroom with a small-scale model of the room and its contents. In one condition children were provided with several pre-placed cue items, but in the second condition, no landmark-like items were present. The accuracy of some aspects of the children's reconstructions increased with landmark availability. The differentiating features or landmarks seemed to function as environmental "pegs" for partially organized mental representations of space.

Although adults as well as children use landmarks to facilitate representation, young children are severely hindered without them. In the absence of differentiating features, young children are unable to maintain orientation and remember position. Acredolo (1977) studied the role of landmarks for preschoolers' representation of a room. Three-, 4-, and 5-year-olds were trained to learn the location of a hidden object in a small room with or without a landmark. Children's orientation within the room was then reversed and they were asked to find the object, still located in the same place. Although the 4- and 5-year-olds were able to coordinate different views of space without landmarks, 3-year-olds were more likely to locate the hidden object correctly when the landmark was present. The effects of such self-landmark relations are particularly salient in familiar environments in which the child has had extensive opportunities to learn the space (Acredolo, 1979).

Further evidence is provided by Acredolo, Pick, and Olsen (1975). Preschoolers and 8-year-olds were taken on individual walks down a hallway. During the walk, the experimenter casually dropped an object. After the walk, children were asked where the experimenter's object had been lost. When the object had been dropped near a distinctive feature, or landmark, preschoolers and 8-year-olds were equally accurate. However, when no distinctive features were present, the preschoolers had more difficulty remembering location than did the older children.

Piaget, Inhelder, and Szeminska (1960) suggest that the use of landmarks for representing the environment is closely tied to the development of projective and Euclidean spatial reference systems. Young children, who lack such conceptual systems, have difficulty remembering spatial position and maintaining orientation unless a landmark is available in the environment. Therefore, wayfinding and representing traveled routes such as a walk through the environment are particularly dependent upon differentiating features. If a landmark is moved, spatial representations become disrupted. As children construct knowledge of projective and Euclidean spatial relations, there is an increasing independence from differentiating features and children are able to maintain an integrated representation even when a landmark is moved.

However, environmental differentiation occurs in a variety of forms. The task confronting the young child is not merely to *use* a feature as a landmark but to select the most appropriate feature to serve that function. A setting may be differentiated by a variety of items, some stable and some movable. Examples of settings with movable landmarks include a parking lot filled with cars or the multipurpose room of a school filled, at various times during the day, with lunch tables, folding chairs, or athletic equipment. Acredolo (1976) demonstrated that at least in some situations, young children, but not older children, choose movable items in the environment as landmarks. Preschoolers and 10-year-olds were brought into a highly differentiated setting, which included patterned walls and a window. Children were asked to stand near a table, the only piece of furniture in the room. They were blindfolded and taken on a short walk while the table was silently moved across the room. After the walk, the blindfold was removed and the children were asked to return to where they had begun the walk. None of the 10-year-olds returned to the relocated table; many of the preschoolers did. Thus it seems that the older children recognized the value of the more permanent features of the room and the younger children relied on a less efficient, more temporary landmark.

Allen, Kirasic, Siegel, and Herman (1979) also provide evidence for children's increasing efficiency and selectivity in their use of landmarks. They examined the types of items children and adults spontaneously chose as landmarks along a city street shown on slides. Second and fifth graders tended to select features that were highly noticeable, such as colored awnings or windows. Adults were more likely to choose features at decision spots for wayfinding: they picked features at intersections or corners where a turn was possible. In a second portion of the study, it was shown that the fifth-grade children but not the second-grade children were able to use adult-selected landmarks for making distance judgments. Thus the fifth graders could benefit from high-information landmarks although they did not spontaneously recognize their value.

In summary, landmarks play an integral role in large-scale spatial cognition and their function in spatial representation is linked to the developmental status of the child's internal spatial reference system. Differentiating features may be critical for maintaining orientation, for maintaining direction of movement, and for marking spatial position. Two complementary trends in children's changing use of differentiating features have been discussed. First, children are increasingly capable of functioning without landmarks when they must. Second, children's use of landmarks becomes more flexible. They are increasingly capable of using features of the physical environment for maintaining orientation, remembering location, and making decisions about wayfinding. Furthermore, an initial tendency to choose perceptually salient features is abandoned as children become older. With age, children simultaneously use the total context more efficiently and become more independent of the immediate context.

Containing Features. Containing features can be defined as physical boundaries in the environment. Perhaps the most obvious physical boundary is a wall. When space is enclosed by walls, this containing feature defines the size of the space. Other boundaries in the physical environment include, for example, markings on a floor, the edge of a rug, fences, pathways, and geographic features.

Containing features facilitate young children's representation of space. Herman and Siegel (1978) asked kindergarten, second- and fifth-grade children to walk through a model of a village. After the walk, children were asked to reconstruct the location of several model buildings. Two boundary conditions were inadvertently created by setting up the model village in a classroom and a large gym. Kindergarten children more accurately reconstructed the model village in the smaller classroom-sized space. While boys performed better than girls in the unbounded, larger room, overall the performances of second and fifth graders were not affected by the boundary variations.

The facilitating effects of boundaries, defined by walls of a room, was tested directly by Liben, Moore, and Golbeck (1982). Three-, 4-, and 5-year old children were asked to reconstruct the layout of their preschool classroom using the real life-sized space (by directing the placement of furniture in the room), and also with a small scale model of the classroom. Several items could be identified as ''bounded'' (near the wall) while others were ''unbounded'' (located near the center of the room and far from other objects). The results supported the hypothesis that the bounded items would be more accurately replaced than the unbounded items. In addition, this boundary effect was found for reconstructions using either the life-sized space or the model.

Why do children have difficulty remembering location in an unbounded space? In part, this may be due to the child's lack of an interiorised spatial reference system. Euclidean spatial concepts that emerge during middle childhood result in the ability to make use of an implicit coordinated reference system for organizing the spatial environment (Laurendeau & Pinard, 1970; Piaget & Inhelder, 1956; Piaget et al., 1960). Prior to the emergence of an interiorised spatial reference system the child can remember locations in space by relating objects to other objects in the environment. However, the child encounters difficulty encoding positions in the absence of objects or landmarks. With the acquisition of Euclidean spatial concepts, the positions of objects in a two-dimensional space, such as the floor of a room, are encoded by mentally constructing an invariant coordinate axes system.

Even rudimentary Euclidean spatial knowledge should lead children to be less dependent upon the structure of the physical environment. This explanation would account for the grade level by boundedness interaction reported by Herman and Siegel (1978). Kindergartners, who presumably lacked Euclidean spatial concepts, had more difficulty reconstructing a village layout in a large, unbounded context than in a small, bounded context. In the bounded context, the walls of the room served as a containing frame and objects could be related directly to the frame. Such a frame was not present in the unbounded room. By second grade, the differences between the bounded and unbounded contexts decreased. Children at this age have mastered some rudimentary Euclidean spatial concepts (DeLisi, 1983), although such knowledge is far from fully developed. In future research this hypothesis should be directly tested by assessing children for Euclidean spatial knowledge in addition to memory for location in bounded and unbounded settings.

The limited processing capabilities of young children may also contribute to their difficulty in remembering spatial location in unbounded space. Cognitive psychologists have suggested that an analogical representation of the spatial environment is used for remembering spatial location. An analogical representation implies some correspondence between the mental representation and the actual physical structure of information in the world (Evans, 1980; Kosslyn, 1975). Representation of a large unbounded space leads to heavy information-processing demands that surpass the limited capabilities of a young child. If the child represents the space by subdividing it into smaller units or subspaces the unbounded space lacks clear reference points for such subdivision and may result in a faulty representation.

Developmental changes in attentional abilities also may account for the effect of boundaries on memory for spatial location. Lane and Pearson (1983) as well as Hoving, Spencer, Robb, and Schulte (1978) have shown that kindergarten children have difficulty locating a stimulus in an otherwise empty field. Although this research employed reaction time to detection of briefly presented visual stimuli as the dependent variable, such attentional difficulties may interfere with large-scale spatial memory. When a spatial array and boundary are separated by a large distance, young children may have difficulty allocating attention to the relationships among the various objects in the stimulus array as well as the relationship between the total array to the boundary. The locus of such attentional deficits might be found at the time of initially processing information about the environmental arrangement or during the completion of the reconstruction task.

All three of these factors—spatial operations, cognitive processing abilities, and attentional skills—may contribute to the influence of containing features upon the accuracy of large-scale spatial representations. With the emergence of concrete operations incorporating Euclidean spatial operations, all cognitive activity including perception, attention, and memory become increasingly organized (Furth, 1969; Piaget, 1970; Piaget & Inhelder, 1973). Neo-Piagetian approaches (e.g., Pascual-Leone, 1976) have emphasized the importance of differentiating developmental changes in processing space from underlying cognitive operations and may be useful here.

Many questions about boundary effects remain unanswered. How close must an object be to a boundary for the effect to occur? How do various types of boundaries differ in their effect? Do children become increasingly sensitive to stable or "good" boundaries as they seem to do with landmarks? In future research, careful attention should be given to containing features and boundaries in the everyday, real-world environment. Within the built environment such boundaries are consciously dealt with by architects, planners, and designers. In classrooms and other public settings the manipulation of containing features and boundaries has been shown to influence the use of space (Canter & Stringer, 1976). Future researchers might address the relationship between changes in the use of space in these settings and changes in the representation of space.

Barrier-like Features. Barriers are the third group of structural characteristics to be considered here. Barriers serve a number of functions. They organize space by dividing it into segments. They also influence the experience of space by restricting movement and by hindering viewing. Barriers are pervasive in real-world environments. In a variety of situations, both children and adults distort the distance between two points when the points are separated by an intervening barrier. However, the effects of barriers on spatial representation interact with a number of variables including the age of the subject, the distance between the locations, experience in the space, and various other task demands. This work is briefly overviewed here.

Kosslyn, Pick, and Farriello (1974) trained preschoolers and adults to learn the locations of a set of objects in an experimental space. The space was divided into quadrants by two transparent and two opaque barriers. After learning the locations, subjects were asked to rank order from memory the distance between objects. Distance judgments were analyzed using multidimensional scaling techniques. Kosslyn et al. found that preschoolers judged distances to be greater when objects were separated by either an opaque or a transparent barrier. Adults overestimated distances only for locations separated by opaque barriers.

Two explanations were offered for the differential effects of transparent barriers. The first assumes barriers influence spatial representation by the structure they impose on the functional distance between points. Since young children exclusively rely on functional distance in estimating distance, their judgments are equally distorted by opaque and transparent barriers. Adults, in contrast, use the visual information available with the transparent barriers to modify functional distance judgments. The second explanation offered by Kosslyn et al. assumes that barriers organize mental images of space. While adults can ignore the transparent barriers and mentally visualize the space in two large units, children's more limited processing capabilities force them to consider the smaller subspaces within each quadrant. Children lack the capabilities to combine subspaces defined by transparent barriers even though the visual information is readily available. Since success on the rank ordering task requires the ability to consider the entire space at one time, children's distance judgments are equally distorted by opaque and transparent barriers.

Newcombe and Liben (1982) further examined the notion that functional distance is more important for children than adults. They reasoned that if functional distance is more salient for children, differential barrier effects should be maintained even after reducing the processing demands of the task. In addition to rank ordering relationships between all objects, subjects were asked to consider a series of individual pairwise interlocation distance estimates. The Kosslyn et al. results were replicated with first graders and college students using the same rank ordering task. However, on direct pairwise interlocation distance estimates, the age by barrier-type interaction was not replicated. Hence, findings failed to support the notion that functional distance or traversed space operated differently for children and adults in the representation of space. Importantly, this is not to say that children and adults are necessarily accurate in their estimations of distance between objects separated by barriers. Rather, transparent barriers do not influence children and adults differently. Newcombe and Liben suggested that children and adults differ in their integrative processing capabilities. Children were better at the pairwise task than the rank ordering task because it required less overall integration of spatial information.

A different approach to functional distance was taken by Cohen and Weatherford (1980). They examined the role of activity and the presence of barriers on spatial representation. Children in second and sixth grade and college students were asked to estimate the distance separating pairs of locations along routes that were or were not separated by barriers. Pairs of locations varied in distance (4, 6, or 8 feet); in whether or not the subject had directly traveled the connecting route and in whether or not the route contained a barrier. Results of the distance estimation task showed a complex pattern of interactions. Directly traveled routes containing barriers were more accurately estimated than comparable routes that were not directly traveled. Hence, activity in space appears to interact with barrier presence to offset distortion (Cohen, 1982). These findings suggest that increased experience in the setting might have reduced barrier effects reported by Kosslyn et al. Similarly, if children were asked to make judgments about the distance between two points in a highly familiar environment, such as their home or classroom, distortions might decrease. This, of course, assumes that children have adequate experience traversing the paths between the points under consideration.

The absolute distance separating two points seems to be related to accuracy in estimating intervening distance. Cohen and Weatherford (1980) found that when points were separated by distances of 4 and 6 feet, barriers led to an exaggeration of distance. However, when points were separated by a distance of 8 feet, this effect was not seen. Newcombe and Liben (1982) also found that the distance separating two points was related to accuracy in the estimation of distance. They found that 3-foot distances were overestimated and 5-foot distances were underestimated. They suggested that items separated by differing distances may have been oriented in different directions and that such orientation differences induced error in distance estimation.

While the results of these two studies are difficult to compare since the age of the subjects, the experimental settings and the experimental tasks differed, it is noteworthy that accuracy in pairwise interlocation distance estimation did not increase as points increased in proximity. This stands in sharp contrast to memory for spatial position and single point location. Performance on these tasks improved with proximity to landmarks and bounding frames. Apparently, the effects of distance between points in the environment upon spatial representation varies with the type of task employed to measure spatial representation.

Cohen, Baldwin and Sherman (1978) examined distance estimation on two different spatial tasks. In addition, they considered the effects of hills as well as barriers on distance estimation. Nine- and 10-year-olds and adults were asked to estimate distance between pairs of items in a familiar, naturalistic setting. Pairs varied in terms of whether or not items were separated by a hill and/or a physical barrier. Subjects were asked either (a) to estimate directly distances between pairs of items, or (b) to reconstruct an environmental layout on a flat map board. Hills and barriers both led to an overestimation of distance on the direct estimation task. Similarly, hills led to overestimation of distance on the reconstruction task. However, barriers showed no such effect on the reconstruction task. Cohen et al. suggested that the reconstruction task, which is presented on a flat board, might uniquely facilitate compensation for barrier effects. Locations separated by hills would still be distorted because hills would not be salient on the flat map board. Results from this study, along with others (Cohen, Weatherford, Lomenick, & Koeller, 1979; Newcombe & Liben, 1982), emphasize the hazards inherent in drawing conclusions from any single task about the effects of barriers upon spatial representation.

Conclusions about the effects of barriers upon spatial cognition have been limited by the narrow range of settings in which the research has been conducted. With the exception of the study by Cohen et al. (1978), all the research described above has been carried out in laboratory-type situations. A closer look at the function of barriers in real-world settings may point to alternative approaches to the study of barrier-like features and their influence on spatial cognition. This would also clarify the definition of barrier-like features. What geographic forms other than hills might function like barriers? Do barriers within interior spaces such as rooms and buildings function differently from barriers in outdoor spaces?

In addition, the influence of barriers in a broader range of spatial representational problems must be examined. Interlocation distance estimation and overall rank ordering of distances are useful measures of spatial representation. However, it is becoming increasingly clear that different measures yield different information about internal spatial representations (Cohen et al., 1979; Liben, 1982).

Organizational Features

Complementing the structural features of the environment is an organization. Landmarks, containing features, and barriers are discrete elements in the physical environment. In the real-world environment, such physical elements exist in meaningful configurations with both patterns of functional use and cultural values determining their arrangement (Canter, 1977). Unlike the structural features described above, an organizational feature is not a discrete element; it refers to the relationship between several items in the environment. The orientation of objects, the shared attributes of items, characteristics of their arrangement and the salience of items with respect to their context are all organizational features. Lynch (1960) offers an example of an organizational feature in a city environment, a district. A district is a relatively large area possessing some common characteristics such as ethnic heritage or architectural style. A district is defined by a clustering of objects or buildings that share attributes. It is quite different from a particular landmark or pathway that is a discrete element in the city environment.

Organizational features also influence environmental cognition. A good example is provided in a recent study by Waddell and Rogoff (1981). Of interest was the role of "contextual organization" upon spatial memory of middle-aged (M = 46 years) and older women (M = 71 years). The women were asked to remember the location of 30 items in a tabletop arrangement. In the contextually organized condition, items were placed on a tabletop "panorama" including mountains, houses, a street, and so forth. In the nonorganized condition the same set of items was placed in a bank of cubicles or cubby holes. Older subjects had more difficulty than the middle-aged subjects remembering the unorganized, cubby-hole arrangement. There were no differences between the older and middle-aged adults for the organized "panorama" task. The authors suggested that the organized task permitted subjects to use a preexisting conceptual structure for remembering previously learned relationships between items. Unclear, however, is what dimensions of the organized task were actually relevant to success. Do subjects have a conceptual structure for "towns" or "villages"? Does the panorama facilitate mental construction of clusters of objects typically found together (e.g., house, three, person)? Can subjects relate personal experiences to the town arrangement, which they were unable to do in the organized task?

In this section the taxonomy of environmental features is expanded to include organizational features. Although it should be possible to discuss organizational features independently of structural features, frequently the two are confounded. For example, in the Waddell and Rogoff (1981) study just described, the two task conditions were not really equivalent in terms of the structural characteristics. The conditions were equivalent in terms of differentiation, but the unorganized arrangement incorporated more containing features and barriers. Acknowledging the inevitability of this type of problem, three organizational features are included in the taxonomy: (1) the clustering of objects in space, (2) the orientation of objects in space, and (3) the saliency and expectancy of item presence. Each of these features influences spatial representation. Each also merits examination from a developmental perspective. As in the earlier discussion of structural features, other organizational features might be added to the taxonomy. This listing need not be viewed as comprehensive.

Clustering.   Typically, items in the spatial environment are not located randomly. Rather, objects often are placed near other objects with which they share attributes. Shared attributes may include common function (e.g., kitchen objects differ from objects located in the living room) as well as common physical properties (e.g., within the kitchen, plates in the cupboard are stacked by size). This nonrandom arrangement of items in the environment is called clustering.

Clustering as an organizational variable in the representation of space has received relatively little direct study. In fact, the impact of clustering may well have been masked by the simple study of structural, as opposed to organizational, variations in the environment. This is illustrated by reexamination of Siegel and Schadler (1977). Children were asked to reconstruct the arrangement of their classroom using a scale model of the room and furniture. Importantly, however, the room contained 40 items that were partially clustered into functionally related groupings such as the playhouse and the teacher's desk. Children provided with cues or landmark-like items reconstructed a higher percentage of items in the general area of the room in which they belonged than did children not given landmarks. However, the percentage of items returned correctly to the precise area of the room in which they belonged did not differ between the landmark and no landmark groups. There are two explanations for the increased accuracy under the cued condition. Children may have used the cue items as spatial landmarks and related objects to others nearby using topological spatial information. Alternatively, a logical clustering strategy may have been used; children may have grouped the objects around the cues because all items shared a common function (e.g., objects in the playhouse area). Although both explanations would lead to predictions of increased accuracy for general location reconstruction, the reconstruction of precise location could be unaffected. Siegel and Schadler (1977) discussed their results in terms of the first type of explanation, but the possibility of clustering by functional similarity is an equally viable interpretation.

The influence of functional relatedness for organizing the environment has received little attention in terms of its relationship to memory for location. Appleyard (1973) discussed an "operational" response to the environment. He suggested that an individual perceives elements in a city in terms of the "operational" roles they play for completing tasks in the environment. Similarly, Werner (1948) described a study by Muchow in which children's descriptions of their environments were examined. The life-space of young children is bound together by personal significance and is centered around the child's activity in the environment. Thus, it may be that an individual's "operational response" to the environment or life-space would predict the types of functional clusters imposed upon the environment.

Golbeck (1983) examined the relationship between environmental clustering and operativity for memory of a room-sized space. Children were asked to reconstruct an arrangement of 16 items of furniture organized in either a clustered or nonclustered fashion. Under the clustered arrangement, items were organized by physical attributes (color and surface pattern) into a two-by-two matrix-like arrangement, shown in Fig. 9.1. Under the nonclustered arrangement the same 16 furniture items were randomly assigned floor locations. It was hypothesized that children with an understanding of logical classification should remember a clustered arrangement better than children lacking such knowledge (Inhelder & Piaget, 1964).

Children ranging in age from 5 to 10 years were pretested for classification knowledge and assigned to one of three groups, or levels, according to ability.

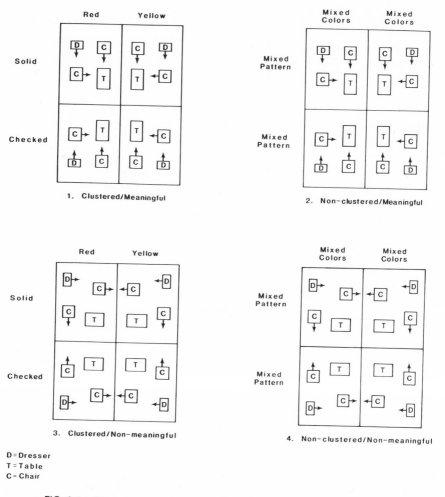

D = Dresser
T = Table
C = Chair

FIG. 9.1.   Illustration of four different environmental organizations. From Gol-beck, S. Reconstruction a large-scale spatial arrangement: Effects of environmental organization and operativity, *Developmental Psychology*, 1983, *19*, 644–653. Copyright by the American Psychological Association. Reprinted by permission of the publisher.

Subsequently, they participated in the memory task under either the clustered or the nonclustered condition. Reconstructions of the room were analyzed for the accurary in the general location of items, specific location of items, and the spatial relations between items. Clustered arrangements were more accurately reconstructed than nonclustered arrangements at all three levels of classification knowledge. This was evident on all three measures of spatial knowledge.

Also, high classifiers out-performed low classifiers for both the clustered and nonclustered rooms. Why should classification skills facilitate performance for the nonclustered environment? Perhaps the development of classification knowledge is related to the development of other cognitive strategies, such as Euclidean spatial concepts, which would be useful for memory of spatial arrangements. This is unlikely since high and low classifiers did not differ in the performance dimension most likely to be related to Euclidean spatial concepts, memory for specific location.

An alternative explanation suggests an interaction between the structural and organizational characteristics of the environment. Even the nonclustered room may have possessed some characteristics that could be understood in terms of a classification strategy. Specifically, both the clustered and nonclustered arrangement contained 16 items divided into four groups. Each group was delineated by the tape floor markings. Those floor markings *contained* or bounded each group of four items; two chairs, one table, and one small dresser. If a child applied a criterion for clustering, "two chairs, one dresser, and one table," even the nonclustered room would become a clustered arrangement. Detecting this organizational strategy is probably a difficult task. It requires the ability to ignore the perhaps more salient physical attributes of color and surface pattern of the furniture. However, it suggests the subtle ways in which clustering of objects in the environment may interact with structural features of the environment to influence representation and memory.

Surprisingly, there was no interaction between type of environmental clustering and level of operativity in classification. The ability to categorize items into distinct clusters is clearly a less complex problem than the ability to simultaneously classify a single object by two or more criteria. The latter requires knowledge of class inclusion, but the former does not. The pretest for knowledge of classification employed by Golbeck (1983) was an adaptation of Inhelder & Piaget's (1964) assessment for multiple classification knowledge. Children in the high group clearly possessed knowledge of multiple classification whereas children in the low group did not. However, children in the low group were able to recognize distinct groups of items. In other words, they possessed some ability to cluster related objects. The ability to cluster physically similar objects should facilitate memory for the clustered as opposed to the nonclustered arrangement, although the ability to detect the overall cross-classified arrangement of the room probably does require multiple classification.

In summary, although many intuitive examples of clustering in the environment can be identified, environmental clustering as a factor in large-scale spatial representation has received very little study. In everyday, real-world settings, the most common and readily identifiable examples of clustering are functional. Closer examination of this phenomenon is essential. Similarly, the cognitive strategies underlying representation and memory for clustered arrangements also call for closer examination. Although knowledge of classification relations are apparently relevant, the ability to appreciate clustering in the environment does not require complete mastery of such classification knowledge as class inclusion and multiple classification. Finally, it is no doubt necessary to examine the impact of clustering as an organizational variable in interaction with structural variations in the environment. For example, landmarks that serve as both physical reference points and also markers for logical clusters may be more salient landmarks than objects lacking such a logical relationship with the surrounding context.

Orientation.   A second feature of environmental organization is the orientation of objects in the environment. Just as the contents of environments are not located randomly neither are they oriented in an arbitrary fashion. Rather, objects tend to be oriented in familiar and meaningful ways. Appleyard (1973) described such expectations about the setting as an inferential or probabilistic response to the environment. Of interest here is how such familiar and meaningful orientation of objects influences memory and representation of space. More specifically, what is the role of the individual's general expectations of how space should be arranged for memory and representation and what happens if expectations are violated?

The role of meaningful orientation in the representation of spatial phenomena has been demonstrated in children's memory for scenes or pictures. Using two-dimensional graphic stimuli, Mandler and colleagues (Mandler & Johnson, 1976; Mandler & Parker, 1976; Mandler & Stein, 1974) studied differences in the retention of organized and unorganized drawings. Some pictures looked like realistic scenes. Others contained the same items oriented differently, lacking an integrated scene quality. Following each scene presentation, children were asked to identify the picture they had viewed before in a forced-choice recognition task. In general, the organized scenes with picture components presented in a familiar spatial orientation were more accurately recognized than unorganized scenes.

Mandler (1979) discussed the role of organization in terms of the schemata that guide the selection and organization of information in a scene. Schemata are knowledge structures or sets of expectations based on past experience. They exist at various levels of abstraction and vary in their complexity. From this perspective, perception, language comprehension, and memory are processes that involve the interaction of new, episodic information with old, schema-based information, and it is assumed that prior experience will influence comprehension and memory for new information. This notion of cognitive structure differs from Piaget's use of structure in its emphasis upon past experience and familiarity per se as factors determining the nature of schemata. In other words, the nature of the environment determines the nature of schemata.

If findings from memory for two-dimensional scene perception can be generalized to memory for three-dimensional environmental arrangements, variations in the spatial orientation of items within an arrangement should influence memory for that arrangement. Such variations should be particularly critical when "familiar" or predictable patterns can be identified. Golbeck (1983) examined the effect of a familiar or meaningful orientation of furniture items upon children's memory for the arrangement. Sixteen items of furniture were placed in a room in a meaningful or nonmeaningful fashion. The meaningful condition included four subgroupings of furniture: two chairs, a table, and a dresser, each placed in a familiar sort of "conversational grouping." In the nonmeaningful condition, items were placed in the floor spots but rotated such that the arrangement resembled a maze more than an ordinary room. (See Fig. 9.1). Based on the research with two-dimensional graphic stimuli (Hock, Romanski, Galie, & Williams, 1978; Mandler & Parker, 1976), the familiar meaningful arrangements were expected to be easier to remember. Finally, to examine the potential relationship between orientation and clustering, the two conditions of spatial orientation were crossed with the two conditions of clustering described earlier.

There was an interesting effect for meaningful spatial orientation. Although the meaningful spatial orientation enhanced scores on the reconstruction task, this effect was seen only when the contents of the environment were also clustered. In other words, the familiar, meaningful orientation influenced memory only in the presence of additional environmental organization. Within the nonclustered setting, there was no difference between the meaningful and nonmeaningful arrangements.

These findings indicate that children may be using something akin to schemata in remembering the arrangement of objects in the environment. The more familiar, previously experienced type of set-up was easier for the child to remember. However, the data also suggest some qualifying conditions for the use of such schemata. In the highly complex, nonclustered setting, a meaningful spatial orientation did not enhance children's ability to remember the arrangement. Familiar, meaningful orientation and clustering may play complementary roles in the representation of real-world settings.

Saliency. A third organizational feature is the salience of items in the environment, or how noticeable an object is. What is noticeable depends upon context. In a study with adults, Brewer and Treyens (1981) contrasted items in an environment in terms of saliency and schema expectancy. Schema expectancy refers to how likely it is that an object will be found in a particular type of setting. An item might have a high schema expectancy rating for a particular room, yet not actually be in the room. Not surprisingly, saliency and schema expectancy ratings were not independent. An object that did not belong in the setting and received a low schema expectancy score was much more noticeable and received a high saliency score.

Brewer and Treyens (1981) went on to study the effect of saliency and schema expectancy for memory. Adults were asked whether or not a variety of objects varying in saliency and schema expectancy were present in a room in which they had spent a brief amount of time. The room was arranged to look like a graduate student's office. In general, objects ranking high in schema expectancy were more accurately encoded and remembered. It is also interesting to note that on several recall tasks, subjects recalled objects that had not been present in the room. These inferred items were nearly always high in schema expectancy. Therefore, in performing on these memory tasks, subjects were drawing upon previous knowledge of what actually belonged in offices, as well as what they had actually seen.

This study has implications for the development of large-scale spatial cognition. Brewer and Treyens (1981) emphasized the importance of distinguishing between saliency and schema expectancy. However, they pointed out further that the discrepancy between the two may be less extreme in a setting for which the subject does not have a strong previously formed schema. Clearly, the subjects had a great deal of knowledge about what did and did not belong in an office. Children may lack the strongly formed schemas of adults and thus saliency, without schema expectancy, may be critical for place memory.

Further examination of the role of object salience in children, along with schema expectancy, is needed. While it seems that for adults, saliency is partially determined by expectancy, very different criteria might determine saliency for children. Techniques for determining saliency in a variety of environmental settings would be most helpful.

Conclusions

In this section of the chapter a taxonomy for describing the physical environment has been presented. This taxonomy is useful as a conceptual tool for articulating relationships between the characteristics of the environment in general and developing representations of the environment. Without this taxonomy, it is difficult to identify features of the environment that are consistently related to emerging conceptions of the environment. Two broad classes of environmental characteristics were identified: structural features and organizational features. Evidence from a variety of large-scale spatial cognition tasks was presented to illustrate how the physical environment itself influences memory and representation of that environment. Also, interactive effects between environmental characteristics and age upon spatial representation were highlighted.

AN APPLICATION OF THE TAXONOMY: YOUNG CHILDREN'S COGNITION AND BEHAVIOR IN CLASSROOMS

Some implications of considering the development of spatial cognition as a function of environmental characteristics are presented in this portion of the chapter. This is done by applying the taxonomy of environmental characteristics to a specific environment, a classroom. This application is an attempt to illustrate two points. The first is that the general environmental features included in the taxonomy are indeed meaningful in the context of a specific setting. The importance of these features is shown by overviewing research on classroom environments. Although researchers studying classroom environments have not been concerned with cognition, they have been interested in features of the environment. It will be shown here that there is a convergence between this research and the taxonomy described in this chapter. The application attempts to illustrate a second point. The features of the environment and their influence on spatial representation of the environment together may relate to children's behavior in the environment. Speculations on this notion are presented here.

Research on Classroom Environments

Researchers studying the physical environment of the school, and more particularly the early childhood classroom, have explicitly focused their attention on direct relationships between characteristics of the physical setting and behavior in the setting. Cognition of the environment has not been of interest. Given this behavioral focus, they have identified variables in the physical environment critical to ongoing activities in the classroom (See Weinstein, 1979, for a review and critique of this literature). These variables include (a) classroom design and furniture arrangement, (b) characteristics of materials and equipment, and (c) places for privacy. Overviewed briefly here is the literature illustrating the significance of each of these variables in educational settings for young children. A more general review of the literature on classroom environments may be found in the chapter by Poag and Goodnight.

Although research on behavior in classroom environments has not addressed issues in cognition, the important environmental variables may be placed in the taxonomy outlined earlier. Table 9.1 illustrates how the classroom variables, or the components of the classroom setting, mesh with the structural and organizational features of the physical environment included in the taxonomy. The following discussion clarifies Table 9.1 by considering each component of the classroom environment and the features of the taxonomy it exemplifies.

Classroom Design and Furniture Arrangement. One of the most comprehensive studies of physical settings in early education is reported by Kritchevsky and Prescott (1969) as part of a larger study of day-care environments carried out by Prescott, Jones, and Kritchevsky (1972). These data serve as a primary source of support for the importance of classroom design and furniture arrangement in the early childhood classroom. Of particular interest to these researchers was the delineation of spatial characteristics and the identification of relationships between the physical setting of the day-care centers and the teachers' and children's

TABLE 9.1
Classroom Components in Relation to Features of the Environment

| Components of Early Education Setting | General Features of the Environment | | | | | |
| | Structural | | | Organizational | | |
	Landmk	Contain	Barrier	Cluster	Orienta	Saliency
Classroom Design & Furniture Arrangement						
(a) Defined activity area	x	x	x	x	x	x
(b) Boundary		x	x			
(c) Path		x				
Materials and Equipment						
(a) Amount	x					
(b) Variety	x					x
(c) Arrangement				x		
(d) Display	x			x		x
Places for Privacy		x	x	x		

behavior. A series of descriptive concepts related to aspects of the space were developed. Several are of interest to the present discussion. A "play unit" is a piece of play equipment and the space around it necessary for its use. A "boundary" is the outer edge of a play unit or play yard. A "path" is the space that children use to move from one place to another. Play yards and centers were rated on several dimensions including the degree of organization. Organization was defined as the relationship between yard boundaries, pathway and yard surface covered with objects.

Well-organized space was termed high-quality space. It was associated with sensitive, friendly teachers and interested, involved children. Other positive classroom interactions were also related to well-organized space. Low-quality space predicted less involved children and insensitive teachers. The authors note that while in general, the quality of the physical space was related to behavior, the staff seemed largely unaware of the factors contributing to successful space. "Adults put things in space for children to play with, but *where* they are put seems related to happenstance structuring factors already present, rather than any rationale determined from goals and purposes" (Prescott et al., 1972, p. 40).

Several recommendations for room or play yard organization were offered. Patterns of movement and thus, paths, from one play unit to the next should be carefully considered. Also, a room or a play yard should be separated into subareas according to intended activity: quiet-active, vehicles-climbing, messy-clean. When the room is arranged into subareas the division between the main areas can become the major paths. Consequently, divisions between areas can be manipulated through the presence of physical barriers as well as by open space. While the data reported by Prescott et al. are correlational, Weinstein (1977) provided stronger support for potential causal relationships between these setting variables and behavior through the use of a time series design.

Three components of classroom design and furniture arrangement are included in Table 9.1: defined activity areas, boundaries, and paths. These classroom components have been identified elsewhere as important factors in the early childhood classroom (Harms & Clifford, 1980; Phyfe-Perkins, 1980; Weinstein, 1979).

Defined activity areas incorporate several features of the environmental taxonomy. The primary characteristic of an activity area is the clustering of curriculum materials. Teachers are routinely advised to create learning centers or activity areas for mathematics, block play, sociodramatic play, and so on. A classroom activity area illustrates the organizational feature of environmental clustering. Furthermore, within each activity area items are organized to create a cohesive grouping of objects, illustrating meaningful orientation. Within an activity area, any single item might function as a landmark. Additionally, a well-designed activity area typically incorporates a variety of containing features. These might be furniture, room dividers, walls, or rugs. Patterned rugs might serve to bound areas of the room as well as to differentiate the space (Fowler, 1980). Finally, the arrangement of furniture also creates barriers. Some of these entirely obstruct vision, while others are low enough for a child to look over. In sum, as shown on Table 9.1, defined activity areas incorporate all the features on the taxonomy.

Boundaries and paths are critical components of the classroom arrangement. The boundaries surrounding activity areas may be obvious examples of containing features or barriers. Paths can also serve as containing features. However, paths also structure movement through the environment. To the extent that a path structures or controls the child's movement through space, it may well influence spatial representations (Cohen, 1982; Herman, Kolker, & Shaw, 1982).

Materials and Equipment.   A second category of variables in the early childhood classroom concerns materials and equipment. For purposes of discussion here, materials may be contrasted with furniture and fixed items in room, while equipment is synonomous with "play units." However, the arrangement of materials is closely related to placement of furniture. Phyfe-Perkins (1980) has described several factors relevant to materials in the early education classroom. These include amount, variety, arrangement, and display.

The amount of materials in relation to the amount of empty space was identified as a component of classroom organization by Prescott and colleagues. It is a good example of variability in differentiation. A classroom with a large number of materials and equipment in relation to the amount of empty space is high in landmark density. Kritchevsky & Prescott (1969) suggested that good organization is typically found in space where the surface is no less than one-third and no more than one-half uncovered. It would be interesting to examine the interaction of density in the physical environment in relation to specific types of organization.

Other evidence concerning the effects of variations in amount of materials has been discussed by Phyfe-Perkins (1980). Typically, researchers have considered the effects of such variables as availability of toys upon the quantity and quality of both social interaction and play activity (Johnson, 1935). Another approach has considered quantity of materials in interaction with other classroom variables, such as daily schedule (Doke & Risley, 1972). As noted in Table 9.1, variations in the amount of materials illustrate the structural feature of landmark presence.

The variety of materials is a notion borrowed from Kritchevsky & Prescott (1969). In their framework, variety refers to the number of different kinds of activity the "play units" provide. Variety is complemented by complexity, or the extent to which "play units" contain potential for active manipulation and alteration by children. Prescott and colleagues (1972) maintain that variety and complexity of materials relate to high quality interactions in the classroom. As Phyfe-Perkins (1980) pointed out, variety is particularly important in a classroom emphasizing children's free-choice of activity. Upon completion of an activity, a child must be able to choose a new activity. If the choice is to be real for the child, the environment must provide *at least* two alternative courses of action for every child in the room at any given point in time.

In contrast to the amount or variety of materials, arrangement specifically concerns spatial placement in the classroom environment. The arrangement of materials, together with furniture placement, comprises classroom organization. Again, Weinstein (1977) and Kritchevsky and Prescott (1969), among others, have identified the importance of the arrangement of materials for effective classroom functioning.

The arrangement of materials is one illustration of clustering in the environment. One characteristic of a defined activity area is a grouping of related curriculum materials. The effect of the arrangement of materials in the preschool classroom was examined by Nash (1981). Classrooms were organized in one of two fashions. Materials and equipment were arranged either according to curriculum activity (language, math, science, etc.) or according to a functional system for the teachers not related to curriculum activity (messy, noisy, needing access to the sink, etc). Nash hypothesized that children would combine materials within each room area more frequently when materials were grouped according to curriculum activity. The results supported the hypothesis that children would use materials more frequently and in more complex and elaborate ways when the learning environment was organized in a rational and sensible fashion for the child.

The display of materials in the classroom is closely related to the amount and arrangement of objects available to children. To the extent that materials are visible and accessible to children, they differentiate the environment. Toys and materials stored on open shelves may also be displayed with varying levels of organization. Not only might an arrangement be described as messy or neat, it might be described as clearly classified or grouped. Materials in the classroom may be displayed to emphasize particular logical and spatial relationships. Such an approach is explicitly espoused in an early childhood curriculum developed by Weikart (Hohmann, Banet, & Weikart, 1979; Weikart, Rogers, Adcock, & McClelland, 1974), although other early educators also have used this approach. Specifically, blocks are stored on open shelves and categorized by size and shape. Toys are displayed on shelves in a similar fashion (e.g., barnyard animals versus zoo animals; wooden cars versus plastic cars). Toys or other materials that can be placed in a seriated relationship are clearly displayed as such (e.g., three pans varying only in size are hung on the wall of the house area to emphasize the progression from large to small).

Labeling is another feature relevant to the display of materials in the classroom. Labels are placed on shelves or other storage areas to indicate the appropriate location for an object (Hohmann et al., 1979). Labels may be presented at varying levels of abstraction: the actual object (e.g., a crayon taped to the crayon holder), a graphic representation (a picture of a crayon), or a word. Such labels might be considered a type of landmark. In addition to functioning as spatial landmarks, they mark logical clusters of objects.

Places for Privacy. The final set of variables to be considered here concerns the provision of places for children to be alone in the classroom. Privacy in the classroom is discussed by Weinstein (1979) and Phyfe-Perkins (1980). Both authors define privacy as the ability to control or regulate interactions with other individuals. Although many educators seem to agree with the notion that providing places for children to be alone in the classroom is a good one, there is little empirical work to substantiate this claim.

In a study of privacy-seeking behavior in an elementary school, Weinstein (1982) found evidence of individual differences as reflected in teacher ratings and children's use of a special privacy booth placed in the classroom. The privacy booth was a three-sided cubicle, constructed of cardboard, which enclosed a desk and a chair. This sort of enclosed area, separated from the rest of the classroom, is typical of arrangements suggested for privacy. Since Weinstein (1981) was interested in elementary school-aged children, the booth enclosed a desk. With younger children, a different arrangement might be created.

Different degrees of enclosure or privacy were also considered by Weinstein (1982). Three types of booths were created, one without windows, a second with a window, and a third with a window that could be covered from the inside with an opaque panel. Although there were no differences in the actual use of the various booths, children expressed a preference for the booth containing a window that could be covered. Such preference for a private space that permits visual access to the environment is consistent with previous research (Gramza, 1970).

Designing classrooms to incorporate places for privacy illustrates the use of two structural features of the environmental taxonomy, as shown in Table 9.1. These include the presence of containing features and the presence of barriers. Such places for privacy might be considered specialized activity areas that necessarily contain barriers.

Since the scant research on privacy in classrooms has focused on simply identifying what private places in a classroom might be and how children differ in their needs for privacy, no clues are available about children's representations of the special places in classrooms in which they can be alone. Simply providing children with locations in which they can watch and perhaps contemplate activities in space may influence their representation. The "barrier effects" described earlier may also differ when a barrier provides a place in which the child may be alone from the rest of the classroom.

Spatial Cognition as an Explanation of Environmental Use

The taxonomy of environmental features was applied to the classroom environment in an effort to reach two goals. The first was to demonstrate that the general taxonomy of environmental features could be applied to a specific setting. This has been done by showing the overlap between components of the classroom environment and the features of the taxonomy. In addition, the relevance of each classroom environment variable for behavior in the environment has been presented.

The second goal in applying the taxonomy was to consider how features of the environment and spatial representation taken together relate to children's behavior in a real-world setting, the classroom. Ideally, one would proceed with this task by showing how children's understanding of the setting influences their use of the setting. Unfortunately, there are little data illustrating ways that spatial representations mediate behavior. Therefore, this section offers some speculations and directions for future research.

Proshansky and Wolfe (1974) have argued that there are two major ways in which the design and arrangement of classroom affect educational goals. First, the physical and spatial aspects of a learning environment communicate a symbolic message about what is supposed to happen in the environment. Second, physical and spatial factors play a pragmatic role by restricting and encouraging particular behaviors. This discussion suggests a third way in which the design and arrangement of the classroom can facilitate educational goals: the ease with which the child can create a mental representation of the environment.

Children's ability to represent a large-scale space improves with age, experience, and variations in the structural and organizational characteristics of the environment. Furthermore, the variations in environmental organization that influence representation also influence children's behavior in classroom settings. Children's ability to detect, or mentally construct, an organization in the environment, to represent the environment, and to employ that representation for planning and carrying our a sequence of actions in the environment should facilitate positive classroom interactions. Across the total classroom, this should result in a more smoothly functioning learning environment. Children should be engaged in more meaningful activity and teachers should experience less stress.

Olds (1979) provides an excellent rationale for a relationship between children's cognition of their classrooms and their actions in the environment. She maintains that children have a basic need that must be met by the physical environment: the need to feel competent. An environment organized in a manner that the child can comprehend will help meet this need.

A classroom organized to facilitate the young child's representation would include particular combinations of environmental features chosen according to the child's level of cognitive development. Such a classroom should maximize the child's sense of competence by providing a physical environment which the child understands both at the level of action and at the level of reflection. accurate representation is outlined here. It is important to note that physical variations in the environment alone are not important. Rather, it is the interaction of each with the child's level of cognitive development, age, and experience in the environment that matter. In general, the younger the child and the less experience in a particular setting, the more important the structural and organizational features of the setting are for the child's representation.

Landmarks. Young children's representations of space are highly dependent upon landmarks, so this structural feature of the environment merits careful attention. Classrooms organized with this notion in mind should lead to more adequate representations. The classroom is filled with objects potentially serving as landmarks. Fixed features of the room such as doors and windows, as well as furniture, floor and wall markings, planfully placed decorations, and accidentally placed boxes and materials all might be landmarks. In choosing landmarks, young children seem to choose perceptually salient objects in the environment even if the object is not positioned in a stable fashion.

Landmarks could play a role in helping the child represent individual activity areas as cohesive units. A salient object nearby or within the activity area might be identified as a landmark. Relationships between landmarks and surrounding items should be emphasized and children systematically alerted to landmark-object relationships. Throughout, care should be given to preserving landmark positions in the environment. It seems likely that younger children would benefit from landmark planning more than older children. Also, as children gain experience in the environment, multiple landmark relationships will be identified and the importance of planned landmarks will decrease.

Containing Features. Within the classroom, containing features such as walls, room dividers and floor markings help to define activity areas and paths. Containing features emphasize the logical clustering of items within an activity area. An activity area lacking well-articulated containing features, or boundaries, may not be recognized by a child. Boundaries may serve to emphasize the logical relationships obvious to an adult teacher, but much less obvious to a child (Golbeck, 1982). Containing features also help conceptually ground objects. Earlier, it was suggested that containing features may help the child mentally separate a large space into subspaces. Walls, room dividers, and rugs might emphasize awareness of activity areas by dividing a large room-sized space into smaller "chunks" or subareas.

An example of the way containing features might influence spatial representation is provided in Fig. 9.2. Rather than representing the entire classroom, the

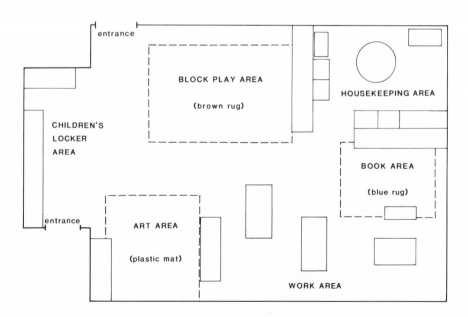

FIG. 9.2.   The layout of an early childhood classroom.

child might conceptualize the room in six subspaces. These subspaces roughly correspond to the activity areas and include the block area, contained by the block shelves and the rug; the art area, contained by the plastic mat; the book area, contained by the blue rug; the housekeeping area, contained by the corner and pieces of furniture; the locker area; and a diffuse area contained on one side by the wall. (In an ideal arrangement, this sixth area might be more clearly bounded.) This subdivision leads to a more accurate representation of each individual activity area, although the young child's representation of the room as a whole may be inaccurate. However, since activities in the classroom are planned and completed within activity areas and not the entire space, representation of the total space may be less important than representations of smaller areas.

Barriers.   Barriers appear to influence spatial representation by distorting distance estimates between two points separated by a barrier. Such distortions might be quite useful in an environment such as a classroom. Classrooms contain multiple activity areas or learning centers. Different activities are going on within each. Increasing the sense of distance between activity areas in the classroom may be important for children's involvement in activities. For example, in Fig. 9.2, the cupboard separating the art area from the adjacent work area both controls traffic flow and psychologically separates children working in the two areas.

Places for children to be alone in the classroom are also important. Although it may not be possible for a child to leave the classroom, an area closed off from the rest of the room may be the next best option. In such situations, the distortions of distance created by the barrier would be desirable.

Clustering.   Activity areas might be described as the systematic grouping of equipment and learning materials. Arranging materials according to a logical criterion of common use should facilitate the completion of meaningful activities on the part of the child. Such an arrangement complements spatial relationships emphasized in landmark planning and the placement of containing features. Olds (1979) suggested accentuating activity areas with common colors. For example, in Fig. 9.2, furniture and floor coverings within the book area might all be blue and those in the art area might be yellow. Clustering furniture and equipment by function and color should emphasize the discrete activity areas as subspaces in the room. This should lead to more stable representations of room areas, and support children's plans for involvement with materials.

Orientation.   In a real-world setting, orientation seems to work closely with clustering and structural features of the environment. Since furniture can only be used from certain positions, shifts in orientation of furniture disrupt a functionally arranged group of objects. For example, the back of an open storage shelf functions not as a shelf but as a room divider. The orientation of furniture items both contains and defines activity areas through clustering.

Orientation might enhance representation in a different manner. The orientation or arrangement of items in the classroom might be modeled after other real-world settings the child has experienced. A book corner similar to the corner of a child's bedroom at home may be approachable because the child has some preexisting scheme for such arrangements. As children gain experience in school settings, unique "school schema" may develop and arrangements dissimilar to those they have come to know may be disruptive.

Saliency. The salience of items in the early childhood classroom also works in interaction with other structural and organizational features to influence representation. Color, lighting, and texture might be used to enhance the salience of particular pieces of furniture, equipment, and materials. In planning landmarks, it would be sensible to choose objects high in saliency and low in schema expectancy (Brewer & Treyens, 1981). Similarly, it would be wise to limit the number of salient and unexpected items in any given activity area. This could be achieved by creating visually homogeneous activity areas, as already described in clustering. Finally, saliency could be structured or planned to overlap with and complement other environmental features such as containing features and barriers.

Conclusions

The taxonomy of environmental features was applied to a specific environment to illustrate how general environmental features might interact with cognitive factors in the formation of a representation of that environment. The classroom environment presented examples of all the structural and organizational features included in the taxonomy, and speculations about the effects of these features along with representation for behavior in the classroom were offered. Although limited research is available on children's cognition of their classrooms, this analysis suggests several avenues for future study. First, variations in environmental features already shown to influence behavior in the classroom may well also influence representation of the classroom environment. Second, these effects may differ depending upon the developmental level of the child. Third, if variations in the physical environment influence representation, variations in representation may play a role in explaining behavior in classrooms.

GENERAL SUMMARY AND CONCLUSIONS

Although researchers from several disciplines have studied large-scale spatial cognition, relatively little attention has been directed toward identifying general characteristics of the environment and the relationship of these characteristics to spatial representation. The purpose of this chapter has been to provide a framework for articulating relationships between representations of the spatial environment and physical characteristics of the environment itself. Toward this end, a taxonomy of environmental features has been proposed. This taxonomy is intended to serve as a tool for conceptualizing the reciprocal relationships between the physical environment and spatial representations.

The set of environmental features included in the taxonomy is intentionally broad and is not necessarily complete. However, by applying the framework to a variety of specific places and spaces, such as classrooms, homes, neighborhoods, and so forth, abstract spatial concepts will be better understood in the context of specific settings. Such findings would enrich theory in the development of children's spatial cognition by bringing it outside the laboratory into the real world. Such enriched and expanded theory in turn would provide researchers in environmental psychology with a better means for examining the relationships between representation and behavior in particular kinds of settings. Working in such a fashion will not only enrich theory in environmental cognition; it will also offer more satisfactory explanations of children's behavior in their everyday environments.

ACKNOWLEDGMENTS

I would like to gratefully acknowledge the contributions of R. Cohen, R. DeLisi and L. Liben. Their thoughtful comments on earlier versions of this chapter were greatly appreciated. I would also like to thank C. Weinstein for her help in expanding my knowledge of classroom environments.

REFERENCES

Acredolo, L. P. Frames of reference used by children for orientation in unfamiliar places. In G. Moore & R. Golledge (Eds.), *Environmental knowing*. Stroudsburg, PA: Dowden, Hutchinson & Ross, 1976.

Acredolo, L. P. Developmental changes in the ability to coordinate perspectives of a large-scale space. *Developmental Psychology*, 1977, *13*, 1–8.

Acredolo, L. P. Laboratory versus home: The effect of the environment on the 9-month old infant's choice of spatial reference system. *Developmental Psychology*, 1979, *15*, 666–667.

Acredolo, L. P. Small-scale and large-scale spatial concepts in infancy and childhood. In L. S. Liben, A. Patterson, N. Newcombe (Eds.), *Spatial representation and behavior across the life-span: Theory and application*. New York: Academic Press, 1981.

Acredolo, L. P., Pick, H. L., & Olsen, M. Environmental differentiation and familiarity as determinants of children's memory for spatial location. *Developmental Psychology*, 1975, *11*, 495–501.

Allen, G. L., Kirasic, K. C., Siegel, A. W., & Herman, J. F. Developmental issues in cognitive mapping: The selection and utilization of environmental landmarks. *Child Development*, 1979, *50*, 1062–1070.

Altman, I., & Wohwill, J. (Eds.). *Human behavior and environment: Vol. 3. Children and the environment*. New York: Plenum, 1978.

Appleyard, D. Notes on urban perception and knowledge. In R. M. Downs & D. Stea (Eds.), *Image and environment*. Chicago: Aldine, 1973.

Baird, J. C., & Lutkus, A. D. (Eds.). *Mind child architecture*. Hanover: University Press of New England, 1982.

Brewer, W. F., & Treyens, J. C. Role of schemata in memory for places. *Cognitive Psychology, 1981, 13,* 207–230.

Canter, D. *The psychology of place*. New York: St. Martin's Press, 1977.

Canter, D., & Stringer, P. *Environmental interaction*. New York: International Universities Press, 1976.

Cohen, R. The role of activity in the construction of spatial representations. In R. Cohen (Ed.), *Children's conceptions of spatial relationships*. San Francisco: Jossey-Bass, 1982.

Cohen, R., Baldwin, L. M., & Sherman, R. C. Cognitive maps of a naturalistic setting. *Child Development, 1978, 49,* 1216–1218.

Cohen, R., & Weatherford, D. L. Effects of route traveled on the distance estimates of children and adults. *Journal of Experimental Child Psychology, 1980, 29,* 403–412.

Cohen, R., Weatherford, D. L., Lomenick, T., & Koeller, K. Development of spatial representations: Role of task demands and familiarity with the environment. *Child Development, 1979, 50,* 1257–1260.

DeLisi, R. Developmental and individual differences in children's representation of the horizontal coordinate. *Merrill-Palmer Quarterly, 1983, 29,* 179–196.

Doke, L. A., & Risley, T. R. The organization of daycare environments: Required versus optional activities. *Journal of Applied Behavioral Analysis, 1972, 5,* 405–420.

Evans, G. Environmental cognition. *Psychological Bulletin, 1980, 88,* 259–287.

Fowler, W. *Infant and child care: A guide to education in group settings*.Boston: Allyn & Bacon, 1980.

Furth, H. *Piaget and knowledge*. Englewood Cliffs, NJ: Prentice-Hall, 1969.

Golbeck, S. Young children's knowledge of the classroom environment. *Journal of Man-Environment Relations, 1982, 1,* 67–78.

Golbeck, S. Reconstructing a large-scale spatial arrangement: Effects of environmental organization and operativity. *Developmental Psychology, 1983, 19,* 644–653.

Gramza, A. F. Children's preferences for enterable play boxes. *Perceptual Motor Skills, 1970, 31,* 177–178.

Gump, P. School environments. In I. Altman & J. Wohlwill (Eds.), *Human behavior and the environment: Vol. 3. Children and the environment*. New York: Plenum, 1978.

Harms, T., & Clifford, R. *Early childhood environment rating scale*. New York: Teachers College Press, 1980.

Herman, J. F., Kolker, R. G., & Shaw, M. L. Effects of motor activity on children's intentional and incidental memory for spatial locations. *Child Development, 1982, 53,* 239–244.

Herman, J. F., & Siegel, A. W. The development of cognitive mapping of the large-scale environment. *Journal of Experimental Child Psychology, 1978, 26,* 389–406.

Hock, H. S., Romanski, L., Galie, A., & Williams, C. S. Real-world schemata and scene recognition in adults and children. *Memory and cognition, 1978, 6,* 423–431.

Hohmann, M., Banet, B., & Weikart, D. *Young children in action*. Ypsilanti: High/Scope Press, 1979.

Hoving, K. L., Spencer, T., Robb, K. Y., & Schulte, D. Developmental changes in visual information processing. In P. A. Ornstein (Ed.), *Memory development in children*. Hillsdale, NJ: Lawrence Erlbaum Associates, 1978.

Inhelder, B., & Piaget, J. *The early growth of logic in the child*. New York: Norton, 1964.

Ittelson, W. Environment perception and contemporary perceptual theory. In W. H. Ittleson (Eds.), *Environment and cognition*. New York: Seminar Press, 1973.

Johnson, M. W. The effect on behavior of variation in the amount of play equipment. *Child Development, 1935, 6,* 56–68.

Kosslyn, S. M. Information representation in visual images. *Cognitive Psychology*, 1975, *7*, 341–370.

Kosslyn, S. M., Pick, H. L., & Farriello, G. R. Cognitive maps in children and men. *Child Development*, 1974, *45*, 707–716.

Kritchevsky, S., & Prescott, E. *Planning environments for young children: Physical space*. Washington, DC: National Association for the Education of Young Children, 1969.

Lane, D. M., & Pearson, D. A. Attending to spatial locations: A developmental study. *Child Development*, 1983, *54*, 98–104.

Laurendeau, M., & Pinard, A. *The development of the concept of space in the child*. New York: International Universities Press, 1970.

Liben, L. Spatial representation and behavior: Multiple perspectives. In L. S. Liben, A. H. Patterson, & N. Newcombe (Eds.), *Spatial representation and behavior across the life-span*. New York: Academic Press, 1981.

Liben. L. S. Children's large-scale spatial cognition: Is the measure the message? In R. Cohen (Ed.), *Children's conceptions of spatial relationships*. San Francisco: Jossey-Bass, 1982.

Liben, L., Moore, M., & Golbeck, S. Preschoolers' knowledge of their classroom environment: Evidence from small-scale and life-size spatial tasks. *Child Development*, 1982, *53*, 1275–1284.

Liben, L. S., Patterson, A. H., & Newcombe, N. (Eds.). *Spatial representation and behavior across the life-space*. New York: Academic Press, 1981.

Lynch, K. *The image of the city*. Cambridge, MA: MIT Press, 1960.

Mandler, J. M. Categorical and schematic organization in memory. In C. R. Puff (Ed.), *Memory organization and structure*. New York: Academic Press, 1979.

Mandler, J. M., & Johnson, N. S. Some of the thousand words a picture is worth. *Journal of Experimental Psychology: Human Learning and Memory*, 1976, *2*, 529–540.

Mandler, J. M., & Parker, R. E. Memory for descriptive and spatial information in complex pictures. *Journal of Experimental Psychology: Human Learning and Memory*. 1976, *2*, 38–48.

Mandler, J. M., & Stein, N. L. Recall and recognition of pictures by children as a function of organization and distractor similarity. *Journal of Experimental Psychology*, 1974, *102*, 657–669.

Moore, R., & Young, D. Childhood outdoors: Toward a social ecology of the landscape. In I. Altman and J. Wohlwill (Eds.), *Human behavior and the environment: Vol. 3. Children and the environment*. New York: Plenum, 1978.

Nash, B. C. The effects of classroom spatial organization on four- and five-year old children's learning. *British Journal of Educational Psychology*, 1981, *51*, 144–155.

Newcombe, N., & Liben, L. Barrier effects in cognitive maps of children and adults. *Journal of Experimental Child Psychology*, 1982, *34*, 46–58.

Olds, A. Designing developmentally optimal classrooms for children with special needs. In S. J. Meisels (Ed.), *Special education and development: Perspectives on young children with special needs*. University Park Press, 1979.

Parke, R. D. Children's home environments: Social and cognitive effects. In I. Altman & J. Wohlwill (Eds.), *Human behavior and environment: Vol. 3. Children and the environment*. New York: Plenum, 1978.

Pascual-Leone, J. On learning and development, Piagetian style: In a reply to Lefebyre-Pinard. *Canadian Psychological Review*, 1976, *17*, 270–288.

Phyfe-Perkins, E. Children's behavior in preschool settings: A review of research concerning the influence of the physical environment. In L. Katz (Ed.), *Current topics in early childhood education* (Vol. 3). Norwood, NJ: Albex, 1980.

Piaget, J. Piaget's theory. In *Carmichael's manual of child psychology*. New York: Wiley, 1970.

Piaget, J., & Inhelder, B. *The child's conception of space*. New York: Norton, 1956.

Piaget, J., & Inhelder, B. *Memory and intelligence*. New York: Basic Books, 1973.

Piaget, J., Inhelder, B., & Szeminska, A. *The child's conception of geometry*. New York: Basic Books, 1960.

Prescott, E., Jones, E., & Kritchevsky, S. *Day care as a child-rearing environment.* Washington, DC: National Association for the Education of Young Children, 1972.

Proshansky, E., & Wolfe, M. The physical setting of open education. *School Review,* 1974, *82,* 557–574.

Runyon, D. K. Histories and futures: Aspects of the child's relation to the land and the city. In K. Riegel & J. Meacham (Eds.), *The developing individual in a changing world* (Vol. 2). Chicago: Aldine, 1976.

Siegel, A. W., & Schadler, M. The development of young children's spatial representations of their classrooms. *Child Development,* 1977, *48,* 388–394.

Waddell, K. J., & Rogoff, B. Effect of contextual organization on spatial memory of middle-aged and older women. *Developmental Psychology,* 1981, *17,* 878–885.

Walsh, D. A., Krauss, I. K., & Regnier, V. A. Spatial ability, environmental knowledge, and environmental use: The elderly. In L. S. Liben, A. H. Patterson, & N. Newcombe (Eds.), *Spatial representation and behavior across the life-span.* New York: Academic Press, 1981.

Weatherford, D. L. Spatial cognition as a function of size and scale of the environment. In R. Cohen (Ed.), *Children's conceptions of spatial relationships.* San Francisco: Jossey-Bass, Inc., 1982.

Weikart, D., Rogers, L., Adcock, C., & McClelland, D. *The cognitively oriented curriculum.* Washington, DC: National Association for the Education of Young Children, 1974.

Weinstein, C. S. Modifying student behavior in an open classroom through changes in the physical design. *American Educational Research Journal,* 1977, *14,* 249–262.

Weinstein, C. S. The physical environment of the school: A review of the research. *Review of Educational Research,* 1979, *49,* 577–610.

Weinstein, C. S. Privacy seeking behavior in the elementary classroom. *Journal of Evnironmental Psychology,* 1982, *2,* 23–35.

Werner, H. *The comparative psychology of mental development.* New York: International Universities Press, 1948.

Wohlwill, J. F. The environment is not in the head! In W. Preiser (Ed.), Proceedings from the Fourth International Conference of the Environmental Design Research Association (EDRA 4), 1973.

10 The Social Cognition of Spatial Cognition: Regulating Personal Boundaries

Judith A. Goodnight
Robert Cohen
Memphis State University

The chapters in this book document the wide range of phenomena associated with spatial cognition. The majority of the issues addressed concern the representation and understanding of physical environments as a function of the nature of the space and the cognitive characteristics of the participants in the space. In many of the chapters there is a consideration of the influence of social interactions on these spatial cognitive processes. Certainly the theoretical positions of Bronfenbrenner (1979) on the ecological systems that influence development and of Siegel (1982) on the importance of social agenda for spatial understanding have led investigators in this direction of broader conceptualizations of spatial cognitive functioning.

In the present chapter we review the literature on the development of spatial boundary regulation. The emphasis of this area of spatial research traditionally has been social in nature, focusing on interpersonal phenomena such as privacy, crowding, and personal space. It seems to us that this set of cognitive processes offers a natural extrapolation to the concerns expressed by Bronfenbrenner (1979) and Siegel (1982). At a simplistic level, the manner in which an individual conceives of and regulates interpersonal distance will certainly influence the opportunities for and the nature of those interpersonal relationships. In addition, as we propose at the conclusion of the chapter, boundary regulation may be related to more general aspects of social development.

CONCEPTUALIZATION OF PRIVACY

A number of theoretical accounts of privacy exist. Westin (1970), a political scientist, focused on the right of an individual to control personal information available to others. For Westin, there are four states of privacy: solitude, anonymity, intimacy, and reserve. These states function to provide the individual personal autonomy, emotional release, time for self-evaluation, or limited and protected communication with others. This view of privacy is similar to that offered by Proshansky, Ittelson, and Rivlin (1970) who emphasize the role of privacy in maximizing an individual's freedom of choice and in controlling activities in relation to self.

Other theorists focus more on situational analyses of privacy (Laufer, Proshansky, & Wolfe, 1976; Laufer & Wolfe, 1977; Wolfe, 1978; Wolfe & Laufer, 1974). These authors propose three dimensions of the concept of privacy: self–ego, which concerns individuation and the development of autonomy; environmental factors, such as culture, traditions, values, sociophysical arrangement of the environment, and life cycle influences such as sociohistorical and developmental changes; and an interpersonal dimension that involves information management and interaction management.

In these theoretical approaches, privacy is closely related to personal autonomy and a sense of individuality. As such, it involves the issue of control in regulating both one's interactions with others and the information that is received by others. One of the most comprehensive theories of privacy to date that integrates these common factors along with other environmental phenomena is proposed by Altman (1975), and is considered in greater detail.

Altman (1975) defined privacy as the selective control of access to the self or to one's group. Such access can be in terms of interaction with others, sharing information with others, or both. Also recognized in this definition is that groups of people may function similarly to an individual in seeking privacy. Privacy is a process, not simply a state of being, with four essential characteristics. First, privacy is a boundary-regulation process. It is through privacy that we pace and regulate our day-to-day encounters with others. Second, privacy is a bidirectional, dialectic process. That is, privacy is directed not only to the restriction of interaction with others but to the seeking of interaction as well. Third, privacy is a dynamic process since neither desired nor achieved degrees of privacy are static. As situations change, the individual's degree of interaction also changes.

As a fourth characteristic, Altman proposed that the regulation of privacy follows an information processing, feedback loop kind of evaluation. For each individual there is an optimal degree of access at any point in time. Each person has a desired level of privacy as a goal—some subjective assessment of the ideal level of interaction with others. This is compared to the individual's achieved level of privacy, or actual degree of contact. When the desired and the achieved levels of privacy are judged to be equal, privacy is at its optimal level. However, when unequal in either direction, an unsatisfactory condition arises. When the achieved level is less than the desired, this is called crowding, i.e., the person is experiencing more contact with others than desired. When the achieved level is greater than the desired, the resultant condition is termed social isolation or loneliness.

The individual seeks to achieve desired levels of privacy through the use of several mechanisms. One of these encompasses various forms of communication. A person may issue a direct statement about privacy to others such as "I want to be alone." Adults may use a different language when children are present. Nonverbal communicators, such as body stance and facial expressions, are also indicators of the desired degree of contact.

A second privacy mechanism is personal space, defined as an invisible boundary zone that surrounds the self into which others cannot inappropriately intrude without causing discomfort (Hall, 1966; Sommer, 1969). Interactions are regulated according to the interpersonal distance between participants. Usually the closer together people are, the more intimacy and less privacy they have in their relationship with each other. When people are spaced farther apart, their relationship with each other is more remote. By moving closer to someone, we signal our wish to establish closer contact, to be more accessible, whereas by moving away from others, we indicate a desire to limit accessibility.

The use and control of territories constitute a third privacy mechanism. While personal space is carried around with the body, territories are fixed, geographical locations, e.g., an office or a bedroom. Territories are frequently marked in some way (a name on a mailbox, a coat left on a chair) to indicate possession or occupancy. Access to the territory and its occupant is often managed through the use of architectural features such as doors, fences, or gates. In the United States, a closed door is one of the most powerful ways of denying access to others.

Finally, at the level farthest removed from the individual is the use of cultural norms of behavior as privacy mechanisms. For example, in cultures where it is difficult to achieve being physically alone, privacy takes the form of psychological withdrawal and reserve.

According to Altman, privacy carries out three functions, similar to the approaches mentioned previously. First is the control and management of interpersonal interactions. Privacy is the central boundary-regulation process under which personal space, territoriality, and so forth are subsumed. Next, privacy aids in the development of plans and strategies for dealing with others and in the development of interpersonal roles. Finally, privacy provides the opportunity for reflection about the self and the development of features of self-identity such as self-respect and personal autonomy.

THE DEVELOPMENT OF PRIVACY

How does knowledge of privacy's characteristics, functions, mechanisms, and so on develop? Wolfe and Laufer (1975) asked 900 children and adolescents 5 to 17 years of age to describe all the possible meanings of privacy, a private time, a private place, a private talk, and experiences with intrusion. The elements of aloneness and managing information were the most frequent definers for all age groups. Aloneness was used significantly more often by those 8 years and older, than by the youngest age group (5 to 7). Responses in the aloneness category for the older children were more complex in meaning, e.g., being alone when you want to be versus just being alone. The oldest group (13- to 17-year-olds) also used managing information as a defining characteristic significantly more often than the younger children. The inability to manage information was reported as a problem more often by the oldest children than the younger children. This information was likely to be related to activities involving sex, smoking, or drugs. Also increasing significantly with age were responses related to autonomy/choice such as "being able to do what you want to and no one knows." These responses were infrequent for children less than 8 years old.

Descriptions of privacy in terms of controlling access to places were highest for children in the 8- to 12-year-old range. This group was also significantly more likely to describe a private place according to the presence of doors or doors with locks and to use "keep out" signs. The one factor that decreased with age was the use of "quiet" as a key element of privacy.

Developmental differences also were found when the subjects were asked to describe the ways in which other family members indicated that they wanted privacy. Respondents of all ages described mothers as giving predominantly verbal cues. Twice as many fathers as mothers were said to use nonverbal cues. Verbal cues from parents were reported as greater than nonverbal cues by children under age 13, with the opposite reported by children over 13.

Three types of verbal cues were reported. Direct commands (e.g., "Go away!") were reported most often at all ages but especially by the 8- to 12-year-olds. Children ages 5 to 7 received more personal statements (e.g., "I need to be alone right now so I can get my work done"); children 13 to 17 received more hints (e.g., "Why don't you find something else to do?"). Nonspecific commands such as "Go away" increased with age, and specific commands like "Be quiet" decreased with age. When personal statements were given, they were more likely to be explanatory when addressed to children less than 13. Parents apparently assumed the child's understanding of privacy needs and did not feel the need to include an explanation for children over 13.

There were also three types of nonverbal cues. Children 13 to 17 years old reported the equivalent use by parents of subtle cues such as facial expressions or ignoring, as well as the use of markers or consistent patterns of behavior (e.g., closing the door, sitting in a certain chair). Children under 13 reported that parents most often went someplace else. When the parent used this type of cue, the choice of location showed a definite trend according to the child's age. For the 5- to 7-year-old children, parents were described as moving to some other nonspecific location within the house. With 8- to 12-year-olds, parents almost always moved into the bedroom, but left the house completely if the children were between 13 and 17 years old.

As part of a longitudinal project at the Fels Research Institute, Parke and Sawin (1979) examined 2- to 17-year-old children's use of privacy rules and markers in regulating the access of other family members within the home, i.e., the ways in which children indicate their privacy needs to others. As they grew older children increased their use of closed doors as privacy markers and their use of rules such as "knock before entering a room," as well as placing more limitations on others' access to a bedroom or bathroom occupied by the child. The greatest shift in all three of these behaviors occurred during early adolescence and was related to the physical maturity of the adolescent, not to chronological age alone.

Age differences also were evident based on the type of activity engaged in by the child, particularly concerning bathroom occupancy. Two- to 5-year-olds showed little differentiation of access according to type of bathroom activity. Older adolescents (14 to 17) placed distinct restrictions on access varying by the type of activity. Most limited access occurred for toilet use, slightly less restricted access during bathing or dressing, with grooming as the activity with least restricted access. Finally, Parke and Sawin (1979) reported that mothers who were restrictive and coercive retained greater control over their children's privacy habits. Affectionate and approving mothers were more likely to have children who sought less privacy during personal activities.

It is evident from both of these studies that the social organization in the home and the child's experiences with privacy change according to the child's developmental level. An important point to remember, however, is that the specific details of such experiences are likely to differ according to the family's social status, culture, and so on. Just as parents modify their speech according to the child's level of understanding (Phillips, 1973; Snow, 1972), it appears that they also regulate their use of privacy cues according to the child's expected level of understanding. The youngest children (up to age 7) received more verbal cues from parents, usually accompanied by explanatory statements and also more specific commands. With adolescents, parents used more nonverbal cues, usually subtle ones. Verbal cues were either nonspecific commands or hints and suggestions. The 8- to 12-year-old children, who were too old to be easily distracted and too young to be left alone in the house, received the greatest amount of direct commands without explanations while the parents retreated behind the closed door of their bedroom. As the child's understanding of the concept of privacy increased, so did their own use of privacy rules and practices. Thus conceptions of privacy follow a developmental progression related to the developmental status of the individual, environmental factors, and sociocultural influences.

The research on the development of privacy appears to have two serious limitations. First, conceptions of privacy and privacy regulation have been addressed, but little work has examined privacy-related behaviors in context. Second, privacy has been assessed for the home environment but not for other environments of children.

In the next two sections we review two important aspects of privacy regulation that have received considerable attention in the research literature. First we examine the condition where privacy regulation is inadequate. Recall that in

Altman's model, the failure of these behaviors to achieve the desired level of privacy results in feelings of crowding. This is followed by a review of perhaps the most studied boundary regulation process—personal space.

CROWDING

Sundstrom (1975) described crowding as a sequential process in which high-population density and/or unwanted social input leads to stress that causes the individual to enact coping behaviors and eventually leads to long-term costs. Stokols (1976) suggested that a distinction be made between neutral crowding and personal crowding. Neutral crowding occurs when a group of individuals through no fault of their own are required to exist in close proximity to each other for an unspecified period of time, e.g., being on a full elevator. Personal crowding occurs when an individual or group deliberately invades another person's privacy. Personal crowding, due to the intention behind the act, should produce more stress than neutral crowding.

Crowding has been studied primarily in terms of physical density—room size and/or group size. For a review of density studies with children in the home and in the school, see the chapter by Poag, Goodnight, and Cohen in this book. The rationale for many of the crowding studies was to expose subjects to a particular density condition and then to assess its effects on either task performance, physiological factors, or social factors.

With adolescents and adults, high-density ("crowded") conditions have had little effect on task performance (Freedman, Klevansky, & Ehrlich, 1971). Sherrod (1974) had groups of eight female high school students serve in one of three density conditions: noncrowded (150 available square feet), crowded (37 available square feet), and crowded with perceived control (same 37 square feet, but subjects were told they could leave if they wanted). Subjects spent one hour in the room working on a series of simple and complex pencil-and-paper tasks. Subsequent to their density exposure, all subjects were assessed for quality of proofreading performance and frustration tolerance (i.e., persistence in attempting to solve unsolvable puzzles). No differences between groups were found for either simple or complex tasks nor on proofreading quality. There was a significant difference in frustration tolerance. Students in the noncrowded room showed the most persistence in puzzle solving. The students with perceived control over the crowding showed less persistence but still significantly more than the students in the crowded condition. Although not demonstrating task differences during high density, Sherrod (1974) did show a behavioral aftereffect.

Physiological effects of crowding have been demonstrated using measures of skin conductance level, palmar sweating, and so forth. Aiello, Epstein, and Karlin (1975) placed undergraduates in groups of six in small and large rooms by a counterbalanced order and measured skin conductance level for each participant. Results showed that while in the smaller room group members exhibited higher skin conductance levels and greater arousal than while in the larger room. In a second experiment, skin conductance levels were measured for individuals in both the large and small rooms. Comparing the individual and group members' data, Aiello et al. found that the presence of others was significantly related to arousal; room size by itself had no effect on arousal. Groups of 4th-, 8th-, and 11th-grade students experienced varying degrees of density in the study by Aiello, Nicosia, and Thompson (1979). Across all grades, males showed higher elevations in physiological stress-related arousal than females. After the crowding experience, subjects were more competitive and reported feeling crowded, tense, and uncomfortable in the situation.

As a third study demonstrating physiological effects of crowding, Aiello, DeRisi, Epstein, and Karlin (1977) varied spatial density and college subjects' interpersonal distance preference, i.e., subjects who preferred interactions at a close range and those who preferred more distant interactions. Higher skin conductance levels were obtained from crowded subjects during exposure. Crowded subjects also reported greater discomfort due to the experimental situation and showed lower performance levels on two creativity tasks immediately after crowding. Subjects who preferred greater interpersonal distances exhibited the most physiological stress and reported greater stress as well.

The effects on social behavior as a function of crowding were demonstrated by Peay and Peay (1983) with adult subjects. Factorial combinations of high and low density in square feet per person (approximately 7.8 versus 29.1) and large and small group size (approximately 10 versus 30) formed the experimental conditions. To ensure the effects of crowding, subjects spent 7½ to 7¾ hours in their assigned condition. A videotaped sample of the locations and interaction patterns of subjects was made at 15-minute intervals throughout the experiment. The greatest amount of social activity between subjects during confinement occurred in the low density-small group condition and the least social activity took place in the low density-large group condition, with both high-density conditions intermediate. In addition, subjects retrospectively rated their feelings of crowding for the beginning, middle, and end of the experiment. Significant effects of crowding and density on the number of negative responses made by subjects occurred only for the end of the experiment in which subjects in the high-density, more crowded condition expressed more negative feelings than subjects in the low-density conditions.

Zeedyk-Ryan and Smith (1983) varied social density in a crowding experiment in which subjects were sequestered for approximately 16 hours as part of a civil defense exercise. Subjects in the crowded room showed significantly more hostility than uncrowded subjects and expressed more negative feelings about the experience. For all subjects, hostility and anxiety increased as the experiment went on.

As a final experiment to report, Chandler, Koch, and Paget (1977) demonstrated the interactive effects of the child's cognitive level and the structural complexity of the environment. They kept both room size (10 by 14 ft) and group size constant. Groups of nine children were given yardsticks and 15 minutes in which to order themselves by height. The setting of the room was varied by using a level floor for half the groups and a floor contoured irregularly by risers for the other half, making the task much more complex. Additionally, children were screened for operative knowledge of seriation and the concept of unit measurement. Level I children showed no understanding of seriation; Level II children had knowledge of seriation only; Level III children understood both seriation and unit measurement. Each group of nine was composed of three children from each level. Measures of palmar sweating, behavioral stress ratings, and estimates of room length, width, and the number of participants were obtained. Children whose cognitive structures did not match the complexity of the setting (i.e., Level II children in the contoured room, Level I children in either room) showed the most physiological stress and most behavioral disorganization, i.e., experienced the most crowding. In addition, these children also underestimated the size of the room while overestimating the number of children in the group.

In summary, crowding represents a condition where boundary control between self and others fails. This brief review suggests that states of crowding can have negative effects on the physiological arousal and the affect an individual experiences in an environment. Since crowding refers to a psychological state of unpleasant density, experiences of crowding will vary as a function of a variety of intra-individual factors. The factor most relevant for the present chapter is that the cognitive level of the child influences how an environment will be perceived and experienced, here in terms of density or crowding.

THE DEVELOPMENT OF PERSONAL SPACE

Personal space, the invisible boundary zone surrounding an individual, has been defined operationally in terms of interpersonal distance. There are three primary techniques used for assessing interpersonal distance: symbolic simulation studies, and observational studies either in the laboratory or in naturalistic settings. The basic paradigm of the simulation studies is to have the subject place a silhouette figure representing self on a board in relation to a target figure. This is assumed to represent the distance from the target that a person would actually maintain. With the observational techniques, the person's actual behavior is examined in settings either controlled by the experimenter or in naturally occurring settings. Following a brief review of the literature on personal space in infancy, we present the research with children, first offering general trends in the development of personal space, then considering a variety of mediating factors such as sex differences, affect, race and socioeconomic status, and physical status. As a final part of this section, we consider the research on reactions to intrusions of personal space.

Personal Space in Infancy

We can speculate that one of the important cognitive accomplishments that serves as a foundation for personal space behavior occurs during infancy— namely, the distinction between what is self and what is the world or non-self. This can be regarded as a basic boundary differentiation. Other developments during infancy can be related as well. Horner (1983) drew on a body of work already established in the social attachment literature, i.e., infant-stranger reactivity. In reviewing several hundred studies using the infant-stranger paradigm, Horner discovered that in studies where the stranger moved toward the child, it was the stranger's approach rather than mere appearance that evoked negative affect in the infants. Specifically, it was the stranger's movement into the immediate space surrounding the child. In infant-controlled studies when the child was free to move, a substantial number of infants (8 to 12 months old) approached to within 4 to 5 feet of the stranger. Shaffron (1974) found that negative responses were lessened when adults maintained an interactive distance for a short time before entering an infant's immediate space. This evidence suggests that infants are sensitive to their spatial relationships with others, although they may lack refined response capabilities.

Burgess and McMurphy (1982) observed children from 6 months to 5 years of age in order to determine when children actively maintain predictable distances toward adult caretakers and peers. The children were divided into three age groups: (1) infants who were 6 to 18 months old and mobile; (2) toddlers (19 to 27 months old); and (3) preschoolers (30 to 60 months old). During free-play situations, it was found that the children's distance from adults increased with age and children's distance from peers decreased with age. Specifically, infants stayed significantly closer to adults than did toddlers and preschoolers. Preschoolers stayed significantly closer to peers than did infants and toddlers. As the child gains independence and expands from adult relationships to peer relationships, there is a corresponding shift in spatial proximities.

Another cue in relation to personal space is eye contact. A study that examined the development of gaze aversion observed the reactions of children to being stared at by an adult in a shopping center (Scheman & Lockard, 1979). Comparisons of the likelihood of eye contact and length of child's gaze were made for infants (less than 18 months old), toddlers (18 months to approximately 5 years), and school-age children (5 to about 9 years). The likelihood of eye contact increased with age. Only 12% of the infants made visual contact with the adult but 62% and 60% respectively of the toddlers and school-age children did.

Personal Space in Children

In simulation studies, Bass and Weinstein (1971), Lerner, Karabenick, and Meisels (1975), and Lerner, Iwawaki, and Chihara (1976) found increased interpersonal distance with age for kindergarten through third-grade children. Beyond the third grade, age trends are not as clear. Lerner, Venning, and Knapp (1975) found no differences due to age using a projective technique with fourth, fifth, and sixth graders, whereas results obtained by Pedersen (1973) showed an increase in personal space for boys until third grade followed by a decrease, and a slight decrease in personal space until fifth grade for girls, with an increase at Grade 6. The high rate of inappropriate figure placements (25%) made by the younger children in Bass and Weinstein (1971), as well as other evidence (see Peterson, Draper, & Roscoe, 1982), suggests that the use of projective simulation techniques with young children may be questionable.

Clearer support for an overall age trend can be derived from observational studies. In general, there is an increase in personal space distance between age 3 and adulthood (Aiello & Aiello, 1974; Argyle & Dean, 1965; Baxter, 1970; Lomranz, Shapira, Choresh, & Gilat, 1975) although one study (Sarafino & Helmuth, 1981) reported a decrease in interpersonal distance between children 25–42 months old and children 43–62 months old. Recall that Burgess and McMurphy (1982) found that preschoolers would stay closer to peers than to adults, the opposite pattern found for infants. In addition, Tennis and Dabbs (1975) found that same-sex pairs of first graders maintained closer interpersonal distance in the corner of a room whereas fifth, ninth, and twelfth graders and college sophomores, maintained closer spacing in the center of the room.

As well as these broad measures of proximity, some researchers have examined the child's sensitivity to cues relevant for personal space. As mentioned previously, Horner (1983) demonstrated that infants were aware of and sensitive to the approach of strange adults. Interactions of preschoolers with an adult showed the persistence of this sensitivity. As the adult leaned toward and away from the child while both were seated at a table, the child moved in synchrony— withdrawing when approached by the adult and approaching when the adult withdrew (Peery & Crane, 1980). It can be hypothesized that this synchronous behavior served to maintain the ongoing interaction.

Several projects have examined the development of the use of eye contact as a cue for regulating personal space and interpersonal interactions. Savitsky and Watson (1975) found that in the dyadic play of same-age, same-sex 3½- to 5½-year-olds, as eye gaze directed at the other peer increased, the rate of verbalization increased. Unlike the adults in the study by Argyle and Dean (1965), no negative relationship was found between eye gaze direction and interpersonal distance for the preschoolers.

The research on making and maintaining eye contact with an adult stranger at a shopping center (Scheman & Lockard, 1979) was mentioned in the previous section. Not only did toddlers and school-age children make more eye contact than infants, but in comparing length of gaze, Scheman and Lockard found that the toddlers stared significantly longer than the other groups. That is, they did not avert their gaze. The school-age children were much more likely to establish eye contact and then quickly avert their gaze. This behavior was similar to adult behavior and appropriate for the setting.

Why don't toddlers avert their gaze? Evidence suggests that they have not learned the social rules for looking away. Post and Hetherington (1974) examined children's ability to use proximity and eye contact cues in judging whether they were liked by another child. Both boys and girls at age 4 were able to use proximity cues in judging liking, although only females increased in accuracy by age 6. However, none of the 4-year-olds exhibited reliable use of eye contact cues in judgments of liking. When 3½- to 4½-year-olds were given discrimination training in the use of proximity cues, once again only the females increased their accuracy in the use of the cue. Overall, accuracy in discerning the relationship of proximity and eye contact cues to liking by others improved from age 4 to age 6, with girls more sensitive to these cues at an earlier age than boys.

Beyond the research on these general trends for distancing and the use of body movement and eye gaze cues, a number of mediating factors for the use of personal space have been identified. We turn to a brief review of these areas and conclude with a consideration of reactions to intrusions of personal space.

Sex Differences.   Although fairly consistent sex differences have been reported in the personal space literature, sex differences have not been an area of central focus. In some cases, the findings regarding sex differences are qualified by the age and race of the subjects and/or the setting being observed.

In general, males (from preschool to college age) are reported as having larger personal space than females whether assessed by projective measures (Guardo, 1969; Pedersen, 1973) or in actual observations (Gifford & Price, 1979). From first grade to college, differences in males' and females' personal space increased with age (Tennis & Dabbs, 1975). Sarafino and Helmuth (1981) reported that the male-female difference in interpersonal distance emerged as a function of the time spent in a day-care environment. Boys showed a greater approach distance than girls only among older preschoolers who had been in school for more than 9 months compared to those attending for 8 months or less.

Lomranz et al. (1975) found that for 3-, 5-, and 7-year-olds, regardless of the sex of the child approaching a peer, females were more closely approached than males. Using projective measures, Lerner, Karabenick, and Meisels (1975) discovered that interpersonal distance to same-sex peers decreased with age. Other work has shown that fourth to sixth graders increased distance to opposite-sexed targets (Lerner, Venning, & Knapp, 1975).

Examining peer relationships using a projective technique with like-sex pairs of sixth-grade boys and girls in dyadic interactions, girls placed silhouettes representing "best friends" and "someone you like very much" closer together than did boys. In addition, girls used larger interpersonal distances than did boys in representing "someone you're afraid of" (Guardo, 1969).

Affect.   One of the assumptions about personal space is that it is indicative of the relationships between people, i.e., the closer together people sit or stand, the more intimate and friendly their relationship. Empirical reports bear out this assumption. Morris and Smith (1980) demonstrated that children show a preference for proximity to adults who exhibit positive affection over adults who are negative. With a projective technique, Meisels and Guardo (1969) discovered that children from Grades 3 through 10 placed greater distances between silhouettes of self and positive affect peers as they got older. In observations of eighth-grade students' dyadic interactions, those who liked each other stood significantly closer than students who disliked each other (Aiello & Cooper, 1972). As the interaction progressed, students who disliked each other adopted less direct body orientations than did students who liked each other.

Race and Socioeconomic Status.   Baxter (1970) observed groups of Mexican-Americans, blacks, and Anglo-Americans visiting a zoo. Consistent differences in interpersonal distance occurred based on the interactants' ethnicity. While outdoors, Mexican-Americans interacted at the closest range, Anglo-Americans at the next closest range, and blacks stood farthest apart. This difference was evident for children (10 years and less) and increased with age. However, while indoors, blacks interacted at the closest range. Sex of the interactants also affected interpersonal distance. For all groups, male-male pairs maintained the greatest distances; male-female pairs were closest among blacks and Anglo-Americans, female-female pairs were closest among Mexican-Americans.

In observations of first- and second-grade children on the school playground, Aiello and Jones (1971) found that middle-class white children stood farther apart than lower class black or Puerto Rican children. However, it was not possible to determine whether race or social class was the primary factor involved. When first, third, and fifth graders were observed in classroom settings at a school with middle-class whites and upper lower class blacks, it was found that in first grade, black children stood closer together than white children (Jones & Aiello, 1973). The difference in interaction distance disappeared by the fifth grade.

Scherer (1974) examined the effects of socioeconomic status and race on children's interaction distance. Race was found not to be a significant factor. Overall, middle-class children stood farther apart than did lower-class children while talking.

Physical Status.   One physical factor that affects personal space behavior is the child's body build. A series of studies (Lerner et al., 1976; Lerner, Karabenick, & Meisels, 1975; Lerner, Venning, & Knapp, 1975) with both American and Japanese elementary school subjects showed that children maintain greater interpersonal distances from children with endomorphic body builds as compared to mesomorphic and ectomorphic types.

Hard-of-hearing children who had limited opportunities to interact with normal-hearing children exhibited greater personal space than both normal-hearing and hard-of-hearing children who had been integrated into a public elementary school for a year term (Mallenby, 1974). The latter groups had similar interpersonal distances.

Reactions to Intrusions of Personal Space

According to Leibman (1970), three types of personal space violations can be distinguished: (1) overly close physical distances, (2) inappropriate body positions, and (3) behaviors that result in excessive symbolic intimacy. When these intrusions occur, an individual has four possible responses. In reestablishment, the individual attempts to restore the situation to the status quo, e.g., by withdrawing when someone approaches too near. Redefinition consists of changing the rules defining the situation, for example, from a business relationship to a social relationship. Alternatively, the person may decide simply to endure the intrusion or if too stressful, to terminate the encounter completely.

Studies with adults have demonstrated that short people are intruded on more often than tall people (Caplan & Goldman, 1981); male-female pairs are intruded on less than female-female pairs followed by male-male pairs, with intrusions increasing as the distance between conversants increases (Cheyne & Efran, 1972; Efran & Cheyne, 1973). People generally go around a group of people talking rather than intruding through; conversing pairs are invaded more than groups of four people. Intrusions are more likely to occur if the group is low status (as indicated by age or dress) than if the group is high status (Knowles, 1973).

An interesting line of research has examined adults' reactions to personal space intrusions by children. In one study (Fry & Willis, 1971), child confederates, ages 5, 8, and 10, intruded on adults waiting in line for theater tickets by standing extremely close to them. It was found that the adults' reaction to this proximity varied with the age of the child. Adults reacted positively to the 5-year-olds, in a tolerant or neutral fashion to the 8-year-olds, and negatively to the 10-year-olds. Dean, Willis, and LaRocco (1976) extended this work by examining both the child's and adult's sex and race. A similar situation was used, namely, waiting in line for refreshments at a drive-in. No effects of either child's sex or adult's sex were found. Also, there was no effect of race except that white adults had a higher frequency of failure to respond than black adults. The only significant effect on type of adult response occurred with age of the child. Facilitative or friendly responses such as smiling, talking, and touching were primarily given to the 5-year-olds. The 8-year-old children received significantly fewer responses of any kind. The 10-year-olds evoked responses such as avoidance (moving or leaning away) and excess motor activity (rocking, shifting weight). These results suggest that adults have differential expectations about children's adherence to personal space norms according to the child's age. Young children are not expected to be fully aware of the rules regarding personal space and do not receive negative sanctions for their intrusions. Conversely, by age 10 it is expected that children both know and obey the rules regarding spatial norms. The 8-year-old child represents a more ambiguous state of rule knowledge, thus they receive neither encouraging nor discouraging responses.

CONCLUSION

The boundary regulation of space develops throughout childhood and is mediated by a variety of sociocultural, intraindividual, and environmental factors. Conceptions of privacy become increasingly complex with age and parents' use of privacy cues varies with the presumed cognitive understanding of the child. Crowding as a psychological experience of intrusions to privacy is experienced differently by young children than older children. Finally, young children operate at smaller interpersonal distances than older children and adults. These progressions emphasize the child's growing awareness of others and the use of space when interacting with others. As we stated in the beginning of the chapter, our goal is to extrapolate beyond this obvious relationship of spatial use to more general concerns of social development.

Damon (1983) noted two complementary functions of social development: socialization and individuation. Socialization refers to the integration of self into the fabric of society. The child must come to adopt behaviors, standards, values, attitudes, and so on deemed appropriate by society. However, the child must also develop in terms of self—a differentiation of one's identity within the society. Adequate socialization can lead to satisfying interpersonal relations; poor socialization can lead to deviance or isolation. Adequate individuation can lead to a sense of control and self-esteem; poor individuation can lead to confusion and despair.

This dialectical tension seems relevant to Altman's (1975) conceptualization of privacy. Privacy as the psychological process whereby the individual regulates accessibility to self would certainly serve as a process in the service of socialization and individuation. On the one hand, privacy can be viewed as the mechanism through which one acquires, represents, and reflects upon interpersonal information. On the other hand, privacy serves as the mechanism through which one can reflect upon self in relation to others.

An important ingredient for this bridge between the regulation of space and the nature of interpersonal interactions would be how the child understands the psychological functioning of others—a concern of interest to social developmental psychologists studying social cognition. Shantz (1975) summarized the research on the development of social cognition in terms of the ability to infer what another person sees, feels, thinks, and intends, as well as what the other person is like. Selman (1973) and Selman and Byrne (1974) provided an overall sequence to these abilities consisting of four levels. At the first level, approximately age 6 and under, the child is egocentric and makes no differentiation between his or her own view and the views of others. The child may recognize the possibility of different points of view, but in general, assumes similarity to his or her own view. Between 6 and 10 years of age, the child shows increasing accuracy at inferring the intentions, thoughts, and so forth of other people. However, the child cannot coordinate the fact that others can do the same. Around 10 or 11 years of age, the child is capable of recognizing that others are making inferences about self while the child is doing the same. Thus, simultaneous and mutual role taking occurs. Beyond age 12, the adolescent can view both self and other as a pair interacting in relation to a greater social system.

These levels of social cognition correlate well with our review of boundary regulation. The egocentrically oriented young child neither infers the psychological aspects of others nor regulates interpersonal distances to facilitate interactions. Crowding is probably understood in terms of the thwarting of personal activities; privacy is not understood in terms of aloneness or managing information since the child is, in a sense, psychologically alone already and furthermore is not capable of dealing with the interpersonal information. The school-age child, able to infer a great deal about the actions or intentions of others, also regulates interpersonal distancing to reflect this greater understanding. This child understands privacy concretely in that controlling access to places is a primary concern. Finally, the adolescent can view social relationships relative to broad social systems. Autonomy and choice are significant descriptors of privacy as is managing information. In sum, the ability to infer the psychological processes of others parallels the individual's knowledge and regulation of space. Both conform to ever-complex resolutions of socialization and individuation.

What makes the above integration of spatial boundary considerations with social cognition research particularly speculative is that the vast majority of research reports on how children reflect on these concerns rather than how they act upon this knowledge in context. Certainly it is important to investigate these cognitive skills in terms of children's developing conceptions of them. We feel that an equally important extension of this work would be to examine the use of these processes across environmental contexts. As a concrete example of this, consider an interesting program of research on children's aggressive behavior that more directly addresses the issue of social cognition in context.

One hypothesis about children's aggressive behaviors is that aggressive children fail to use cues about other children's intentions or to integrate intention information in their own behavior. Alternatively, aggressive children may use intention cues but distort the intentions of others. Presumably, then, the more ambiguous another child's intentions, the more distortion there is likely to be by the aggressive child.

To assess these hypotheses, Dodge (1980) exposed aggressive and nonaggressive boys from Grades 2, 4, and 6 to a situation that ended in a frustrating negative outcome as a result of the behavior by some unknown peer. Specifically, the child was led to believe that the other child disrupted a puzzle that the subject had been working on. The intentions of the other child were manipulated such that the intent of the action was either benign, hostile, or ambiguous. All subjects responded more aggressively to the hostile intent peer than to the benign intent peer. The aggressive and nonaggressive boys differed only when the peer exhibited an ambiguous intent. Nonaggressive boys interpreted the ambiguous intent as benign and the aggressive boys responded as if the intent was hostile. Dodge and Newman (1981) suggested that this hostile attribution bias of aggressive boys was due to an inhibition deficit; that is, the aggressive child responded quickly with retaliation rather than contemplating alternatives.

Dodge (1980) also indicated that a child's reputation as aggressive had an important influence. Using hypothetical negative-outcome ambiguous episodes, Dodge again found that aggressive boys were more likely to attribute hostile intent to the peer target. In addition, when the peer target was an aggressive child relative to a nonaggressive child, he was more likely to have hostile intentions attributed to him, was more likely to be the object of proposed retaliation by aggression, and was expected to continue in his aggressive actions. This reputation-based decision by nonaggressive children was increasingly important with age; sixth graders attributed hostility to the aggressive peer over the nonaggressive peer more so than fourth graders, who did so more than second graders.

Importantly, Dodge and Frame (1982) found that in naturally occurring situations, aggressive boys initiate and receive more aggressive acts than other boys. Thus, the attribution bias of aggressive children has a basis in their experiences, setting up a dynamic cycle. Once a child displays some unknown amount or types of aggressive acts and becomes known as "aggressive," the child sees the world as hostile when cues do not clearly show otherwise. Those around the child do the same to him; if the cues in a situation are ambiguous, they assume the child intended harm. Thus the child becomes set to aggress and the social world around the child is prepared to acknowledge and retaliate in kind.

The implications of this research are quite interesting. It is not that the deviant aggressive child is particularly deficient in social cognitive ability. Rather the context of social acts influences a bias toward hostility when that context does not offer clear cues as to intent. It would be interesting to find out, in terms of the relationships proposed in this chapter, how aggressive children regulate interpersonal boundaries and how others regulate boundaries with aggressive children. The obvious hypothesis is that aggressive children, relative to nonaggressive children, regulate space so that they are less accessible (physically and psychologically) to others and vice versa. Regulating space in this manner would of course feed into the cycle above of the aggressive child set to aggress while others are set to interpret the child's actions as hostile.

As a final consideration, the relationship of thinking involving physical objects and thinking involving social phenomena has received a great deal of attention recently. This issue is particularly pertinent in the present chapter given that the majority of research on spatial cognition involves the mental manipulation of physical information, whereas the research on boundary regulation involves both physical and social information. Three different views on this relationship can be identified.

One view of this relationship is that these two types of thinking are totally similar, both being derived from the same structural base (Piaget, 1950). As support for this position, Bearison (1982) suggested that the distinction is inappropriate because all knowledge, by its very nature, is social. Without social discourse and exchange, even physical knowledge would be meaningless because we derive meaning from shared social contexts. The opposite view holds that physical objects are so different from social objects in the world, thinking about these two domains must be quite different (Glick, 1978). Physical knowledge of objects in the world is based on logic while social knowledge of people's interactions is probabilistic and reflects cultural beliefs and stereotypes. Social knowledge is structured differently in order to reflect the mutual intentionality of people in an interaction that does not exist for the actions of a person with an object.

A compromise position between these extremes recently has been offered. Shultz (1982) suggested that social and nonsocial thought share a common view of causation, a view termed generative causality. Rather than determining causality empirically (i.e., in terms of associating assumed regularities of cause and effect), Shultz proposed that children are inclined to construe causation in terms of event generation (i.e., that causes create their effects). Thus causality is a necessary condition, not a coincidental one. From this common conception of causality, social and nonsocial reasoning involve differences in the manner in which causal inferences are drawn. Inferences for nonsocial phenomena involve energy transmission, whereas inferences for social phenomena involve intentions and plans. He suggests that some inferencing rules are probably common to both domains, such as covariation, and temporal and spatial contiguity.

We tend to agree with the position offered by Shultz (1982). Although the physical world and the social world offer some unique qualities with which the child must come to grips, we prefer to believe that the bottom line rationales are similar across the domains. What we would stress in this conceptualization is the influence of context, an influence where thinking about physical and social phenomena must be coordinated.

In conclusion, we have tried to present the case in this chapter that boundary regulation processes, while involving the use of physical space for social affairs, is related to more than simply boundary concerns. Regulating interpersonal distancing is intimately related to the socialization and individuation functions inherent to all social development. The child must interact with others in a variety of contexts. The child must learn the social agenda that govern these interactions. Boundary regulation both mediates these interactions and reflects the child's understanding of others and contexts.

REFERENCES

Aiello, J. R., & Aiello, T. D. The development of personal space: Proxemic behavior of children 6 through 16. *Human Ecology*, 1974, *2*, 177–189.

Aiello, J. R., & Cooper, R. E. *The use of personal space as a function of social affect*. Proceedings of the Annual Convention of the American Psychological Association, 1972, *7*, 207–208.

Aiello, J. R., DeRisi, D. T., Epstein, Y. M., & Karlin, R. A. Crowding and the role of interpersonal distance preference. *Sociometry*, 1977, *40*, 271–282.

Aiello, J. R., Epstein, Y. M., & Karlin, R. A. Effects of crowding on electrodermal activity. *Sociological Symposium*, 1975, *14*, 43–57.

Aiello, J. R., & Jones, S. E. Field study of the proxemic behavior of young school children in 3 subcultural groups. *Journal of Personality and Social Psychology*, 1971, *19*, 351–356.

Aiello, J. R., Nicosia, G., & Thompson, D. E. Physiological, social, and behavioral consequences of crowding on children and adolescents. *Child Development*, 1979, *50*, 195–202.

Altman, I. *The environment and social behavior*. Monterey, CA: Brooks/Cole, 1975.

Argyle, M., & Dean, J. Eye-contact, distance, and affiliation. *Sociometry*, 1965, *28*, 289–304.

Bass, M. H., & Weinstein, M. S. Early development of interpersonal distance in children. *Canadian Journal of Behavioural Science*, 1971, *3*, 368–376.

Baxter, J. C. Interpersonal spacing in natural settings. *Sociometry*, 1970, *33*, 444–456.

Bearison, D. J. New directions in studies of social interaction and cognitive growth. In F. C. Serafica (Ed.), *Social-cognitive development in context*. New York: Guilford Press, 1982.

Bronfenbrenner, U. *The ecology of human development: Experiments by nature and design*. Cambridge, MA: Harvard University Press, 1979.

Burgess, J. W., & McMurphy, D. The development of proxemic spacing behavior: Children's distances to surrounding playmates and adults change between 6 months and 5 years of age. *Developmental Psychobiology*, 1982, *15*, 557–567.

Caplan, M. E., & Goldman, M. Personal space violations as a function of height. *Journal of Social Psychology*, 1981, *114*, 167–171.

Chandler, M. J., Koch, D., & Paget, K. F. Developmental changes in the responses of children to conditions of crowding and congestion. In H. McGurk (Ed.), *Ecological factors in human development*. New York: North-Holland, 1977.

Cheyne, J. A., & Efran, M. G. The effect of spatial and interpersonal variables in the invasion of group control territories. *Sociometry*, 1972, *35*, 477–489.

Damon, W. *Social and personality development*. New York: W. W. Norton, 1983.

Dean, L. M., Willis, F. N., & LaRocco, J. M. Invasion of personal space as a function of age, sex, and race. *Psychological Reports*, 1976, *38*, 959–965.

Dodge, K. A. Social cognition and children's aggressive behavior. *Child Development*, 1980, *51*, 162–170.

Dodge, K. A., & Frame, C. L. Social cognitive biases and deficits in aggressive boys. *Child Development*, 1982, *53*, 620–635.

Dodge, K. A., & Newman, J. P. Biased decision making processes in aggressive boys. *Journal of Abnormal Psychology*, 1981, *90*, 375–379.

Efran, M. G., & Cheyne, J. A. Shared space: The cooperative control of spatial areas by two interacting individuals. *Canadian Journal of Behavioural Science*, 1973, *5*, 201–210.

Freedman, J., Klevansky, S., & Ehrlich, P. Effects of crowding on human task performance. *Journal of Applied Social Psychology*, 1971, *1*, 7–25.

Fry, A. M., & Willis, F. N. Invasion of personal space as a function of the age of the invader. *Psychological Record*, 1971, *2*, 385–389.

Gifford, R., & Price, J. Personal space in nursery school children. *Canadian Journal of Behavioural Science*, 1979, *11*, 318–326.

Glick, J. Cognition and social cognition: An introduction. In J. Glick & K. A. Clarke-Stewart (Eds.), *The development of social understanding*. New York: Gardner Press, 1978.

Guardo, C. J. Personal space in children. *Child Development*, 1969, *40*, 143–151.

Hall, E. T. *The hidden dimension*. New York: Doubleday, 1966.

Horner, T. M. On the formation of personal space and self-boundary structures in early human development: The case of infant stranger reactivity. *Developmental Review*, 1983, *3*, 148–177.

Jones, S. G., & Aiello, J. R. Proxemic behavior of black and white first, third, and fifth grade children. *Journal of Personality and Social Psychology*, 1973, *25*, 21–27.

Knowles, E. S. Boundaries around group interaction: The effect of group size and member status on boundary permeability. *Journal of Personality and Social Psychology*, 1973, *26*, 327–332.

Laufer, R. S., Proshansky, H. M., & Wolfe, M. Some analytic dimensions of privacy. In H. M. Proshansky, W. H. Ittelson, & L. G. Rivlin (Eds.), *Environmental psychology: People and their physical setting*. New York: Holt, Rinehart & Winston, 1976.

Laufer, R. S., & Wolfe, M. Privacy as a concept and a social issue. *Journal of Social Issues*, 1977, *33*, 22–42.

Leibman, M. The effects of sex and race norms on personal space. *Environment and Behavior*, 1970, *2*, 208–246.

Lerner, R. M., Iwawaki, S., & Chihara, T. Development of personal space schemata among Japanese children. *Developmental Psychology*, 1976, *12*, 466–467.

Lerner, R. M., Karabenick, S. A., & Meisels, M. Effects of age and sex on the development of personal space schemata toward body build. *Journal of Genetic Psychology*, 1975, *127*, 91–101.

Lerner, R. M., Venning, J., & Knapp, J. R. Age and sex effects on personal space schemata toward body build in late childhood. *Developmental Psychology*, 1975, *11*, 855–856.

Lomranz, J., Shapira, A., Choresh, N., & Gilat, Y. Children's personal space as a function of age and sex. *Developmental Psychology*, 1975, *11*, 541–545.

Mallenby, T. W. Personal space: Direct measurement techniques with hard-of-hearing children. *Environment and Behavior*, 1974, *6*, 117–122.

Meisels, M., & Guardo, C. J. Development of personal space schemata. *Child Development*, 1969, *40*, 1167–1178.

Morris, E. K., & Smith, G. L. A functional analysis of adult affection and children's interpersonal distance. *Psychological Record*, 1980, *30*, 155–163.

Parke, R. D., & Sawin, D. B. Children's privacy in the home: Developmental, ecological and child-rearing determinants. *Environment and Behavior*, 1979, *11*, 87–104.

Peay, M. Y., & Peay, E. R. The effects of density, group size, and crowding on behavior in an unstructured situation. *British Journal of Social Psychology*, 1983, *22*, 13–18.

Pedersen, D. M. Developmental trends in personal space. *Journal of Psychology*, 1973, *83*, 3–9.

Peery, J. C., & Crane, P. M. Personal space regulation: Approach-withdrawal-approach proxemic behavior during adult-preschooler interaction at close range. *Journal of Psychology*, 1980, *106*, 63–75.

Peterson, K. L., Draper, D. C., & Roscoe, B. Utilization of appropriate projective techniques in assessing preschool children's personal space and body orientations. *Perceptual and Motor Skills*, 1982, *54*, 67–70.

Phillips, J. R. Syntax and vocabulary of mother's speech to young children: Age and sex comparisons. *Child Development*, 1973, *44*, 182–185.

Piaget, J. *The psychology of intelligence*. London: Routledge & Kegan Paul, 1950.

Post, B., & Hetherington, E. M. Sex differences in the use of proximity and eye contact in judgments of affiliation in preschool children. *Developmental Psychology*, 1974, *6*, 881–889.

Proshansky, H. M., Ittelson, W. H., & Rivlin, L. G. Freedom of choice and behavior in a physical setting. In H. M. Proshansky, W. H. Ittelson, & L. G. Rivlin (Eds.), *Environmental psychology: Man and his physical setting*. New York: Holt, Rinehart & Winston, 1970.

Sarafino, E. P., & Helmuth, H. Development of personal space in preschool children as a function of age and day-care experience. *Journal of Social Psychology*, 1981, *115*, 59–63.

Savitsky, J. C., & Watson, M. J. Patterns of proxemic behavior among preschool children. *Representative Research in Social Psychology*, 1975, *6*, 109–113.

Scheman, J. D., & Lockard, J. S. Development of gaze aversion in children. *Child Development*, 1979, *50*, 594–596.

Scherer, S. E. Proxemic behavior of primary school children as a function of their socioeconomic class and subculture. *Journal of Personality and Social Psychology*, 1974, *29*, 800–805.

Selman, R. L. *A structural analysis of the ability to take another's perspective: Stages in the development of role-taking ability*. Paper presented at the biennial meeting of the Society for Research in Child Development, Philadelphia, 1973.

Selman, R. L., & Byrne, D. F. A structural-developmental analysis of levels of role-taking in middle childhood. *Child Development*, 1974, *45*, 803–806.

Shaffron, R. Modes of approach and the infant's reaction to the stranger. In T. DeCarie (Ed.), *The infant's reaction to strangers*. New York: International Universities Press, 1974.

Shantz, C. U. The development of social cognition. In E. M. Hetherington (Ed.), *Review of child development research*. (Vol. 5). Chicago: University of Chicago Press, 1975.

Sherrod, D. R. Crowding, perceived control, and behavioral aftereffects. *Journal of Applied Social Psychology*, 1974, *4*, 171–186.

Shultz, T. R. Causal reasoning in the social and nonsocial realms. *Canadian Journal of Behavioural Science*, 1982, *14*, 307–322.

Siegel, A. W. Toward a social ecology of cognitive mapping. In R. Cohen (Ed.), *New directions for child development: Children's conceptions of spatial relationships*. San Francisco: Jossey-Bass, 1982.

Snow, C. E. Mother's speech to children learning language. *Child Development*, 1972, *43*, 549–565.

Sommer, R. *Personal space*. Englewood Cliffs, NJ: Prentice-Hall, 1969.

Stokols, D. The experience of crowding in primary and secondary environments. *Environment and Behavior*, 1976, *8*, 49–86.

Sundstrom, E. Toward an interpersonal model of crowding. *Sociological Symposia*, 1975, *14*, 129–144.

Tennis, G. H., & Dabbs, J. M. Sex, setting and personal space: First grade through college. *Sociometry*, 1975, *38*, 385–394.

Westin, A. F. *Privacy and freedom*. New York: Atheneum, 1970.

Wolfe, M. Childhood and privacy. In I. Altman & J. F. Wohlwill (Eds.), *Children and the environment*. New York: Plenum Press, 1978.

Wolfe, M., & Laufer, R. S. The concept of privacy in childhood and adolescence. In D. H. Carson (Ed.), *Man-environment interactions: Evaluation and application*. (Part II, Vol. 6: S. T. Margulis, Vol. Ed.), Washington, DC: EDRA, 1974; and Stroudsburg, PA: Dowden, Hutchinson, & Ross, 1975.

Zeedyk-Ryan, J., & Smith, G. F. The effects of crowding on hostility, anxiety, and desire for social interaction. *Journal of Social Psychology*, 1983, *120*, 245–252.

V METHODOLOGICAL AND META-METHODOLOGICAL ISSUES

11 Methods for the Study of Spatial Cognition

Nora Newcombe
Temple University

Researchers who wish to study the nature of people's memory and knowledge of spatial information have worried off and on for years about what methods to use to accomplish this goal. Initially, methods to study spatial knowledge of environments generally involved asking subjects to draw sketch maps or to make models of specified areas (e.g., Lynch, 1960). These tasks have the advantage of producing spatial representations as products directly, with points related to each other simultaneously in two or three dimensions. But because people seem to differ in their graphic or modeling ability, and because freely drawn maps can be difficult to classify or study quantitatively (e.g., Walsh, Krauss, & Regnier, 1981), investigators have been ingenious in seeking other means of studying spatial knowledge. Several techniques have been used. People can be asked to reconstruct spatial information, that is, to place a pair or array of objects where they belong. The framework for this task can be the original space (be it a room or other spatial framework) or another framework, on a same or different scale as the original one. People can be asked to estimate distances, in absolute or ratio terms, or in terms of travel time. They can be asked to rank-order distances or locations; to move around in real or imagined space and find detours, new routes, and shortcuts; or to point to locations from a variety of positions, allowing inference about location through projective convergence (triangulation). Many of these last methods have been evolved to get around the difficulties raised by the graphic demands of sketching and modeling tasks.

Since spatial representations are hypothetical internal entities, of which individuals may or may not be aware, the enterprise of "extracting" or "externalizing" them obviously raises difficult philosophical as well as methodological issues. (For further discussion, see Downs, 1981; Liben, 1981; Newcombe,

1981). Several discussion of methods to study spatial knowledge exist (Evans, 1980; Golledge, 1976; Siegel, 1981), as well as a variety of papers comparing results obtained with different dependent variables (e.g., Cohen, Baldwin, & Sherman, 1978; Newcombe & Liben, 1982). The purpose of the present chapter is to go beyond a listing of techniques and the cataloging of the strengths and weaknesses of each, to a systematic literature review of comparisons of available methods of evaluating spatial knowledge. The review is organized in three sections, corresponding to three different criteria for comparing methods.

A major contention throughout is that "comparing" methods ought not to imply deciding which are good and which are bad. All existing methods seem to have both strengths and drawbacks. The important point is that different tasks call for different types of spatial processing. We need to understand the nature of the task demands, as an integral part of understanding the nature of spatial representation. In fact, "representation" may be a poor term, if it is taken to imply the existence of a static, passive entity, to which processes are applied. ("Spatial storage" has been suggested as an alternative by Liben, 1981).

The first question that is often asked in evaluating dependent variables is, which method leads to greater accuracy? Greater accuracy is defined as greater correspondence of subjects' judgments about locations to a set of measures of actual physical distances, or to a cartographic map. This correspondence may be assessed in several ways: correlating subjective with actual distances; looking at the relationship between subjective and actual distance in terms of Stevens' power law (e.g., Baird, Merrill & Tannenbaum, 1979), in order to assess whether methods lead to over-estimation or under-estimation of actual distances; calculating the congruence between an overall map derived from subjects' estimates by multidimensional scaling and a cartographic map of the area; performing analysis of variance of the degree of error in judgments.

The first question, of correspondence between subjective and cartographic maps, while certainly worth asking, has one important limitation, however. It begs a second question, Which technique better captures the subjective knowledge, or "what's in the head"? Subjects' knowledge of spatial relationships may well be substantially different from physical reality as traditionally measured, and as mapped by cartographers. This is true for several reasons. Downs (1981 and the present book) draws our attention to the nonabsolute nature of cartographic convention. That is, there can be many different ways of representing spatial information within cartography, each of which is legitimate given its aims. A familiar example is the distortion in polar regions common when the globe is represented on a rectangle. Thus, the type of physical measurement that should be used as a criterion of accuracy may not be obvious. Second, even if some physical measure is selected, what people know about spatial relationships may well be systematically distorted from the "physical reality." A measure that revealed this psychological structure would be preferable to one that did not, even if the latter corresponded better to physical reality. Third, subjective knowledge about space may not even be internally consistent. Tversky (1981) concludes that "cognitive maps may be impossible figures" (p. 432) because they can consist of fragmentary information that contains contradictory information when integrated. Kuipers (1982) makes a similar point, adding that another fact indicating that cognitive maps may be impossible figures is that people's knowledge of routes may be asymmetric: a route can be followed in only one direction. This state of affairs is difficult to represent on a cartographic map.

Thus, a second question to ask when evaluating dependent variables is whether a "less accurate" representation in the physical sense might be psychologically better. To do this, some investigators have asked subjects which of several maps (each derived from a different type of data, often through multidimensional scaling) the subjects prefer, or *believe* to be more accurate representations of their spatial knowledge.

This second line of investigation, while again worth pursuing, has the limitation that subjects may not be aware of the spatial representations they actually use, and may prefer some maps over others on the basis of extraneous factors such as symmetry or neatness. Or, their knowledge may not be easily represented by map-like figures at all. Further, when multidimensional scaling is used, two facts must be remembered: (1) not all data lend themselves to multidimensional scaling; a relatively exhaustive set of paired comparisons or rank orderings is required, which may be beyond the capacity of some subjects (e.g., children, the elderly); (2) even when MDS is possible, it may not fully capture the data, as can be revealed by high stress values in two-dimensional solutions. That is, if cognitive maps are indeed sometimes "impossible figures," representing them in two dimensions will "distort" them.

The third question to ask in comparing dependent variables involves whether other variables affect each dependent variable in the same way. That is, one can look for evidence of convergent validity. The variables examined for their relationship to spatial representation may be subject variables like age, sex, spatial ability, or area of residence; environmental variables (either existing in the natural world or assigned by the experimenter), such as straightness or crookedness of routes or presence or absence of barriers; or behavioral variables such as frequency of use of an environment. If the variables examined have the same relationship to measures based on two different modes of externalizing spatial knowledge, one has evidence of the convergent validity of the methods.

If one dependent variable, however, shows an effect of an independent variable while another does not, or even shows an opposite effect, one has an interpretive problem. One of the methodologies may be invalid (but which one?) or both may be invalid. It is, however, also possible that both are valid, and the traditional logic of convergent validity is not applicable. Spatial knowledge may be paired with two different sets of processing demands to yield two different sets of data. The different data sets are troublesome if one believes that there exists a single spatial representation, a thing-in-the-head which should have only one characterization. But if one instead takes the view that spatial knowledge is used in different ways in different tasks, there is less of a problem. One gives up "stalking the elusive cognitive map," and instead begins to formulate hypotheses about how people use knowledge to solve spatial problems.

Two other issues are considered throughout the chapter. One is the importance of examining individual as well as aggregate data in investigating the three questions above. Although some investigators have argued that spatial representations based on data averaged across subjects are adequate (Magana, Evans, & Romney, 1981), other investigation and commentary suggest this is not the case (Ewing, 1981; Mackay & Olshavsky, 1975). A second theme is that early pessimism about modeling and drawing tasks may have been overdone, and enthusiasm for rank ordering techniques or paired comparisons, with spatial knowledge inferred from multidimensional scaling, misplaced. The demands of the latter tasks are also quite extensive; they do not require graphic ability, but they do require considerable information-processing capacity, and are not everyday or well-practiced tasks. They require sequential processing of information that either is or ought to be simultaneous and integrated.

CORRESPONDENCE BETWEEN SUBJECTIVE SPATIAL KNOWLEDGE AND MEASURED SPATIAL RELATIONSHIPS

The first question to be addressed is, What methods of studying spatial knowledge show the best correspondence between subjects' knowledge and spatial layouts as traditionally measured and mapped? Studies that evaluate the accuracy of subjects' spatial representations and compare two or more methods within a single study are listed in Table 11.1. This table also indicates what dependent variables were compared by this method, what statistical technique was used, what the subjects' ages were, and what kind of spatial environment was being assessed. The conclusions are presented in the text.

Correlational Studies

Several studies have adopted the approach of correlating subjective distances, arrived at by different methods, with actual distances. The sizes of the correlations for the different methods were then compared. Howard, Chase, and Rothman (1973) had subjects perform one of four tasks: (1) make a sketch map including eight points on their college campus, with the distance between two locations given to provide a scale; (2) place scale models of the eight buildings, again with the distance between two of them provided; (3) make estimates of distances in metric units between all possible pairs of the eight buildings, with one distance given to them in yards; (4) make estimates of distances between all

TABLE 11.1
Studies Comparing Methods for Accuracy

	Dependent Variables	Statistics	Ages and Settings
Baird, Merrill, and Tannenbaum, 1979	(1) magnitude estimation (on scale of 1 to 100) (MDS) (2) mapmaking	Power functions; congruence in terms of average deviation	Adults (college campus and town)
Cadwallader, 1976	(1) distance estimates in miles; (2) time estimates; (3) magnitude estimation (standard = 100)	Correlation (individual and aggregate)	Adults (cities in L. A. area)
Canter, 1977	(1) distance estimates; (2) time estimates	Correlation (aggregate)	Adults (London Underground)
Cohen, Weatherford, and Byrd, 1980	(1) active distance estimates (card-placing); (2) passive distance estimates (directed card-placing)	ANOVA	Grades 2 and 6 (5 locations in room)
Howard, Chase, and Rothman, 1973	(1) sketch maps (2) scale models (3) distance estimates (units chosen by subject) (4) ratio distance estimates	Correlation (aggregate)	Adults (college campus)
Kirasic, Siegel, Allen, Curtis, and Furlong, as cited in Siegel, 1981	(1) rank ordering (MDS); (2) projective convergence	CONGRU	Adults (college campus)
Liben, Moore, and Golbeck, 1982	(1) modeling (2) reconstruction	ANOVA	Preschoolers (classroom)
Mackay, 1976	(1) sketch maps (MDS); (2) distance estimates (MDS)	COMPARE (aggregate)	Adults (cities in U.S.)
Mackay and Olshavsky, 1975	(1) sketch maps (MDS); (2) rank ordering of paired locations for proximity (MDS)	COMPARE (individual and aggregate)	Adults (local supermarkets)

(*continued*)

TABLE 11.1—*Continued*
Studies Comparing Methods for Accuracy

	Dependent Variables	Statistics	Ages and Settings
Magana, Evans, and Romney, 1981	(1) free sketch maps (MDS); (2) sketch maps, landmarks specified (MDS); (3) absolute distance estimation (MDS); (4) triadic distance comparison (MDS)	CONGRU (aggregate)	Adults (college campus)
Sherman, Croxton, and Giovanatto, 1979	(1) magnitude estimation (standard = 100) (2) mapmaking	Correlation and power functions (individual and aggregate)	Adults (college campus)
Siegel, Herman, Allen, and Kirasic, 1979	(1) modeling (2) reconstruction	ANOVA	Kindergarten, grades 2 and 5 (large or small-scale space)
Tversky, 1981	(1) sketch maps (2) compass directions (drawing arrow through circle with one location at center, to indicate orientation of second location)	t-test	Adults (locations learned from artificial map)

possible pairs of the eight buildings, by marking a line so that the distance would be proportional to the amount represented by a reference line representing the distance between two buildings. Correlations of subjective distances *averaged across subjects,* with actual distances, were above .98 for all four methods!

Although at first glance the Howard et al. data seem to suggest that accuracy is very high for sketch mapping, modeling, absolute distance estimation, and ratio distance estimation, such a conclusion is not completely justified. Since from 29 to 32 subjects performed each of the four tasks, averaging their estimates might eliminate a considerable amount of individual error from the data. If errors were systematic and shared by subjects, the error would remain in the averaged data, but to the extent that error is random or idiosyncratic, it would be eliminated by averaging. For instance, if all subjects believed Building A was much further from Building B than it actually was, this would be evident in the average estimate also, but if some subjects overestimate the distance from A to B, while others underestimate it, the average estimate for distance AB might appear quite accurate. In the latter case, correlation of averaged subjective distances with physical distances would overestimate the degree of accuracy achieved.

A similar criticism can be made of the work of Canter (1977), who had people make both estimates of distance "as the crow flies" between points on the London Underground, and estimates of travel times, by Underground, between these points. Average estimated distance was correlated highly (.8) with actual distance, whereas average estimated travel time was not significantly correlated with actual travel times (−.1). But Ewing (1981) provides graphic illustrations showing how Canter's use of aggregate data could well produce correlations much different from the individual correlations for most people in the sample.

The contrast between individual and aggregate data is evident in the data of Cadwallader (1976). He asked subjects, for a set of 30 cities in the Los Angeles area, to estimate distance of the cities from their home: (1) in miles, (2) in terms of travel time, and (3) in terms of a ratio of a standard distance assigned the value of 100 by the experimenter. Although aggregate data showed correlations of .94 to .96 with the actual values, correlations for individuals varied quite widely, with median values in the .81 to .85 range.

Cadwallader (1976) observed no differences in size of correlations for the three methods. However, the slope of the regression line of actual and subjective judgments was close to unity for mileage and time estimates, but less for ratio estimates. For ratio estimates, scaled subjective distances increased linearly, but more slowly than actual scaled distances. That is, the high correlation for subjective and actual scaled distances concealed the fact that as actual distances grew increasingly larger, they were increasingly underestimated using the ratio methodology.

Baird et al. (1979) and Sherman, Croxton, and Giovanatto (1979) also examined regressions of subjective on actual distances, for individuals as well as groups. Both studies compared direct mapping (placing stimuli on a board or computer screen) to magnitude estimation. For the latter task, Baird et al. did not give a standard reference, while Sherman et al. did set a specific distance equal to 100.

Baird et al. found greater individual variability in correlations and slopes of regression lines for distance judgments as opposed to direct mapping. Median values of correlations were, however, comparable and fairly high: .87 for distance judgments and .92 for direct mapping. Average slopes were close to 1 (.97 and .92 respectively), indicating some underestimation of distance for both methods.

Sherman et al. do not report in detail on individual variability, although they claim it was not large. Correlations of subjective and actual distance were again comparable to each other and high for both methods: .96 and .94 respectively.

Data on slopes were, however, somewhat different from those of Baird et al. The value of .89 for direct mapping indicated underestimation and some compression of points, especially for larger actual distances, as in Baird et al. However, the value of 1.05 for distance judgments indicated overestimations.

Baird and Wagner (1983) have recently examined these sets of data and proposed several models of how subjects might use knowledge of distances to perform the mapping task. Computer simulation of these models indicated that the slope for distances derived from mapping was always less than 1, whether the slope for distance judgments was set at values more or less than 1. Thus, subjects in Baird et al.'s (1979) study may have been underestimating distance, and subjects in Sherman et al.'s (1979) overestimating, for unknown reasons. But the fact that their slopes for distances derived from mapping were less than 1 may follow inevitably from their procedures for performing the task. The psychological reality of the Baird and Wagner model has yet to be directly assessed, however. In particular, whether or not subjects base their map placements primarily on distance estimates, without considering angle or orientation, seems questionable.

Consideration of these studies leads to several conclusions. One is that correlations based on aggregate data are not a good tool for assessing correspondence to measured distances, unless supplemented by individual correlations and knowledge of the slope of the regression line. A second suggestion, based on the work of Cadwallader (1976), is that adults' mileage and travel time estimates for a familiar area may be quite accurate. Use of magnitude estimation procedures led to underestimation in Cadwallader's (1976) and Baird et al.'s (1979) studies, but to overestimation in the paper by Sherman et al. (1979). The unfamiliarity of the task of magnitude estimation may be important here; while at first glance it appears less numerically demanding than mileage or time estimation, it requires considerable abstraction and use of scaling. Mileage and time estimation is a more everyday task for most adults, and for a familiar area may even have been memorized. Thirdly, in two studies direct mapping seemed to lead to compression of distances. However, Baird et al. found it was associated with less individual variability in accuracy than magnitude estimation. Finally, it should be noted that none of the studies involved children, the elderly, or other special populations. The reasonably good accuracy found may depend on the use of adults judging familiar environments.

Congruence Studies

Several studies used multidimensional scaling to produce "maps" based on different kinds of dependent variables, and then compared these maps to cartographic maps using various overall indices of congruence. Another study (Tversky, 1981) compared the accuracy of orientations indicated on a sketch map with the accuracy of orientation on a line-and-circle task in which subjects imagined one location in the center of a circle and north at the top, and drew an arrow in the direction of the second location, but did not compare overall congruence of sketch maps with a "map" derived from the line-and-circle orientation data.

Three studies (Kirasic, Siegel, Allen, Curtis, & Furlong, as cited by Siegel, 1981; Mackay, 1976; Mackay & Olshavsky, 1975) converge on the conclusion that MDS (Multi-Dimensional Scaling) solutions based on rank ordering of distances produce "maps" lower in accuracy than sketch maps (Mackay, 1976; Mackay & Olshavsky, 1975) or projective convergence (Kirasic et al.). Baird et al. (1979) found equivalent accuracy for MDS solutions based on magnitude estimations and maps made by placing locations on a computer display. Tversky (1981) found greater accuracy for the orientation of locations on a sketch map than for orientations indicated by drawing a line through one location at the center of a circle toward a second location.

The studies of Mackay, Mackay and Olshavsky, and Tversky suggest that sketch mapping may have been underrated as a method for studying spatial knowledge, at least in adults. A somewhat different conclusion was reached by Magana, Evans, and Romney (1981), although their data seem actually to support the conclusion. Magana et al. asked college students to do one of four tasks: (1) draw a sketch map of their campus; (2) draw a sketch map of their campus, containing 13 specified landmarks; (3) give distance estimates, in metric units, for all possible pairs of 13 campus locations; (4) choose the one location of a triad that was most distant from the other two; this was done for 70 triads, involving 13 campus locations. MDS of the triad data showed a higher error index and higher stress than MDS of the other three kinds of data, which were equivalent to each other.

Magana et al. concluded that MDS techniques are desirable tools in research on spatial representation, without addressing the low accuracy and high stress found for their triad data. It may be that the triad judgment task, while less demanding of graphic ability than sketch mapping, and not requiring the numerical ability of metric distance estimation, is an abstract task requiring simultaneous consideration of several imagined spatial relationships. Furthermore, it may be a less common everyday task than sketch mapping or estimating distance.

These studies, then, agree in suggesting a surprising degree of accuracy for various mapping tasks in adults, as well as a good degree of accuracy for projective convergence, metric distance estimation, and magnitude estimation. By contrast, tasks that are less concrete, less common and more demanding of information-processing capacity, such as rank ordering or triadic distance comparison, seem to lead to inferences of less accurate and coherent spatial representations.

A second limitation of many rank ordering techniques, as well as distance estimation, noted by Mackay (1976; Mackay & Olshavsky, 1975) is that they do not ask directly about angularity or orientation information. Rather, investigators rely on the MDS procedure to allow inferences as to angle and orientation. This may underestimate subjects' actual configurational knowledge. In fact, of several measures of accuracy examined by Mackay, it was a cosine measure of angle that most clearly indicated superiority of sketch maps over MDS maps derived from ranking procedures. Similarly, Baird, Wagner, and Noma (1982) show mathematically that if in recalling unidimensional distances, people systematically show a power function between judged and actual distance either more or less than 1, transforming the judgments back into two-dimensional Euclidean space will distort angular relationships, and often result in fragmented or "impossible" figures.

It should be noted again that, like the correlational studies, several of the MDS studies used aggregate data, and thus may have overestimated the accuracy of the inferred representations, as well as the coherence of the individual subjects' data points. Magana et al. defend their aggregation of data on the basis of expense, because they claim that error indices for individuals could not be compared, and because Evans, Marrero, and Butler (1981) drew similar conclusions based on individual and aggregate data. Mackay and Olshavsky (1975), however, compared error indices for individual subjects as well as for aggregate data. The aggregate data showed higher congruence to actual maps than did individual data. Also, aggregate data revealed no difference between sketch maps and MDS solutions of rank ordering, although individual data, as noted above, did show a superiority of sketch maps over rank ordering.

All of the comparative MDS studies above involved young adult subjects. Studies of children, the elderly, and other special populations might well lead to different conclusions. As often remarked, for instance, children's graphic ability develops with age, so that inaccurate drawings produced by young children may underestimate their spatial knowledge. It is equally true that techniques such as rank ordering may be exceptionally demanding for children. Newcombe and Liben (1982) found that 12 of 20 children, but only 4 of 20 adults, had unacceptably high stress values for MDS solutions in two dimensions of rank orderings of 10 locations. This finding also reinforces the importance of examining individual as well as aggregate data. The rank ordering portion of the Newcombe and Liben study replicated a study by Kosslyn, Pick, and Fariello (1974), which had performed MDS only of aggregate data, finding acceptable stress levels for children as well as for adults. Acceptable stress levels for MDS solutions of aggregate data were also found for the Newcombe and Liben data (although not reported in the published article). But as noted above, this concealed unacceptable stress values for many individual subjects.

In sum, studies of the accuracy of spatial judgments made with different techniques indicate that adults are often fairly accurate in performing tasks that are common requirements in dealing with space: making estimates of distance or travel time, and making maps, perhaps especially if they are asked to place locations in a framework rather than to sketch freehand, although no studies have contrasted these techniques specifically. Adults' apparent difficulty with tasks like rank ordering, triadic comparison or ratio estimation may be due to lack of practice with these tasks. It may also be that these techniques tend to require sequential consideration of information that needs to be integrated; they are thus demanding of processing capacity. With what techniques children perform better is not known, although the Newcombe and Liben study suggests that a rank ordering task is certainly quite difficult, and even more difficult than it is for adults.

ANOVA Studies

Two studies with children that compared techniques using analysis of variance were concerned with issues of translation of scale (Liben, Moore, & Golbeck, 1982; Siegel, Herman, Allen, & Kirasic, 1979). Siegel et al. had children from three grade levels learn the layout of eight buildings through a 4.6 × 6.1 m area, or by moving a truck through an 81.3 × 101.6 cm model. Half the children from each condition subsequently reconstructed the town in the large space and the remainder reconstructed the array on the model board. Analysis of variance of accuracy of placement showed that performance in the two conditions that required simple reconstruction (expose large-construct large and expose small-construct small) was equivalent to that in the condition that required miniaturization (tabletop modeling of a larger space). But performance that required an enlargement of scale (expose small-construct large) was less accurate than the other three kinds.

Siegel et al.'s work suggests that the traditional modeling task, involving miniaturization rather than expansion of scale, does not lead to significantly lower accuracy for children than reconstruction at the same scale. However, Liben, Moore, and Golbeck (1982) report data that show the opposite. Preschoolers were asked either to replace furniture in their classroom or to place models of furniture in a miniaturized classroom. They performed significantly better in the former task, which did not require translation of scale.

Of course, any of several factors could account for the discrepancy between the conclusions of Siegel et al. and Liben et al. Preschoolers, used by Liben et al., may have more difficulty than older children with translation of scale. Changing scale for very familiar spatial layouts, such as a preschool, could involve set breaking more difficult than changing of scale for experimental layouts viewed much more briefly. Or, there may be a real detrimental effect of translation of scale not detected by Siegel et al.; although the difference was not statistically significant, the means indicated lower performance in the modeling condition of that study.

Cohen, Weatherford, and Byrd (1980) were concerned with another factor affecting children's ability to make judgments using their spatial knowledge—

the effect of activity on accuracy of children's distance estimations. Second and sixth graders learned the location of five objects in a room, either by walking among the locations, or looking at them from a fixed position. In a second room, they then placed cards representing objects along a straight line from a constant start position. They did this either by walking (actively) or by directing the experimenter (passively).

For second graders, Cohen et al. found that congruency between acquisition and response (active-active or passive-passive) resulted in greater accuracy than incongruency and that within the incongruent conditions, active-passive was better than passive-active. For sixth graders, all four conditions were comparable. The reason may be that action (or its absence) is more important for younger than older children, allowing correct placement through sensorimotor or visual matching. However, another interpretation of the Cohen et al. data is that performance of the older children was at ceiling, since errors of estimation were less than 10% in all four conditions for the sixth graders.

It is surprising that so few studies of comparative accuracy exist using children. The demands of various externalization tasks are surely even more problematic with children than with adults; for instance, one would not even presume to ask children to give distance estimates in miles or yards, since their accuracy would, self-evidently, be extremely low. Children may well have substantial problems with other techniques as well, and studies of their relative accuracy with drawing, modeling, distance estimation, rank ordering, and so on are sorely needed.

SUBJECTS' PREFERENCES

The three studies of what representations subjects prefer (that is, believe to be closer to their idea of the spatial array) are listed in Table 11.2, and are easily summarized. Baird et al. (1979) found that although directly made maps seemed objectively equal in accuracy to MDS-derived maps, subjects preferred the directly made maps. This preference was shared by a new group of subjects, who had not participated in either kind of task but were simply asked to judge the representations. The subjects of Mackay (1976) likewise showed very marked preferences for hand-drawn over MDS-derived maps, based on rank orderings, although in this case the sketch maps were also objectively more accurate. Thus, the preference data support the accuracy data discussed above: directly made maps seem better to subjects than maps derived indirectly from piecemeal judgments, as well as sometimes being objectively more accurate.

Summers and Mackay (1976) did not compare preferences for representations based on different dependent variables. Their study bears on the issue of preferences for maps based on individual versus aggregate data. They asked college students to rank their preference for their own MDS-derived map of 11 campus

TABLE 11.2
Studies Comparing Methods for Subjective Preference

	Dependent Variables	Age and Settings
Baird, Merrill, and Tannen-baum, 1979	(1) distance estimates (MDS) (2) mapmaking	Adults (college campus and town)
Mackay, 1976	(1) sketch maps (MDS) (2) distance estimates (MDS)	Adults (cities in U.S.)
Summers and Mackay, 1976	(1) rank ordering (MDS)	Adults (college campus)

locations, an MDS map based on aggregate data, and a display corresponding to the actual physical distances. Interestingly, and surprisingly, the aggregate map was ranked significantly preferable to both the individual's own MDS map and the actual map. Preference for the actual and the individual map did not differ.

This study supplies a corollary to the point made above that aggregation of data may be misleading. Although aggregation apparently leads to spuriously high accuracy as objectively assessed, it can also lead to higher subjective preference. Perhaps the aggregate map captured a common, but inaccurate, belief about the campus that struck many subjects as accurate, just as a prototype derived from visual stimuli may seem familiar even when never actually presented before (Posner & Keele, 1968).

It is also interesting that subjects in the Summers and Mackay study did not prefer the objectively accurate map to the aggregate MDS map. This substantiates the point made in the introduction that since people's spatial knowledge may not correspond to physical reality, asking which dependent variables lead to the highest objective accuracy is but one of several important questions that must be asked about dependent variables.

CONVERGENT VALIDITY

Table 11.3 contains information on papers that have examined the impact of one or more independent variables on two or more dependent variables, within a single study.

Several of these investigations have found evidence of convergent validity, that is, of parallel results with different dependent measures. Cohen and Nodine (1980) found that how people acquired spatial information about a museum (by actual tour, by film, or by slide sequence) influenced the accuracy of placement and identification of elements in both written descriptions and sketch maps.

TABLE 11.3
Studies Evaluating Convergent Validity of Methods

	Dependent Variables	Independent Variables	Ages and Settings
Briggs, 1976	(1) distance estimates (2) ratio distance estimates	(1) towards/away from town; (2) straight/bending routes	Adults (Columbus, OH)
Cohen and Nodine, 1980	(1) sketch maps (2) written descriptions	(1) acquisition experience (tour, film, slide sequence)	Adults (museum)
Cohen, Baldwin, and Sherman, 1978	(1) distance estimation (number of steps) (2) reconstruction	(1) barriers (2) hills; (3) age	9- and 10-year-olds; adults (summer camp)
Cohen, Weatherford, Lomenick, and Koeller, 1979	(1) reconstruction (2) distance estimation (number of steps) (3) distance estimation (along specified line)	(1) age; (2) environmental familiarity	Grades 1 and 5 (6 objects in room)
Howard, Chase, and Rothman, 1973	(1) sketch maps (2) scale models (3) distance estimates (metric) (4) ratio distance estimates	(1) travel time (2) number of environmental features	Adults (college campus)
Kirasic, Siegel, Allen, Curtis, and Furlong, cited in Siegel, 1981	(1) rank ordering (2) projective convergence	(1) year in college	Adults (college campus)
Liben, Moore, and Golbeck, 1982	(1) item placement in model (2) life-size placement	(1) boundedness	Preschoolers (classroom)
Liben and Newcombe, 1981	(1) modeling (disc placement); (2) rank ordering	(1) barriers (2) distance (3) sex	Adults (20 toys)
Mackay and Olshavsky, 1975	(1) sketch maps (2) rank ordering	(1) consumer preference; (2) visits per month	Adults (local supermarkets
Maki, 1982	(1) distance estimates (2) mapping (dot placement)	(1) boundaries	Adults (locations learned from artificial maps)
Newcombe and Liben, 1982	(1) distance estimation;	(1) barriers (2) distance	Grade 1 and adults (10 toys)

TABLE 11.3—*Continued*

	Dependent Variables	Independent Variables	Ages and Settings
Sherman, Croxton, and Giovanatto, 1979	(2) rank ordering (1) magnitude estimation (standard = 100) (2) mapmaking	(1) area of residence on campus	Adults (college campus)
Tversky, 1981	(1) sketch maps (2) compass directions (drawing arrow through circle with one location at center, to indicate orientation of second location)	(1) rotation and alignment errors	Adults (locations learned from artificial maps)
Walsh, Krauss, and Regnier, 1981	(1) mapping (disc placement); (2) sketch maps	(1) sex; (2) health; (3) district; (4) education; (5) driving frequency; (6) ease of walking; (7) size of neighborhood	Elderly (neighborhood)

Tours resulted in greatest accuracy, followed by films and slide sequences in that order. Liben, Moore, and Golbeck (1982) found that preschoolers' placement of individual items in either scale models or life-size spaces was more accurate for bounded items (those near permanent topological cues) than for unbounded items. Briggs (1976) found that both mileage estimates and ratio distance estimates were larger for distances toward as opposed to away from the downtown area of Columbus, Ohio, and for routes with bends as opposed to straight routes.

Although these three cases show some evidence of convergent validity (and more evidence could be gleaned if we included cross-study comparisons as well as within-study comparisons), there are several limitations to the conclusion that measures show convergent validity. Most obviously, the range of methods compared is quite limited, and the two methods used by Liben et al. and by Briggs are quite similar: placements differing in scale and two types of distance estimation, respectively. A second serious limitation is that establishing convergent validity is, as Howard, Chase, and Rothman (1973) point out, tantamount to trying to prove the null hypothesis. One may always fail to find differences among measures because of failures of design or measurements, rather than the true absence of differences. For instance, Howard et al. found that lower travel times and larger numbers of environmental features on a route both added to explanation of variance in subjective distances, whether these distances were derived from sketch maps, scale models, metric distance estimates, or ratio distance estimates. This, apparently, is convergent validity. But the two independent variables (travel times and environmental features) were added to regression equations predicting subjective distances after entry of the actual distances. The actual distances, as noted above in the first section, accounted for large amounts of variance in these data. Thus, the amount of additional variance explained by travel times and environmental features was small, and it may be that differences among the four methods in the size of the effects of the two independent variables were thereby masked.

A second version of the "null hypothesis problem" in convergent validity studies arises when two measures "agree," in that neither detects a statistically significant effect of an independent variable. Kirasic et al., as cited in Siegel (1981), failed to find an effect of year in college (freshman or senior) on spatial representations of a college campus, using MDS maps derived either from rank ordering or from projective convergence data. But these results are difficult to interpret, since other studies have found that year in college does relate to the nature of spatial representations (e.g., Evans, Marrero, & Butler, 1981; Schouela, Steinberg, Leveton, & Wapner, 1980).

A third aspect of the "null hypothesis problem" arises as one considers the results of studies in which independent variables had similar effects on dependent variables, but these effects differed in magnitude. Mackay and Olshavsky (1975) found that distances among supermarkets derived by MDS from rank ordering data correlated more highly with consumer behavior (visits per month) than did distances on sketch maps although both correlations were significant. (There was no difference in the size of the correlations of the two measures with consumer preference.) Tversky (1981) found that spatial errors caused by rotation of frames of reference into congruence, and by alignment of locations within groups, occurred both with a sketch map task and when subjects were asked to indicate the orientation of one location relative to another by drawing an arrow. But errors were significantly greater with the latter technique. Both Mackay and Olshavsky, and Tversky found evidence of convergent validity of measures, but in each case the difference in magnitude of the effects serves to remind us that with less powerful designs, one might have found significant results with one variable but not another.

A similar situation arose in the data of Maki (1982). Maki was interested in subjects' knowledge of distances separating cities, and how this is affected by categorization (the imposition of state boundary lines). Subjects learned the location of 12 cities, organized into only one state or into two. Distance estimates were made either in miles, after being told that the largest distance was 75 miles, or by marking the location of two cities at a time on sheets of paper already marked with the most distant cities. This second measure showed the predicted pattern of pairs of cities in different states being judged further apart than those in the same state. The first measure showed a similar pattern, but there was a puzzling finding that for some city pairs, the same effect also occurred when all cities had been presented as located in a single state, and there was no basis for expecting a difference. The distorting effect of the border was also less apparent with the distance estimation data than with the mapping data. Although Maki does not speculate on the point, her findings may indicate that subjects are more able to make their spatial knowledge manifest when asked to produce judgments in a similar format to that in which they originally learned the information. But again, that is a post hoc interpretation.

Patterns of data are, of course, most interpretable when one has a plausible explanation for the findings. This should go without saying, but because most studies have not been designed to examine dependent variables, and instead included multiple measures merely in the hope of establishing convergent validity, explanations for differences are not always readily available. Tversky suggests that her arrow task is less constrained than sketch mapping and hence perhaps more prone to error. Although this may explain the differences between the tasks, the explanation has a somewhat post hoc air. Mackay and Olshavsky's findings can also be explained post hoc: perhaps subjects inadvertently used knowledge of their preferences for (and use of) the supermarkets in doing rank orderings of proximity. While sketch mapping, they could have been more continuously aware that their task was to reproduce spatial relationships.

The remaining studies to be discussed either found different results with different dependent variables, or found mixed agreement among different variables. In cases where convergent validity seems challenged, the need for a theoretical framework for predicting performance patterns is even more pressing than when convergent validity seems present, although effect sizes differ.

Walsh, Krauss, and Regnier (1981) had elderly adults make neighborhood sketch maps and rated the maps for accuracy on a scale of 1 to 10. They also asked subjects to place discs representing neighborhood landmarks on a large sheet of paper to make a map. The disc placements were then compared to the correct placements, and the stress remaining after best fit was achieved was taken as a measure of accuracy. Accuracy of sketch maps was significantly related to being male, being healthy, and living in the community of Long Beach rather than Westlake. Accuracy of disc placements was related to being healthy and having better education. The only overlap in these two sets of data is the effect of health on accuracy, but it is hard to speculate on what the lack of convergent validity might mean. Perhaps the two techniques make differential demands on subjects' abilities, but since different sample sizes and different methods of evaluating accuracy were used as well, it is hard to be sure.

Sherman, Croxton, and Giovanatto (1979) examined college students' knowledge of campus layout, using groups of freshmen from three different residence locations. Students gave magnitude estimates alone, or else first performed a map-board task and then gave magnitude estimates. Relative distortion of north-south relative to east-west axes was examined as a function of residence. It was found that different conclusions would be reached looking at map-board data or at magnitude estimations, and also by looking at magnitude estimations after mapping as opposed to those performed without that prior experience. No theoretical interpretation was offered for these results.

The data of Cohen, Weatherford, Lomenick, and Koeller (1979) are easier to interpret and serve well to make the point that differences among dependent variables can be substantively interesting, rather than merely a nuisance. Cohen et al. asked first and fifth graders to estimate distances among six objects in novel or unfamiliar environments, using one of three techniques: (1) reconstruction (placing two colored cards representing objects, in any orientation); (2) distance estimation (in number of steps between locations); (3) distance estimation (placing colored cards in a specified orientation). Age increases in accuracy were found for the second two measures, but not for free reconstruction. This makes sense, since the reconstruction task does not demand rescaling or metric estimation (as does the number-of-steps task) nor does it require reorientation (as does the specified-orientation task). Since age differences in metric estimation and reorientation are theoretically predicted, the Cohen et al. study does not so much show lack of convergent validity as provide substantive information concerning the nature of developmental changes in spatial representation and the ability to operate on spatial information. The study thus provides a model of how the study of multiple dependent variables can be substantively interesting, if performed within an adequate theoretical model.

The three remaining studies in Table 11.3 all concern the effect of barriers on spatial representation. This line of research was begun by Kosslyn, Pick, and Fariello (1974), who found that rank orderings of preschoolers and adults reflected overestimation of distances between objects separated by opaque barriers, relative to objects without intervening barriers. Preschoolers, but not adults, also overestimated distances between objects separated by transparent barriers. Cohen, Baldwin, and Sherman (1978) followed up these findings using a natural environment, a summer camp in which locations were separated by hills, and by buildings and trees. Spatial representations of 9–10-year-olds and adults were measured in two ways: (1) distance estimation (number of steps between locations); (2) reconstruction (placement of tiles on a featureless board). For both measures, the absence of the hills led to underestimations of distance, whereas the presence of hills led to overestimations. This effect was more marked for distance estimation than reconstruction, however.

The presence or absence of trees or buildings had more complex effects. For distance estimation, the pattern of barriers leading to overestimation was replicated. But for reconstruction, a precisely *opposite* effect was found: distances between locations separated by trees or buildings were underestimated, and those not so separated overestimated.

It should also be noted that, overall, judgments on the reconstruction task were extremely accurate, and significantly more accurate than distance estimations. Thus, this study could also be included among those listed in the first section and used to support the conclusion that modeling tasks are surprisingly easy, perhaps because of the contextual support and the ease of representing angular, as well as distance, information. But the pattern of interactions of the type of dependent variable with the presence of hills, and of trees and buildings, indicates the necessity of a more complex view. Cohen et al. note that subjects were asked to place tiles corresponding to buildings, but not to represent hills in any fashion. The act of placing these barriers could have alerted subjects to the dangers of distortion, and led to overcompensation. An alternative interpretation is that trees and buildings served as landmarks, to which other locations tended to be attracted (Sadalla, Burroughs & Staplin, 1980).

Newcombe and Liben (1982) asked first graders and adults either to rank order the proximity of 10 toys in an environment containing both transparent and opaque barriers (a straightforward replication of Kossyln et al.) or to estimate distances between pairs of objects by directing the experimenter in placing objects along a line of specified orientation. Rank ordering data replicated Kosslyn et al., with opaque barriers leading to overestimations at both age groups, and transparent barriers having the same influence only for the children. The distance estimation data, however, showed a different picture of barrier effects and developmental change. Adults were more accurate than children, at least among males. Only adult males showed any evidence of barrier effects in distance estimations.

Newcombe and Liben suggest that rank ordering is an abstract task with considerable processing demands, a conclusion supported by many of the studies reviewed in this chapter. Children cope with these demands either with uncertainty and random responding, or by clustering their rankings by quadrant, a pattern that would create or exaggerate barrier effects. Thus, developmental differences in response to barriers on this task may represent, at least in part, the processing demands of the task used to study spatial representations.

Liben and Newcombe (1981) examined adults' rank orderings when asked to learn locations of 20 toys. The rank ordering results were contrasted with results of a disc placement task. Subjects placed discs on a piece of cardboard already marked with representations of the opaque and the transparent barriers, to form a map. Although barrier effects were found in distances marked by disc placement, the effects were quite different from those in the rank-ordering data. Distances involving transparent barriers were less underestimated (91% of correct value) than distances with no barriers (84%) or opaque barriers (86%). The general underestimation found may reflect a tendency for the boundary lines to act as landmarks attracting objects, as shown for natural environments by Sadalla et al., and for a circle and dot task by Nelson and Chaiklin (1980). It was certainly true that closeness to boundaries facilitated overall correctness of placement; distance of locations from barriers correlated .69 with distance off in inches in the placement of those points by subjects. Why the distances involving transparent barriers were less underestimated is not known, but may reflect the fact that the locations involved tended to be closer to barriers.

In sum, studies that have looked at dependent variables in an effort to establish convergent validity have had mixed outcomes. Although some have been successful, the overall picture is that different techniques frequently reveal different results. The question is what to do with that fact. If viewed simply as failure to establish convergent validity, it is certainly most discouraging to work in spatial cognition. But such discouragement would be unwarranted. First, conclusions may simply need to be more limited in generalization. We should not assume we have discovered facts about spatial knowledge per se, having used only one dependent variable. For instance, barriers or boundaries may lead to overestimation of distance in some tasks, but perhaps to underestimation in others, as when they are used as reference points that seem to attract locations in a placement task. Each conclusion, however, may be perfectly reliable in itself and allow prediction of behavior in analogous real-world situations, as when people are asked to estimate distance between towns separated by a mountain ridge, as opposed to making a model of the terrain. Second, differences in the processing demands of various tasks can actually be used as tools for making predictions about substantively interesting issues. For instance, Cohen, Weatherford, Lomenick, and Koeller (1979) and Newcombe and Liben (1982) both present evidence that developmental differences in spatial cognition in the grade-school age range may reflect, in part, age differences in ability to cope with task demands such as rescaling, metric estimation, and information-processing capacity. These are important age-related differences, but somewhat different in flavor from the qualitative, stage-like change sometimes assumed to be most important (see Newcombe, 1982). Other such substantive hypotheses can surely be tested using the strategy of *predicting* when and how results obtained with different dependent variables *ought* to differ.

One example of the kind of work that can result from adopting this strategy is provided by a paper by Thorndyke and Hayes-Roth (1982). These authors were interested in examining differences in the kind of spatial knowledge gained when people learn about an environment from a map as opposed to when they learn about the environment through actual navigation. Thorndyke and Hayes-Roth used five tasks: (1) estimating distances of routes; (2) estimating Euclidean distances between locations; (3) pointing to target locations from reference locations; (4) pointing to target locations while imagining being at a certain reference location; (5) placing a location on a page on which two locations were already entered to indicate the scale and orientation of the "map."

In terms of the first question reviewed in this chapter ("Which method is more accurate?"), Thorndyke and Hayes-Roth found that the answer often depended on whether the subjects had learned the space from maps or navigation. For instance, for map subjects, orientation was more accurately indicated using the dot location task than using the pointing task. For navigation subjects, on the other hand, there was no difference. In terms of the third question reviewed in this chapter, convergent validity of methods, the data showed that navigation subjects were more accurate than map subjects at performing some tasks (route distance estimation, the two pointing tasks) but less accurate at performing others (Euclidean distance estimation, dot location).

To the investigator not concerned with building processing models, these results would be disappointing. No one method is the "best"; there is no one answer to the question of whether navigation or map learning results in more accurate spatial representations. However, the main point of Thorndyke and Hayes-Roth's paper is the *prediction* of these complex patterns by the building of performance models that include hypotheses about both the representations built by subjects exposed to the environment in different ways and the processes the subjects use to solve the various problems the investigators posed. Given the goal of understanding spatial processing as well as the nature of representation, variations in performance on different tasks become the focus of interest, the means of testing the models that have been formulated.

CONCLUSION

Several conclusions can be drawn from this literature review. The first conclusion concerns the empirical gaps made obvious by the review, for instance, the simple need for more research comparing methods at the individual as well as the aggregate level, and the need for more such research especially with special groups like children and the elderly. Research along these lines clearly needs, however, to be more guided by theory, cast more in the guise of hypothesis testing. A second recommendation is that researchers interested in spatial knowledge need to get beyond the idea that a spatial representation is a "thing in the head," more or less well externalized by a given methodology. Especially in attempts to establish convergent validity, this tends to lead to problems with null results, and to confusion and discouragement if measures do not lead to the same conclusions. If we are able to predict when and why various measures *should* show differential distortions as a result of environmental and subject variables, however, the "failure" to establish convergent validity is seen in a whole new light. Different results with different measures become facts to be explained in future investigations of spatial processing, "clues" to the nature of spatial cognition.

There have been various efforts (e.g., Golledge, 1976) to suggest a taxonomy of dependent variables used to tap spatial representation. Golledge suggested three dimensions for categorization: whether behavior is natural or experimenter-controlled, whether behavior is observed by the experimenter or reported by the subject, and whether spatial representations are directly produced by the subject, or inferred from indirect judgmental tasks. Many other such dimensions could be added: Does the task require rescaling? reorientation? the use of metrics? the use of symbolization? knowledge of mapping conventions, such as aerial view? Are prior judgments perceptually available to the subject? What degree of contextual support (e.g., landmarks still present in a room, or drawn on a map) is provided?

These dimensions all seem important. Since there are so many relevant points of difference between tasks, however, efforts to establish a cross-cutting, mutually exclusive set of taxonomic categories seem difficult. Thus, a third recommendation for future research is to look analytically at dimensions such as those listed above. We should, as much as possible, compare along abstract dimensions rather than compare tasks per se.

A fourth conclusion is perhaps more specific than the first two. There is considerable evidence that pessimism about the use of sketch maps and modeling tasks has been overdone, and the promise of indirect judgmental techniques and of MDS correspondingly exaggerated. Mapping and modeling are certainly correlated with spatial and graphic ability, are susceptible to instruction (e.g., Wood & Beck, 1976), and change developmentally. But they have the advantage of being easy-to-understand, everyday tasks, which provide context for judgments through the perceptual availability of prior judgments, and a natural means of representing orientation and distance information simultaneously. Ranking, triadic comparison, and so on are more abstract, more piecemeal tasks which demand considerable attention and memory capacity. These indirect means of inferring spatial representation should be used with a good deal of care.

ACKNOWLEDGMENT

I would like to thank Lynn Liben, Robert Weisberg, and Robert Cohen for commenting on earlier drafts of this chapter.

REFERENCES

Baird, J. C., Merrill, A. A., & Tannenbaum, J. Cognitive representation of spatial relations: II. A familiar environment. *Journal of Experimental Psychology: General*, 1979, *108*, 92–98.

Baird, J. C., & Wagner, M. Modelling the creation of cognitive maps. In H. L. Pick & L. P. Acredolo (Eds.), *Spatial orientation: Theory, research, and application*. New York: Plenum Press, 1983.

Baird, J. C., Wagner, M., & Noma, E. Impossible cognitive spaces. *Geographic Analysis,* 1982, *14,* 204–216.

Briggs, R. Methodologies for the measurement of cognitive distance. In G. T. Moore & R. G. Golledge (Eds.), *Environmental knowing: Theories, research and methods.* Stroudsburg, PA: Dowden, Hutchinson & Ross, 1976.

Cadwallader, M. T. Cognitive distance in intraurban space. In G. T. Moore & R. G. Golledge (Eds.), *Environmental knowing: Theories, research and methods.* Stroudsburg, PA: Dowden, Hutchinson & Ross, 1976.

Canter, D. *The psychology of place,* New York: St. Martin's Press, 1977.

Cohen, M. E., & Nodine, C. F. *Modes of representation in cognitive mapping.* Paper presented to the American Psychological Association, Montreal, August 1980.

Cohen, R., Baldwin, L. M., & Sherman, R. C. Cognitive maps of a naturalistic setting. *Child Development,* 1978, *49,* 1216–1218.

Cohen, R., Weatherford, D. L., & Byrd, D. Distance estimates of children as a function of acquisition and response activities. *Journal of Experimental Child Psychology,* 1980, *30,* 464–472.

Cohen, R., Weatherford, D. L., Lomenick, T., & Koeller, K. Development of spatial representations: Role of task demands and familiarity with the environment. *Child Development,* 1979, *50,* 1257–1260.

Downs, R. M. Maps and mappings as metaphors for spatial representation. In L. S. Liben, A. H. Patterson, & N. Newcombe (Eds.), *Spatial representation and behavior across the life span: Theory and application.* New York: Academic Press, 1981.

Evans, G. W. Environmental cognition. *Psychological Bulletin,* 1980, *88,* 259–287.

Evans, G. W., Marrero, D., & Butler, P. Environmental learning and cognitive mapping. *Environment and Behavior,* 1981, *13,* 83–104.

Ewing, G. O. On the sensitivity of conclusions about the bases of cognitive distance. *Professional Geographer,* 1981, *33,* 311–314.

Golledge, R. G. Methods and methodological issues in environmental cognition research. In G. T. Moore & R. G. Golledge (Eds.), *Environmental knowing: Theories, research, and methods.* Stroudsburg, PA: Dowden, Hutchinson & Ross, 1976.

Howard, R. B., Chase, S. D., & Rothman, M. An analysis of four measures of cognitive maps. In W. F. E. Preiser (Ed.), *Environmental design research.* Stroudsburg, PA: Dowden, Hutchinson & Ross, 1973.

Kosslyn, S. M., Pick, H. L., & Fariello, G. R. Cognitive maps in children and men. *Child Development,* 1974, *45,* 707–716.

Kuipers, B. The "map in the head" metaphor. *Environment and Behavior,* 1982, *14,* 202–220.

Liben, L. S. Spatial representation and behavior: Multiple perspectives. In L. S. Liben, A. H. Patterson, & N. Newcombe (Eds.), *Spatial representation and behavior across the life span: Theory and application.* New York: Academic Press, 1981.

Liben, L. S., Moore, M. L., & Golbeck, S. L. Preschoolers' knowledge of their classroom environment: Evidence from small-scale and life-size spatial tasks. *Child Development,* 1982, *53,* 1275–1284.

Liben, L. S., & Newcombe, N. *Barrier effects and processing demands.* Paper presented to the Psychonomic Society, Philadelphia, November 1981.

Lynch, K. *The image of the city.* Cambridge, MA: MIT Press, 1960.

Mackay, D. B. The effect of spatial stimuli on the estimation of cognitive maps. *Geographical Analysis,* 1976, *8,* 439–451.

Mackay, D. B, & Olshavsky, R. W. Cognitive maps of retail locations: An investigation of some basic issues. *Journal of Consumer Research,* 1975, *2,* 197–205.

Magana, J. R., Evans, G. W., & Romney, A. K. Scaling techniques in the analysis of environmental cognition data. *Professional Geographer,* 1981, *33,* 294–301.

Maki, R. H. Why do categorization effects occur in comparative judgment tasks? *Memory and Cognition*, 1982, *10*, 252–264.

Nelson, T. O., & Chaiklin, S. Immediate memory for spatial location. *Journal of Experimental Psychology: Human Learning and Memory*, 1980, *6*, 529–545.

Newcombe, N. Spatial representation and behavior: Retrospect and prospect. In L. S. Liben, A. H. Patterson, & N. Newcombe (Eds.), *Spatial representation and behavior across the life span: Theory and application*. New York: Academic Press, 1981.

Newcombe, N. Development of spatial cognition and cognitive development. In R. Cohen (Ed.), *New directions for child development: Children's conceptions of spatial relationships*. San Francisco: Jossey-Bass, 1982.

Newcombe, N., & Liben, L. S. Barrier effects in the cognitive maps of children and adults. *Journal of Experimental Child Psychology*, 1982, *34*, 46–58.

Posner, M. I., & Keele, S. W. On the genesis of abstract ideas. *Journal of Experimental Psychology*, 1968, *77*, 353–363.

Sadalla, E. K., Burroughs, W. J. & Staplin, L. J. Reference points in spatial cognition. *Journal of Experimental Psychology: Human Learning and Memory*, 1980, *6*, 516–528.

Schouela, D. A., Steinberg, L. M., Leveton, L. B., & Wapner, S. Development of the cognitive organization of an environment. *Canadian Journal of Behavioral Science*, 1980, *12*, 1–16.

Sherman, R. C., Croxton, J. & Giovanatto, J. Investigating cognitive representations of spatial relationships. *Environment and Behavior*, 1979, *11*, 209–226.

Siegel, A. W. The externalization of cognitive maps by children and adults: In search of ways to ask better questions. In L. S. Liben, A. H. Patterson, & N. Newcombe (Eds.), *Spatial representation and behavior across the life span: Theory and application*. New York: Academic Press, 1981.

Siegel, A. W., Herman, J. F., Allen, G. L., & Kirasic, K. C. The development of cognitive maps of large- and small-scale space. *Child Development*, 1979, *50*, 582–585.

Summers, J. O., & Mackay, D. B. On the validity and reliability of direct similarity judgments. *Journal of Marketing Research*, 1976, *13*, 289–295.

Thorndyke, P. W., & Hayes-Roth, B. Differences in spatial knowledge acquired from maps and navigation. *Cognitive Psychology*, 1982, *14*, 560–589.

Tversky, B. Distortions in memory for maps. *Cognitive Psychology*, 1981, *13*, 407–433.

Walsh, D. A., Krauss, I. K., & Regnier, V. A. Spatial ability, environmental knowledge, and environmental use: The elderly. In L. S. Liben, A. H. Patterson, & N. Newcombe (Eds.), *Spatial representation and behavior across the life span: Theory and application*. New York: Academic Press, 1981.

Wood, D., & Beck, R. Talking with Environmental A, in experimental mapping language. In G. T. Moore & R. G. Golledge (Eds.), *Environmental knowing: Theories, research, and methods*. Stroudsburg, PA: Dowden, Hutchinson & Ross, 1976.

12

Strengthening Weak Links in the Study of the Development of Macrospatial Cognition

Gary L. Allen
Old Dominion University

As an interdisciplinary research area, the study of the development of macrospatial cognition is facilitated by the sharing of concepts and techniques from different groups of researchers. Considerable progress has been made toward understanding how knowledge of the spatial attributes of large-scale environments is acquired and how such knowledge affects human behavior, and much of this progress has been stimulated by an exchange of information among psychologists, geographers, sociologists, and urban planners. However, not everything transmitted across disciplinary boundaries has contributed to progress. In fact, some concepts with widespread application have actually had the effect of impeding advances in the area. These weak links provided the impetus for this chapter. The chapter has two objectives. The first is to advance the proposition that the concept of the cognitive map has become a weak link in the sense that it provides an ineffective interface between the study of the development of macrospatial cognition and the experimental study of human cognition. The second is to suggest a number of theoretical constructs that may prove to be of greater heuristic value than the cognitive map concept has been.

Before these objectives are pursued, it should be made clear what is meant by the term "macrospatial cognition." In this chapter, macrospatial cognition refers to those hypothesized processes that are involved in the acquisition and use of knowledge from and about the spatial attributes of large-scale environments. A large-scale environment is one in which an individual cannot perceive its entire structure from a vantage point within the confines of the environment itself. Knowledge of the spatial attributes of a large-scale environment has been classified according to various taxonomies, but theoretical consensus indicates three general types. Landmark knowledge implies the ability to recognize environmental features encountered previously and to use such features as navigational aids and reference points. Route knowledge implies the ability to match a series of locomotor maneuvers with a specific sequence of environmental features and to provide information about the temporospatial relationships among those features. Configurational or survey-type knowledge implies the ability to infer spatial relationships among a set of environmental features from vantage points either within or outside of the environment itself and to provide information about these relationships. It may be added that a developmental progression from landmark knowledge to route knowledge to configurational is also widely accepted. This progression is meant to imply that although all three types of macrospatial knowledge can co-exist, over the course of ontogeny, capability for landmark knowledge precedes capability for route knowledge, which in turn precedes capability for configurational knowledge. This same general progression has also been posited in microgenesis, which can be thought of as a short-term knowledge acquisition process (e.g., learning a new spatial environment as an adult).

CAUSES AND EFFECTS OF A WEAK LINK

An examination of the causes and effects of a weak link must be preceded by evidence that such a problem exists in the study of the development of macrospatial cognition. Such evidence is largely in the form of statements from recent empirical and theoretical literature. The difficulties involved in advancing a general understanding of cognitive development in the spatial domain are frequently outlined in introductions to empirical studies (e.g., Allen, Kirasic, Siegel, & Herman, 1979; Hazen, Lockman, & Pick, 1978). Commentaries and discussion often include the proposition that crucial issues concerning the processes involved in macrospatial cognition are not being addressed (e.g., Downs, 1976; Siegel, 1981). Occasionally, there are wholesale indictments of the state of the art in this research area, such as the following quote from Downs and Siegel (1981): "The field has been characterized by a relatively innocent form of low level empiricism, simple-minded data gathering and classification, co-existing with an abundance of speculative frameworks, each of which is grounded in what amounts to anecdote and common sense" (p. 237–238).

Clearly, some investigators believe that progress in this research area has been impeded. Most criticism points to weaknesses of a conceptual nature. There has been no shortage of empirical effort, but that effort has been motivated by hypotheses that are either too limited to have implications outside of macrospatial cognition or too general to have been questioned in the first place. Similarly, there has been no shortage of descriptive theories, but these have been either too specific to relate to cognition in general or too vague to give rise to testable hypotheses. It appears that the weakness in these efforts can be traced to the lack of satisfactory theoretical constructs that provide the conceptual link between theories and testable hypotheses.

The etiology of this state of affairs is not too difficult to delineate. The study of the development of macrospatial cognition has been greatly influenced by the synthetic overviews of Hart and Moore (1973) and Siegel and White (1975). These works were similar in the sense that the majority of their content was devoted to a marriage of developmental theory—Piagetian (Piaget, 1954, 1970), Wernerian (Werner, 1948, 1957), or both—and an emerging field of study that now is identified as social ecology or environmental psychology. The remainder of these works was comprised of philosophical, anthropological, sociological, and psychological findings that supplemented and supported the aforementioned synthesis.

Although these theory-oriented works were concerned with the acquisition of macrospatial knowledge by children and adults, they included only limited attempts to integrate the existing literature on the experimental study of human learning and memory. There are two major reasons for this lack of integration. The first reason is philosophical. For the most part, developmental theory reflects a philosophy of science that is organismic, rationalistic, and structure-oriented. In contrast, experimental psychology is based on a philosophy of science that is mechanistic, empiricistic, and process-oriented (see Pepper, 1970). Because early conceptualizations of the acquisition of macrospatial knowledge embodied developmental theory, they did not readily lend themselves to the generation of experimental hypotheses. A second reason for the lack of integration was practical rather than philosophical. The information-processing view of human cognition, which had become dominant in the preceding decade, did not show much promise in terms of constructs applicable to a developmental analysis of macrospatial learning. Even today it is not a straightforward matter to incorporate the concepts of different types of memory (e.g., semantic vs. episodic), different memory stores (e.g., short-term vs. long-term), and different levels of processing (e.g., orthographic vs. semantic) into a coherent account of macrospatial cognition and its development. Also, while researchers in macrospatial cognition were enthused by an opportunity to study ecologically significant cognitive activity, many contemporary cognitive psychologists were turning in the opposite direction toward the study of mechanical information processing, or artificial intelligence. For these reasons, the experimental approach to the study of human cognition was not well integrated into the emerging research area.

This situation resulted in a void in terms of constructs to relate theoretical tenets to experimental hypotheses. Yet, researchers needed a label to apply to a collection of psychological processes that play a role in macrospatial learning and behavior. This need was met by resurrecting the concept of a cognitive map, a relic from psychology's past. In essence, the cognitive map became the "black box" within the Behaviorists' famous "black box," as researchers felt the need to refer to poorly defined processes that guided an organism's spatial behavior from within that organism's nervous system. Initially, there was considerable caution in using this term originated by Tolman (1948), particularly among psychologists. Recently, however, use of the expression has proliferated both in frequency and breadth. Currently, the term can be used to refer to everything from cartographic sketches (Beck & Wood, 1976) to theoretical knowledge states (Siegel, Kirasic, & Kail, 1978). It can assume the status of intervening variable, metaphor, or hypothetical construct (Moore & Golledge, 1976). Generally speaking, it is used as a metaphor to convey the expectation of a knowledge state concerning the spatial attributes of an environment (Downs, 1981). It is in this regard that it has been referred to as "a convenient fiction" (Siegel, 1981).

Although this description may not be appropriate in the case of some work, such as that of O'Keefe and Nadel (1978) on the role of the hippocampus in spatial memory, it is particularly apt for describing many usages of the term. In a number of instances, cognitive map has been used as a convenient fiction, an all-encompassing unrestricted construct to fill the void that should ideally be occupied by more rigorous constructs from the study of cognition. The major problem with convenient fictions is that they have no practical constraints or boundaries. The cognitive map became an all-purpose entity. A cognitive map was that which permitted way finding, route planning, detouring, map drawing, and model building. It made it possible to identify aerial photographs, to avoid getting lost, to imagine places that were outside of immediate perceptual range, and to estimate distances from memory. What was offered as an explanation for how such a utilitarian knowledge state came into being? Using impeccable logic, it was reasoned that if the final product was a cognitive map, the process that gave rise to it must be cognitive mapping! Cognitive mapping became the expression used to describe the process by which cognitive maps grow more complex and accurate over repeated transactions between an individual and the environment. Several descriptive models (e.g., Downs & Stea, 1973; Hart & Moore, 1973; Siegel et al., 1978) offer characterizations of this change, but they provided at best a nebulous account of the cognitive mechanisms underlying such development.

References to cognitive maps and cognitive mapping became ubiquitous and ambiguous. The broader the boundaries of definition were stretched, the less meaningful the terms became. Currently, these terms may contribute more to misunderstanding than to progress. Not accidentally, the use of these terms is correlated with the low-level empiricism and armchair speculation decried by Downs and Siegel (1981). True to the famous dictum, this correlation does not imply causation. In this case, both the use of these expressions and the lack of satisfactory progress may be tied to an absence of more precise theoretical constructs.

Some researchers have sought to avoid the problems associated with the terms cognitive maps and cognitive mapping by substituting the terms "image," as in Downs and Stea's (1973) *Image and Environment,* and "spatial representation," as in Liben, Patterson, and Newcombe's (1981) *Spatial Representation and Behavior Across the Life Span.* While these terms represent movement away from the "map-in-the head" connotation, they also have some disadvantages. The study of imagery has re-emerged in cognitive psychology amid considerable debate (e.g., Kosslyn, 1980), and it may well be the case that "reproductions" of perceptual experiences play a role in macrospatial cognition. Siegel and White's (1975) idea of recognition-in-context memory could serve as a case in point. However, there seems to be little gained by substituting the concept of "pictures-in-the-head" for the notion of "maps-in-the-head." Neither concept provides much in the way of medium-level theoretical constructs for translating theoretical propositions into testable hypotheses. If image is to retain integrity as a concept in macrospatial cognition, then its role must be defined with consideraly more precision than it has been thus far. As an all-encompassing term, it is no stronger than cognitive map.

The term "representation" is a respectable one among developmental psychologists and lately among cognitive psychologists. The problems associated with use of the term spatial representation stem from its multiple connotations. As Liben (1982) pointed out, the term can refer to spatial storage, i.e., the creation of a spatial data base in memory; spatial thought, i.e., the application of principles or procedures to perceived or stored spatial information; and spatial products, i.e., the observable or perceivable results of a state of knowing. Recognition of this ambiguity is an important step toward the implementation of more effective theoretical constructs. Representation can be an effective concept only when its meaning is limited to a specific phenomenon or set of circumstances. It can be used to describe some aspect of macrospatial cognition without extending its use to cover all aspects, as would be done in substituting spatial representation for cognitive mapping.

CONSTRUCTS FOR STRENGTHENING WEAK LINKS

The only worthwhile purpose in pointing out weak links is to facilitate efforts to strengthen them. Accordingly, several examples of theoretical constructs that could contribute to these efforts are provided in this section. The first two are described within the context of specific experimental studies in which they proved useful. The latter two are examined in terms of their general impact.

Metamemory

One aspect of the development of macrospatial cognition is related to the concept of metamemory (Flavell & Wellman, 1977), particularly that facet which Brown (1975) referred to as "knowing how to know." An illustration of the utility of this construct in macrospatial cognitive research was provided by Allen et al. (1979). These investigators were initially interested in studying children's ability to make ordinal judgments of distances along real-world routes. To benefit from the control and convenience of a laboratory study, the experimenters used a series of color slides made during a walk through a commercial section of an urban neighborhood to provide a visual approximation to actual experience in a macrospatial environment. During testing, subjects made ordinal distance judgments among specific places portrayed in a set of test slides selected from the original series. In planning the study, the question arose as to how these test slides should be selected. Ample evidence indicated that adults generally agreed on which environmental features were memorable along a route (Carr & Schissler, 1969) and that children apparently selected (Moore, 1976) and used (Acredolo, Pick, & Olsen, 1975) environmental landmarks to maintain orientation and to specify locations. However, it was not known whether children and adults would use the same landmarks along a route for these purposes.

To address this question, subjects from different age groups selected a set of photographs from the pictorialized route which they believed would best serve them as reminders for where they were along the course of the walk. In the study, 7-year-olds, 10-year-olds, and college-age adults first viewed the walk and then selected a set of pictures that best served as reference points. This quality was referred to as high-landmark potential. Results indicated that agreement as to which scenes had high-landmark potential increased across age groups. The set of scenes selected most frequently by adults depicted actual or potential changes in heading, in other words, either a turn or an intersection where a turn was possible. Such scenes could have been selected on the basis of their perceptual qualities, e.g., the fact that intersections and turns altered the texture of the optical flow field (Gibson, 1966) portrayed by the slide series, or they could have been chosen on the basis of convention, i.e., that such features are basic elements for organizing and communicating macrospatial information (Lynch, 1960; Sadalla & Staplin, 1980). Regardless of the adults' basis for selection, it was clear that children generally did not share their criterion. Less than one half of the scenes selected most often by the 10-year-olds and less than one fourth of those selected most often by the 7-year-olds depicted actual or potential changes in heading. Instead, most of their scenes portrayed views from the middle of blocks, often containing colorful window displays and striped awnings. These features were distinctive in a visual sense, but because there were numerous such displays and several such awnings, they were not distinctive in a spatial sense.

The fact that children and adults in this study did not make the same selections did not by itself imply that the children chose scenes that were low in landmark potential. It is very likely that children's view of a route differs significantly from that of adults (Siegel et al., 1978). It could have been that their selections reflected a "child's eye" view of the walk but not a view that resulted in poorer choices of potential landmarks. To examine this issue, groups of 7-year-olds and 10-year-olds were tested on a distance judgment task using the scenes selected by their same-age peers from the initial study, while comparable groups of 7-year-olds and 10-year-olds were tested on the same task using the scenes selected by adults in the initial study. For purposes of comparison, a group of college-age adults was also was also tested with the adult-selected scenes.The results were fairly clear-cut (see Fig. 12.1). Performance was poor for the 7-year-olds regardless of which set of scenes they referred to in making their distance judgments. Performance was equally poor for 10-year-olds tested with scenes selected by other 10-year-olds Unlike the younger children, the 10-year-olds performed significantly more accurately when they were tested with the scenes selected by adults as being high in landmark potential. In fact, their performance with these pictures was comparable to that of the adults tested with the same scenes.

This pattern of results suggested an application of Flavell's (1970) distinction between a production deficiency and a mediational deficiency in the use of mnemonics. According to this interpretation, the 7-year-olds exhibited a production deficiency in that they did not spontaneously select the scenes that were high in landmark potential (i.e., the best visual mnemonics for distance information), and they exhibited a mediational deficiency in that they did not increase the accuracy of their distance judgments when such scenes were provided. The 10-year-olds also provided evidence for a production deficiency in their selection of

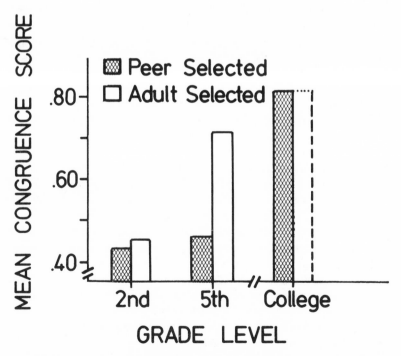

FIG. 12.1.   Effect of peer-selected versus adult-selected reference scenes on the accuracy of distance judgments (Allen et al., 1979).

scenes. However, they showed no evidence of a mediational deficiency in that their distance judgments were virtually as accurate as those of adults when they were provided with scenes that were high in landmark potential.

These findings illustrate the utility of concepts from the literature on metacognitive phenomena, a feature that other investigators (e.g., Acredolo, 1977; Siegel et al., 1978) have also noted. In this instance, metamemory as "knowing how to know" was shown to be an important factor in the relationship between landmark knowledge and route knowledge. The evidence indicated that the selection of environmental reference points affected directly the quality of the temporospatial information comprising route knowledge (cf. Sadalla, Burroughs, & Staplin, 1980). The concept of "knowing how to know" is applicable not only to studies of age-related developmental changes in macrospatial knowledge but also to studies of expert–novice differences in macrospatial skills such as orienteering and map reading (Chase & Chi, 1981). "Knowing about knowing," the other aspect of metamemory mentioned by Brown (1975), may also be an important construct in future research on macrospatial knowledge and skills. For example, Herman (1980) demonstrated that the ability to judge accurately when a spatial array has been memorized changes dramatically over childhood. It seems reasonable to speculate that failure to assess accurately one's own macrospatial knowledge is a major contributing factor in children's and adults' becoming disoriented or getting lost. In view of its overall heuristic potential, metamemory is a promising construct with which to work toward strengthening the weak links between the development of macrospatial cognition and human cognition.

Linear Order Representations

Another construct that may be useful is that of "linear order representations." This term, or one of its variants, has been used in reference to memory for a set of sequentially related stimuli. Thus, the number line (Holyoak, 1978), the alphabet (Klahr & Chase, 1978) and lists of verbal and nonverbal stimuli (Potts, 1974) serve as examples. The most interesting features of linear order representations are some characteristic effects that appear when subjects are required to learn and then use the ordered information in an experimental task. The acquisition of an ordered set of stimulus elements typically gives rise to the familiar recency and primary effects in which the first and last elements in a set are learned more rapidly than the central elements. Also, certain elements within the interior of the order may, because of their semantic properties, be learned prior to others and come to serve as reference points. Once a linear order is represented in memory, it generally gives rise to some distinguishing reaction time effects in experimental tasks requiring judgments of relative proximity or magnitude along some dimension. Decisions that involve the first or last elements in a sequentially ordered set are made more rapidly than are those not involving these "end anchors'' (Moyer & Dumais, 1978; Potts, 1972; Woocher, Glass, & Holyoak, 1978). The same holds true of decisions involving reference points (Holyoak & Mah, 1982).

Perhaps the most pervasive effect is referred to as the symbolic distance effect (Moyer & Bayer, 1976). This robust effect refers to the finding that the time required to make some judgment involving two elements within an ordered set decreases as the distance between the elements increases. The phenomenon of categorization, however, apparently can provide an exception to this rule. Judgments made involving elements within the same category typically show the symbolic distance effect, whereas judgments involving elements from adjacent categories do not (Maki, 1981). Categorization can lead to counterintuitive results in those instances in which two elements from different categories were closer along the linear order than are two elements from the same category.

It should be fairly clear from this brief characterization of linear order representations that they might prove useful in the study of route knowledge, which has frequently been descirbed in terms of a sequence of locomotor actions associated with specific environmental cues (e.g., Siegel & White, 1975). A recent study by Allen (1981) illustrated how the concept of categorization effects in spatial linear orders could be applied to the study of route knowledge. It has been proposed that route representations are organized into ''chunks'' of macrospatial information for the sake of cognitive economy. The idea of route segmentation (Downs & Stea, 1973) is very similar to the concept of categorization along linear order representations. If this similarity is strong, some indication of route segmentation should be evident in judgments of distance along routes. Based on inferences from the reaction time studies cited, it would be posited that locations within segments will be judged to be nearer to each other than they actually are and locations in different segments would be judged to be farther apart than they actually are.

This possibility was tested as an experimental hypothesis in a series of two studies involving groups of 7-year-olds, 10-year-olds, and college-age adults. In the initial study, subjects divided a pictorialized walk into segments. They first viewed a series of slides portraying a walk that began in a park, continued through a college campus, and ended in a residential neighborhood. Subsequently, they examined a set of sequentially ordered photographs from the slide series and were asked to designate different parts to that walk. They were instructed to divide the walk into as many parts as desired and were told that they would be required to explain their divisions. From these data, boundaries between divisions were determined on the basis of frequency of designation. Eight out of ten subjects in each age group agreed upon the same six route segments. These segments, which reflected changes in surroundings that had intentionally been made a part of in the pictorialized route, included the following: a park, two parts of a college campus, and three residential areas. The segments designated by the subjects were used to select proximity judgment problems for the second study.

The proximity problems involved one reference scene and two comparison scenes. The subject's task in the experiment was to decide which of the two comparison scenes was nearer the reference scene in terms of walking distance along the route. Three varieties of this problem were constructed. In the first variety, the reference scene and both comparison scenes were from the same route segment. In the second variety, the reference scene and the more distant comparison scene were from the same segment and the closer reference scene was from an adjacent segment. In the third variety, the reference scene and the closer comparison scene were in the same segment and the more distant comparison scene was in an adjacent segment.

If subjects' distance judgments were based exclusively on route segmentation, then their performance on problems of the first variety would be at or around chance level because all three scenes were from the same segment; their performance on problems of the second variety would be very inaccurate in a strictly metric sense because the metrically more distant scene was from the same segment as the reference scene; and their performance on problems of the third variety would be extremely accurate in a metric sense because the closer scene was in the same segment as the reference scene. If subjects ignored route segmentation in making their judgments, then the accuracy of their performance would be determined by their ability to estimate and compare the two distances involved in each problem. The influence of route segments was examined by constructing easy problems, in which the ratio between the shorter and the longer distances was 1:3 (e.g., 20 m versus 60 m), and difficult problems, in which the ratio between the two distances was 1:1.5 (e.g., 30 m versus 45 m), for each of the three problem varieties. Subjects not relying on route segmentation for their proximity judgments would be expected to perform more accurately on 1:3 ratio problems than on 1:1.5 ratio problems regardless of which variety of problem was involved. In contrast, subjects relying on route segmentation for their judgments of which comparison scene was nearer the reference scene would not be affected by distance ratio. An interesting question arose with regard to the expected performance of children. There was evidence that children in these age groups are capable of making judgments of macrospatial distance (e.g., Cohen, Weatherford, & Byrd, 1980; Curtis, Siegel, & Furlong, 1981). However, it was not clear how route segmentation would affect their judgments. Categorization generally is taken to be a hallmark of cognitive development, the classic example of hierarchical organization (see Rosch & Lloyd, 1978). However, route segmentation did not seem to be the semantic equivalent of categorization in this regard. Instead, segmentation suggested what in Gibsonian terms could be called a failure—not necessarily an inability, but a failure—to differentiate among discrete environmental features (cf. Gibson, 1969). In Piagetian terms, responding on the basis of segmentation could be thought of as relying on a topological concept of spatial relations, governed by principles of enclosure, similarity, or "belongingness," as opposed to a Euclidean or metric concept of spatial relations, governed by principles of abstract space and standardized units of measurement (Piaget & Inhelder, 1967; Piaget, Inhelder, & Szeminska, 1960). In either of these views, the children would be expected to rely heavily on segmentation in making their proximity judgments.

The results of the study confirmed this expectation (see Table 12.1). The 7-year-olds performed as though they relied exclusively on segmentation for all three varieties of problems. In the case of the first variety, this meant that the accuracy of performance did not differ from chance level. In the case of the second variety, this meant that the metric accuracy of their performance was significantly below chance level. For problems of the third variety, accuracy was significantly above chance level. Distance ratio had no effect for any of the varieties. Route segmentation apparently influenced the distance judgments of 10-year-olds and adults as much as it influenced the younger children. These two groups were also extremely inaccurate (in a metric sense) on problems of the second variety and extremely accurate on problems of the third variety. Distance

TABLE 12.1
Performance in the Two-alternative Proximity Judgment Task
(Allen, 1981)

	Type of Problem		
Grade Level	*Relationship of Distances Compared*	*Distance Ratio*	*Observed Proportion Scores*
Second	Both intrasegment	1:3	.58
	Both intrasegment	1:1.5	.39
	Intrasegment > intersegment	1:3	.27**
	Intrasegment > intersegment	1:1.5	.22**
	Intrasegment < intersegment	1:3	.88*
	Intrasegment < intersegment	1:1.5	.75
Fifth	Both intrasegment	1:3	.83*
	Both intrasegment	1:1.5	.55
	Intrasegment > intersegment	1:3	.20**
	Intrasegment > intersegment	1:1.5	.23**
	Intrasegment < intersegment	1:3	.97*
	Intrasegment < intersegment	1:1.5	.91*
College	Both intrasegment	1:3	.92*
	Both intrasegment	1:1.5	.53
	Intrasegment > intersegment	1:3	.30**
	Intrasegment > intersegment	1:1.5	.23**
	Intrasegment < intersegment	1:3	.88*
	Intrasegment < intersegment	1:1.5	.95*

*significantly above .50.
**significantly below .50.

ratio had no effect for these two varieties of the proximity problem, i.e., both the 1:1.5 ratio and the 1:3 ratio problems resulted in the same accuracy levels.

In a departure from the pattern of the younger children's performance, however, the 10-year-olds and adults performed above chance level on the easy problems (1:3 ratio) of the first variety, that is, problems in which all three scenes were from the same route segment. This was not the case with the difficult problems (1:1.5 ratio) of this variety. Thus, the findings indicated that subjects from all three age groups relied on route segmentation when possible in making judgments of comparative distance. When this source of information was not available, the older children and adults relied on a more difficult process involving the estimation and comparison of distances. Apparently, the younger children did not, or could not, exercise this ability. As in the previous section, these experiments can serve as a case study illustrating how a hypothetical construct can serve as an impetus for research on the development of macrospatial cognition. In this case, the proposition that route knowledge could be viewed as a form of linear order representation served as a point of departure for a developmental investigation of how route segmentation affects judgments of macrospatial distances. Recent work by Holyoak and Mah (1982), Maki (1981), and others on symbolic spatial linear orders provides an indication that this link to cognitive psychology will grow to be a profitable one for researchers studying macrospatial cognitive processes.

Clearly, the concept of linear order representations of macrospatial information has its most potent application to the study of route knowledge. However, it should be noted that effects similar to categorizational influences have been reported in macrospatial tasks other than the studies of distance judgments along routes presented above. Stevens and Coupe (1978) found that directional judgments were distorted when subjects were asked to determine the directional relationship between two locations in adjacent superordinate spatial regions. The directional relationship of the two locations were generally distorted to conform to the directional relationship of the two regions. For example, Reno, Nevada, was typically judged to be east of San Diego, California, when in fact it is north-northwest of that city. Thus, the idea of macrospatial categorization might itself serve to stimulate further progress in the study of macrospatial cognition.

Frames of Reference

The concept of frames of reference has already had a significant impact on research in macrospatial cognitive development. As described by Pick, Yonas, and Rieser (1979), a frame of reference is a locus or set of loci with respect to which spatial position is defined. The concept of frames of reference is extremely versatile—applicable across scales of space, age spans, and even species. Also, as pointed out by Pick et al. (1979), the expression has been used in theoretical contexts apart from spatial cognition, such as Minsky's (1975) work on artificial intelligence and Piaget's (1970) work on perspective taking. Yet, despite its versatility, the term has retained its integrity.

Hart and Moore (1973) outlined an ontogenetic progression in frames of reference used for macrospatial orientation that began with egocentric or body-centered orientation in infancy (e.g., left/right of self), added a fixed or object-centered system of reference in early childhood (e.g., toward/away from an environmental feature), and resulted in a coordinated or abstract system of reference in late childhood (e.g., north/south and east/west axes). The progression describes the order in which the ability to use these frames of reference is acquired and does not imply the elimination of a more primitive mode with the acquisition of a more advanced one. Thus, all three frames of reference are available in adulthood.

This general framework has been of significant benefit in motivating research. Particularly noteworthy have been studies of infants' (Acredolo, 1978; Cornell & Heth, 1979; Rieser, 1979) and young children's (Acredolo, 1976, 1977) use of different frames of reference in establishing a spatial relationship between themselves and the site of an environmental event. For the most part, these studies support the proposition that infants and children shift from an egocentric basis for determining the relationships between self and an event (e.g., looking, reaching, or moving left/right to observe an event) to an object-centered frame of reference (e.g., looking, reaching, or moving in a direction specified by an environmental cue). However, more research is needed to specify the role of environmental familiarity and task characteristics in these shifts. Studies of adults' orientation in large-scale environments (e.g., Bøøk & Gärling, 1981; Kozlowski & Bryant, 1977) are also amenable to a frames of reference interpretation.

The concept of frames of reference is relevant most directly to the study of configurational knowledge. Certainly, it is difficult to conceive of the ability to provide accurate information regarding the spatial interrelationships among a set of environmental features within a large-scale environment in the absence of a coordinated, abstract frame of reference. Yet, the concept is also applicable to studies of route knowledge. For example, instructions for following a route often include a combination of body-referenced directives (e.g., "turn left, then right, then right again"), object-referenced directives (e.g., "go past the two-story brick building"), and abstractly referenced directives (e.g., "continue traveling west for 2 miles").

Production Systems

Another construct with considerable heuristic promise is the production system (Newell & Simon, 1972), which ironically reflects Tolman's idea of "means-end readiness" (see Clayton & Woodyard, 1981). The production system has been shown to be a useful conceptual tool for specifying plans for locomoting through macrospatial environments (Kuipers, 1978). Some of its potential is currently being realized in studies of route planning and land navigation (Thorn-dyke, 1980). Actually the usefulness of the production system extends beyond the task of representing macrospatial knowledge per se. It will also serve as a powerful tool for investigating the components of macrospatial skills, including map interpretation, orienteering, navigating, and verbally communicating macrospatial information.

BEYOND "COGNITIVE MAPPING"

It would be improper to suggest a pot pourri of "useful" theoretical constructs for advancing empirical research in the area of the development of macrospatial cognition without also offering some idea of how these constructs could be part of an integrated conceptual scheme. Unfortunately, such a scheme would be speculative, held together by logical inference, informal analogy, and wishful thinking. Given this caveat, it is interesting to anticipate the components of an information-processing account of macrospatial cognition that goes beyond the nonspecific notion of cognitive mapping. Liben's (1982) three facts of spatial representation serve as an aid in previewing these components. Accordingly, metamemory, linear order representations, frames of reference, and production systems are considered in relation to spatial storage, spatial thought, and spatial products.

Spatial Storage

When regarded strictly as "cold storage," spatial memory plays a rather limited role in macrospatial cognition. When divorced from control and encoding mechanisms that fall under the category of spatial thought, spatial storage is involved only in low-level macrospatial activity, such as wayfinding based on recognition. Such activity would be of a reactive rather than an anticipatory nature, dependent upon a feature match between incoming perceptual information and data stored in memory. Developmental change in the capacity for this primitive activity, which can be related to Bruner's (1964) iconic representation or Piaget's (1970) sensorimotor intelligence, should be minimal. There is some evidence for developmental improvement in recognition memory (e.g., Kirasic, Siegel & Allen, 1980; Mandler & Robinson, 1978). However, such improvement can usually be attributed to the influence of conceptual factors influencing encoding. Improvement in children's recognition-based wayfinding could reflect increased skill in differentiating among environmental features with regard to their reliability within a particular spatial context. The same could be said for the observed shift from egocentric responding to responding based on an objective frame of reference in studies involving infants and young children (Acredolo, 1982).

Spatial Thought

A number of simple and complex processes are involved in spatial thought. These processes are responsible for most of the activity that can be referred to as spatial cognition. The most influential processes are those that are involved in the control of information. These control processes work in synchrony with attentional and encoding processes to create an information-seeking system. Attention is directed toward those environmental features that provide reliable information regarding the spatial environment. Of course, it must be assumed that the reliability and informativeness of features can be determined only through prior experience. Control mechanisms make reference to encoding schemes abstracted from past experience in directing attention to certain environmental features, or to be more precise, to certain qualities of those features. When viewed in this manner, control processes are synonymous with metamemory or metacognition, particularly in the "knowing how to know" sense. As discussed previously, developmental change in this aspect of metacognition appears to be dramatic over the early and middle childhood years. However, a great deal of research remains to be directed toward the question of how children acquire these control processes and apply them to various macrospatial tasks.

Once attention is focused on environmental features, information must be encoded if it is to be accessible on demand. Encoding encompasses some powerful cognitive operations—to use Piagetian terminology—including spatial concepts (e.g., topological, projective, and Euclidean space) and spatial relations (e.g., temporospatial order, comparative orientation, horizontality/verticality). The development of knowledge of these concepts and relations was the focal point of major theoretical and empirical work in the Piagetian tradition (e.g., Laurendeau & Pinard, 1970; Piaget & Inhelder, 1967), but its role in large-scale spatial cognition and behavior has been more a matter of conjecture rather than empirical investigation (see Newcombe, 1982).

It is in the context of schemes for encoding spatial relationships that the constructs of linear order representations and frames of reference fit into this speculative framework. Linear orders are conceptual constructions the capacity for which develops in early childhood (Brown, 1976). In primitive form, they provide the basis for simple anticipatory route following; in more complex form, they can serve as the basis for interlocational distance estimates along routes. This change in complexity, which reflects the influence of different, progressively acquired concepts of space, is for the most part undocumented by research. In contrast, quite a bit of research has been conducted on frames of reference, the developmental progression for which has been described earlier. The voluntary selection of one frame of reference over another actually reveals the influence of control processes, but the application of a frame of reference is a matter of encoding spatial location (Pick et al., 1979). As in the case of linear orderings, the developmental changes in this mode of encoding spatial relations reflect the acquisition of different concepts of space.

Once information is encoded, it is stored until needed to perform some task. Retrieval processes are employed to access stored information, and it is plausible to suggest that control processes again play an important role in interacting with these mechanisms for successful retrieval. It is also reasonable to propose a close relationship between encoding schemes and retrieval processes. For example, recalling a landmark should be facilitated if it were originally encoded in the context of a linear ordering. Information is typically retrieved for purposes of wayfinding. However, other tasks require some complex transformations of macrospatial information. Perspective-taking tasks (e.g., Siegel, 1981), for example, would require some combination of translation and comparison processes. These processes may reflect unique spatial abilities (McGee, 1979), but they also are influenced by the development of spatial concepts (Huttenlocher & Presson, 1973, 1979).

Spatial Products

The expression of macrospatial knowledge in the form of sketch maps, environmental models, or verbal instructions involves a set of executive processes applied to information that has been retrieved, and possibly transformed, from the spatial knowledge system. All products of macrospatial knowledge will necessarily be influenced by encoding processes. It is unlikely that spatial information not encoded originally will be available at a later date, particularly if encoding schemes have not been altered in the interim (see Liben, 1977). However, executive processes have their own unique influence on spatial products. For example, Siegel (1981; Siegel et al., 1978) has long argued that skill in map drawing can have a profound effect on assessments of macrospatial knowledge that are based on map scoring. In other words, sketch maps reflect knowledge of a particular area plus generalized skill in map drawing. Likewise, one could contend that verbal descriptions or instructions reflect specific macrospatial knowledge plus generalized verbal communication skills. In the final analysis, it must be acknowledged that performance on any task used by researchers to assess macrospatial knowledge is influenced to some extent by various demonstration or communication skills represented by executive processes.

In any event, the graphic, verbal, or even motoric expression of macrospatial knowledge can be characterized by a sequence of cognitive activities known as a production system. As indicated earlier, the production system provides an exhaustive listing of "condition–action" pairings designed to document the steps toward achievement of a desired goal state. Several researchers cited earlier have applied this construct to various aspects of macrospatial cognitive skill. It is interesting to note that Thorndyke (1981) suggested this conceptualization of macrospatial knowledge as a means of bridging the gap between cognitive psychologists and environmental psychologists studying spatial cognition. Unquestionably, it is a powerful tool for specifying the processes and activities that are presumed to be involved in an expression of macrospatial knowledge, and as such it represents a departure from the vagueness that has characterized previous process-oriented accounts of these activities. However, the extent to which the concept of production systems will actually serve to stimulate developmental research on macrospatial cognition remains to be seen.

Summary

The purpose of this section was to demonstrate how the four theoretical constructs identified earlier could fit into a single framework for conceptualizing macrospatial cognitive processes. The speculative framework that was offered could be considered an end unto itself, or it could be taken as a rough outline for a more comprehensive view of the development of macrospatial cognition from an information-processing perspective. Regardless of its heuristic potential, this brief sketch illustrates some of the conceptual and empirical challenges that lie beyond the era of the cognitive map.

THE COGNITIVE PROCESSING APPROACH IN PERSPECTIVE

This chapter has been concerned with establishing stronger ties between the study of the development of macrospatial cognition and the experimental investigation of human cognition. In closing, it is important to add a few disclaimers in order to keep this endeavor in proper perspective. First, experimentation is not construed to be the only valid scientific method for gaining a better understanding of how children and adults learn about and behave in their spatial environments. Certainly, our understanding is advanced as much—if not more—by comprehensive field study (e.g., Hart, 1979) as by experimentation. Nevertheless, the experimental approach affords obvious advantages in terms of the control and manipulation of experience that cannot be found in other methods, and thus it makes a unique contribution to scientific inquiry. Experimental work and field work in the study of macrospatial cognitive development should complement each other so that better experimental research leads to more effective, better focused field work, and improved field studies, in turn, lead to more clear-cut issues for experimental investigation.

A second matter, related to the first, involves the frequent complaint that experimental studies of children's macrospatial cognition ignore motivational and situational factors that influence cognitive performance in real-world settings. It is undeniable that macrospatial cognition, as well as reading and mathematical operations for that matter, occurs in a social ecological context and that this context has an impact on the quality of cognitive activity that takes place (Siegel, 1982). Accordingly, more concern is being shown for introducing experimental tasks in realistic contexts (e.g., Cohen, 1982). However, at the heart of experimentalism is the practice of reducing the complexity of the phenomenon under study in order to build a body of evidence based upon a foundation of certainty. More complex issues are addressed on the basis of findings from research on simpler issues. In the absence of both the necessary experimental technology and the foundation of evidence from earlier studies that would permit the examination of macrospatial cognition within the psychosocial milieu, experimentalists study performance on tasks abstracted from that milieu. As mentioned previously, this strategy yields the greatest dividends when it is complemented by other scientific approaches. As the state of the art improves, experimentalists should be able, as Siegel (1981) put it, to "ask better questions."

A final point should be made regarding the theoretical constructs suggested as being useful in this research area. These constructs were not selected because of their universal acceptance or uniform definition. Instead, they were pointed out because (a) they differentiate among a number of phenomena that in the not too distant past could have been lumped under the rubrics "cognitive map" and "cognitive mapping," and (b) they are applicable to, and in fact were developed in, different research areas. These qualities heighten the likelihood of their utility in strengthening the link between the experimental study of human cognition and the developmental study of macrospatial cognition.

REFERENCES

Acredolo, L. P. Frames of reference used by children for orientation used in unfamiliar spaces. In G. Moore & R. Golledge (Eds.), *Environmental knowing*. Stroudsburg, PA: Dowden, Hutchinson, & Ross, 1976.

Acredolo, L. P. Developmental changes in the ability to coordinate perspectives of a large-scale space. *Developmental Psychology, 1977, 13,* 1–8.

Acredolo, L. P. Development of spatial orientation in infancy. *Developmental Psychology,* 1978, *14,* 224–234.

Acredolo, L. P. The familiarity factor in spatial research. In R. Cohen (Ed.), *New directions for child development: Vol. 15. Children's conceptions of spatial relations.* San Francisco: Jossey-Bass, 1982.

Acredolo, L. P., Pick, H. L., & Olsen, M. G. Environmental differentiation and familiarity as determinants of children's memory for spatial location. *Developmental Psychology, 1975, 11,* 495–501.

Allen, G. L. A developmental perspective on the effects of "subdividing" macrospatial experience. *Journal of Experimental Psychology: Human Learning and Memory, 1981, 7,* 120–132.

Allen, G. L., Kirasic, K. C., Siegel, A. W., & Herman, J. F. Developmental issues in cognitive mapping: The selection and utilization of environmental landmarks. *Child Development, 1979, 50,* 1062–1070.

Beck, R. J., & Wood, D. Cognitive transformations from urban geographic fields to mental maps. *Environment and Behavior, 1976, 8,* 199–238.

Bøøk, A. & Gärling, T. Maintenance of orientation during locomotion in unfamiliar environments. *Journal of Experimental Psychology: Perception and Performance,* 1981, *7,* 995–1006.

Brown, A. L. The development of memory: Knowing, knowing about knowing, and knowing how to know. In H. W. Reese (Ed.), *Advances in child development and behavior* (Vol. 10). New York: Academic Press, 1975.

Brown, A. L. The construction of temporal succession by preoperational children. In A. D. Pick (Ed.), *Minnesota Symposium on Child Psychology* (Vol. 10). Minneapolis: University of Minnesota Press, 1976.

Bruner, J. S. The course of cognitive growth. *American Psychologist,* 1964, *19,* 1–15.

Carr, S., & Schissler, D. The city as a trip: Perceptual selection and memory in the view from the road. *Environment and Behavior,* 1969, *1,* 7–35.

Chase, W. G., & Chi, M. Cognitive skill: Implications for spatial skill in large-scale environments. In J. Harvey (Ed.), *Cognition, social behavior, and the environment.* Hillsdale, NJ: Lawrence Erlbaum Associates, 1981.

Clayton, K., & Woodyard, M. The acquisition and utilization of spatial knowledge. In J. Harvey (Ed.), *Cognition, social behavior, and the environment.* Hillsdale, NJ: Lawrence Erlbaum Associates, 1981.

Cohen, R. The role of activity in the construction of spatial representations. In R. Cohen (Ed.), *New directions for child development: Vol. 15. Children's conceptions of spatial relationships.* San Francisco: Jossey-Bass, 1982.

Cohen, R., Weatherford, D. L., & Byrd, D. Distance estimates of children as a function of acquisition and response activities. *Journal of Experimental Child Psychology,* 1980, *30,* 464–472.

Cornell, E. H., & Heth, C. D. Response versus place learning by human infants. *Journal of Experimental Psychology: Human Learning and Memory,* 1979, *5,* 188–196.

Curtis, L., Siegel, A. W., & Furlong, N. E. Developmental differences in cognitive mapping: Configurational knowledge of familiar large-scale environments. *Journal of Experimental Child Psychology,* 1981, *31,* 456–469.

Downs, R. M. Cognitive mapping and information processing: A commentary. In G. Moore & R. Golledge (Eds.), *Environmental knowing.* Stroudsburg, PA; Dowden, Hutchinson, & Ross, 1976.

Downs, R. M. Maps and mapping as metaphors for spatial representation. In L. Liben, A. Patterson, & N. Newcombe (Eds.), *Spatial representation and behavior across the life span.* New York: Academic Press, 1981.

Downs, R. M., & Siegel, A. W. On mapping researchers mapping children mapping space. In L. Liben, A. Patterson, & N. Newcombe (Eds.), *Spatial representation and behavior across the life span.* New York: Academic Press, 1981.

Downs, R. M., & Stea, D. Cognitive maps and spatial behavior: Process and products. In R. Downs & D. Stea (Eds.), *Image and environment.* Chicago: Aldine, 1973.

Flavell, J. H. Developmental studies of mediated memory. In H. W. Reese & L. P. Lipsitt (Eds.), *Advances in child development and behavior* (Vol. 5). New York: Academic Press, 1970.

Flavell, J. H., & Wellman, H. M. Metamemory. In R. V. Kail & J. W. Hagen (Eds.), *Perspectives on the development of memory and cognition.* Hillsdale, NJ: Lawrence Erlbaum Associates, 1977.

Gibson, E. J. *Principles of perceptual learning and development.* New York: Appleton-Century-Crofts, 1969.

Gibson, J. J. *The senses considered as perceptual systems.* Boston: Houghton Mifflin, 1966.

Hart, R. *Children's experience of place.* New York: Irvington/Halsted, 1979.

Hart, R. A., & Moore, G. T. The development of spatial cognition: A review. In R. Downs & D. Stea (Eds.), *Image and environment.* Chicago: Aldine, 1973.

Hazen, N. L., Lockman, J. J., & Pick, H. L. The development of children's representations of large-scale environments. *Child Development,* 1978, *49,* 623–636.

Herman, J. F. Children's cognitive maps of large-scale spaces: Effects of exploration, direction, and repeated experience. *Journal of Experimental Child Psychology*, 1980, *29*, 126–143.

Holyoak, K. J. Comparative judgments with numerical reference points. *Cognitive Psychology*, 1978, *10*, 203–243.

Holyoak, K. J., & Mah, W. A. Cognitive reference points in judgments of symbolic magnitudes. *Cognitive Psychology*, 1982, *14*, 328–352.

Huttenlocker, J., & Presson, C. C. Mental rotation and the perspective problem. *Cognitive Psychology*, 1973, *4*, 277–299.

Huttenlocker, J., & Presson, C. C. The coding and transformation of spatial information. *Cognitive Psychology*, 1979, *11*, 375–394.

Kirasic, K. C., Siegel, A. W., & Allen, G. L. The development of basic processes in cognitive mapping: Recognition-in-context memory. *Child Development*, 1980, *51*, 302–305.

Klahr, D., & Chase, W. G. *Developmental changes in latency patterns for access to the alphabet.* Paper presented at meetings of the Psychonomic Society, San Antonio, November 1978.

Kosslyn, S. M. *Image and mind.* Cambridge: Harvard University Press, 1980.

Kozlowski, L., & Bryant, K. Sense of direction, spatial orientation, and cognitive maps. *Journal of Experimental Psychology: Perception and Performance*, 1977, *3*, 590–598.

Kuipers, B. J. Modeling spatial knowledge. *Cognitive Science*, 1978, *2*, 129–153.

Laurendeau, M., & Pinard, A. *The development of the concept of space in the child.* New York: International Universities Press, 1970.

Liben, L. S. Memory in the context of cognitive development: The Piagetian approach. In R. Kail & J. Hagen (Eds.), *Perspectives on the development of memory and cognition.* Hillsdale, NJ: Lawrence Erlbaum Associates, 1977.

Liben, L. S. Children's large-scale spatial cognition: Is the measure the message. In R. Cohen (Ed.), *New directions for child development: Vo. 15. Children's conceptions of spatial relationships.* San Francisco: Jossey-Bass, 1982.

Lynch, K. *The image of the city.* Cambridge: MIT Press, 1960.

Maki, R. H. Categorization and distance effects with spatial linear orders. *Journal of Experimental Psychology: Human Learning and Memory*, 1981, *7*, 15–32.

Mandler, J. M., & Robinson, C. A. Developmental changes in picture recognition. *Journal of Experimental Child Psychology*, 1978, *16*, 122–136.

McGee, M. G. Human spatial abilities: Psychometric studies and environmental, genetic, hormonal, and neurological influences. *Psychological Bulletin*, 1979, *86*, 889–918.

Minsky, M. A. A framework for representing knowledge. In P. H. Winston (Ed.), *The psychology of computer vision.* New York: McGraw-Hill, 1975.

Moore, G. T. Theory and research on the development of environmental knowing. In G. Moore & R. Golledge (Eds.), *Environmental knowing.* Stroudsburg, PA: Dowden, Hutchinson, & Ross, 1976.

Moore, G. T., & Golledge, R. G. Environmental knowing: Concepts and theories. In G. Moore & R. Golledge (Eds.), *Environmental knowing.* Stroudsburg, PA: Dowden, Hutchinson, & Ross, 1976.

Moyer, R. S., & Bayer, R. H. Mental comparison and the symbolic distance effect. *Cognitive Psychology*, 1976, *8*, 228–246.

Moyer, R. S., & Dumais, S. T. Mental comparison. In G. H. Bower (Ed.), *The psychology of learning and motivation* (Vol. 12). New York: Academic Press, 1978.

Newcombe, N. Development of spatial cognition and cognitive development. In R. Cohen (Ed.), *New directions for child development: Vol. 15. Children's conceptions of spatial relationships.* San Francisco; Jossey-Bass, 1982.

Newell, A., & Simon, H. A. *Human problem solving.* Englewood Cliffs, NJ: Prentice-Hall, 1972.

O'Keefe, J., & Nadel, L. *The hippocampus as a cognitive map.* New York: Oxford University Press, 1978.

Pepper, S. C. *World hypotheses.* Berkeley: University of California Press, 1970.

Piaget, J. *The construction of reality in the child.* New York: Basic Books, 1954.

Piaget, J. *Genetic epistemology.* New York: Norton, 1970.

Piaget, J., & Inhelder, B. *The child's conception of space.* New York: Norton, 1967.

Piaget, J., Inhelder, B., & Szeminska, A. *The child's conception of geometry.* New York: Basic Books, 1960.

Pick, H. L., Yonas, A., & Rieser, J. Spatial reference systems in perceptual development. In M. H. Bornstein & W. Kessen (Eds.), *Psychological development from infancy: Image to intention.* Hillsdale, NJ: Lawrence Erlbaum Associates, 1979.

Potts, G. R. Information processing strategies used in the encoding of linear orderings. *Journal of Verbal Learning and Verbal Behavior,* 1972, *11,* 727–740.

Potts, G. R. Storing and retrieving information about ordered relationships. *Journal of Experimental Psychology,* 1974, *103,* 431–439.

Rieser, J. J. Reference systems and the spatial orientation of six month old infants. *Child Development,* 1979, *50,* 1078–1087.

Rosch, E., & Lloyd, B. B. (Eds.) *Cognition and categorization.* Hillsdale, NJ: Lawrence Erlbaum Associates, 1978.

Sadalla, E. K., Burroughs, W. J., & Staplin, L. J. Reference points in spatial cognition. *Journal of Experimental Psychology: Human Learning and Memory,* 1980, *6,* 516–528.

Sadalla, E. K., & Staplin, L. J. The perception of traversed distance: Intersections. *Environment and Behavior,* 1980, *12,* 167–182.

Siegel, A. W. The externalization of cognitive maps by children and adults: In search of ways to ask better questions. In L. Liben, A. Patterson, & N. Newcombe (Eds.), *Spatial representation and behavior across the life span.* New York: Academic Press, 1981.

Siegel, A. W. Towards a social ecology of cognitive mapping. In R. Cohen (Ed.), *New directions for child development: Vol. 15. Children's conceptions of spatial relationships.* San Francisco: Jossey-Bass, 1982.

Siegel, A. W., Kirasic, K. C., & Kail, R. V. Stalking the elusive cognitive map: The development of children's representations of geographic space. In J. F. Wohlwill & I. Altman (Eds.), *Human behavior and the environment* (Vol. 3). New York: Plenum, 1978.

Siegel, A. W., & White, S. H. The development of spatial representations of large-scale environments. In H. W. Reese (Ed.), *Advances in child development and behavior* (Vol. 10). New York: Academic Press, 1975.

Stevens, A., & Coupe, P. Distortions in judged spatial relations. *Cognitive Psychology,* 1978, *10,* 422–437.

Thorndyke, P. W. *Performance models for spatial and locational cognition* (R-2676-ONR). Santa Monica, CA: The Rand Corporation, December 1980.

Thorndyke, P. W. Spatial cognition and reasoning. In J. Harvey (Ed.), *Cognition, social behavior, and the environment.* Hillsdale, NJ: Lawrence Erlbaum Associates, 1981.

Tolman, E. C. Cognitive maps in rats and men. *Psychological Review,* 1948, *55,* 189–208.

Werner, H. *Comparative psychology of mental development.* New York: International Universities Press, 1948.

Werner, H. The concept of development from a comparative and organismic point of view. In D. Harris (Ed.), *The concept of development.* Minneapolis: University of Minnesota Press, 1957.

Woocher, F. D., Glass, A. L., & Holyoak, K. J. Positional discriminability in linear orderings. *Memory and Cognition,* 1978, *6,* 165–173.

13 The Representation of Space: Its Development in Children and in Cartography

Roger M. Downs
The Pennsylvania State University

INTRODUCTION

If we look carefully at the progress of recent work on the development of spatial cognition, we can see a research tradition emerging. The tradition consists of basic concepts, models, techniques, and data sources. For example, many of the central ideas are built on the theoretical position introduced by Piaget (Piaget & Inhelder, 1967; Piaget, Inhelder, & Szeminska, 1960), a position subsequently elaborated and refined by Hart and Moore (1973) and by Siegel and White (1975). Without question, this tradition has served us well. It has generated a remarkable volume of interesting work in a relatively short period of time, and it has provided a comfortable context within which we can organize our teaching, research, and publishing. In short, there is a conventional wisdom emerging, one that is collectively subscribed to and tacitly accepted.

This chapter is both a critical reflection on this tradition and a speculation about some alternative ideas that we might want to consider before the conventional wisdom becomes too firmly entrenched. Given the normal dynamics of a conventional wisdom, many things are taken as obvious and/or as given: as a consequence, they escape critical attention. I want to question one important part of the conventional wisdom, that surrounding the understanding of maps and cartography. The centrality of the map idea to work on spatial cognition is beyond dispute. It is interesting, for example, to look at the impact of some basic mapping studies. We might turn to the original Piagetian "coordination of perspectives" task involving the three mountains study (Piaget & Inhelder, 1967). To this, we could add the mapping tasks based on the sandbox school model (Piaget et al., 1960). Underpinning both of these tasks are a series of linked ideas: the use of spatial models as environmental representations; the importance of scale change and perspective change as properties of the cognitive mapping process; the view of the child as being a maker and user of map-like representations of space. The creative elaboration of these tasks has been a central concern; they form the basis for the subsequent work by Hart (1979) and Siegel (1981). The elaboration of the work on the coordination of perspectives is a testimony to the strength of the empirical method: equally well, it shows the subtle way in which a tradition of work feeds on itself and becomes entrenched.

In a similar vein, we could discuss the extent to which our thinking about basic cognitive concepts has been influenced by the use of the map idea (Downs, 1981a). Both the real world and the world in the head can be captured conveniently by the idea of a map. Although the precise interpretation of the cognitive map is unclear (that is, its metaphorical and/or analogical character), its centrality is beyond question. Clearly, therefore, to speak about the development of spatial cognition is to speak in terms of maps and mapping. Equally clearly, this is based on a presumed level of understanding of maps and cartography on the part of thinkers about spatial cognition.

The basis for this presumed level of understanding is the use of maps and cartography as means of expressing and representing space and spatial relationship. I am interested in the ways in which the conventional wisdom *has* made use of maps and cartography, *and* the ways in which we *might* make use of maps and cartography in order to understand the development of spatial cognition. Specifically, I am interested in the questions that we are and are *not* asking, in the expectations that we do and do *not* have, and in the data that we do and do *not* choose to accept. In these respects, the conventional wisdom acts as a guide and as a constraint. I want to highlight both roles by drawing on an understanding of maps and cartography that goes considerably beyond the incomplete and impoverished version that is currently accepted and presumed.

To this end, I begin with a basic *thesis*. I believe that cartography has played and continues to play a central role in the attempt to understand spatial cognition and its development. However, many facets of this central role are hidden in the sense of being overlooked and ignored. If we consider this central role in detail, three significant points emerge. First, there has been, and continues to be, a considerable amount of serious misunderstanding about the nature of maps and cartography. Second, the relationship between spatial cognition and cartography is incredibly complex; there are similarities, parallels, interdependencies, and interactions that border on paradoxes. Third, the potential value of cartography as a source of alternative ways of understanding has not been fully appreciated.

The remainder of this chapter is a first attempt to sketch in the outlines of this thesis, with a particular emphasis being placed on the third point. The chapter is organized in the following way: we (a) explore the meaning and importance of cartography; (b) analyze the current uses of cartography in understanding spatial cognition in general; (c) detail some points of contact between cartography and the development of spatial cognition in particular; and (d) review some alternative ways of understanding the development of spatial cognition. These alternatives focus on the goals and nature of the process of development.

THE MEANING OF CARTOGRAPHY

Cartography is broadly defined here. I would like to include not just cartography in the traditional meaning of the theory and practice of graphic map making, but also include computer cartography, architectural and engineering drawing, modern interactive C.R.T. graphics, photogrammetry, and remote sensing. In going beyond the narrow base of the traditional view of cartography, we see a field that is bound together by three essential concerns: (1) a concern with the intrinsic geometrical properties of space and thus the relationships between objects in space; (2) a concern with the extrinsic geometrical relations between spaces and their representations; and (3) a concern with the technical possibilities and limitations of different modes for the representation of space.

Working definitions of maps are surprisingly hard to find, even in cartography! At the heart of any definition is that always useful, though somewhat artificial, distinction among form, structure, and function. Rather than following the traditional path that begins with the ostensible form of a map, let me start my definition instead with the function of a map as a representation.

By setting cartography in a broad base, we can see that underpinning all three of the above concerns is the *essential function of a map*: that is, rendering the experience of space comprehensible. As Treib (1980, p. 22) argues, "maps are the projections of experience." That experience can be direct and personal—the neighborhood sketch map—or indirect and impersonal—a Landsat-3 satellite image based on a remote, multispectral scanner. Whatever its specific form, the map as a representation must evoke appearances in a manner sufficient to create (or if one chooses, reflect) a world that is convincing, that is thought to be *real*. Even in the case of the satellite image, the map is convincing because it maintains that essential hypothetical property: "This is what the world would look like if. . . ." Such realism does not depend necessarily upon a literal, pictorial verisimilitude. The map is neither mirror nor miniature; it is a model of the world. The map is a representation, and thus a carefully controlled symbolic abstraction.

From the point of view of *structure,* there are two ways of looking at a map. As a representation *of a* space *in* space, the map itself possesses an intrinsic geometry. As a representation of some other space, the map shares an extrinsic geometry that specifies its relation to the original space. Both extrinsic and intrinsic properties are defined by the mapping function that generates the map. (For more detailed discussions of these ideas, see Callahan, 1976, and Downs, 1981a). It is worth stressing that the nature of the particular geometry or mapping function does not have to be specified in a general definition of a map. Maps can be based on a wide variety of geometries: metric, projective, and topological. It is the ostensible *form* of a map that normally commands our attention and thus dominates most attempts to define a map. Thus we become overly concerned with a limited expression of form: the "standard" cartographic map becomes the printed road map with its particular symbols, key, scale, orientation, and so on. The broad base for definition removes this constraint and offers an alternative sense of map form. Form is expressed through the technology of cartographic production. Techniques, what we might call *cartographics*, are particular systems for rendering the experience of space comprehensible. There is a wide range of systems of cartographics. Lines, for example, can be the basis for a contour interpretation of landform and relief; alternatively, lines can portray the "transparent," skeletal structure for the rotating representation of the surface of a three-dimensional object on a C.R.T. screen. In both instances, the use of the line as the basis for a cartographic form is an exercise in persuasive rhetoric. The map reader is convinced that this *is* an acceptable and comprehensible representation.

The key to this broad definition of cartography is the view of a map as a persuasive representation that we accept as real. A map is a representation, *not* the thing being represented. A map can take a wide range of representational forms. A map is persuasive to the extent that its cartographics convey a form that evokes appearances; in order to convince, it does not have to mirror appearances. A map is real to the extent that we find the rhetoric acceptable and see a world made comprehensible. Above all else, the ideas of rhetoric and persuasion remind us that a map is a shared exercise in communication. Before we try to make use of this definition in understanding the development of spatial cognition, it is worth reflecting on the current relationship between the general field of spatial cognition and cartography.

THE CURRENT ROLE OF CARTOGRAPHY IN UNDERSTANDING SPATIAL COGNITION

There seem to be four major ways in which the presumed understanding of cartography influences work on spatial cognition. The first three of these are easy to understand, and while the fourth is more ambiguous and indeterminate, it is the most significant. For the sake of this discussion, I identify these four aspects as the *science*, the *art*, the *products*, and the *metaphysics* of cartography.

Science of Cartography

The science of cartography refers to the theory of mapping, and it is useful to consider this theory as being composed of two parts. On the one hand is the conceptual structure of maps as analog models, which leads to the attendant ideas of generalization, schematization, and symbolization (see Downs, 1981b). On the other hand is the geometrical/mathematical theory of map projections, with ideas of projection points, surfaces, and the relations between points, surfaces, and the object to be mapped (see Downs, 1981a).

Cognitive psychologists have drawn on the theory of mapping extensively. It provides an essential part of the context for understanding the "appropriate" geometrical model for describing the properties of cognitive representations of space. Thus researchers talk about Euclidian models, locally Euclidian models, or non-Euclidian models. "Good" maps are ones whose essential properties can be specified in terms of an intrinsic *metric* geometry; the same seems to be true for "good" cognitive models of space. Here I am thinking of the adaptation of Piaget's ideas, of the long-standing debate over the topological-projective-Euclidian developmental sequence. Extending this rationale, the idea of "good" maps leads directly to the numerous attempts to calculate error and/or distortion as they exist in cognitive models and as these characteristics change with either microgenesis or ontogenesis.

Art of Cartography

The art of cartography refers to the technical possibilities of graphic construction, to the sense of graphic design, and to the map as an exercise in rhetoric and persuasion. The ideas of graphic construction and graphic design might be thought of as a continuum that ranges from explicit understanding with its attendant quality of precision, to implicit, intuitive judgments and rules of thumb with their attendant imprecision. The precision of graphic construction comes from the quantified psychophysical relationships that have been established between apparent and absolute magnitude scalings for texture, color value, color intensity, and area and volume symbols. The imprecision of graphic design rests on the injunctions that are issued to cartographic novices: delete the reference coordinate grid "under" the land masses to "lift" the land out of the water; avoid parallel lines because they "hurt" the eyes; and the one that is my favorite, avoid "wiggly" lines because they are indecisive.

Again, there are innumerable points of contact between these ideas and the understanding of spatial cognition. Braille maps for the blind depend upon adapting an understanding of spatial symbol systems (see Leonard & Newman, 1970; Rosencranz & Suslick, 1976). There is a major body of work dealing with the comprehension of terrain relief (see Wood, 1977). For obvious reasons, there is a practical concern with the ability to comprehend terrain relief patterns. Does one use a digital coding system, with spot numerical values for height? An analog coding system, with hachuring to indicate slope angle, shadow effects, and color gradations? Or is the answer a hybrid digital-analog system, with contour lines, spot values, and color gradations?

Products of Cartography

The products of cartography are specific maps. These may be either particular types of maps (for example, topographic maps) or they may be maps of a particular place. Once again, the ties with our understanding of spatial cognition are strong. There are attempts to understand the way in which exposure to a limited class of map projections, modified Mercator projections, leads to a pervasive misunderstanding of proportional area relationships (the famous "Greenland" effect); minimum distance relationships (the Great Circle effect); and orientation (the North-Up, South-Down effect). For recent examples of this work, see Evans and Pezdek, 1980, and Tversky, 1981. A second body of work deals with the success and failure of maps as devices to aid in human wayfinding. Examples are Henry Beck's 1931 London Underground map, a much-imitated success, and Massimo Vignelli's 1972 New York Subway map, a failure that was rapidly abandoned. Good introductions to this literature can be found in Treib (1980) and Levine (1982).

Metaphysics of Cartography

I find the most interesting use of cartography to be the metaphysics of cartography, yet it is an elusive idea, one that is difficult to convey. By metaphysics, I mean the way in which we automatically and unquestioningly accept ideas of maps and mapping as logical and obvious ways of expressing the idea of space and of representing the world in which we live. In a sense, cartography is a "natural" way of thinking. The use of spatial expressions is fundamental to the structure of natural language and thinking. There is an apparently perfect match between experience, language, and thought. We can, and therefore do, readily borrow the logic, the concepts, the language, and the techniques of cartography to express and understand spatial cognition.

To illustrate the extent of this borrowing, consider the genesis of three of the most recent major attempts to model the structure and function of cognitive representations of space. O'Keefe and Nadel (1978), Kuipers (1978), and Lieblich and Arbib (1982) all base their arguments on the idea of the spatial or cartographic map. There is an inescapable connection between cartography and spatial cognition—cartography as a way of thinking is both pervasive and persuasive.

For my part, I have absolutely no wish to escape from this connection, nor do I believe that it is possible to do so. There are, however, three pertinent questions that I explore in succeeding parts of this chapter. First, to what extent *is* it appropriate to borrow so extensively and readily? In effect, this question is a restatement of the problem of the use of formal systems to explore the nature of psychological reality. Does the psychological reality correspond to the structure of the formal system? Sternberg (1980) points out that such formalisms often have proved to be red herrings. Thus an understanding of the structure of the formal systems of logic, probability, and statistics did not necessarily assist in, and often hindered, attempts to understand everyday propositional, syllogistic, and statistical reasoning. We must, therefore, ask whether the formal system of cartography is an appropriate base from which to consider the development of spatial cognition.

This leads immediately to the second question: What *is* the formal system of cartography that we have presumed in our attempts to understand spatial cognition? In essence, I believe that not only is cartography misunderstood, but cartography is far more *in*formal and *un*systematic than is commonly believed. Moreover, cartography is a representational system that has undergone, and continues to undergo, some dramatic transformations. Far from being a stable, well-articulated system of theoretically grounded knowledge and practice, cartography itself bears a striking resemblance to what we know about a child's attempts to come to terms with and to master the experience of space. The next section of the chapter shows that the history of cartography and the development of spatial cognition have much in common: we can talk about both in similar ways.

From this discussion emerges the third question about the cognition-cartography nexus: Are there some alternative ways of interpreting the development of spatial cognition using a much broader understanding of the history of cartography? The final section is a detailed answer in the affirmative, which suggests that a misunderstanding of cartography has often led to a misunderstanding of the development of spatial cognition.

CARTOGRAPHY AND THE DEVELOPMENT OF SPATIAL COGNITION

Given the cognition-cartography nexus, it is not surprising to find some complex points of contact between the history of cartography and the study of the development of spatial cognition. Three levels of statements exist: similarities, parallels, and interdependencies. Examining these levels will allow us to see ideas that we might wish to pursue and phenomena worthy of explanation.

The most obvious *similarity* concerns the goal of cognition and of cartography. They both render the experience of space comprehensible and useful to the self and to others. Moreover, both change in ways that we choose to see as a progressive form of development. One form is called ontogenesis, the other history or evolution. (Wood, 1977 uses the term "ethnogenesis" for the latter.) These two deceptively simple similarities are fraught with a number of unresolved problems. Progressive development toward what goal? It is difficult to specify the goal of the development process and cope with its teleological character.

Since the reader is likely to be familiar with this issue from the cognitive development perspective, let me interpret it in a cartographic context. What is the "goal-as-destination" of cartography? Better maps obviously—but in what sense? There is a range of candidates: a quantitative answer would suggest an increasingly comprehensive coverage of the earth's surface at a smaller and smaller scale. Qualitative answers might include more accurate maps, more realistic maps, a greater variety of map forms, maps which are more effective, and so forth. In each instance, the goal is nebulous and imprecise. Assuming that a goal could be specified, how is it being attained? What is the character of the developmental process in cartography? Is the change continuous and incremental, or discontinuous and discrete? Is it cumulative and hierarchical, or full of radical restructurings? Is it purposive or accidental?

These questions have *not* been answered in the history of cartography, although Harvey (1980) makes an admirable first effort. For cognitive development, these questions are precisely those at the heart of the Piagetian tradition. If developmental theorists are assuming that the understanding of the formal system of cartography is well grounded from a historical-genesis point of view, they will be disappointed. There are cartographic histories that arrange significant events in a chronological order—but these beg the question. Virgil Thompson's (1981) comment about the history of music finds an appropriate echo here:

> Though repeating patterns do seem to recur in any such narrative, organic development is notoriously difficult to identify. In the arts, certainly, the creating, elaborating, and transmitting of techniques are basic procedures, but among these there are few long-term growths. They are more like inventions—say the fish net, the wheelbarrow, or pie crust—which once they have come miraculously into being stay on. (p. 47)

And yet we have allowed our chronological understanding of techniques of cartographics to influence our interpretations of children's maps. As shown in the next section, answers to questions about the goals and character of the developmental process are crucial to the interpretations that we make, to the questions that we ask, and to the data that we are willing to accept.

Beyond these obvious similarities, a second level of statements denotes some fascinating *parallels* between cognition and cartography. If the term "map" designates the products of both cognition and cartography, then four issues are evident. (Of course, equating the products of cognition with maps begs a fundamental question that lacks anything approaching a satisfactory answer.) In exploring these parallels, I focus on the cartography side of the argument. First, maps are everywhere within a culture and occur across all cultures. Recognizing the limitations of the archival and archaeological record, and the spotty nature of the evidence, it appears that no culture, past or present, is without map forms that would fit any ostensible definition. Second, maps can appear "early" in human ontogenesis and do appear early on in cultural development. Harvey (1980) has an excellent discussion of the earliest cartographic maps, and offers rock carvings from the Valcamonica area of north Italy, dating from the second millenium B.C., as candidates for the earliest known maps. Third, in discussing developmentally "early" or culturally "primitive" map forms, we must be careful not to make inappropriate relative judgments. Taken in context, it is as sensible to call children's maps or Australian aboriginal maps "sophisticated" as to call them "inaccurate" and "distorted." Fourth, at the most basic level the structure and functions of maps have remained essentially constant through time. It is the technology of map production, cartographics, that is most noticeably variable. Cartographic development, for example, is very much concerned with the rhetoric of cartographic persuasion, with the design of symbols and the establishment of graphic conventions that allow the expression of a comprehensible, realistic view of the world. Could the same set of statements be made with respect to children's cartographic representations as these change with age, education, and spatial experience? We consider this question in the next section of the chapter.

The third level of statements about points of contact between spatial cognition and cartography is the most problematical because it deals with the complex *interdependencies* between the study of spatial cognition and cartography. Let me identify the two most important of these interdependencies. The first points to the relation between conventional views of the world and beliefs about the world. Thus we find that our view of the world is shaped by the way that we map it, and in circular fashion, it is no less true that our maps of the world are shaped by the way that we view it. The second points to the relations between the current practice of cartography, our expectations about the world, and the way that we study views of the world. Thus we find that, on the one hand, cartography and its products shape the nature of expectations about what the world *does* and therefore *should* look like. On the other hand, cartography (in the senses of its science, art, and metaphysics) shapes the procedures and criteria by which we study and analyze the products of the cognition of the world. As a result of these interdependencies, one could say that cartography is at once descriptive . . . and prescriptive, generative . . . and interpretive.

ALTERNATIVE WAYS OF UNDERSTANDING THE DEVELOPMENT OF SPATIAL COGNITION

Thus, there is a complex interaction between cartography and the representation of the world. This complexity can take on the character of a paradox when we return to the argument that cartography itself can, and I would argue must, be set in a developmental context. Thus the formal system, the "yardstick," for assessing, interpreting, and understanding the development of spatial cognition is itself undergoing developmental change. At the same time, this changing yardstick may be affecting the very same thing that we are trying to calibrate, namely the ontogenesis of spatial cognition.

This is a highly speculative and contentious argument, but one with significant implications for the nature of work on the development of spatial cognition. As an illustration, consider children's graphic representations of space. A typical set of judgments would suggest that these graphic representations are arbitrary, inconsistent, and inaccurate. These maps fail, as an act of persuasion, at least from our adult point of view. Specifically, the basis for these judgments is the use of strange pictorial symbols, multiple perspectives, and multiple scales within the same representation. These three characteristics support the adult judgments of arbitrariness, inconsistency, and thus inaccuracy, *if* we accept that the conventions of abstract symbols, a single perspective (preferably orthographic), and a simple linear scale are part of the conventions of "standard" cartography.

There is an alternative interpretation of these graphic representations that renders the typical set of judgments as itself being arbitrary and inconsistent. One could argue with equal force that the child has not yet learned to (or is it agreed to?) accept the constraints and power of another, conventional mode of cartographic representation. In this view, development becomes a process of self-limitation, and therefore progressive attainment could be considered as the progressive acceptance of conventional constraint. What the typical judgments are really saying is that the child is not following the "normal" dictates of cartographic convention. The irony of this position is the relativism of a judgment based on cartographic conventions that have themselves undergone continuous developmental change (Downs & Siegel, 1981).

This alternative interpretation might be built around a rebuttal of the arbitrary and inconsistent components of the judgment. Suppose that we were to view the use of multiple perspectives and multiple scales not as a failure to conform but as a creative response to some fundamental problems of representation—the problem of continuity and the problem of simultaneity. In my attempt to define the structure of a map, the properties of continuity and simultaneity are central. They arise in part in contradistinction to the properties of time as a principle for ordering information. Whereas we normally treat time as linear, unidimensional, and directional, the map arrays information in a two-(or more) dimensional matrix or surface. There is no necessary direction for reading the information, although there is a left-right scan bias that probably derives from textual material. The surface of the map is continuous. The multiple perspectives and scales of children's maps seem to violate these essential continuity and simultaneity properties.

It is fascinating, therefore, to see that these "violations" are present in medieval art and cartography. Rees (1980) has argued that early maps lack a uniform scheme of geographic space, even in those areas that have been traversed and observed. His argument continues:

The idiosyncracies of medieval cartography characterized medieval art. Paintings might indicate clearly the sequence in which objects were meant to be seen, as well as their orientation relative to the picture plane, but might offer no clues as to the size and spacing. As on the portolan charts, angles and directions were reliable, but distances were not. Relative sizes usually depended less on actual size than on the emphasis that the artist chose to give to the depicted objects; thus important figures and features, like important places on maps, were magnified. There was also a tendency to let objects "float" to the foreground of the paintings and to show them from different viewpoints. Space, in other words, was "naive" or discontinuous and so rarely penetrated that there were few vistas. (p. 66, reference footnotes omitted)

Substituting "child cartography" for "medieval art" we arrive at the conventional view once again, thus emphasizing the idiosyncratic and naive qualities of child cartography as an expression of space.

Consider the following representations of space. Architectural renderings present a multiplicity of views of a structure: a plan, an elevation, a side view, vertical and horizontal cross-sections, and so on. This would suggest the need for multiple renderings, with a variety of perspectives and scales, in order to reach an adequate (read accurate?) comprehension of a structure. The cubist movement in art was partly concerned with the multiple representation of the spatiality of objects in space. Thus one could "see through" something because, while the other facets were obscured, they still existed and they could be depicted within a single representation. Many of the city maps used for wayfinding and for tourists are a cross between a plan (or orthographic map) and a view (or perspective map). Treib (1980) discusses the dimetric graphic techniques that incorporate plan and view elements simultaneously. This list of representations could also include surface geological maps with fault lines that depict stratigraphical discontinuities, maps that portray Pangea and the subsequent patterns of continental drift, and graphical interpretations of catastrophe theory that permit an expression of discontinuity. From these representations we could proceed to the use of hypergraphics in order to visualize *n*-dimensions and so-called impossible figures (Brisson, 1978; Rucker, 1977).

Perhaps the point can be made best by Treib's comment about the use of dimetric graphical systems: "What all these systems make clear is the vast difference between the world as described through scale geometry and the world as experienced" (Treib, 1980, p. 10). Adults and children alike struggle with this vast difference, with its comprehension and representation. What we might be seeing, therefore, is a creative, sophisticated effort to come to terms with this difference, with multiple scales and perspectives as one possible graphic response. If we insist that children's maps are full of violations and are naive, then so are many "adult" representations. Given this alternative view, the judgments of inconsistency and arbitrariness become impossible to support.

For the moment, let me leave the judgment of inaccuracy as it stands and turn immediately to one of the common reactions to the implications of this alternative interpretation. It is possible to render this alternative of little importance by denying, in effect, the value of these graphic representations of space as data. This can be seen in our curious, inconsistent reactions to graphic sketch maps, for example. At best, the maps themselves are useful vehicles from which we can draw inferences to other phenomena of more significance. A classic example of this procedure is the use of the standardized road map test of direction sense for detecting cases of Turner's syndrome in teenaged girls (Money, Alexander, & Walker, 1965). I recognize that this is an extreme case of the ''at best'' position, but it presents a striking contrast to the ''at worst'' position, which views graphic modes of representation as being confounding variables. The maps, far from being data, are merely artifacts.

This is certainly a curious position. While maps in general are an acceptable base to work from (the metaphysics of cartography), children's maps in particular are highly suspect for the following three reasons. First, a sample of maps from children of approximately the same age group shows wide variations in manual graphic competence, familiarity with cartographic convention, and competence in representing space. Yet analogous variations are present in natural language, and, in this latter context, become an important object of study rather than a confounding variable. Second, as data, the resultant maps are difficult to handle: scoring, coding, and analysis are problematical and idiosyncratic. But do such practical considerations deny the value of the maps as data? These are precisely the challenges that hard-core empiricists thrive on. And third, one gets the implication, if not explicit statement, that these maps do not look like ''real'' maps should. Their unfamiliarity shades into unrecognizability and thus leads to the judgment of inaccuracy. Children's maps often do not evoke a reality that is acceptable to the conventional knowledge of adults.

We are faced with an awkward confusion. The concept of a map, the map as a model, is useful for thinking about the child's representation of space. The production of a map, the map as technique, is problematical as a means of studying the child's representation of space. We can accept the former but we tend to reject the latter as unacceptable. A logical consequence of my alternative position is that we can and should take maps-as-data seriously. As a way of doing so, let me go back to the development of cartography and show how it might provide one way of understanding the ontogenesis of spatial cognition. The discussion based on Rees's comment about medieval cartography suggests that such an approach might be fruitful.

Of the many issues emerging from the historical interpretations of cartography, two are closely linked to the development of spatial cognition. The first issue centers on the types of changes that are apparent in the structure, functions, and cartographics of maps. The second issue attempts to account for these changes. Why have they taken place? What has ''driven'' them?

If one looks specifically at the history of Western cartography, two key sets of changes are being worked out over a long period of time. In saying this, there is no implication that these changes are complete, and neither can they be complete since this would invoke some ultimate goal or destination. The first set of changes are a function of the disentangling of cartography from art. (I will not detail the changes here; for discussions of the loss of pictorialism in cartography, see Rees, 1980, and Harvey, 1980.) Concurrent with these changes are those which lead to the establishment of cartographic conventions. (No single source can adequately reflect these changes. Two journals, *The International Yearbook of Cartography* and *Imago Mundi* offer fascinating introductions to this complex topic.)

These two sets of changes occurred simultaneously and interacted with each other. The value of looking at these changes from the perspective of the ontogenesis of spatial cognition has been demonstrated most effectively by Denis Wood (1977). Wood was concerned with the means of landform and relief representation (hill-form symbols) throughout the history of cartography and within the development of children. His data consisted of a large number of landscape maps produced by children of varying ages. The results of his work are captured by Fig. 13.1, Ethnogenesis, and Fig. 13.2, Ontogenesis.

From the point of view of this argument, what is of interest is the series of ordered sequences that Wood identified. Although intertwined and interacting, there are three sequences. The first deals with a picture-to-abstraction shift which "begins" with concrete pictures, "moves" to abstractions based on the shadow-throwing properties of objects, and "ends" with abstractions based on elevation. The second sequence, profile-to-plan, begins with an egocentric view (profile or elevation), rotates through to a bird's eye (or oblique) view, and ends with an overhead, plan view. The third sequence, generic-to-unique, traces the shift from generic hill signs (any and all hills), to signs differentiated into types or classes, to signs that are capable of representing a specific, unique place.

Using the definition of cartography that was discussed previously, these three sequences can be interpreted in a variety of ways. For instance, the structure of a map undergoes some complex transformations. The picture-to-abstraction and the profile-to-plan sequences offer alternative ways of specifying the extrinsic geometrical relations between spaces and their representations. They allow for alternative "projections of experience." Similarly, all three sequences relate to the basic function of a map in that they permit alternative ways of evoking reality, of providing a world that is convincing and real. Interestingly, the "ends" of the three ethnogenetic sequences represent the current view of cartographic convention, and the popular expression of the way that maps "should" be.

Wood's work allows us to explore the interaction between cognition and cartography, to see that the similarities and parallels are more than coincidence. But documentation and description of the nature of developmental change is not

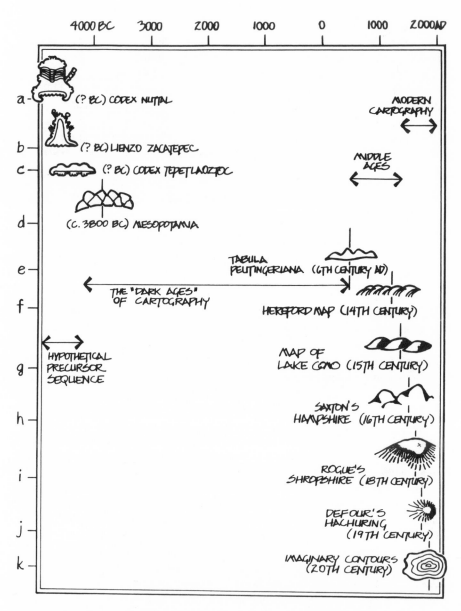

FIG. 13.1. The Ethnogenesis of Hill Signs. (This is a reproduction of Fig. 2 in Wood 1977, p. 154. Reproduced by permission of Denis Wood.)

School age

Group	No.	Shape	Pre-school n=50 %	Kindergarten 28 %	1st grade 30 %	3rd grade 26 %	5th grade 25 %	9th grade 29 %	10th grade 44 %	College sophomores 38 %	Graduate students 30 %
Elevation	1	(scribble)	16								
	2	≡	4								
	3	(house)	6	7							
	4	○	38								
	5	△	14								
	6	◠	4	11			4				
	7	∩	42	50	7	8		24	28	16	3
	8	∧	6	14				7		18	
	9	⌒		61	50	15	72	27	38	42	36
	10	⌒			7	30	4				
	11	⊓	8					10		5	
	12	∿				7	23	7	14	8	
	13	∿				10		7		8	7
	14	⌒⌒	8			20	27	8		3	
	15	(zigzag)			13	49	84	17	10		
	16	∧∧∧						3	2		
	17	Other		4							
Oblique	18	(shaded curve)							10	13	20
	19	(shaded oblique)				7	4			3	7
	20	(hatched)					8	16	10	14	
	21	(textured)							2		
	22	Other									
Plan view	23	(shaded zigzag)						17	19		
	24	♡						14	24		10
	25	⌣						14	12		7
	26	⊛							5	8	
	27	✳							14	11	
	28	⊛							2	3	3
	29	◎						3	12	71	40
	30	●						14	2	3	
	31	Other							2	3	7

FIG. 13.2.   The Ontogenesis of School Signs. School age is shown on the horizontal axis; hill-sign type on the vertical axis. (This is a reproduction of Fig. 5 in Wood 1977, p. 159. Reproduced by permission of Denis Wood.)

sufficient: We must also ask why these changes have taken place. What are the "driving" mechanisms? Let me again try to answer these questions in the context of the development of cartography.

There are at least two ways of viewing the forces or driving mechanisms that underpin the development of cartography. For convenience, I will call these the *instrumentalist* and the *constructivist* interpretations.

The instrumentalist interpretation sees cartography as developing in response to the opportunities and constraints of technology. The responses range from the dramatic (e.g., the impact of aerial and satellite imagery on mapping), to the radical (e.g., the impact of computers on map production), to the fundamental (e.g., the 18th and 19th century preoccupation with cadastral surveying), to the subtle (e.g., the response to plate-engraving techniques. Rees, 1980, argued that the 16th century use of copper engraving led to the abandonment of pictorialism that demanded complex, intricate plate engraving. In its place emerged simplified, abstract, all-purpose symbols).

The constructivist interpretation sees cartography as developing in response to the need for alternative ways of representing space. Again we can document a range of responses. Satellite imagery, for example, has had a tremendous impact on popular, everyday cartography. Maps in advertisements now depict the curvature of the earth, the penumbra of the atmosphere, exaggerated vertical relief, ocean currents, polar ice caps, star patterns, and even cloud formations in "lifelike" colors and forms. City maps display an incredible variety of projections (for example, isometric or axonometric views), symbols, fish-eye lens panoramas, nonlinear distance scales, and so on. Treib (1980) analyzes a variety of these maps.

The instrumentalist interpretation treats cartographic development as a drive for accuracy, detail, completeness, and comprehensiveness, whereas the constructivist interpretation is a search for realism. There is a tension between these two drives, a tension built on partial incompatibility and on the ever-present potential for misunderstanding. Consideration of this tension in the context of cartography might be useful in the context of the development of spatial cognition. More importantly, this examination provides instances where we might have been guilty of some misunderstandings already.

There is an ultimate absurdity, a paradox, in the compulsive search for accuracy that seems to be a key motivating force behind much of the work in cartography. In their search for ever-more accurate maps, cartographers are in danger of losing sight of the essential nature of maps as representational models. To reiterate, in essence, a map is a representation of space; it is not, and cannot be, the same as the space itself. It must always be, in some crucial sense, "less" than the original space. The map is a model and it owes its significance to the properties of a model. Thus it must always be a simplification and a generalization that is less than the original. It is for these purposes of simplification, generalization, and comprehensibility that we construct the map-as-model in the first place.

To lose sight of this vital point is to fall into the fallacy best expressed by this now-famous quote about 17th century cartography. (By way of an aside: I have seen this quote used by a variety of people and it has been attributed to a variety of sources. What is ironic is that its message seems to have been missed. It is almost as though the humor and the incongruity prevent people from seeing and accepting the point that is being made.)

> In that Empire, the Art of Cartography achieved such Perfection that the Map of one single Province occupied the whole of a City, and the Map of the Empire, the whole of a Province. In time, those disproportionate Maps failed to satisfy and the Schools of Cartography sketched a Map of the Empire which was of the size of the Empire and coincided at every point with it. Less addicted to the Study of Cartography, the Following Generations comprehended this dilated Map was Useless, and, not without Impiety, delivered it to the Inclemencies of the Sun and of the Winters. In the Western Deserts there remain piecemeal Ruins of the Map, inhabited by Animals and Beggars. In the entire rest of the country there is no vestige left of the Geographical Disciplines.

There is a sense in which cartographers seem to deny the very reason for their being; they denounce the arts and skills that they practice. Cartographers try to remove themselves from the process of mapping by a complex form of instrumentalism in which they become instruments on a par with press-on lettering and parallel rulers. By such means, objectivity is acquired and ensured.

This preoccupation with objectivity and accuracy extends to work on spatial cognition. First, cartographic maps guide our thinking about the likely (and perhaps necessary) form, structure, and functions of internal and external representations of space. Thus what I have called the metaphysics of cartography provides a convenient, readily understood and obvious language for expressing our thoughts. In addition, maps and cartography serve as a base for expectations and help to generate hypotheses about cognitive representations of space. Finally, maps and cartography provide methodologies for collecting and analyzing data. Thus in this operational context, internal representations become maps. Second, the cartographic map stands for the real world, and therefore it becomes a baseline or yardstick against which the form, structure, and function of cognitive representations can and should be measured. Cartography becomes a formal system against which we can evaluate psychological reality, an argument that has a circular quality to it. Third, there is an easy transition to *naive cartographic realism*. That is, the belief that the map *is* the real world. It portrays things as they "really" are. Admittedly, the map is smaller than the real world, but this is only a matter of convenience and portability. Given this belief, therefore, the cartographic map is *the only* yardstick for comparisons between cognitive representations of space and the real world. The logic of cartography as a formal system controls the process of analysis and it gives rise to judgments about the accuracy and distortion of cognitive spatial representations. The argument thus acquires a spherical, almost seamless quality.

Clearly, this is an over-simplification of research practice. Equally clearly, it points to a major problem. An earlier argument called into question the judgments that children's maps are arbitrary and inconsistent. Now we can question the judgment about accuracy: accurate with respect to what criteria? We must recognize that the comparison is always going to be between a map-as-model and a map-as-model, not a map-as-model and *the* map-as-the-real-world. The over-simplification also points to the question of realism: to what extent can we view the development of cartography as being a drive for realism? More importantly, why do we succumb to the idea of naive cartographic realism?

In the context of a map, we might interpret realism as the result of a map being credible and persuasive. That is, it must look like what we think the world would look like *if* it were (on) a map. We might say that the map substitutes direct and immediate perception for the impossible feat of direct perception! In other words, accepting the classic distinction between perception-cognition, the map brings the unperceivable extent of the world at large into the perceivable bounds of the map. The world achieves a reality and comprehensibility that is otherwise not available. The map is a self-supporting statement: This *is* what the world would look like if we were up there because this is what we know (read believe) the world *does* look like from up there. This idea fits with our definition of the function of a map. It must evoke appearances. It also points to the interdependency between maps and views of the world: convention and belief interlock.

Before we explore the implications of this view of realism, some examples might help to clarify the discussion. Representational realism is not confined to maps. In discussing Susan Sontag's (1977) *On Photography,* John Berger (1980) offers this argument about the impact of photography:

> It was not, however, until the 20th century and the period between the two world wars that the photograph became the dominant and most "natural" way of referring to appearances. It was then that it replaced the world as immediate testimony. It was the period when photography was thought of as being most transparent, offering direct access to the real. . . . (p. 48)

Maps have a preeminence and have possessed this quality of direct access to the real (world) for far longer than photographs. Seen from the naive cartographic realism position, the map *is* the real world. This is shown most strikingly in a review by J. H. Elliott (1978) of *The Times Atlas of World History:*

> For the best part of five centuries Western man's vision of the world has been conditioned by the map. It was the advent of the printed map that made it possible

for sixteenth-century Europeans to conceptualize global space, allowing them to replace an odd assortment of known details, vague impressions, and wild imaginings with the image of a world that could be grasped and known. In 1556 the son of St. Francis Borgia wrote to thank his father for sending him a map or sphere of the world. "Before seeing it," he wrote, "I was still ignorant of how small the world is." No sooner mapped, the world began to shrink. (p. 14)

The reaction of the son captures the essential function of the map as a means of *realizing* an understanding of the world. There are two important senses of the word realize. The first is that of making real, giving form to something that was previously intangible. There is a thing, a map, that permits, if not encourages, a series of possible manipulations: detailed inspection, rotation, extrapolation, interpolation, and so on. This obviously shades into the second sense, realize as in understand. The map allows one to comprehend relationships that were previously unsuspected but that become apparent through the structural properties of the map. Understanding follows from relationship, continuity, coherence, scale change, perspective change, and so forth. We realize that the experience of the world is comprehensible.

The drives for realism and accuracy interact most dramatically in the cartographic responses to remotely sensed imagery. This imagery includes aerial and satellite images that are generated either by photo-optical means or by electronic scanning. The most obvious example is the superimposition of state and national boundaries on NASA weather satellite photographs. A second example involves the increasing use of cartographically enhanced photomaps of the earth's surface. The photomaps, which by definition contain radial distortion due to the central perspective of the camera, are converted into orthophotos based on parallel perspective. The addition of cartographic information (names, resymbolization, recoloring, etc.) creates an orthophotomap, a map-photograph hybrid which is "realistic," readable, and plausible. It is interesting to see how this "realism" is artfully contrived by the cartographer. Remotely sensed color images are becoming commonplace. Yet the color component presents a range of possible forms of expression: normal color, simulated normal color, pseudo color, and false color. Normal color is just what it claims to be—the "standard" color photographic spectrum. Simulated normal color is an attempt to reconstruct what the surface colors would be like *if* there were no scattering, and hence no light loss due to atmospheric interference. The interference is greatest at the short wave-lengths of visible light. These "missing" wave-lengths are replaced by either digital or optical simulation. In other words, "realistic" colors (vegetation appearing green, soil brown, etc.) are based on creating a world without atmosphere. The colors are those that would be seen at ground level, although it is worth remembering that photograph and retinal color norms are in themselves different. In brief, pseudo color takes one sensing wave band, converts it into a range of grey tones, and assigns colors to these tones. False color deals with the reflected or photographic infra-red bands. Thus the color red is assigned to infra-red, the color green to red, and the color blue to green. Hence the interpretation problem that people face. Both pseudo and false color images are appropriately named; the images have lost some of their immediate power to evoke appearances.

There are two points to be made from this argument. First, the ideas of accuracy and realism are inextricably intertwined. Second, neither property is an objective quality that is somehow present in the world and that must be preserved and brought to the map. Instead, these are subjective qualities that are present to the extent that we agree that this is how the world would look if. . . . The map is a model that is credible to the observor.

The translation of these ideas into the work of development of spatial cognition is straightforward. In looking at the graphic representations of space that children produce, we do not expect to find either photographic or pictorial realism. We do seem, however, to fail to carry this argument to its logical conclusion because we tend to think in terms of cartographic realism. Moreover, this conception of cartographic realism is itself a very limited one. To borrow a common phrase, it is the world according to Rand McNally. But that cartographic conception of the world has itself undergone and continues to undergo change. There are changes in the cartographic techniques that permit alternative representations. There is change in our views of what the world looks like, and this change in turn demands alternative representations. Accuracy defined in planimetric and geometrical terms has increased; so has realism if this is seen in relative terms.

The development of cartography cannot be seen as the progressive attainment of some fixed, absolute goal. The concept of a good or a better map is difficult to specify. The concept of the right or correct or best map is impossible. As a formal system, cartography is *not* the stable, well-defined structure that we imagine it to be. The understanding of cartography that is presumed when we make use of the metaphysics of cartography bears close scrutiny. There are numerous misunderstandings and missed opportunities.

CONCLUSION

At the beginning of this chapter, I spoke of the need for questioning a tradition, for critically examining the conventional wisdom that grounds the tradition. The process of questioning has followed a series of steps. The first step has been built around the need to disentangle our understanding of spatial cognition from a presumed understanding of cartography. In effect, I have tried to contrast two ideas: the development of spatial cognition and the development of cartography. Each idea itself has been further broken down: Thus we can talk about how a child develops an understanding of space *and* we can also consider how we, as researchers, have looked at the development of spatial cognition. In a similar fashion, we can consider the development of cartography *and* the historical interpretation of the development of cartography. The essential point is to disentangle what happens from what we think happens and separate the phenomena of interest from our understanding of those phenomena. This obvious point is particularly important as we turn to the second step in the argument. Since we use cartography in order to understand spatial cognition, we need to look carefully at cartography as a formal system: What is cartography and how did it develop? Is our knowledge of the formal system of cartography useful for interpreting the development of spatial cognition? The answer to this question lies in accepting that the ontogenesis of spatial cognition and the development of cartography share the common aim of representing space; thus we can use the latter to understand the former. This step depends upon accepting a much broader definition of cartography, one that goes beyond the rather simplistic definition that is currently incorporated into the conventional wisdom. The proposed definition is built around an understanding of the relation between function, structure, and cartographics.

Accepting this basic argument allows us profitably to ask a series of questions about the development of spatial cognition. For instance, why do we so often treat children's graphic representations as artifacts? If we were to treat them as a legitimate source of data, then we might see that modes of graphic representation (cartographics) merit study in and of themselves. The work of Wood (1977) demonstrates this point, and the work of Goodnow (1977) on the development of children's art provides a model for the analysis of child cartography and the development of cartographics.

Central to such work is the way that we think about the nature and goals of the developmental process. Again, some alternative questions suggest productive lines of reasoning. What difference does it make if we treat development as a process of self-limitation and progressive acceptance of constraint? How do we consider the struggle to disengage from pictorialism, and the drive to maintain a sense of realism? What is the interaction between beliefs about the nature of space and ways of representing space? What is the interaction between the striving for accuracy and for realism? At the heart of all of these questions is an alternative characterization of the process of development. It takes the constructivist interpretation at its face value, and explicitly considers the impact of cultural norms and conventions on the representation of space.

As can be seen from these questions, the objective of my argument is a simple one. I have tried to step out of what I see to be the mainstream of work on the development of spatial cognition, and to ask some questions that may alter the assumptions that we work from, the expectations that we have, and the data that we accept.

REFERENCES

Berger, J. *About looking.* New York: Pantheon Books, 1980.

Brisson, D. W. (Ed.), *Hypergraphics: Visualizing complex relationships in art, science, and technology.* Boulder, CO: Westview Press, 1978.

Callahan, J. J. The curvature of space in a finite universe. *Scientific American,* 1976.

Downs, R. M. Maps and mappings as metaphors for spatial representation. In L. S. Liben, A. Patterson, & N. Newcombe (Eds.), *Spatial representation and behavior across the life span.* New York: Academic Press, 1981. (a)

Downs, R. M. Maps and metaphors. *The professional geographer,* 1981, *33,* 287–293.

Downs, R. M., & Siegel, A. W. On mapping researchers mapping children mapping space. In L. S. Liben, A. Patterson, & N. Newcombe (Eds.), *Spatial representation and behavior across the life span.* New York: Academic Press, 1981.

Elliott, J. H. Global vision: *The Times atlas of world history. The New York Review of Books,* 1978, December 7, 14–15.

Evans, G. W., & Pezdek, K. Cognitive mapping: Knowledge of real-world distance and location information. *Journal of Experimental Psychology: Human Learning and Memory,* 1980, *6,* 13–24.

Goodnow, J. *Children drawing.* Cambridge: Harvard University Press, 1977.

Hart, R. *Children's experience of place.* New York: Irvington Publishers, 1979.

Hart, R., & Moore, G. The development of spatial cognition: A review. In R. M. Downs & D. Stea. (Eds.), *Image and environment: Cognitive mapping and spatial behavior.* Chicago: Aldine, 1973.

Harvey, P. D. A. *The history of topographical maps: Symbols, pictures and surveys.* London: Thames & Hudson, 1980.

Kuipers, B. J. Modelling spatial knowledge. *Cognitive Science,* 1978, *1,* 265–295.

Leonard, J. A., & Newman, R. C. Three types of "maps" for blind travel. *Ergonomics,* 1970, *2,* 165–179.

Levine, M. You-are-here maps: Psychological considerations. *Environment and Behavior,* 1982, *14,* 221–237.

Lieblich, I., & Arbib, M. A. Multiple representations of space underlying behavior. *The Behavioral and Brain Sciences,* 1982, *5,* 627–659.

Money, J., Alexander, D., & Walker, H. T., Jr. *A standardized road-map test of direction sense.* Baltimore: Johns Hopkins Press, 1965.

O'Keefe, J., & Nadel, L. *The hippocampus as a cognitive map.* Oxford: Clarendon Press, 1978.

Piaget, J., & Inhelder, B. *The child's conception of space.* New York: Norton, 1967.

Piaget, J., Inhelder, B., & Szeminska, A. *The child's conception of geometry.* New York: Basic Books, 1960.

Rees, R. Historical links between cartography and art. *The Geographical Review,* 1980, *70,* 60–78.

Rosencranz, D., & Suslick, R. Cognitive models for spatial representations in congenitally blind, adventitiously blind, and sighted subjects. *New Outlook for the Blind,* 1976, *70,* 188–194.

Rucker, R. V. *Geometry, relativity, and the fourth dimension.* New York: Dover, 1977.

Siegel, A. The externalization of cognitive maps by children and adults: In search of ways to ask better questions. In L. S. Liben, A. Patterson, & N. Newcombe. (Eds.), *Spatial representation and behavior across the life span.* New York: Academic Press, 1981.

Siegel, A., & White, S. H. The development of spatial representations of large-scale environments. In H. W. Reese, (Ed.), *Advances in child development and behavior* (Vol. 10). New York: Academic Press, 1975.

Sontag, S. *On photography.* New York: Farrar, Straus & Giroux, 1977.

Sternberg, R. J. Capacities of young children [A review of Gelman and Gallistel's *The child's understanding of number*]. *Science,* 1980, *208,* 47–48.

Thompson, V. Music does not flow. *The New York Review of Books,* 1981, *28,* December 17, 47–51.

Treib, M. Mapping experience [Whole issue]. *Design Quarterly,* 1980, *115.*

Tversky, B. Distortion in memory for maps. *Cognitive Psychology,* 1981, *13,* 407–433.

Wood, D. Now and then: Comparisons of ordinary American's symbol conventions with those of past cartographers. *Prologue,* 1977, 151–161.

14

The Symbolizing and Symbolized Child in the Enterprise of Cognitive Mapping

Alexander W. Siegel
Jennifer H. Cousins
University of Houston

The general observation of child-life about one, the gathering of unrelated observations and incidents. . . . the study of children's diaries and letters, and the wide reading of autobiographies, will quicken our interest, broaden our sympathies, and give us a larger understanding of special instances. However, if such a work is not accompanied by direct and well-ordered observation, by experimentation and statistical study, leading to some general quantitative results, it is apt to leave us with a feeling that human life is not amenable to law.
—Earl Barnes, *Studies in Education,* 1896 (p. 10)

He [the American] was accustomed to prosperity. . . . Whatever promised to increase wealth was automatically regarded as good. . . . All this tended to give a quantitative cast to his thinking and inclined him to place a quantitative valuation upon almost everything. . . . His solution for most problems was therefore quantitative—and education, democracy, and war all yielded to the sovereign remedy of numbers.
—Henry Steele Commager, *The American Mind,* 1950 (p. 7).

In the past decade, a new production emerged on the stage of developmental psychology: The development of cognitive mapping of large-scale environments. In a sense, the production was not really new. There had been a few early papers by Trowbridge (1913) and Lord (1941) on the spatial orientation systems used by school children; Maier (1936) had examined children's spatial learning in a large maze. But these early papers did not provoke a sustained interest. Two theoretical papers by Hart and Moore (1973) and Siegel and White (1975) and two empirical studies by Kosslyn, Pick, and Fariello (1974) and Acredolo, Pick, and Olsen (1975) appeared to "kick off" the enterprise afresh. Empirical pieces appeared in the journals in increasing numbers over the next several years, until, by the time of this writing, the study of cognitive mapping of large-scale environments had become an industry.

Our purpose in writing this chapter is not to review the theories and data generated by this polyglot industry, but rather to consider the empiricism within a broader epistemological and social context. The chapters in the present volume address nearly discrete pieces of the jigsaw puzzle of cognitive mapping research. The various authors are seriously involved in trying to articulate their pieces of the puzzle. Their well-designed, and frequently elegant, empirical efforts are like landmarks in the terrain of cognitive mapping, with connections to other landmarks gradually beginning to be made. Perhaps it is time to step back and, from a distance, try to see the larger map or puzzle in which these landmarks are embedded. In order to do this, we first try to articulate some assumptions underlying research on the development of cognitive mapping. Next, we discuss the issue of ecological validity in the design of research, and argue that a more functional perspective is needed. After briefly reviewing techniques that have been used to externalize children's spatial knowledge, we address the problem of "accuracy" of cognitive maps and in doing so consider issues of competence and performance. Finally, we try to set the production of cognitive mapping research within the larger context of the dramaturgy of science.

ASSUMPTIONS

Any theory that attempts to explain, and any methodological approach that attempts to investigate, cognitive mapping involves some underlying assumptions regarding the nature of the phenomenon under study. These assumptions are discussed at length elsewhere (Siegel, 1981), but since they are implicit in most of the research on the development of cognitive mapping (represented in this volume and elsewhere) they warrant a brief recapitulation.

1. Since neither children nor adults typically consult road maps or use compasses to find their way, and typically do not get lost, it is assumed that environmental navigation is guided by some internal representation of (some piece of) the environment. These representations are often distorted, fragmented, and probably not "maplike" (Appleyard, 1970; Siegel & White, 1975). Nonetheless, the term "cognitive map" is a useful descriptor, and has a long and honorable history (Tolman, 1948; Trowbridge, 1913).

2. The term "cognitive map" is used extensively throughout this chapter, and thus we may have (inadvertently) seemed to reify the term. Cognitive map is an inferred construct; it is a state description of a process at a moment in time, and like other state descriptions (e.g., the labels for various cognitive-develop-

mental stages) may be misleading. "Maps" are not static realities, fixed in form or content, residing somewhere in the right parietal lobe. Like cognitive stages, cognitive maps are hypostatizations—abstractions that we create and use in understanding the sequence and development of the continual activity of cognitive mapping (Downs & Stea, 1977; Kaplan, 1967; Siegel & White, 1975). In this sense, cognitive maps are convenient fictions.

3. The process of cognitive mapping is constructive and develops in both children and adults. As the products of cognitive mapping, cognitive maps will reflect these developmental changes. The maps do not change simply by accretion, but rather by progressive transformation both over ontogenesis and over repeated experience in adults and children. Like any learning, the acquisition of cognitive maps is not a process of "getting full," but rather a process of becoming unconfused (Gibson, 1969; White & Siegel, 1976).

4. The study of the development of cognitive mapping need not be confined to a particular time span (e.g., years) nor to particular organisms (e.g., children). The process of development—of cognitive mapping or any other phenomenon—can be studied fruitfully in children over months and years, and in adults and children over shorter periods of time, e.g., over repeated encounters with environments (Kaplan, 1967; Wapner, Kaplan, & Ciottone, 1981; Werner, 1957).

It should be noted that these four assumptions are paradigmatic for a constructivist position in any psychological or behavioral domain (Reese & Overton, 1970; Siegel, Bisanz, & Bisanz, 1983).

5. The nature and development of cognitive maps in particular, and environmental cognition in general, can be investigated productively within the context of a broadly experimental approach. Further, it is possible and necessary to design procedures that are "representative" (Brunswik, 1956) of the everyday situations of children and adults.

A fundamental problem in understanding the acquisition and development of cognitive mapping is the externalization of cognitive maps—getting the spatial knowledge out in some public medium. These externalized products are, in effect, "re-representations" (Jackson, 1884/1958, pp. 45–75; Spencer, 1855) of spatial experience. A second major problem involves the criteria against which these "re representations" are measured, evaluated, and interpreted.

The extent of cognitive mapping and the nature of the resultant representation are, to a large degree, a function of the agenda (purposes) of the individual doing the mapping. For example, a casual visitor to a city and a prospective home buyer will probably differ in the extent to which they actively and selectively map the environment. Thus, the nature and detail of their respective cognitive maps will differ (Wapner et al., 1981; Wapner, Kaplan, & Cohen, 1973). Although much lip service has been paid to the importance of the traveler's agenda, developmental research has devoted empirical attention to it only in the form of intentional-incidental instruction manipulations (e.g., Acredolo et al., 1975).

THE NEED FOR A THEORY OF SITUATIONS

The research reported in this volume reflects an increasing sensitivity to characteristics of the physical environment in which cognitive mapping occurs, e.g., size and scale of the environment, distinctiveness of landmarks, a laboratory or a field setting, or the familiarity of the setting. Investigators are becoming more concerned with how various aspects of environmental settings influence and interact with the resulting representations (or "re-representations") of that environment. (This was Kevin Lynch's major concern in his classic *Image of the city*, 1960.) The performance of children seems to vary dramatically as a function of the setting toward which their thought and action are directed—familiar are better represented than relatively novel settings, settings-in-context are better represented than isolated settings, and so on. These findings in cognitive mapping research reflect two major issues currently being discussed in the larger arenas of cognitive and developmental psychology: (1) the dilemma of situation-specific versus universal cognitive competencies, and (2) the meaning of ecological validity.

Situational versus Universal competencies: The Need for a New Functionalism

From the mid 1960s to the late 1970s, the central issues of research on children's cognitive development have focused on structural models of cognitive competence. Arguments that the structural development of competence must be *adaptive* have been exceedingly vague concerning adaptation *for what*. With some exceptions, the research movements of this period have not seriously attempted to explore those contexts toward which adaptation is daily directed. Life is not primarily a matter of getting along in laboratory cubicles or school classrooms— the two contexts in which children have been most frequently studied—or even in navigable small-scale spaces. We need a new functionalism that must include, in some broad sense, an analysis and theory of the contexts of children's behavior. A long line of theorists from John Dewey (1902) to Kurt Lewin (1935) to Roger Barker (1968) to Michael Cole (Cole, Hood, & McDermott, 1979) and Urie Bronfenbrenner (1979) have argued that a naturalistic developmental psychology (or cognitive development) can only be achieved through the creation and use of a theory of situations.

Our everyday knowledge is that children travel from place to place. Cognitive changes in growing children depend on the functional demands imposed on them during travel, and by the requirements of communication and cooperation with people that children experience as they enter adult society. White and Siegel (1984) have discussed the cognitive development of children as they travel among natural contexts of human interaction, both face-to-face contexts, and contexts distal in time and space. In discussing cognitive development in this way, we needed to question and modify some assumptions about just what cognitive development is, and what the study of cognitive development needs to entail.

Contemporary research on child development is a response to the necessities of modern societies and their new behavior settings (White & Siegel, 1984). It is doubtful that for children in a modern society any single kind of environment should be regarded as natural, privileged, or authentic *uber alles* for the determination of a child's behavior and thought (White, 1980). It is not obvious to us that a tachistoscope or a layout of a town on the floor of a gym is any less natural to a child than Sunday school or flute lessons. Nor does a classroom seem any less natural than Friday night dinner at Grandma Clara's. What does seem obvious is that children "live" in many situations, and a typification of a child may not automatically be valid across any pair of them.

With minor exceptions, the contexts in which children live are social contexts. (Seymour Papert, 1980, has recently argued that children's individual encounters in programming microcomputers require that the child develop a theory about how the computer—the other—works, and thus these are inherently social situations.) When we abstract the cognitive part of a social adaptation we do so at the risk of losing or distorting the texture and meaning of the cognitive phenomenon. To understand cognitive development in any full-blooded way, we need to understand it as being deeply embedded in a social world full of formalities, etiquettes, and occasions (Douglas, 1973).

Linked with the traditional notions of a general cognitive development are notions of a general socialization. Socialization frequently is treated as a universal process through which a common stock of knowledge, beliefs, and social forms are acquired by all children in a society. But this is a simplistic view of what happens as a group of age-mates finds niches and roles in any society. Children live in multiple and diverse settings. A major part of each child's socialization involves the negotiation of a viable and unique set of social contexts to be used and lived in by that child. In that negotiation, children make different adaptations to different contexts. We see partial developments of what might best be termed "multiple personalities." For example, the moderate correlations frequently obtained between parent and teacher ratings of children on a variety of instruments are probably *not* primarily due to the instruments' unreliability, but rather due to the fact that the child-at-home and child-at-school are not entirely the same child.

White and Siegel (1984) have argued that a properly functional view of cognitive development must envision it as being embedded in the child's movement and travel across the social contexts of society. If this is valid, then socialization must be viewed as involving a second kind of travel using symbols. The capacity for symbolic travel, in some major sense, depends on the fact that we require the growing child to travel and to think about things at a distance. Children learn to engage (via reading, writing, telephone, television, and now, the microcomputer) in cooperative activity with people that are far away in space (e.g., talking on the phone with Aunt Sophie in Minneapolis) and time (e.g., reading about the adventures of Robinson Crusoe). The often talked-about trend in cognitive development toward more abstraction, decontextualization, and distancing of children's thought (Sigel & Cocking, 1977; Werner & Kaplan, 1963) must be regarded as an expression of the child's increasing capacity for long-range communication and cooperation with others.

Finally, a new functionalism must entail an enlarged view of children's knowledge of self. As children move from one setting to another, they not only experience other people in those settings, they experience themselves in other settings. Multiple adaptation of the young child is surely accompanied by knowledge-about-self that directs the child toward some settings as "promising" or "secure" and away from others that have proved threatening (see Acredolo, 1981, this volume).

Beyond Ecological Validity

Rallying cries under the banner of "Ecological Validity" have typically called for a focus on research in naturalistic environments with a concomitant de-emphasis on research in artificial experimental settings. Both Bronfenbrenner and Cole have long argued that studying children in their everyday environments will permit us to establish reasonably valid and authentic estimates of how children think. One hears today additional voices that advocate joining this new direction for developmental research—naturalistic, ecological, ethological studies of children in their natural settings.

But there are some problems that prevent most psychologists from embracing this position. What is a natural environment for a young child? School-age children live and perform in a variety of behavior settings: Home, school, the playground, cub scouts, shopping malls, and so on. Should we regard some of these various settings as more natural and essential than others? How do we sample? The open and uncontrolled nature of these everyday environments make most psychologists uncomfortable. The research tools in the armamentarium of most psychologists are based on precision and control, and in order to use them we tend to create simple environments in which to study children. The intellectual paraphernalia of psychological research all lose precision rather rapidly when too many variables are free to wander in a research environment. Although the advantages of working with children in everyday environments are obvious, the difficulties of doing so have kept most of us at work in the controlled environments of the laboratory (White, 1980).

It seems to us that the term ecological validity is often poorly understood and badly used. "Ecological representativeness" was initially used by Brunswik (1956) "as an antidote to the artificial 'tying' of variables in the laboratory, and to the artificiality of the control over 'extraneous' variables in laboratory experimentation" (Wohlwill, 1981). In most current discussions "An investigation is regarded as ecologically valid if it is carried out in a natural setting and involves objects and activities from everyday life'' (Bronfenbrenner, 1979, p. 28). Viewing the issue of ecological validity as a choice between natural versus laboratory environments is a misleading oversimplification. A field versus laboratory dichotomy implies the assumption that in some ideal situation it will be possible to ''attribute underlying capacities or processes to internal functioning of people without concern for the context of their activity'' (Rogoff, 1983, p. 4). That is, this dichotomy implies that we can find universal, context-free theories of thought and behavior. In fact, the term ecological validity, as it is used most frequently in the literature, often has little relation to an ecological approach to developmental research.

A more satisfactory definition is implicit in Cole's work (Cole et al., 1979) and is formalized by Bronfenbrenner: ''Ecological validity refers to the extent to which the environment experienced by the subjects in a scientific investigation has the properties it is supposed or assumed to have by the investigator'' (Bronfenbrenner, 1979, p. 29). For Bronfenbrenner, an ecological approach is defined by the underlying conceptual model of the environment, not by the nature of the environment in which the research is conducted. Bronfenbrenner's (1979) model—in which the individual, the environment, and the relationship between them are conceptualized in terms of nested systems—is congruent with a contextual, or transactional, model (Ogbu, 1981; Overton & Reese, 1973; Rogoff, 1983) in which the context and the individual's actions are viewed as jointly producing the psychological event.

Such an ecological approach has several implications for how we might investigate the development of cognitive mapping. Methodologies that go ''beyond ecological validity'' entail a number of characteristics (Bronfenbrenner, 1977):

1. The traditional assumption is that an experimental situation involves a unidirectional, causal relationship between the experimenter and the subject. In an ecological approach, the interaction is reconceptualized as a process that goes both ways.

2. An ecological approach allows for and investigates ''second-order effects,'' i.e., how other people or situations mediate the relations between the child and the environment.

3. A comparative perspective is the defining core of an ecological approach. What are the joint effects and interactions *between* different settings? How do events in one situation or environment influence the child's behavior and development in another? In this perspective the environment is not considered a nuisance variable that is to be controlled, but rather a variable of legitimate interest (Rogoff, 1983).

4. This approach views child-environment relationships from a dynamic, transactional perspective rather than either a static or an interactional one (Rogoff, 1983; Wapner, et al., 1973). If the functioning of the individual and the

environment are conceptualized as aspects of a larger system that defines and relates the elements, then it is insufficient to look at separate elements of the system and then put the pieces back together. A further implication is that attention must be paid as well to the larger systems that encompass the immediate environment of the child.

5. An ecologically minded approach to the study of cognitive mapping (or any psychological phenomenon of interest) demands that we not only look at objective behaviors of the child (be they responses to the experimenter's task or some naturally occurring behavior), but also try to understand the meaning of a particular setting to the child functioning within it.

THE EXTERNALIZATION OF COGNITIVE MAPS

Procedures

As mentioned earlier, a central concern in the literature of cognitive mapping has been the development and refinement of techniques that enable the child to externalize his spatial knowledge and permit the investigator to assess that knowledge. In this section we discuss briefly a number of procedures used to externalize cognitive maps and some of the problems inherent in their use.

Verbal protocols of spatial experience or sketch maps of the environment were used in the early studies on cognitive mapping (Appleyard, 1970; Lynch, 1960; Piaget & Inhelder, 1967; Piaget, Inhelder, & Szeminska, 1960). It is now well known that developmental differences in spatial representation and differences in verbal and drawing skills are almost completely confounded in such tasks (Brown, 1976; Goodnow, 1977; Kosslyn, Heldmeyer, & Locklear, 1977). An early attempt to avoid this confounding employed children's reconstructions from memory of small-scale models of their classroom (Siegel & Schadler, 1977). But the use of tabletop models has its own problems. These include (1) assuming (often incorrectly) that the child knows that a model "stands for" some piece of the real world; (2) the difficulty of translating one's cognitive map, derived from experience within large-scale environments, from one scale of space to another. Siegel, Herman, Allen, and Kirasic (1979) have demonstrated discrepancies in representational accuracy that are attributable to this requirement of translation.

More recently, investigators have used model construction tasks in which the environment and the model of it are experienced and reconstructed on the same scale (e.g., Herman & Siegel, 1978). This method alleviates the problems encountered using small-scale models, but is not problem free. Performance of young children in large-scale model construction tasks has been shown to be dependent on the larger environment in which the model is embedded and reconstructed, i.e., whether the model environment is isolated in the middle of a large room or close to its walls.

Photographic simulation of environmental journeys through the use of slide presentations has been used successfully to study both route (Allen, Kirasic, Siegel, & Herman, 1979; Allen, Siegel, & Rosinski, 1978; Siegel, Allen, & Kirasic, 1979) and configurational knowledge (Cohen & Schuepfer, 1980). In conjunction with this and other techniques, multidimensional scaling (MDS) procedures have also proved feasible and valuable. MDS involves a powerful set of statistical procedures for extracting a metric representation from non-metric proximity judgments (ordinal distances) between pairs of environmental landmarks. MDS procedures have also been used to investigate route (Allen et al., 1978; Siegel et al., 1979) as well as configurational knowledge (Herman, Kail, & Siegel, 1979; Kosslyn, et al., 1974).

However, Kirasic, Siegel, Allen, Curtis, and Furlong (1982) reported evidence that the use of MDS techniques may underestimate subjects' knowledge of the environment when compared to direct distance and bearing estimates. In 1976, Hardwick, McIntyre, and Pick developed a technique they termed "triangulation" by obtaining bearing estimates from three locations to a set of targets in a school library room. Triangulation has also been used successfully to assess children's configurational knowledge of large-scale areas (Anooshian & Young, 1981). Curtis, Siegel, and Furlong (1981) extended this technique by obtaining both bearing *and* distance estimates from children. This has proven to be a feasible method of externalizing cognitive maps of large-scale areas of both adults (Kirasic et al., 1979) and children (Cousins, Siegel, & Maxwell, 1983; Curtis et al., 1981).

Much of the research just discussed was generated from Siegel and White's (1975) model of the development of cognitive mapping. In a recent study, Cousins, Siegel, and Maxwell (1983) assessed the validity of the model's proposed hierarchical sequence of components by determining the extent to which individual performance patterns conformed to the model. Cousins et al. (1983) addressed two other issues as well. Age-group differences on children's externalized representations found in previous research tend to portray young children as being spatially incompetent or egocentric, or lacking even routelike knowledge or Euclidean concepts (Cohen & Schuepfer, 1980; Piaget et al., 1960). Yet our everyday experience indicates that young children are spatially competent in the sense that they are rather skilled way-finders in their own neighborhoods by age 4 and can quite easily get to school and back home by age 6. We assessed children's environmental way-finding competence in the same environment in which their cognitive mapping competence was assessed. Finally, Cousins et al. (1983) had the opportunity to investigate the relationship between grade level and familiarity on each of the component measures in an environment where subjects' familiarity with subsets of the school campus varied by grade level.

First, fourth and seventh graders were given a series of tasks to assess both their way finding competence and their cognitive mapping of their school campus. Children were asked to create and walk three novel and efficient routes (way finding), to select photographs of scenes belonging to the three routes (landmark knowledge), to correctly order and then metrically relate those scenes (route order and metric knowledge), and to make bearing and distance estimates from several sighting locations to six targets within the campus (configurational knowledge). Guttman scale analysis indicated that 93% of the children exhibited performance patterns congruent with the sequence predicted by the model, i.e., landmark to route to configuration. A few reversals in the developmental trend on some component measures were found, however, between fourth and seventh graders for whom performance differences were strongly related to differences in familiarity within different sections of the campus. In spite of the significant differences found in the accuracy of children's externalized maps, all children tested were extremely competent way finders. These results indicate a need for further research on within-subject differences on different components of spatial knowledge and on the relationship between environmental experience and developmental differences in cognitive mapping.

Conceptual Issues

Cognitive Maps and the Problem of "Accuracy."   As noted, we need to be cautious in interpreting the externalized cognitive maps of children and adults— the "public" products of cognitive mapping activity. Spatial environments are experienced by or "presented" to the organism, and cognitive maps are representations of these experiences. The externalized cognitive maps are "re-representations," and thus two levels removed from actual spatial experience.

But, given that we obtain these cognitive maps from children, it is of critical interest to pose questions of interpretation: How are the maps of children and adults different? What developmental differences are found between younger and older children? In what ways do the maps change across age or with experience? What should be the standard against which performance is assessed?

Most psychologists have implicitly adopted the cartographic map as the metaphor that guides our thinking about the structure and function of cognitive maps and shapes our methodologies for externalizing them (Downs, 1981; Downs & Siegel, 1981). Further, the cartographic map has become *the* standard against which performance is typically compared. In the main, researchers have asked, "Under what conditions and to what extent can adults and children produce models of their environment that look like (or conform to the properties of) cartographic maps representing that environment?" The extent to which the performance (i.e., the externalized product) conforms to the cartographic map is assessed in terms of "accuracy." In most of the papers in the present volume, "accuracy" of performance is a focal concept; further, "accuracy" is used in a value-normative way: Accuracy is "good" and implies being more developed; inaccuracy is "bad" and implies being less developed.

What is it that is more or less accurate than what? How can we reconcile the apparent paradox between children's accurate spatial behavior and their "inaccurate'' cognitive maps? What is accuracy? Agreement with an external standard. But what standard? The real world, of course. But from a constructivist position there is no such thing as *the* real world (Pepper, 1970; Reese & Overton, 1970). From this perspective, reality is a construction by an individual and by a society. At all levels of analysis—phylogenetic (Jerison, 1976; von Uexkull, 1957), ontogenetic (Bruner, 1964; Piaget, 1971; Werner, 1957), and sociocultural (Berger & Luckman, 1967; Mead, 1934)—there are multiple real worlds, each of which is a potential standard against which to assess accuracy-as-agreement (Downs & Siegel, 1981). By acknowledging what Downs (1981) has termed "cartographic relativism," any map—cognitive or cartographic—is a *possible* world model.

Cartographic maps are *one* kind of model—the world according to Rand McNally—in which the earth's surface if transformed into a two-dimensional grid having abstract axes of latitude and longitude, quantified in the metric of degrees. Yet most of us act and write as if a cartographic map is the *best* model of reality, and as if a cartographic-map-in-the-head is the most useful form of knowledge. These presumptions are, at best, questionable.

The major function of cognitive maps is to facilitate way finding in the large-scale environment and to prevent getting lost (Downs & Stea, 1977; Lynch, 1960); they also function as dynamic data stores, as organizers of social and emotional experience, and as devices for inferring novel spatial and nonspatial relationships (Siegel & White, 1975). Surely there are other models of the world—perhaps less elegant and cognitively economical than a cartographic map—that can serve these same functions.

In *East is a Big Bird* (1970), Gladwin described the navigational system of the Puluwat Islanders; in *We, the Navigators* (1972), Lewis described that of the Santa Cruz Islanders. Both of these systems are used to navigate extensive expanses of open ocean successfully. The navigators using these systems do not require compasses, and cartographic maps make little sense to them, yet they never get lost. The contrast to "modern" compass-based navigational systems (based on the cartographic map, in which one orients oneself by using bearings like North and South that radiate out from the self), both of these systems can be described as home-centered and/or local-reference systems. In these systems one orients onself with respect to geographic points such as home, an island, wave formations, and star positions. These systems are simple-minded (in a nonpejorative sense), practical, and have built-in flexibility and redundancy. They involve not-terribly-elegant algorithms to prevent getting lost; they are not "pretty" systems and require much rote memorization, but they're safe. They are conservative in the sense that, while being cumbersome, they absolutely minimize the possibility of getting lost. Clearly, way finding can be based on models of the world different from that of the cartographic map. Just as clearly, cognitive-maps-in-the-head need not be cartographic.

Gatty's (1958) description of such home-centered systems seems, curiously, to reflect the travel experiences of the developing child:

As early peoples ventured forth in search of food they maintained a constant anxiety about their home and would often look back to see where they were in relation to their point of departure. Each time they went out more territory would become familiar to them; and they would proceed further . . . never once losing the thread. (p. 46)

Gatty constrasted these systems with modern compass-based navigational systems, which are more elegant but riskier.

Notice that, frequently, linguistic descriptions of non-compass-based reference systems are similar to descriptions of "immature" and/or "primitive" frames of reference attributed to young children by Piaget, Werner, and Hart and Moore (1973). Yet is is clear that these "immature" or "primitive" systems are enormously useful and adaptive. In contemporary discussions of cognitive development, competence is frequently defined in "adultomorphic" terms; the same kind of "egocentric" error is made by equating competence in cognitive mapping to compass-based navigational systems or the use of abstract, coordinated frames of reference inherent in cartographic maps.

The Competence-Performance Problem(s).   Cognitive competence occupies a central role in the cognitive mapping research enterprise. Internal representations are externalized, and evaluated in terms of accuracy (usually with the cartographic map as the standard). From the attainment of some qualitative or quantitative level of accuracy, a particular level of competence is inferred or assigned. There is a problem with this approach, both in cognitive mapping, and, more generally, in cognitive development. This problem is acutely present and well exemplified in contemporary Piagetian research.

Piaget's work has generated an enormous number of replication studies, many of which have yielded findings consistent with those reported by Piaget. But an increasing number of studies are showing that if Piaget's original procedures are modified, even in apparently insignificant ways, then results are apt to appear that are not consistent with Piaget's original outcomes. Repeatedly, researchers are finding that children appear to have certain competencies (e.g., perspective taking, conservation) long before Piaget describes them as occurring. If the procedures used to assess those abilities are made simpler and less complex (e.g., less distraction, shorter and clearer instructions, the presence or use of concrete prompts), then children perform better. They appear to have a higher level of competence. Thus, variable procedures seem to yield variable levels of competence.

One proposed solution to the challenge of "wandering competencies" pose to Piagetian theory is to distinguish between observable performance and underlying, unobservable competence (Flavell & Wohlwill, 1969). Performance wobbles; competence remains stable. That cognitive mapping reserchers rely on this kind of cognitive-performance distinction is attested to by the emphasis placed on developing externalization procedures that will somehow minimize performance variables while permitting a better glimpse of the "true" underlying competence.

Cole (1984) and Stone and Day (1980) have discussed the difficulties involved in invoking this dual model of cognitive functioning. The most obvious difficulty is that we have no agreed-upon way to separate performance (task-specific) factors from competence (task-nonspecific) factors. Nor do we have a theory to analyze various settings that would specify what simpler or more complex means in the distribution of possible settings in which children live.

As a first approximation to this specification, White (1980) has proposed that children's performance, and thus their apparent competence, influenced by three broad groups of factors that tend to introduce "load" or "noisiness" into a particular setting. Internal factors include a variety of idiosyncratic, rhythmic and reactive, endogenous psychophysiological state changes. External situational factors include such things as task procedures, type and arrangement of cues, memory demands, and concrete prompts. Factors of agenda—cognitive, social, and emotional (White, 1980)—involve the match or mismatch of what the child wants to do with what the experimenter has in mind as the "serious" business of the situation. Many of the externalization procedures that we described earlier can be viewed as representing attempts to decrease situational load factors: Use of large-scale rather than tabletop environments (reducing representational demands), increased reliance on direct estimates of distance and bearing rather than reliance on verbal accounts or drawn products (reducing verbal and praxic demands), etc. These are all situational "load" factors. Vygotsky (1978) has talked about the "zone of proximal development" as the difference in performance between what the child can do on his or her own and what the child can do with the help of adults. In general, Vygotsky talked about this kind of assistance as being mediated by social interaction. But it is clear that nonsocial situational factors (particular ways of posing problems, elimination of distraction, arrangement of cues) can also serve as "scaffolding" devices to extend the range and robustness of children's performance on a variety of tasks.

We would argue that attempts to separate competence and performance factors tend to obscure the phenomenon (and its development) under study. Competence implies a context-free capability, i.e., what the individual can do in the ideal situation. Again, borrowing from Vygotsky, we suggest that a more appropriate unit for analysis is the action or performance itself in the context of a particular task, rather than the individual's presumed situation-independent capability. The action, or context, incorporates the person, the situation, and the goals involved. As pointed but by Cole et al. (1979), a shift from person analysis to action or context analysis is more than semantic: "it precludes talking about the skills which people carry around 'in their heads' " (p. 108).

Rather than pursuing the Holy Grail of Platonic, context-free, universal competencies, we should begin to specify the range and features of situations in which children act to acquire and use environmental information to satisfy their needs and agenda.

Cognitive Mapping is More Than Cognitive

What is it that children need or want to do as they perform a specific task set by an experimenter? Although this is probably unanswerable in the general case, we know enough from the literature on cognitive mapping to permit us to estimate some of what the children's agenda are as they cognitively map the everyday world through which they travel.

The role of travel is a crucial element in the development of cognitive mapping (a point made repeatedly in the papers in this volume, and by White & Siegel, 1983). What do we know about where children travel? In their classic work *Midwest and its children* (1954), Barker and Wright attempted to lay a foundation for what we have called a theory of situations by collecting massive and meticulous data of children in and among the settings of a midwestern American town. Their data suggest some general trends that are obvious to developmental psychologists (but largely ignored by them—perhaps because they are so obvious).

Children spend their earliest years predominantly at home. As they enter school age, they move out into the community; they experience a more differentiated set of psychological environments and begin to establish secondary "home bases." As they get older they enter more centrally into community activities of adults to become increasingly central performers. What do children learn as they travel in ever-widening geographic and social circles?

Obviously, children map the physical characteristics of the environment as they travel in it. The growth of cognitive mapping in children reflects directly the range and variety of travel that has been permitted them. Hart (1979) has shown that preschoolers and kindergarteners can produce sophisticated maps—survey maps—of their homes, but more distal settings are not well represented. Herman (1980) and Wapner et al. (1981) have found that when children build maps they start with home; they then put in places that can be seen or easily reached from the home; finally they put in less visually and physically accessible places. Hart (1979, 1981) reports similar results.

Cognitive maps are not isolated targets of learning. Children remember the places that are meaningful in their everyday lives, and not these places as landmarks on the maps they make (Wapner et al., 1981). Adults and children are purposive. The knowledge that people take in on their journeys and the maps they construct selectively enhance those things that seem important to them in the light of their purposes (Siegel, 1981, 1982). The agenda of the traveller is of direct relevance to Acredolo's (1981) distinctions between intentional and incidental learning, and between active and passive experience. The process of cognitive mapping is only in part cognitive: As children travel, they encode social information in their maps. They learn where different behavior settings are, where to go to find things, people, personal involvements, or help. They learn who some of the other people are in the community and thus become aware of the range of the social, physical, and behavioral differences that people in the community present to them. They develop normative expectations about social life and social forms. Children learn how to act properly and skillfully in a number of community behavior settings. Training in style, manner, and etiquette is an integral part of socialization and skill training in community settings (such as a department store or the YMCA), just as it is in school and at the family dinner table (Bossard, 1948, Ch. 17). These settings are by no means randomly chosen. Whiting (1980) has argued cogently that the power of socializing agents to shape social behavior lies largely in their role in the assignment of children to settings.

Children's situational learning also centrally involves attitudinal and motivational aspects. Community settings differ in the emotional atmospherics they maintain or offer to a child who enters. In Midwest, Barker and Wright observed 6-year-old Roy Eddy enter 17 community behavior settings in one day. In some settings Roy was ignored, restricted, and coerced; in others he was warmly welcomed, helped, and given great social approval and self-esteem (Barker & Wright, 1954, p. 96). Children also experience changes in tempo in different settings (Wapner, 1980) and must learn how to manage their own behavior to function within those settings. As children pick up the emotional tones, tempos, and the self-management demands of diverse behavior settings, places in their environment are given emotional tags on their cognitive maps. In what settings does the child feel secure? Which settings are unsafe, threatening, or anxiety provoking?

Thus, as children cognitively map their environment, they also map it socially and emotionally to satisfy their multiple agenda. Piaget acknowledges the relationships among movement, knowledge, and agenda:

> At seven, a child knows several roads; those which take him to school where he now goes himself and those which he walks along with his family when they go on their customary walks; he can *therefore* describe several fragmentary routes, and he can draw a plan showing a number of discrete areas. At nine or ten, a child is free as a man and can roam at will all over town; he *therefore* answers all the questions satisfactorily. (Piaget, Inhelder, & Szeminska, 1960, pp. 23–4)

Piaget talks of the child of nine as "free as a man"; Barker and Wright talk about the increased freedom and responsibility of the older child. Rogoff, Sellers, Pirotta, Fox, and White (1975) surveyed cross-cultural reports of children's entries into adult roles and responsibilities in the school years: Mobility, freedom, responsibility, status, and power seem to rise together as children gradually enter and map the behavior settings of the adult world. Children and adults, then, satisfy a variety of agenda as they cognitively map a physical and social world.

THE DRAMA OF RESEARCH AND THE AGENDA OF SCIENTISTS

We have spent a good deal of time trying to characterize cognitive mapping research, a relatively recent production on the stage of developmental psychology. Up to this point we have focused mainly on children, both in the laboratory and in the larger social world. Using the terminology of a dramatistic perspective (Burke, 1945; adapted by Wapner et al. in their "genetic dramatism," 1981), we have looked at Agents (children) performing Actions (way finding) in Scenes (laboratory or town) via Agencies or Instrumentalities (cognitive mapping) to achieve certain Purposes (agenda). As in a good newspaper story, the other authors in this volume have explored issues of who does what, where, and when. But little explicit attention is given to "why?"

Consider the possibility that what we have been describing thus far is really a play within a play. Just as in Shakespeare's *Hamlet,* the audience for one play becomes the Actors in another. In our case, the audience for the "play" of cognitive mapping—the developmental psychologists and others observing and interpreting children engaged in cognitive mapping—can alternatively be looked at as the Actors in a surrounding play. It seems worthwhile to elaborate this notion, to try to describe the what, when, where, how, and particularly the why of this larger play.

We have already described some of the elements of this play. The Actors or Agents are researchers (cognitive and developmental psychologists, geographers, etc.). The Actions undertaken are the research moves and procedures involved in the Scenes of the laboratory, the classroom, a gymnasium, or summer camp. The Agencies are the techniques employed to externalize spatial knowledge and to render the child's performance in a communicable form. The Purposes of the Agents—the "why"—are somewhat less clear.

What does the researcher actually do? Bringing with him a host of assumptions about the phenomenon he wishes to study, the researcher creates a situation in which a child is to perform, and as the child performs, the researcher makes notations about that child's performance. The situation is designed so that certain aspects of performance are central and can be recorded easily (whatever is "business-like" and "serious"), while other aspects of performance are incidental and less readily recorded. Whatever children do that is not business-like—a child fidgets, daydreams, wanders around the room, interjects a story about the new toy his sister just got—is excluded from the research record. In short, the researcher defines what is "serious" and what is less serious about the child's performance, and then records the serious. How? By marks on paper (or other mark-recording devices). Since it is impossible to capture everything that a child does during a given half-hour session, the recording is highly selective. In effect, what the researcher records is not the child's behavior, but rather the researcher's own purposes!

Further, most scientists (in cognitive mapping, in psychology more broadly, or in the social and behavioral sciences most broadly) notate the "serious" aspects of the child's performance either directly in numbers (e.g., "It took the child 5 minutes to construct the model," "3 buildings were off by 4 feet or more," "3 recognition errors were made") or in a way that permits quantification. Using statistical procedures, the scientist then concatenates the selected performance of groups of children (or repeated performances of individual children). The scientist goes from accounts of individual children to accounts of numericized children—the average child, the symbolized child. The performances of these mythical children are then reported in the public form of, say, a journal article.

Why do researchers engage in this complex ritual? What are their purposes? Just as children cognitively map their environments to satisfy cognitive, social, and emotional agenda, so scientists do research to satisfy these same agenda. Realizing that these agenda are complexly interwoven, it seems useful to list some of them:

• We want to survive in our chosen professions (Deans and Evaluation Committees are highly sensitive to, and often reckon worth according to, a particular class of marks on paper, i.e., publications).

• We want to improve the human condition (But beware. Albert Szent-Gyorgi was quoted to have advised: "If any student comes to me and says he wants to be useful to mankind and go into research to alleviate human suffering, I advise him to go into charity instead" [Holton, 1978, p. 235]).

• We want to find out something about how a particular phenomenon works and how it develops, and we want to understand that "something" *precisely* (one is reminded of Johannes Kepler's statement in 1597 that "the mind comprehends a thing the more correctly the closer the thing approaches toward pure quantity as its origin").

• We want to, even for an instant in time, know something no one else knows ("Research wants real egotists who seek their own pleasure and satisfaction, but find it in solving the 'puzzles of nature' " [Albert Szent-Gyorgi, cited in Holton, 1978, p. 235]).

• We want recognition from our peers. Put another way, we want to communicate with and receive support from what Donald Campbell (1979) has called "the tribal society" of psychology.

In order to gain this recognition, support, and communication with others, scientists must follow certain rules, conventions, customs, and rituals that bind a tribal society (the scientific community) together:

• We transform "hot" knowledge, gained in face-to-face interaction with flesh-and -blood children and retained in images, into "cool" knowledge

(White, 1978) gained by interaction with symbolized children and expressed in numbers (e.g., means) and in statements about the average child, e.g., "Fifth graders were better able to . . . than were first graders."

- We translate our own convictions about a phenomenon (retained in images of particular children's performances) into numerical statements regarding publicly and consensually accepted criteria of conviction, e.g., $F(2,36) = 5.01, MSe = 1.45, p < .05$; these symbols of conviction formally substantiate our own image of what has gone on.

- We move from individual accounts (observed) toward universal accounts (inferred or postulated). We create the symbolized child, the average child. We elevate accounts of particular children to accounts of children-in-general.

Just as, with development, the child extends his thought in time and space, so research permits us to extend our own thoughts in time and space. We do research so that our purposes, our marks on paper, can be communicated from the proximal situation of our laboratories to the distal situations of other tribal members whose support we need and value.

REFERENCES

Acredolo, L. P. Small- and large-scale spatial concepts in infancy and childhood. L. A. Liben, A. H. Paterson, & N. Newcombe (Eds.), *Spatial representation and behavior across the life span.* New York: Academic Press, 1981.

Acredolo, L. P., Pick, H. L., & Olsen, M. G. Environmental differentiation and familiarity as determinants of children's memory for spatial location. *Developmental Psychology, 1975, 11,* 495–501.

Allen, G. L., Kirasic, K. C., Siegel, A. W., & Herman, J. F. Developmental issues in cognitive mapping: The selection and utilization of environmental landmarks. *Child Development,* 1979, *50,* 1062–1070.

Allen, G. L., Siegel, A. W., & Rosinski, R. R. The role of perceptual context in structuring spatial knowledge. *Journal of Experimental Psychology: Human Learning and Memory,* 1978, *4,* 617–630.

Anooshian, L. J., & Young, D. Developmental changes in cognitive maps of a familiar neighborhood. *Child Development,* 1981, *52,* 341–348.

Appleyard, D. Styles and methods of structuring a city. *Environment and Behavior,* 1970, *2,* 100–118.

Barker, R. G. *Ecological psychology.* Stanford, CA: Stanford University Press, 1968.

Barker, R. G., & Wright, H. F. *Midwest and its children: The psychological ecology of an American town.* Evanston, IL: Row, Peterson, 1954.

Barnes, E. *Studies in education: A series of ten numbers devoted to child-study and the history of education.* Stanford, CA: Stanford University Press. (1896–7).

Berger, P. L., & Luckmann, T. *The social construction of reality.* New York: Anchor, 1967.

Bossard, J. H. S. *The sociology of child development.* New York: Harper, 1948.

Bronfenbrenner, U. The ecology of human development in retrospect and prospect. In H. McGurk (Ed.), *Ecological factors in human development.* New York: North-Holland, 1977.

Bronfenbrenner, U. *The ecology of human development: Experiments by nature and design.* Cambridge: Harvard University Press, 1979.

Brown, A. L. The construction of temporal succession by preoperational children. In A. D. Pick (Ed.), *Minnesota Symposiam on Child Psychology* (Vol. 10). Minneapolis: University of Minnesota Press, 1976.

Bruner, J. S. The course of cognitive growth. *American Psychologist, 1964, 19,* 1–15.

Brunswik, E. *Perception and the representative design of psychological experiments.* Berkeley: University of California Press, 1956.

Burke, K. *A grammar of motives.* Berkeley: University of California Press, 1969. (Orig. published, 1945.)

Campbell, D. T. A tribal model of the social system vehicle carrying scientific knowledge. *Knowledge: Creation, diffusion, and utilization,* 1979, *1,* 181–201 (Sage Publications, Inc.)

Cohen, R., & Schuepfer, T. The representation of landmarks and routes. *Child Development, 1980, 51,* 1065–1071.

Cole, M. Society, mind, and development. In F. S. Kessel & A. W. Siegel (Eds.), *Houston Symposium IV. Psychology and society: The child as a cultural invention.* New York: Praeger, 1984.

Cole, M., Hood, L., & McDermott, R. *Ecological niche picking: Ecological invalidity as an axiom of experimental cognitive psychology.* Laboratory of Comparative Human Cognition and Institute for Comparative Human Development, The Rockefeller University, 1979.

Commager, H. S. *The American mind: An interpretation of American thought and character since the 1880's.* New Haven: Yale University Press, 1950.

Cousins, J. H., Siegel, A. W., & Maxwell, S. E. Way finding and cognitive mapping in large-scale environments: A test of a developmental model. *Journal of Experimental Child Psychology,* 1983, *35,* 1–20.

Curtis, L. E., Siegel, A. W., & Furlong, N. E. Developmental differences in cognitive mapping: Configurational knowledge of familiar large-scale environments. *Journal of Experimental Child Psychology,* 1981, *31,* 456–469.

Dewey, J. *The educational situation.* Chicago: University of Chicago Press, 1902.

Douglas, M. (Ed.). *Rules and meanings: The anthropology of everyday knowledge.* New York: Penguin, 1973.

Downs, R. M. Maps and mappings as metaphors for spatial representation. In L. S. Liben, A. H. Patterson, & N. Newcombe (Eds.), *Spatial representation and behavior across the life span.* New York: Academic Press, 1981.

Downs, R. M., & Siegel, A. W. On mapping researchers mapping children mapping space. In L. S. Liben, A. H. Patterson, & N. Newcombe (Eds.), *Spatial representation and behavior across the life span.* New York: Academic Press, 1981.

Downs, R. M., & Stea, D. *Maps in minds.* New York: Harper & Row, 1977.

Flavell, J. H., & Wohlwill, J. F. Formal and functional aspects of cognitive development. In D. Elkind & J. H. Flavell (Eds.), *Studies in cognitive development: Essays in honor of Jean Piaget.* New York: Oxford University Press, 1969.

Gatty, H. *Nature is your guide.* London: Collins, 1958.

Gibson, E. J. *Principles of perceptual learning and development.* New York: Appleton-Century-Crofts, 1969.

Gladwin, T. *East is a big bird.* Cambridge: Harvard University Press, 1970.

Goodnow, J. *Children drawing.* Cambridge: Harvard University Press 1977.

Hardwick, D. A., McIntyre, C. W., & Pick, H. L. The content and manipulation of cognitive maps in children and adults. *Monographs of the Society for Research in Child Development,* 1976, *41,* (3, Serial No. 166).

Hart, R. A. *Children's experience of place.* New York: Irvington, 1979.

Hart, R. A. Children's spatial representation of the landscape: Lessons and questions from a field study. In L. S. Liben, A. H. Patterson, & N. Newcombe (Eds.), *Spatial representation and behavior across the life span.* New York: Academic Press, 1981.

Hart, R. A., & Moore, G. T. The development of spatial cognition: A review. In R. M. Downs & O.

Stea (Eds.), *Image and environment: Cognitive mapping and spatial behavior.* Chicago: Aldine, 1973.

Herman, J. F. Children's cognitive maps of large-scale spaces: Effects of exploration, direction, and repeated experience. *Journal of Experimental Child Psychology,* 1980, *29,* 126–143.

Herman, J. F., Kail, R. V., & Siegel, A. W. Cognitive maps of a college campus: A New look at freshman orientation. *Bulletin of the Psychonomic Society,* 1979, *13,* 183–186.

Herman, J. F., & Siegel, A. W. The development of cognitive mapping of the large-scale environment *Journal of Experimental Child Psychology,* 1978, *26,* 389–401.

Holton, G. *The scientific imagination: Case studies.* Cambridge: Cambridge University Press, 1978.

Jackson, J. H. Evolution and dissolution of the nervous system. (Croonian Lectures). Published in parts in the *British Medical Journal, Lancet,* and *Medical Times and Gazette,* 1884. Reprinted in J. Taylor (Ed.), *The selected writings of John Hughlings Jackson* (Vol. 2). New York: Basic Books, 1958.

Jerison, J. H. Paleoneurology and the evolution of mind. *Scientific American,* 1976, *234,* 90–101.

Kaplan, B. Meditations on genesis. *Human Development,* 1967, *10,* 65–87.

Kirasic, K. C., Siegel, A. W., Allen, G. L., Curtis, L. E., & Furlong, N. A comparison of methods of externalizing college students' cognitive maps of their campus. *Environment and Behavior,* 1979, unpublished manuscript, University of Pittsburg.

Kosslyn, S. M., Heldmeyer, K. H., & Locklear, E. P. Children's drawings as data about internal representations. *Journal of Experimental Child Psychology,* 1977, *23,* 191–211.

Kosslyn, S. M., Pick, H. L., & Fariello, G. R. Cognitive maps in children and men. *Child Development,* 1974, *45,* 707–716.

Lewin, K. *A dynamic theory of personality.* New York: McGraw-Hill, 1935.

Lewis, D. *We, the navigators.* Honolulu: University Press of Hawaii, 1972.

Lord, F. E. A study of spatial orientation in children. *Journal of Educational Research,* 1941, *34,* 481–505.

Lynch, K. *The image of the city.* Cambridge: MIT Press, 1960.

Maier, N. R. F. Reasoning in children. *Journal of Comparative Psychology,* 1936, *21,* 357–366.

Mead, G. H. *Mind, self, and society.* Chicago: University of Chicago Press, 1934.

Ogbu, J. Origins of human competence: A cultural ecological perspective. *Child Development,* 1981, *52,* 413–429.

Overton, W. F., & Reese, H. W. Models of development: Methodological implications. In J. R. Nesselroade & H. W. Reese (Eds.), *Life-span developmental psychology: Methodological issues.* New York: Academic Press, 1973.

Papert, S. *Mindstorms: Children, computers, and powerful ideas.* New York: Basic Books, 1980.

Pepper, S. C. *World hypotheses.* Berkely: University of California Press, 1970.

Piaget, J. *Biology and knowledge.* Chicago: Univeristy of Chicago Press, 1971.

Piaget, J., & Inhelder, B. *The child's conception of space.* New York: Norton, 1967.

Piaget, J., Inhelder, B., & Szeminska, A. *The child's conception of geometry.* New York: Basic Books, 1960.

Reese, H. W., & Overton, W. F. Models of development and theories of development. In L. R. Goulet & P. Baltes (Eds.), *Life-span developmental psychology: Research and theory.* New York: Academic Press, 1970.

Rogoff, B. Approaches to integrating context and cognitive development. In M. E. Lamb & A. L. Brown (Eds.), *Advances in developmental psychology* (Vol. 2). Hillsdale, NJ: Lawrence Erlbaum Associates, 1983.

Rogoff, B., Sellers, M. J., Pirotta, S., Fox, N., & White, S. H. Age of assignment of roles and responsibilities to children: A cross-cultural survey. *Human Development,* 1975, *18,* 353–369.

Siegel, A. W. The externalization of cognitive maps by children and adults: In search of ways to ask better questions. In L. S. Liben, A. H. Patterson, & N. Newcombe (Eds.), *Spatial representation and behavior across the life span.* New York: Academic Press, 1981.

Siegel, A. W. Towards a social ecology of cognitive mapping. In R. Cohen (Ed.), *New directions for child development: Vol. 15. Children's conceptions of spatial relationships.* San Francisco: Jossey-Bass, 1982.

Siegel, A. W., Allen, G. L., & Kirasic, K. C. Children's ability to make bi-directional distance comparisons: The advantage of thinking ahead. *Developmental Psychology,* 1979, *15,* 656–657.

Siegel, A. W., Bisanz, J., & Bisanz, G. L. Developmental analysis: A strategy for the study of psychology change. In D. Kuhn & J. A. Meacham (Eds.), *On the development of developmental psychology.* Basel: Karger, 1983.

Siegel, A. W., Herman, J. F., Allen, G. L., & Kirasic, K. C. The development of cognitive maps of large- and small-scale space. *Child Development,* 1979, *50,* 582–585.

Siegel, A. W., & Schadler, M. Young children's cognitive maps of their classroom. *Child Development,* 1977, *48,* 388–394.

Siegel, A. W., & White, S. H. The development of spatial representations of large-scale environments. In H. W. Reese (Ed.), *Advances in Child Development and Behavior* (Vol. 10. New York: Academic Press, 1975.

Siegel, A. W., & White, S. H. The child study movement: Early growth and development of the symbolized child. In H. W. Reese (Ed.), *Advances in Child Development and Behavior* (Vol. 17). New York: Academic Press, 1982.

Sigel, I. E., & Cocking, R. R. *Cognitive development from childhood to adolescence: A constructivist perspective.* New York: Holt, Rinehart and Winston, 1977.

Spencer, H. *The principles of psychology* (Vol. 1) (3rd ed.) New York: Appleton, 1894 (First edition, 1855).

Stone, A., & Day, M. C. Competence and performance models and the characterization of formal operational skills. *Human Development,* 1980, *23,* 323–353.

Tolman, E. C. Cognitive maps in rats and men. *Psychological Review,* 1948, *55,* 189–208.

Trowbridge, E. C. Fundamental methods of orientation and "imaginary maps." *Science,* 1913, *38,* 888–897.

von Uexkull, J. A stroll through the worlds of animals and men: A picture book of invisible worlds. In C. H. Schiller (Ed. & Transl.), *Instinctive behavior.* New York: International Universities Press, 1957.

Vygotsky, L. S. *Mind in society.* Cambridge: Harvard University press, 1978. (Edited by M. Cole et al.).

Wapner, S. *Toward an analysis of transactions of persons-in-a-high-speed-society.* Paper presented at a symposium on "Man and a high speed society" sponsored by the International Association of Traffic and Safety Science, Tokyo, Japan, September 1980.

Wapner, S., Kaplan, B., & Ciottona, R. Self-world relationships in critical environmental transitions: Childhood and beyond. In L. S. Liben, A. H. Patterson, & N. Newcombe (Eds.), *Spatial representation and behavior across the life span.* New York: Academic Press, 1981.

Wapner, S., Kaplan, B., & Cohen, S. B. An organismic-developmental perspective for understanding transactions of men and environments. *Environment and Behavior,* 1973, *5,* 255–289.

Werner, H. *Comparative psychology of mental development.* New York: International Universities Press, 1957. (Orig. published, 1948.)

Werner, H., & Kaplan, B. *Symbol formation.* New York: Wiley, 1963.

White, S. H. Psychology in all sorts of places. In R. A. Kasschau & F. S. Kessel (Eds.), *Houston Symposium I. Psychology and society: In search of symbiosis.* New York: Holt, Rinehart & Winston, 1978.

White, S. H. Cognitive competence and performance in everyday environments. *Bulletin of the Orton Society,* 1980, *30,* 29–45.

White, S. H., & Siegel, A. W. Cognitive development: The new inquiry. *Young Children,* 1976, *31,* 425–435.

White, S. H., & Siegel, A. W. Cognitive development in time and space. In B. Rogoff & J. Lave

(Eds.), *Everyday cognition: Its development in social context.* Cambridge, Mass: Harvard University Press, 1984.

Whiting, B. B. Culture and social behavior: A model for the development of social behavior. *Ethos,* 1980, *8,* 95–116.

Wohlwill, J. F. (1981, April). Ecological representativeness in developmental research: A critical view. Paper presented at the meetings of the Society for Research in Child Development, Boston.

Author Index

369

Subject Index